In DEFENCE *of*
TROTSKYISM

In DEFENCE *of* TROTSKYISM

The communists fight for the attainment of the immediate aims, for the enforcement of the momentary interests of the working class; but in the movement of the present, they also represent and take care of the future of that movement.

Karl Marx & Friedrich Engels, the Communist Manifesto

socialist books

In Defence of Trotskyism by the Committee for a Workers' International

With an introduction by Peter Taaffe

© Socialist Publications 2019

First Edition November 2019

Classification: Marxism & Trotskyism

Politics/Sociology

ISBN 9781870958882

A catalogue record for this book is available
from the British Library

Published by Socialist Books, an imprint of
Socialist Publications

Printed and bound by CPI Group (UK) Ltd, Croydon,
CR0 4YY

CONTENTS

The TRADE
UNIONS

The NATIONAL
QUESTION

RE-FOUNDING
the CWI

Appendices

INTRODUCTION

The great scientific socialists, beginning with Karl Marx and Friedrich Engels, defended the role of the working class as the main agency for fighting capitalism and establishing a new socialist society. This was a thread running throughout their works. The working class, organised and disciplined by mass production, is the only class capable of developing the necessary collective consciousness through their organisations to achieve this task.

However, they and we recognise that the working class is not composed of one homogenous, undifferentiated whole. It historically involves, for example, men and women workers, the skilled and unskilled, and in our day is made up of many new layers involved in a number of different sectors with their own demands and agenda. Nevertheless, the CWI and Militant (now the Socialist Party), as this book demonstrates, successfully engaged in many different sectional struggles but always emphasised the decisive role of the working class, and their organisations, the trade unions and political parties, as the unifying force against big business.

The ruling class from the outset has tried to play on differences within the working class, to widen them as a means of cementing its rule. In recent years what has become known as 'identity politics' has come to the fore in general in society. Women's struggles bursting onto the scene again and again, protests against sexual harassment, the fight for LGBT+ rights and other struggles have impacted on all manner of organisations in society. Indeed, the ruling classes quite consciously, through their ideological factories the universities and 'places of learning', have encouraged identity politics as a means of splitting and weakening the ability of the working class and its organisations to fight back. Even self-proclaimed 'revolutionary left' organisations, like the US International Socialist Organisation (ISO) have split on this issue and have virtually disappeared from the political arena.

Unfortunately, the former CWI section in the US, Socialist Alternative, has also turned in an opportunist direction towards the Democratic Party, and made concessions to identity politics. This has involved watering down its programme and actions to accommodate to the Democratic Socialists of America (DSA). This organisation has the false, utopian view that the ingrained pro-capitalist Democratic Party can be turned into a 'workers' party'. Undoubtedly, some who split from the DSA can move in this direction but the overwhelming majority for a new workers' party in the US will come from fresh layers, alongside trade unionists and other activists looking towards a fighting, anti-capitalist, workers' or even 'pre-workers' party. A theoretical or political error inevitably can lead to a big price being paid by those organisations claiming to be 'Marxists' or 'Trotskyists'.

Something similar to what has happened to the ISO has affected sections of the CWI in the course of the last period. Serious political differences arose towards the end of 2018, continued throughout 2019 in our ranks and developed into a full-blown dispute as a clearly petty-bourgeois opportunist trend raised its head within the CWI.

The delay in an upsurge of mass movements also contributed to this. A similar political trend to that which confronted Trotsky in 1939-40, but over different issues, arose within the CWI seeking an 'easier', in reality opportunist, road – a 'short cut' to gaining greater influence amongst 'specially oppressed' groups and a turning away from the working class and its organisations to 'more revolutionary' forces.

The issues under dispute centred on the crucial role, the primacy and centrality, of the working class and its organisations in the struggle against capitalism and for socialism. The leadership of the CWI – like Trotsky in the late 1930s – confronted head-on these major political and organisational diversions from genuine Marxism. The spark for the dispute arose from young members of the Socialist Party in Ireland who implied at an international school that it was not the working class and its organisations but allegedly 'new' forces – women, LGBT+ people, etc – which constituted a new 'vanguard of the working class'. Rather than correcting these young people, even gently, the Irish leadership dug in and defended their mistaken formulations. They compounded their error when they stood in the European elections of 2019 under the slogan of a 'socialist feminist' candidate. This was calculated to appeal to just one a small section of the working class. The consequences of this mistaken slogan and political orientation were that, unfortunately, their vote dropped dramatically in the European elections and they were reduced to four councillors from the previous 14 in the local elections held the same day.

This represented a sharp departure from the political traditions of the CWI which was actually born in 1965 when Ted Grant and myself came into conflict with the Mandelite United Secretariat of the Fourth International (USFI) on similar issues. We were delegates to their world congress but walked out and politically turned our backs on them in protest at the abandonment of a consistent Marxist approach based upon the power and potential of the working class.

Representing small forces at the time, we separated ourselves politically from Ernest Mandel's USFI. For them it was also the 'new forces', allegedly new methods of struggle through rural and urban guerillaism pursued by charismatic popular leaders at the time, or those like Tito in Yugoslavia, Mao in China and of course Fidel Castro in Cuba, who had, they argued, replaced the political power of the working class in carrying through socialist change. We recognised the changes that had been effected in some areas of the world through these radical popular leaders, like Castro and Guevara, who although not rounded -out Marxists played a significant role in social change. Nevertheless we stubbornly but correctly defended the historic role and potential of the working class in the forthcoming battles that were likely to open up internationally.

We were very soon vindicated in action in the mass revolutionary upheavals that erupted, particularly in France in 1968 with the working class reaching out for power through a general strike and organised occupations of the factories. This scepticism of Mandel about the potential of the working class was answered in action and resulted in the greatest general strike in history, with ten million workers occupying the factories. The French workers undoubtedly had the possibility of taking power relatively peacefully, at least initially, but for the obstacle of the perfidious French Communist Party and so-called 'Socialists'.

Our general approach allowed us to subsequently face up to winning and mobilising the best working-class youth, and at the same time winning a significant layer of student youth in the universities who put themselves politically and historically on the standpoint of the working class.

This in turn laid the basis for us to effectively intervene in Britain by establishing a significant force amongst the Labour Party Young Socialists and eventually winning the majority. We followed this up with consistent, assiduous work in the Labour Party itself and built a powerful trade union base. This work was carried out initially through our very few cadres and journal, the Militant. This became an example for others in Britain and internationally who were in turn attracted to the banner of the CWI.

Unfortunately, while Herculean methods were used to try and establish a similar basis elsewhere, it was only in Britain that Marxism/Trotskyism managed to break through to the degree to which it did, to become a significant force that was able to powerfully influence events. We were not just a 'factor' but on some crucial issues a decisive factor in some of the big battles of the working class, recruiting 500 miners during their strike of 1984-85. This was also the case in the epic Liverpool struggle and the poll tax battle. It was not the pathetic 'official leadership' of the Labour Party at that time, under the hapless and treacherous leadership of Neil Kinnock, nor the Trades Union Congress (TUC) or the completely ineffective little sects on the outskirts of the labour movement, which led the way.

It was Militant that led the hugely successful mass movement to defeat Thatcher in the 1980s in Liverpool, winning in the process significant concrete reforms for the working class. Moreover members of the present leadership of the real CWI formulated and carried through the strategy and tactics that were employed to gain a great victory. Many other comrades joined us later in these battles. If the methods employed in Liverpool had been emulated in other cities and towns in Britain by the labour movement, then undoubtedly the Thatcher government's savage council cuts would have been swept away. Rather than one victory in a triumphant city – Liverpool, supported by Lambeth council – numerous councils involved in struggle could have inflicted an even greater defeat on the Tory government.

Nevertheless the achievements of Liverpool were enormously impressive and attracted support from elsewhere. This in turn led to a rise in the political profile and the support amongst increasing layers of workers for the ideas of Militant of a fighting Marxist/Trotskyist organisation both in Britain and internationally, especially as this was aligned to the mass organisations of the Labour Party and the leftward-moving unions.

The mass rallies under Militant's banner involving thousands of young people and workers, which numbered from 5,000 to 8,000, were organised first at the Wembley Conference Centre, then in the Albert Hall culminating in the spectacularly successful rally of almost 8,000 in Alexandra Palace in 1988 (at this event we had almost 500 children in the crèche – similar in size to a primary school!).

At the same time in Merseyside we had – in addition to Militant, our weekly paper – a local weekly paper and had a thousand members, which was the effective leadership of the labour movement in the city. Dozens of councillors were in our ranks alongside the heroic member of parliament, the late Terry Fields. He was jailed with the complicity of Neil Kinnock for defying Thatcher's poll tax!

Alongside Terry in parliament were the other colossal class fighters, Coventry South-East MP Dave Nellist and Bradford North MP Pat Wall. Dave was expelled from the Labour Party for the 'crime' of defying Thatcher and refusing to pay his poll tax! Additionally we had 34 members amongst the hundreds of nonpayers jailed as Thatcher tried to crush the poll tax resistance. In vain! We organised through the Anti-Poll Tax Federation 18 million people not to pay the tax. It was this non-payment campaign – not the so-called 'Battle of Trafalgar Square', which was important as a symbol of resistance but not decisive – that finished off the poll tax and in the process consigned Thatcher to history. It was these examples that indicated the huge potential for the bold alternative of Marxism and Trotskyism under the leadership of Militant – now known as the Socialist Party.

Very few specifically working-class Trotskyist forces have achieved this kind of success elsewhere in the world, and none other than the CWI in Britain. Some managed to establish a largish base among students but did not succeed as Militant did in penetrating into the ranks of the working class and its organisations, the trade unions. The Trotskyist Morenoite organisation in Latin America did make a significant semi-mass breakthrough in Argentina and Brazil, as well as a separate Trotskyist organisation in Bolivia through the group led by Lora.

It was Militant's gains in Britain that set the alarm bells ringing in the corridors of bourgeois power and which led to a series of underhand, vicious attacks combined with openly repressive measures employed by the capitalist state and its stooges in the labour movement against Militant and the CWI. This involved collaborating with the right wing in the trade unions and sending police spies into our ranks in an attempt to undermine our influence and growth. None of these methods would have succeeded but for the unexpected and unfavourable turn of events for the Labour movement and us, represented by the collapse of Stalinism and its aftermath in the ideological fallout. A massive campaign to discredit 'socialism' took place in the early 1990s.

It is necessary to make these points here, not just to repeat the historical record of the present leadership of the CWI, but to underline the completely false, bombastic claims made by our opponents. They are trying to undermine and distort the real traditions, programme, perspectives and methods of our organisation – the CWI – that led to this significant success. Moreover, this example and tradition can lead to further mass breakthroughs if those seeking a Trotskyist road remain firmly committed to the ideas which we have defended and still represent.

The discussion and differences in our international originally arose with the leadership of the Irish section of the CWI – which revealed a serious opportunist adaptation by them to identity politics, as well as their underhand organisational methods. This group has belatedly admitted that they deployed an 'intervention' into fellow comrades' email accounts. This was to gather information that they were in political opposition to the leadership. This is what Eric Byl, a leader of the Belgian section, and Stephen Boyd, a leader of the Irish section, admitted to in a letter sent to the Nigerian comrades:

"In July of 2018 there was a serious suspicion that emails of leading members were violated by a councillor comrade. If this was the case (and it proved to be so), the comrade would have to be removed as a public representative as he couldn't be trusted politically. However, that is a serious sanction and so we needed to have evidence and proof.

"Therefore three IEC members and Joe Higgins essentially made two decisions. The first was that the potential 'breach' had to be investigated. The investigation was carried out by the comrade who had discovered the original suspicious activity on the computer he used in a party office. Secondly, that it would look at the Chrome browser history on the computer, and also a limited scan of the email account of the comrade suspected of the 'breach', to see if there was any evidence of a 'breach' in his emails. Both of which were readily accessible when the comrade had opened Chrome on his computer…

"The investigation was justified and necessary and got to the truth of a serious attack on the party." A clear admission of 'spying on the ranks' of the organisation!

Paul Murphy was originally the main target for this, the Irish leadership's underhand 'secret' methods of surveillance of 'oppositional' comrades. The IS opposed this and defended his right as a party member and a public representative for the party to put forward his views openly to the membership. He had a record in the public domain, particularly in the water charges campaign, and had been threatened with jailing and a long prison sentence. The Irish party leadership, in our opinion, had not been conducting a sufficiently energetic public campaign, either in Ireland or internationally, to prevent the imprisonment of Paul and the others charged. The IS therefore intervened, particularly CWI Secretary Tony Saunois, to step up the defence campaign, which along with the strenuous campaign waged in Ireland we believe did significantly contribute to staying the hand of the judges and the police in their attempts to jail him and others.

The same principled approach was not reciprocated by Paul Murphy in the course of the struggle over the internal methods of the Irish leadership. He was originally the target, not the IS, for the attacks of the Irish leadership. Now he has separated himself from the IS and, unfortunately in the process, from Trotskyism itself. He has announced that he is separating himself from the Irish organisation – splitting – and would like to link up opportunistically with others on the left including the Greens and Sinn Féin. The IS did at one stage pose the question of perhaps not standing in the way of Sinn Féin participating in a 'left government' in the South of Ireland while at the same time continuing to criticise the inadequacies of its programme. This was raised in perspectives documents and agreed at the conference of the Irish section, but because this situation did not arise, this proposal was not pursued. However, the discussion of the issues inside the party revealed a sectarian approach of the Irish party leadership towards the question of limited agreements with opposition 'left' parties.

This did not imply that we politically endorsed Paul Murphy or his arguments in favour of a 'united front' with Sinn Féin and others, but rather a limited practical technical agreement not to stand in the way of a government in which Sinn Féin participated, if that was the wish of significant sections of the Irish electorate and particularly of the working class. A united front usually pertains to an agreement between specific workers' organisations to fight for a clear programme of demands, while maintaining our own programme, and on some occasions could even include the idea of a 'radical revolutionary government'. None of that was proposed in the case of Ireland. Now Paul Murphy has taken this idea a step further and given it a massive opportunist twist. This involves attempting to link up with other opportunist forces, some of them with a chequered record in the trade union movement.

This bloc will merely be a further deepening of the opportunist trends, already evident in the evolution of the policies of the Irish leadership. The suspicion will be that Paul Murphy is trying to save his seat in the Dáil at any cost. Moreover he is quite clearly linked to Philip Locker in the US who broke from the CWI for similar opportunistic reasons and whose small group has now collapsed into the DSA.

They politically subsist on ideas borrowed from us. For instance, Paul Murphy's latest document lauds the 'dual tasks', which is an idea that we first formulated in the aftermath of the collapse of Stalinism. Consciousness had been thrown back, not just in terms of programme but also of organisation: the need for a mass party of the working class. We therefore had to champion the idea of new mass parties of the working class, as well as the need for a clear revolutionary Trotskyist programme – hence the dual tasks.

During the last debates on this issue in Ireland, supporters of the Irish leadership argued that the IS and the leadership in England and Wales were also promoting 'identity politics' by emphasising the essential role of the working class! As if the working class and trade unions, the mass organisations of the working class, can be put on the same level as sectional struggles and organisations!

This issue of the trade unions reflected a big difference between us – the IS – and the opportunists within the CWI, as is revealed in the documents reproduced in this book. Marxists, Trotskyists, are duty bound to seek out and politically convince and educate workers in the trade unions, the basic organisations of the working class. The discussion revealed that in some sections, like Ireland in the South, and Greece, while lip service was paid to this idea, in practice they had abandoned attempts at systematic work in the unions and workplaces. In Greece they even criticised the gold miners, suggesting they should give up their jobs to "protect the environment" without suggesting alternative employment.

This had been preceded by a whole period when not just political issues arose, but also the method upon which the Irish organisation was being built, with a top-down, out-of-touch apparatus – largely subsidised by the state – substituting for an educated, ideologically solid organisation. The differences expressed were not just with the IS but with the majority of the CWI, including some who opportunistically supported them in the latest dispute.

The Irish organisation undoubtedly has a commendable, courageous past record historically in many campaigns: water charges, leading the significant strike of Turkish workers employed by the multinational Gama, a protracted struggle in the Irish Labour Party against the right wing and then a successful period of open work. All of this was undertaken with the support of the CWI, notwithstanding the criticisms of some aspects of their work and their lack of a real transitional programme in later years. Their participation and role in the victory to legalise abortion in Ireland in 2018 was recognised by us.

We duly commended them at international meetings while at the same time raising the necessity for us to combat and defeat manifestations of identity politics in general and particularly within their ranks. These ideas emanate, as we mentioned, in the main from US universities, and contain a strong element of separatism. Leading proponents of these ideas pretend to be 'progressive' but in reality are aimed at separating and dividing the working class and its struggles, harking back to the beginnings of the labour movement when workers were very often divided. The labour movement played a decisive role in bringing workers together as a cohesive, decisive force.

Marxism historically has consistently first sought to unify the working class in action – and particularly women workers with their male counterparts – at the point of production in the factories, the workplaces, in the localities and in general society. Our opponents – the long-term sectarians, together with those on the right wing of the labour movement and their quasi-left political cousins – of course deny that is their aim. But in practice this is what invariably takes place.

In war – including the class war – the first casualty is truth! This bourgeois maxim is taken for granted amongst the ruling class. However, with the labour movement, and particularly those who claim to be Marxists or Trotskyists, it behoves those who seek to represent the working class to tell the truth both about the objective situation and to seek to answer criticisms honestly. However, Lenin stressed that in Russia he had never come across a really honest labour movement tendency outside of the ranks of the Bolsheviks, the genuine representatives of Marxism and the working class.

It is impossible to answer all the myriad lies used against us. This should be kept in mind when reading some of the slanderous documents, and the language and shameful behaviour of those who supported identity politics in the ideological struggle.

And if there is any doubt that these former comrades did not put forward identity politics, then read a recent statement of Eljeer Hawkins, one of their members who supported the position of the leadership of the US organisation against us. He wrote recently in relation to a comment of US Democratic Party representative Alexandria Ocasio-Cortez, covered uncritically in their paper: "See I have a problem with this statement and the implicit identity politics in her comments. How do we build a united working-class and poor peoples' movement? A universal solidarity politics and a class analysis that doesn't negate special oppression but centres capitalism and the capitalist class as the enemy that uses racism, sexism and homophobia etc as a tool of division, subjugation, alienation and violence."

And yet the leadership of our former US organisation has now joined the queue of those departing from the CWI who engage in colossal distortions and slander when it comes to the policies of the majority of the CWI, with highly personalised attacks similar to Stalinism's against the Left Opposition. There is nothing new in this. Lenin was invariably accused of being a 'dictator', 'bureaucratic', in favour of 'one-party rule', telling lies, etc by the Mensheviks – the opportunists in the Russian Social Democratic Labour Party in the dispute in 1904 with Martov, Plekhanov and others. Trotsky was later accused of harbouring the same methods and views by the Stalinists and reformists. He was accused of lecturing his opponents from the "heights of Oslo", where he did not live and there were no heights in any case!

The former leadership of our Scottish and Liverpool organisations, when they were breaking from Trotskyism in earlier periods, made similar accusations and they gained absolutely no traction, either with the ranks of our organisation or in the wider labour movement. Their slanders became merely ineffectual weapons to be used against us by bourgeois and petty-bourgeois opponents when they needed them. For instance, Alan McCombes, a former leader of our Scottish organisation, in our dispute with its leadership made a similar accusation. The CWI was allegedly seeking to lecture them from the heights of Leytonstone in East London, where we had our centre. This had as much effect as a drop of water on a hot stove! We have always striven to tell the truth no matter how unpalatable, both to our own membership and the broad labour movement, when the situation required it – something that has, unfortunately, not been the method of the leaders of our former Irish organisation and their international supporters.

For instance in the course of the Liverpool struggle we openly in our press – and in the book Liverpool: A City that Dared to Fight – expressed our differences with the comrades in Liverpool on the issue of 'redundancy notices'. They had been pressurised by the situation – and for very good but incorrect reasons – to introduce the 'tactic' of redundancy notices to gain time for the struggle. We disagreed with them at the time and predicted that Kinnock would disloyally use this to attack the councillors, which he duly did at the infamous Labour Party conference later in 1985! Similarly there were disputes in our ranks over the appointment of Sam Bond as the council's principal race relations officer.

There is here in this book an abundance of material which spells out our record in Britain in defending women workers in particular and women in general. We did this very effectively in the 1990s, launching the Campaign Against Domestic Violence, whose programme was in turn taken up by the broad labour movement in Britain and translated into action with the setting up of special refuges and action to help the victims of domestic abuse. The reality is the recent general capitalist offensive through austerity has meant that right-wing councils, including Labour-run authorities, have sabotaged and undermined this work through cuts, leading to the closure of many of the special units which sought to defend women from violence and domestic abuse. This underlines that gains amongst different groups and sections are linked to the general fight of the working class and labour movement.

Moreover, where women have acted in the defence of their own interests, as with the magnificent strikes of women workers in Glasgow in 2018, we have engaged with and supported them, and encouraged male workers to take action alongside the women. These initiatives were welcomed by the women on strike. A similar situation occurred in the strikes in Birmingham where mainly male refuse workers organised their strike alongside that of the mainly female home care workers. They realised the vital need for class unity in the defence of all sections of the working class.

The starting point of the sectarians and advocates of identity politics is firstly to hone in, to seek to emphasise and magnify any differences in consciousness between sections of the working class. A Marxist and Trotskyist approach does the opposite: it seeks to emphasise what unites working people in struggle. Of course, we recognise the special oppression of different groups and accordingly formulate specific demands. But we at the same time always seek to unify in action the struggles of working people through a common programme, instilling confidence in their ranks with a strategy for victory. We recognise the points of difference where they exist, which means supporting particular demands, but also we have the responsibility to seek to enhance the general struggles of the working class, to free them from opportunist and sectarian leaders and unify them on a fighting programme.

All the charges levelled at the CWI on matters of organisation and how the party functions on a day-to-day basis we believe are answered in this book, which seeks to honestly deal with our history, something which many of our opponents know very little about because they did not participate in the work that built the CWI. The breakthroughs that we made in the 1980s and in the 1990s, of helping to create the outline of future mass formations and an international, have been maintained in the revolutionary core that forms the nucleus of our England and Wales organisation and in those in the CWI who are politically aligned with our international.

Our reconstituted international will be developed in the heat of struggle and largely composed of new forces that will leave behind sectarians and opportunists on the sidelines of history.

A central idea for us is that the capitalist system has drained the cup of optimism to its last drop in the economic field, where the productive forces – science, technique and labour – are in a blind alley. Also in politics, this is revealed through the splits in the ruling class – more like a splintering in Britain and Europe as a whole, as Brexit and its aftermath have shown. It is also to be found in the huge discontent which is brewing not just in the ranks of the most important class, the working class, but also in broad layers of the middle class, who are increasingly thrown into a pit of despair by crisis-ridden capitalism.

One measure of the mass revolt that is coming is that the majority of the young in the US – the millennials – are already in favour of the idea of 'socialism', as the brutal journalism of capitalism, the Economist, admitted in a recent leader column: "Socialism is storming back because it has formed an incisive critique of what has gone wrong in Western societies... Some 51% of Americans aged 18-29 have a positive view of socialism, says Gallup." Marxists/Trotskyists, if they are to find a road to the working class, must base themselves in a principled manner on that class.

Capitalism is in a blind alley having already experienced the worst slump since the 1930s! We witnessed the world economic crisis of 2007-08, second only in its effects to the Great Depression of the 1930s. Moreover, all the economic indicators now point towards another great crash in the next period with all its attendant miseries for the masses.

We want to create an international mass party aimed against all capitalist regimes which presently dominate the planet, thereby initiating a democratic socialist confederation of Europe and the world. Only in this way will we be able to fully utilise and develop all the great resources of the planet built up by the ingenuity and labours of the working class, thereby eradicating hunger and privation, and at the same time through a great socialist world plan avoiding environmental and climate catastrophe.

Deteriorating and unacceptable living conditions are not enough to effect serious change. Nor is the willingness of the working class to fight against its immediate conditions, even against capitalism as a whole, which is evident in the constant upheavals, and in the environmental movement.

Only when all the conditions for revolution are present – a split in the ruling class; the middle layers in revolt and looking towards the working class for a way out; a feeling amongst the mass of the working class that "we cannot live like this any longer" – will it be possible to effect what would be the greatest social overturn in history, the socialist revolution.

However, all these conditions can be present, yet if the most vital one is absent, a mass party, revolution can be derailed. Leon Trotsky called this the "subjective factor", a mass revolutionary party, with a trained, far-sighted political leadership, able to withstand the pressures of capitalism and their agents in the working-class movement, the sell-out 'reformist' trade union and labour leaders. Even the most favourable of revolutionary situations can be lost unless a mass revolutionary party is present. This must be systematically built with the fundamental idea of socialist revolution, with the working class in a central, dominant role. This is the only way to liberate humankind from capitalism, a system which is dragging us into the abyss of increasing poverty, degradation and misery. Moreover, humanity can only save the planet itself from catastrophic climate change through revolution, socialist revolution.

"Say what needs to be said; do what needs to be done," said Trotsky. He does not just platonically advocate the necessity for a mass workers' party with a revolutionary leadership. He is very attentive to all the basic tasks involved even in the assembling of the building blocks for such a force. He does not minimise obstacles: "The selection and education of a truly revolutionary leadership, capable of withstanding the pressure of the bourgeoisie, is an extraordinarily difficult task." Difficult but not impossible! The record of the real Committee for a Workers' International – and its parties and formations – has demonstrated this clearly.

The consistent class analysis in this book is particularly timely and relevant to the situation facing all socialists and revolutionaries today – including those assembled in the ranks of the CWI. We have faced many hostile class pressures, at times, unfortunately, reflected in our ranks, particularly in the period after the collapse of Stalinism. This invariably arose, as we have pointed out, from those seeking 'short cuts', like the recent departures from our ranks, invariably buttressed with the argument that we need 'allies', particularly when the working class and its organisations do not appear to be active or moving into an immediate collision with capitalism.

There is nothing new in an attempt to find an 'easier' road to influence the working class by watering down the approach and programme of Marxism. Usually, this means building on sand. Many Trotskyists have in the past and even today struggled against great odds but because of a certain isolation arising from contemporary unfavourable conditions – particularly in the advanced industrial countries in the post-Second World War upswing – the working class appeared on the surface to be politically quiescent and even accepting of capitalism.

Militant – even before the creation of the CWI – turned its back on false methods and faced up squarely to the task of winning workers, young workers first of all, and then, through them, seeking to find a road to the mass of the working class. We have to combat and defeat all ideologically petty-bourgeois political trends which seek to divide, to introduce separatism into the workers' movement. While Marxists support the rights of all oppressed minorities, and fight their special oppression, we repeat, we always emphasise and strive for the maximum unity of the working class.

Despite the many revolutions and revolutionary situations over the last 150 years, why is it that only in Russia so far was a successful working-class, democratic socialist revolution carried through? The dialectic of history meant that a Marxist party with the most modern ideas developed first in an economically 'underdeveloped' country because of the unique circumstances that Trotsky anticipated in his famous 'theory of the permanent revolution'. This and the existence of the leadership of the Bolshevik party – led by Lenin and Trotsky – resulted in the victory of the 1917 Russian Revolution, whose immediate effects were felt internationally.

Rotted capitalism will not automatically disappear from the scene of history. This is a system which is dominated now not by your 'average' millionaire, as in the past, but by a handful of oligarchs – billionaires – who now wield as much power as whole states and confederations of states wielded previously. It will take a mighty movement of the working class, mobilising behind them all the oppressed layers, who are already alienated from and ready to revolt against and defeat outmoded capitalism and replace it with world socialism.

The answer to how to undertake this colossal task can be found – particularly by the new generation – in reading and absorbing the lessons of this book and the method of Trotsky and Lenin to forge the political weapons that will create a new socialist world.

Peter Taaffe
October 2019

Publisher's Note

We have brought together these documents to present to all those fighting back against capitalism our assessment of several key questions. It should be viewed not only as the product of a debate, but first and foremost as statements on some of the fundamental questions facing our movement today.

This book is a selection of documents and articles, which were mainly written in the course of a debate, and therefore largely for an internal audience. A certain amount of knowledge is assumed, especially around internal bodies. We have included a short explanation of the Socialist Party and CWI structures on page 248. We have also included a number of articles from Socialist Party magazine Socialism Today, to make clear our general stance on some of the key questions.

The documents are presented in thematic sections. This is to allow readers to more closely examine the CWI's stance on various key topics, rather than constantly switching. However there is, naturally, some overlap, and many documents refer to others. We have included a chronological index of the debate documents on page 250. Many document titles have been changed to more clearly reflect their contents.

We have also edited a number of the documents. Overwhelmingly, documents produced in the heat of the moment were not proof-read. We have tried to correct errors, while also being aware that the documents in their original form are matters of record.

This book features contributions from across the world, including a number of authors who do not have English as their first language. Because there was a need for speedy translation, there was insufficient time to carry out thoroughgoing translations. In consultation with the original authors, we have worked to more directly convey their meaning.

This selection of documents represents many of the key documents produced by the In Defence of a Working-Class, Trotskyist CWI faction. These are not the full documents from the debate, which together run longer than Trotsky's classic History of the Russian Revolution. The CWI is aiming to share more of these documents, from the faction and its opponents, on Marxist.net. Readers will also find the documents from the 'open turn' debate, the late-nineties debate in Scotland, and other crucial discussions that have taken place within the CWI and with other forces on the left.

We would like to thank Alison Hill, Barbara Clare, Alexis Edwards, John Edwards and James Ivens for proofreading, as well as the various authors for giving us permission to reproduce their documents. We would also like to pay tribute to all the militants worldwide who took a principled stand in this debate, and defended the Marxist ideas and programme that built the CWI. We are certain that these ideas and programme are key tools in the fight for a socialist world, and hope that this book's publication aids that fight.

Ben Robinson
Socialist Books

1. PARTY & PROGRAMME

IN DEFENCE OF A WORKING-CLASS, TROTSKYIST CWI

Faction platform

*A*t the recent meeting of the International Executive Committee (IEC), twenty four comrades took the very considered decision to declare a faction in the CWI. This important step was not taken lightmindedly, but because we believe that there was no alternative given the deep political differences that were revealed in the highest level of the leadership of the CWI, the IEC.

We believe that two main political trends emerged at the meeting, revealing sharp differences on principled questions for the international. They include democratic centralism and its application to internal democracy and the membership, the methods needed to build revolutionary parties and a Trotskyist international, and key issues related to political perspectives and our orientation and tactics needed to intervene in the class struggle.

This development will undoubtedly come as a big shock to comrades throughout the CWI. At root, this crisis has an objective basis. It reflects the contradictory political situation in the class struggle internationally, which has developed since the crisis of 2007-08. In many countries, an extremely polarised situation is opening up, reflected in Trump's victory, Modi's rule in India, the coming to power of Bolsonaro in Brazil, AMLO in Mexico, and now the explosive situation in France and the Spanish state. These illustrate the character of the period we have entered. Reflected in the debate in the CWI is the issue of preparing the revolutionary party to be ready to face up to the new era which has opened up.

At the same time, the working class has not yet put itself at the head of the movement, with a conscious socialist programme. The new radical left forces that emerged from the crisis of social democracy and the communist parties have demonstrated not only their reformist confusion but also their incapacity to lead the mass movement and orientate it towards a struggle for the socialist transformation of society. At this stage, the crises within capitalism, the turn towards the left, and advances in an anti-capitalist consciousness among layers of the masses, especially the youth, have not yet resulted in the emergence of powerful, distinct new workers' parties. A strong socialist consciousness has not yet emerged as a viable alternative to the global crisis of capitalism. This is the price we are still paying for the consequences of the collapse of Stalinism, the bourgeoisification of social-democratic parties, and the opportunism of the new left formations, which inevitably creates difficulties for the development of a Marxist force such as ours.

Under these conditions, the pressure to look for opportunist shortcuts is extremely strong. It has affected other organisations on the left, including the revolutionary left, which have dissolved or partially dissolved as a result. The CWI is not immune from these pressures. This is a central aspect of the debate which has now opened up. It can, and has, led to a tendency to lower the profile and programme of the party to accommodate to these pressures. This is not necessarily a conscious decision but happens as a result of the objective pressures.

The crisis that erupted at the IEC emerged initially because of criticisms raised by the International Secretariat (IS) of the methods used by the majority of the Irish leadership when it confronted indefensible actions taken by a member of the Irish section. These criticisms were not raised in order to question the great achievements of the Irish section in crucial struggles, such as the anti-water charges and Jobstown Not Guilty campaigns and, more recently, the intervention comrades made in the recent Repeal the 8th campaign. All of these are recognised as great achievements throughout the CWI.

In spite of these achievements, the IS has, for a period of years, had serious concerns regarding the political orientation and methods used by the Irish leadership. In the opinion of the IS, Philip Stott (PS – Scotland), who has participated in the work of the Irish section, and other comrades, there has been a marked tendency to lower the profile of our party and our socialist programme for a period.

From our point of view this reached an alarming point during the Irish section's election campaign in 2016, and again during the recent campaign on abortion.

In the 2016 election, the programme the Irish comrades put forward in the AAA (Anti-Austerity Alliance) and in their media appearances to a mass audience advocated the central demand for tax rises on the corporations and the rich. The Socialist Party had little profile during the entire campaign. In general, the comrades did not go further, to put forward a socialist programme, including the nationalisation of the banks or strategic sectors of the economy. Nor did they raise how a socialist government would respond to the attacks that it would confront from the ruling class and the EU. This was particularly important following events in Greece in 2015. After a series of sharp discussions with the IS and PS, in which comrades said they were "indignant" that such issues were being raised with them, they formally accepted that the IS had a valid point of view. Following these discussions there were some changes in the Irish comrades' public material. Socialism was mentioned more frequently, although often in an abstract way and not as part of a transitional programme.

However, even today, much of the public material on the website of Solidarity (the successor to AAA) still does not include a socialist programme, despite our overwhelming influence within Solidarity. The same weakness in programme was revealed during the recent abortion campaign. Rosa – the comrades' socialist feminist platform – was the main vehicle through which the comrades participated in the Repeal movement. Yet the primary Rosa campaign leaflet was completely devoid of any mention of socialism, capitalism or even the working class. It did not include any of Rosa's anti-capitalist and anti-austerity demands, which formally Rosa stands for, or explain how the fight for a woman's right to choose is also a class issue, linked to the fight against social cuts and for better child care, a living wage, equal pay, etc.

The tendency to downplay class and socialist demands is evident in the Irish comrades' material when they engage in mass campaigning. Rather than use the mass audience they have to raise consciousness of the tasks facing the working class in fighting capitalism, they tend to limit themselves to reflect existing consciousness and to adapt to ideas which could be advocated by the new reformist left.

In our view, one of the crucial issues that emerged at this IEC is the centrality of the collective role of the working class and our orientation towards it. Linked to this is how we engage in the women's liberation movement – which in the last period has been a very important axis of social mobilisation and the class struggle in a large number of countries – and other movements, such as those in defence of refugees, LGBTQI people, and on the environment.

The IS majority and supporters of the 'In Defence of a Working-Class, Trotskyist CWI' faction are fully convinced of the importance of these movements and of intervening in them with the view of trying to push them forward, on the basis of a working class, socialist revolutionary programme, and without bending to petty bourgeois prejudices and identity politics which attempt to separate these movements from the broader workers' movement. We must support the legitimate rights and demands of women, LGBTQI and trans people but maintain a class approach and oppose tendencies to split these movements from the working class. Petty bourgeois prejudices are common in the movements and organisations, and often dominate the outlook of the leadership. In order to ensure we have the strongest possible intervention, and to educate our own members, we need a scientific, Marxist analysis of these movements and how they are expressed in different countries.

The main characteristic of movements of this kind is that they are multi-class in nature, and it cannot be otherwise. It is important that we recognise this when we plan how to intervene and what our central slogans should be, and how to confront the confused petty bourgeois prejudices and ideas which are present.

We must ensure that we intervene with the aim of winning, in particular, working class layers and young people from working class backgrounds to the banner of revolutionary socialism. We need to intervene with a view to using the methods of the working class in struggle and to link up with other sections of the working class. This has been exemplified in the demands of the Spanish section and how it has driven the call for general and students' strikes.

The traditional sections of the industrial working class have been numerically weakened due to the decline of manufacturing industry in many countries of Europe and the USA. Yet in parts of Asia, Africa and Latin America there has been a strengthening of the working class. Globally, the working class remains the most powerful force because of its collective role in social production and in the international division of labour. We have also seen that other sectors, including transport, communications, etc, are also potentially extremely powerful sections of workers. In addition, new sections of the working class are beginning to emerge, in logistics and other sectors, and there is an increasing proletarianisation of other social layers that formally comprised layers of the middle class.

Another crucial aspect of this discussion is our attitude towards the trade unions. This is an issue which has arisen in the debate with the comrades from Ireland and in the IEC. In Ireland, as in most countries, the situation in the trade unions is one of increased bureaucratisation and a weakening of the active membership base. There are exceptions to this of course. The bureaucracy in the trade unions has, in general, acted as a gigantic brake on the workers' movement and has often become the guarantee of 'social peace', resulting in the bureaucracy losing authority in the eyes of many workers and young people because of their collaboration in cuts and austerity. In many countries, traditional unions have lost support among some layers of workers, with the majority of young people and precarious workers not organised in the main. This has resulted in some workers' struggles taking place outside the official union apparatus or even in opposition to the bureaucracy. In such conditions, we cannot of course adopt a policy of waiting for the official trade union apparatus to be transformed. Where necessary it is correct to circumvent the official apparatus, organising opposition groupings of workers to take unofficial action, etc. We have done this on many occasions. Even during the anti-poll tax struggle in Britain, the movement we led did not go through the official trade union structures, which refused to act.

At the same time, the trade unions are – or, in some countries, potentially – the mass organisations of the working class and retain a mass base. It is essential that we maintain a consistent orientation by placing demands on them, and by attempting to build rank-and-file opposition groups.

Unfortunately, this has not been the approach of comrades in southern Ireland or as expressed by some other comrades at the IEC. It was argued that the comrades in Ireland had previously drawn the conclusion that the mass anger against austerity would not be reflected in the trade unions because of the sell-out by the leadership. It was also argued at the Irish NC and the IEC that comrades turned away from the unions, with a plan to return later, and that it was not necessary to maintain a consistent, systematic orientation towards them. This was clearly reflected in the political propaganda of Rosa in the south of Ireland during the campaign for abortion rights. There were no concrete, consistent demands made on the trade unions to mobilise the working class in defence of that right. Our approach to the trade unions was even equated to the 'Open Turn' away from the bourgeoisified British Labour Party that we undertook in the 1990s, which meant an end to our entry work. This is mistaken. We have always argued that our orientation to the trade unions' base and workplaces is strategically necessary to sink roots in the working class, while fighting against any adaptation to the union bureaucracy and its policies. That has always been a Marxist approach.

The CWI must – in our programme, activity, campaigns and propaganda – reassert the centrality of the role of the working class for us in the struggle for socialism. This is now even more necessary when a conscious movement of the working class has not yet placed itself at the head of the struggle.

We have always emphasised the importance of youth for the revolutionary party. We are in favour of building a strong base in the universities and among school students. We are in favour of winning students to the revolutionary party, including those from a middle class background. In the initial stages of building our sections, it may be necessary, sometimes, to begin with a base among students. Yet it is essential they put themselves on the standpoint of the working class and strive to win a working class base for our sections.

It is essential that a revolutionary party builds its strongest base among the working class, especially young workers. We do not agree, as some comrades argued at the Irish NC, that students in higher education from a working class background have the same consciousness as the working class. While in many countries more students from a working class background are in higher education, their role in the struggle will never be comparable to the role of young workers in the workplaces, who develop a collective consciousness as a class.

Other issues of disagreement have also emerged in relation to the national question. Comrades from the Irish leadership explained their disagreement with the position adopted by the Spanish section on the crisis and revolutionary movement that developed in Catalonia. This was fully discussed at the IEC in November 2017, and has been covered in many political publications and statements not previously challenged. At the same time, other differences have emerged between the IS and the Irish leadership on the application of elements of the method of the united front, particularly how it applies when dealing with petty bourgeois or bourgeois nationalist parties which have a significant base among sections of the working class.

All these political issues were questioned by the majority of the Irish leadership and by some IEC comrades. In addition, comrades from Sweden, Belgium, Greece and others strongly criticised the IS for not understanding the importance of the new women's movement, the LGBTQI movement and the environmental movement, and of not giving sufficient emphasis to them. One Swedish comrade even argued that we lack a political strategy to intervene into these movements. We entirely reject these allegations and re-state our position on them, as we have argued. These movements can and do have a radicalising effect on the consciousness of significant layers of workers, young people and the layers of the middle class who participate in them. However, we need to intervene to assist the most advanced layers to draw more rounded-out conclusions about the role of capitalism as the cause of their oppression, the need for a socialist programme, and the central position of workers in the struggle against any kind of oppression, while linking these movements to the broader working class movement which is the decisive force to change society.

In our opinion, these are fundamental questions for the CWI and its sections. The leaders of the Irish section, together with the comrades from some of the sections which supported them against the position put by the IS, complained about the 'tone' of the debate and also about the fact that we have used the term 'Mandelism' in the course of the debate or have warned about the danger of a degeneration of our party similar to what happened to the former Scottish section in the 1990s. The comrades have protested insistently against our use of these terms. However, for the IS and the supporters of this faction, these terms are a political characterisation. Mandelism has represented a trend which has weakened or loosened the Marxist programme to the point of abandoning it, advocating methods of building the party which represent the liquidation of the revolutionary party. This trend developed in our former Scottish section. In our opinion, the pressures and dangers of such petty bourgeois trends affecting some sections of the CWI are clearly emerging as a reality that we need to confront and were clearly reflected at the IEC meeting. Defending the CWI from this threat was the reason we took the step of forming the faction and to raise the level of the debate onto a clearer political foundation.

The present crisis initially erupted because of the methods used by the majority of the Irish leadership and the stand taken by the IS in opposing them. As a response to the indefensible and reprehensible action by one comrade, a part of the Irish leadership took counter-measures which the IS believed to be totally alien to our democratic norms and regime. These actions were taken by this small group of leaders without being discussed or approved on any of the democratically elected structures of the party or international – and who were not informed of the situation for almost two months. The majority of the Irish NEC and the IS were not made aware until September, despite this small group of leading comrades taking those measures in July and discussing it amongst themselves at the CWI school. In our opinion, this and the other steps taken by this group in the leadership of the party in Ireland broke the norms of democratic centralism and constituted a threat to the democratic rights of the party.

The IS majority attempted to discuss and resolve these issues with the Irish leadership. A meeting with the IS took place in London in mid-September [see page 230]. Then two IS comrades went to meet the Irish NEC. Following this, a full debate took place at the Irish NC in October, involving four IS members and PS from Scotland. However, despite these discussions and debates, the Irish NEC comrades remained insistent in defending their actions. At the Irish NC meeting, the NC endorsed the actions of the group of NEC members. When the methods used were challenged some comrades defended them on the grounds that the successful struggles of the Irish section showed that the comrades who led the party must have had correct methods. We do not accept this argument. In other meetings, the actions of the NEC grouping were defended as "proletarian methods". The IS was not prepared to agree or endorse such methods which broke the norms of democratic centralism.

The differences were then taken to the IEC meeting. It became clear at the beginning of the IEC that a group of leaders from a number of sections – initially, Belgium, Sweden and Ireland, then Greece and the USA – had been co-ordinating to oppose the IS's handling of this question, which is their right. This grouping acted to defend the Irish leadership from criticism, arguing that the IS wanted to discredit and even "crush" the Irish leadership and provoke a split in the CWI. In discussion with IEC comrades, IS members had simply stated that, given the significance of the differences on methods and programme, a split was possible, depending on how the discussion unfolded. At the IEC, the IS simply proposed that the debates with the Irish leadership were discussed openly and publicly. There was no proposal for a vote or decision on any issue.

From the beginning of the IEC, this group of leaders organised numerous meetings among themselves outside of the plenary and acted in a coordinated way against the proposals and interventions of the IS. They denied they were, or are, part of a faction but operated as a 'non-faction faction' in the run-up to the IEC meeting and during it.

It was in this context that the political issues emerged during the IEC. The supporters of this platform reached the conclusion that we had no alternative but to declare a faction. This was done to oppose the methods and ideas of the political trend that had developed around the leaders of the Irish section during the IEC, and also to allow the political differences on method and programme to be raised in the clearest possible manner throughout the whole of the CWI and its membership.

This step provoked angry protests from the Greek, Belgian, Irish, American and Swedish leaders, and from some other sections. They refused – then and now – to recognise that some IEC members were acting as a faction, even though they had not openly declared one. Lenin, in July 1911, pointed out: "In these circumstances the shouts against 'factionalism' are so empty, especially when coming from those who have just formed their own faction. Surely it is time to understand that shouts against factionalism are meant to distract attention from the really important question – that of the party or anti-party content of the activity of the various factions." (The State of Affairs in the Party, July 1911)

Then, at the end of the IEC, we were presented with a resolution from a leading Greek IEC comrade. Arguing for this resolution, he demagogically congratulated the IEC, especially younger members, for taking a stand against the IS: "And it has happened with very young comrades with little experience [as] members of the IS. This means that in the CWI there's a powerful cadre being developed". He argued: "We think we had an obligation to send a very strong message to the IS that if they are determined to crush the Irish leadership, because this was the plan... If they are determined to crush the Irish leadership, they would have to crush the Greek leadership. Then they would have to crush the Belgian and Swedish leadership, and they would have to crush the US leadership." Yet all the IS had proposed was that a full discussion and debate take place on the methods used by the Irish leadership, which we think were indefensible and not in line with the methods of the CWI.

Previously, over two days of discussion at the IEC the majority of Irish comrades had defended their investigation. Yet, on the IEC's last day, this Greek resolution, stated that the Irish leadership recognised many of the criticisms that had been made of how the confidential investigation had been conducted, criticisms that had originally raised by the IS in September. However the resolution also stated that the paragraph dealing with the criticism of the investigation should only be circulated to the ECs of the sections and the Irish NC. Why such fear of informing the members of the international of this conclusion? We find it unacceptable that such conclusions should be kept from, at least, the leading NCs/CCs of all the sections of the CWI. Moreover, following the IEC, the subsequent meeting of the Irish NC took no decision regarding the criticisms made of the Irish leading group by the IEC. The Irish comrade who reported on the IEC meeting to the Irish NC did not mention the IEC resolution's criticisms of the Irish NEC and the investigation, but concentrated most of his remarks on attacking the IS. The Irish NC's previous decision, to endorse the actions taken by the leading group as "democratic and principled", has not been corrected or modified. The Greek resolution – adopted at the IEC by a majority of three full IEC members – was, in effect, a protective shield placed around the undemocratic methods used by the leading group of the Irish leadership. The IS majority and supporters of this platform find this unacceptable in a Trotskyist international.

The IEC comrade who moved the Greek resolution argued that the IS had to accept the decision of the Irish NC to endorse the actions of the leadership in Ireland and that, while maintaining its criticism, the IS had to move on. Yet the same comrade was moving a resolution – carried by the IEC – that made criticisms of the Irish leadership – criticisms that had been previously rejected by the Irish NC in October. The IS majority and supporters of this platform find these methods unacceptable and undemocratic. These methods by some IEC members provide a cover for actions which broke with the methods of democratic centralism and created the basis for the emergence of cliques. We are not prepared to accept this.

This goes to the issue of the type of international we want to build and the methods that should be used. The CWI is not a federation of parties and groups. It is a revolutionary international based on the methods of democratic centralism. The leadership, the IS and IEC, have never adopted the method of bureaucratically imposing a position on national sections. Yet this does not mean that the leading bodies of either the international or its national sections should be party to 'moving on' and covering up serious mistakes in method or programme. The role of the IS is to intervene politically when important political and organisational issues arise in sections, to clearly express its views and opinions, and make proposals.

During this debate some comrades have argued that the IS should intervene to provide political leadership and 'mediate' in disputes which arise. We do not agree with this approach.

While sometimes it is correct to attempt to mediate between comrades, the primary responsibility of the international leadership is to state its political opinion in any debate or dispute. We do not aim to build a looser international where the role of the IS is to make general political comment but not to intervene in a concrete way in the work of the sections. This is not the concept of a unified revolutionary international, based on democratic centralist ideas that we can agree with.

Where a leadership thinks a serious mistake has been made on programme, tactics or method, it has a revolutionary obligation to say so, and to debate the issues out. When principled issues are on the table for discussion, such debates should be conducted in a comradely manner. However, where serious issues are at stake, the debate will inevitably assume a sharper character. Diplomatic formulae should not be used as a means of masking or obscuring serious political or tactical questions. This issue also consistently emerged at the IEC meeting, with some comrades complaining about the tone of the debate. In any polemic or debate there should be an effort to avoid exaggerations or excesses, but they are inevitable. However, the central issue is not the 'tone' but the political content and the character of the international. It is very significant that those comrades insisted on the 'tone' of the IS and accused it of not understanding that the Irish section has a 'very special' position because of its mass influence and lack of cadres. But, at the same time, these comrades remained silent about the fact that the party apparatus in southern Ireland is soon to be comprised of 27 full-timers, plus three TDs, overwhelmingly financed by the state via the elected positions we hold. A majority of full-timers are connected to work associated with the elected positions.

The debate has now opened up throughout the CWI. We look forward to an open and honest political discussion which we believe can clarify the decisive issues and tasks we face in order to build revolutionary parties in the era which has now opened up. We urge comrades to engage in it to clarify all of the political and organisational issues, and draw the necessary conclusions in relation to the methods we use, and the tasks we are involved in, as we face up to the working class battles in the coming period, such as we see developing in France, Belgium, Spain, Brazil, Mexico, the Spanish state and many other countries. This is a debate to prepare the revolutionary forces for the era which has now begun, and to discuss and clarify the programme, tactics and methods we need to build a revolutionary Trotskyist International, based on the working class and using the methods of democratic centralism.

IEC members and alternates

Weizmann Hamilton (South Africa), Michael Koschitzki (Germany), Philip Stott (Scotland), Clare Doyle (IS), Peter Taaffe (IS), Sascha Staničić (Germany), Hannah Sell (England & Wales, IS), Judy Beishon (England & Wales, IS), Shaun Arendse (South Africa), Babara Areal (Spanish state), Juan Ignacio Ramos (Spanish state), Victor Taibo (Spanish state), Carla Torres (Mexico), Miriam Municio (Spanish state), Miguel Campos (Spanish state), Félix Martínez (Veneuela), Christine Thomas (Italy), Jagadish Chandra (India), Niall Mulholland (IS), Ravi Chandra (Malaysia), Srinath Perera (Sri Lanka), Siri Jayasuriya (Sri Lanka), Bob Labi (IS), TU Senan (IS), Tony Saunois (IS)

We ask to be able to address all sections' CC/NCs and meetings
where the international debate is being discussed.

In Defence of a Working-Class Orientation

Peter Taaffe, for the IS majority

*I*t is necessary to call things by their right name. Barely a month has passed since the IEC and yet it is already quite clear that the CWI faces an opposition to the policies and programme of the CWI with tendencies towards petty bourgeois Mandelism. This opposition originated with the leadership of the Irish section, but it is also present in the leadership of a number of sections of the CWI who support them. This is most prominently displayed in the recent lengthy Greek Executive Committee's resolution written by Andros Payiatsos (AP), which represents an open political retreat from the policies and analysis of the CWI.

This is a complete apologia – both organisational and political – for the false methods, policies and perspectives of the Irish organisation. We have characterised this as representing substantial concessions to 'Mandelite' political positions on identity politics, the abandonment of the need for a revolutionary organisation based upon the movement of the working class and the internal regime and democracy of the revolutionary party, and the revolutionary programme and perspectives that flow from such an approach.

The Greek EC loudly denounces myself, Peter Taaffe, for drawing a clear comparison between the policies and perspectives of the present Irish leadership with those of the Mandelite USFI in the past and today. In the 1960s Ted Grant and I walked out of their world congress and subsequently broke with these opportunists. We turned our backs on them and faced up to the task of winning the working class, above all the youth, to our banner, despite being a very small organisation at the time. All of our present 'critics' would never have been able to discover the revolutionary perspectives and programme of the CWI if we had not resorted at that time to this bold move.

What are the policies of Mandelism then and today? Abandonment of the centrality of the idea of the working class as the main force for socialist change and, in its place, the hunt for other forces to play this role: students as the 'detonator' of revolution, false illusions in the guerrilla movements and leaders like Tito, Fidel Castro, Che Guevara and Mao. The Mandelites did not at the outset present a clear repudiation of the working class as the main force for socialist change. They downplayed its role only gradually. We need to remember here the incident in 1968 when I confronted Ernest Mandel himself at a big public meeting in London where I raised the perspective of the possibility of a working-class revolt in Western Europe that could take place 'at any time'. His riposte was to rule out such an 'exaggerated' perspective, famously declaring that the working class was unlikely to move for at least 20 years! This was on the eve of the mighty French revolutionary events of 1968, resulting in the greatest general strike in history, when 10 million workers went on strike and occupied the factories.

The USFI argued that the working class was dormant, that its organisations were empty, that we had to 'seek support' from other 'oppressed layers', that we should not bang our heads against 'reality' but look for more 'fruitful' areas of work amongst students, intellectuals and 'other social forces' who were coming into collision with capitalism. Does this sound familiar? Yes, unfortunately – it is echoed in the arguments of the Irish leadership and others, like the Greek leadership, and is used to justify their abandonment of systematic organised trade union work both in Ireland and in Greece. Read what the Irish leadership has argued – now reinforced by the false arguments of the Greek leadership – that the trade unions are empty, in the unchallengeable grip of right-wing leaders, etc. and therefore it is necessary to seek a point of reference and work outside of these 'moribund' organisations. Of course, there is some truth in this because of the overall corrosive effect of the trade union right-wing, reinforced by the ineptitude of the 'left' during a severe capitalist economic crisis, although there have been a number of important strikes in recent years in southern Ireland, including an impending nurses' strike. But it is not the whole truth and moreover there was an element of this in the 1960s when Militant in Britain was formed – as the pioneers of the CWI – and still in the 1970s with the formation of the CWI.

While building our influence amongst the youth we nevertheless continued to work assiduously and patiently in the unions, assembling small forces, linking together with other workers to form a left point of attraction, broad lefts, as part of the process of transforming the unions. Without this patient, long-term approach we would never have conquered some important leaderships of some trade unions, like the civil servants' union PCS where we managed to win the leadership with a left majority on its national executive after a battle that lasted for decades. The bourgeois were terrified of such a development as they were over our growing influence within the Labour Party, which was only achieved by a patient but effective approach. This is what a recently released 'secret report' about Thatcher's approach towards this development says. The Thatcher government "was clearly most concerned with members of Militant Tendency, reporting that it was 'the largest and most threatening Trotskyist group in Britain', and that its membership had quadrupled over six years to 6,300. 'Its greatest strengths have been the dedication of its members and its strong internal discipline,' it said.

"The [Inter-departmental group on Subversion in Public Life] SPL also reported in 1985 that 284 members of Militant were civil servants. Three years later, the figure had grown to around 450. Most 'subversives' were found to be working in junior clerical positions. The SPL recommended in its initial report that they should, where possible, 'be identified and distanced from such work'. It added that mounting a purge of suspect individuals would not be possible, but 'it might sometimes be possible covertly to move individuals to posts where they would have less potential for disruption'…

"Senior civil servants were informed that they should consult MI5 [the British secret service] before moving 'subversives' to any new post. 'It would need to be a covert process, because any systematic barring of known subversives from certain work would be contentious,' they were told. Armstrong recorded that he was most concerned about computer operators, revenue collectors and people who had contact with the public.

"The need for the utmost secrecy is stressed repeatedly throughout the files that have been made available at Kew. One SPL chair, John Chilcot, [who later gained notoriety for his white-washing inquiry into the Iraq war] wrote in June 1988: 'It is right on balance to continue with this exercise, despite its acute sensitivity and the high risk of embarrassment in the event of any leak.' The papers also show that MI5 mounted an operation to identify 'subversives' teaching at eight schools in inner London. The Office for Standards in Education said school inspectors had not reported directly to MI5 since it took over the work of HM Inspectors in 1992." [Guardian, London, 24 July 2018]

AP also states in relation to the members of parliament (TDs in Ireland): "The Irish section has re-established traditions about what it means to be a public representative of the working class, long forgotten and unknown to the new generations, like for example MPs going to jail in order to serve the class which they represent." It is astonishing that he completely passes over the 1991 jailing of Terry Fields, Tommy Sheridan and 34 other comrades, for non-payment of poll tax in Britain, a mass movement with 18 million refusing to pay the tax that eclipsed the movement in Ireland in the numbers involved and its effects, especially by bringing down Thatcher. These MPs had a total of three full-time workers assisting them – not the big numbers working for the Irish TDs. These parliamentary full-timers were part of the full-time team of the organisation reported to the membership. We should also say here that Dave Nellist, who was also expelled from Labour for refusing to pay his poll tax, has donated his entire parliamentary pension to the party.

The Irish leadership is completely wrong when they compare their approach today towards the unions – in which, they have admitted, they have effectively abandoned systematic work in the trade unions for a period – to the 'open turn'. The open turn was necessitated by the empty-ing out of the traditional parties of the working class, particularly social democracy, and hence a period where we made a direct appeal for workers to join our organisations and parties.

But all the great leaders of the working class – Marx, Engels, Lenin and Trotsky – em-phasised the absolute necessity even in difficult periods for organised systematic work in and around the trade unions, sometimes even in 'yellow' trade union structures as seem to exist in Greece at the present time. This is as a precondition for assembling a serious working class force both on the trade union field and politically.

We fully recognise the difficulties in Ireland and in Greece of this work. We have expe-rienced similar problems in Britain in the past; for instance in the 1950s and early 1960s when the biggest, heavily bureaucratised union, – the Transport and General Workers Union – frustrated so many militants that they resorted to what was at that time an ultra-left approach of trying to create new, 'pure' unions. We always argued against this in favour of a systematic approach in the larger, more viable union, which was borne out at a later stage when this union shifted sharply towards the left. In the form of Unite it is now the biggest left union in Britain and one of the most important props for Corbyn and the left in the current battle that has opened up between left and right both in the unions and in the Labour Party itself. Even if, in practice, the official structures prevent active engagement with the unions we should then seek to use any positions we build up amongst workers in the factories and workplaces to put forward a plan of action to systematically change the union structures. In addition, there have been the development of new formations amongst the overwhelmingly young 'precariat' in industries like hospitality, logistics, etc, to which we can turn.

This was not the case in southern Ireland where there was little or no attempt by the Socialist Party to link the work amongst women to demanding action by the trade unions. In Spain the comrades did automatically take up the idea of the general strike of both students and workers against the vicious sexual violence, including the rapes carried out by the infamous 'wolfpack'. Unfortunately, no similar call was made either in the factories or to the trade unions in Ireland for concrete workers' action. And this was not at all accidental. It seems this has never even occurred to either the leadership of Rosa or the Irish party because they did not have a clear orientation towards the working-class organisations and forces in the campaign in favour of abortion rights. We all agree that they carried out tremendous work in their participation in this campaign, but it was not through clear working-class methods and orientation.

The fundamental reason for this is that the leadership of the Irish majority did not think there was any possibility of mobilising independent working class support and moreover did not think that the working class was the most decisive force for change. Hence, as the Irish comrades have now admitted in the light of the discussion at the IEC, the idea had grown amongst some of the comrades in Rosa and in the leadership of the Irish organisation that the new 'vanguard' for change is not the working class, but the forces around the movement for women's and LGBTQ+ rights.

We have been clear on the issues of women's rights and LGBTQ+ rights: from the beginnings of our organisation in Britain – over 60 years ago – we have unflinchingly conducted a struggle against the discrimination and sexual harassment of women; not just of working-class women but of all women. We also support the legitimate demands of the LGBTQ+ movement, so long as they do not conflict with the rights of others, and can be resolved by democratic discussion. We have championed the demands of all oppressed groups and strata including the LGBTQ+, for instance against the anti-trans position of Mark Serwotka, the leader of the PCS. However, we have always sought to situate this in a class analysis linked to class demands. This is not the case even with our own organisation in Ireland. This was shown in relation to the recent magnificent strike in Glasgow of 10,000 women. Some comrades quite wrongly rushed to praise this as an example of a purely 'feminist' strike. Our Scottish comrades correctly saw it primarily as class action by women workers that appealed successfully for solidarity action from male workers. This is just one illustration of the different approach we have to those who support or are influenced by identity politics.

We have a long history of opposition to what was in effect identity politics, although not called that at the time, for instance in the 'Black Power' movement in the US and elsewhere in the 1960s. We produced thoroughgoing analyses, for instance of the Black Panthers movement, signifying what was progressive and could be supported and what was not. This movement undoubtedly represented a step forward but largely because of a lack of experience there were tendencies towards separatism that sometimes were reinforced by some alleged US 'Trotskyists', which we opposed and sought to influence in a class direction. The success of our approach was shown in Britain by the fact that we later built the biggest black organisation of youth and workers in the form of the Panther UK. It organised the biggest indoor rally of 2,000 with Bobby Seale, one of the most prominent leaders of the Black Panthers, as a speaker. We discussed with Bobby on his visit to Britain.

Moreover, the evolution of Malcolm X was a tremendous demonstration of how under the blows of events a movement can begin with separatist tendencies, with utopian demands such as 'black power' but then can then seek to finally embrace a class analysis. All of this we explained in our material on Malcolm X, the Black Power movement, etc. The present leadership of the American organisation, particularly the editor of its paper has chosen not to reproduce this material for the new generation of US Marxists moving into struggle, even when they have published other later material on the issue.

However it was not just in terms of theory but in the practice that flows from this that we demonstrated the correctness of a clear Marxist approach. It is well-known that we had major successes in Britain in the Campaign Against Domestic Violence – which the Irish leadership effectively now dismiss as "in the past". This is not the case because it is particularly relevant in relation to the cuts in Britain that are being made against these gains that were won not least because of the work and influence of our party. Moreover it would have been impossible to achieve this if we had had some of the one-sided positions that pass for a Marxist approach and which are now advocated by some comrades who make concessions to identity politics.

'Theory is a guide to action'. When we held effective power at local level in Liverpool we put these ideas into practice – through working-class control by the council unions of hiring and firing – we made clear proposals on the issue of full-time employment of a layer of long-term unemployed, particularly black youth, in deprived areas of Liverpool.

AP spends endless pages and interminable words to try and refute what all of us clearly heard in his contribution on the last day of the IEC when he acted as an apologist for the Irish comrades. In his usual manner, he also viciously attacked the IS. We all remember how he launched a similar, completely unprovoked verbal assault on comrade Lynn Walsh at the CWI summer school over a relatively minor issue when we were discussing the possibilities for an 'alternative currency' in Greece coming out of the crisis over the euro at the time.

This naturally caused outrage, not just amongst the British comrades but many others who noted his lack of sense of proportion in the way he attacks perceived political opponents. I intervened to try and bring comrades together – which flies in the face of the impression that is now given by him and others that we want to split or that we are organising for a split.

He did act in an intemperate fashion at this IEC when he attacked the IS for allegedly trying to 'crush' the Irish leadership and others. He characterised the IS minority comrades as 'independent-minded young comrades' who had stood up to older IS members. The phrase 'independent minded' is precisely that favoured by petty-bourgeois academics in Britain and elsewhere to define those who are 'independent' from class pressures, who seek a middle and unprincipled political position between the pressures of the working class and the labour movement and the bourgeois.

AP attempts in an extremely tortuous manner to separate himself from what he actually said at the IEC, that the IS should effectively capitulate to the decisions of the Irish leadership. He first of all denies that he actually said what he said and then admits that "When the IS meet such an opposition from the NEC of a section, like it did in Ireland, it must retreat, it must take a step back, without however abandoning its views and criticisms, and look for alternative ways to argue for its position and opinion, including with other leading bodies of the International such as the IEC." This is exactly how we behaved on many occasions – first of all trying to persuade the Irish leadership – but on this occasion, having met a brick wall from them, only then deciding to take the issue to the IEC, particularly because the 'cover-up' had created a new situation. To our shock and surprise AP and the Greek organisation supported the Irish on the cover-up of this shameful incident. Ultimately, the Irish leadership admitted 'mistakes' even though this was exactly the wording that we used when we originally discussed this issue in London – which they rejected and continued to reject right up to the time of the IEC [see page 230]. If they had admitted their 'mistake' over the 'cover-up' at the beginning then this whole issue would not have taken on the sharpened form that it has.

AP, along with others, now acts as an apologist for the scandalous behaviour of the Irish leadership on this issue. We warned them at the time that this could have serious legal consequences, particularly for our public representatives. This was brushed aside and now they seek to sweep this further under the carpet. The resolution that they moved at the IEC to 'redact' any mention of the 'cover-up' was in effect an attempted gagging order, a cover-up of the unacceptable behaviour of the Irish leadership in answer to the reprehensible hack of a comrade who has been disciplined for this. The Irish leadership accepted with relief this cover-up initiated by AP, which they hoped would allow them to suppress and hide this issue from the broader membership of the sections and the CWI as a whole. We are not prepared to collaborate in such shameful practices with which now AP and the Greek EC have associated themselves. Moreover, the actions of AP then allowed them to ignore the hack. It remains a fact that the Greek leadership and particularly AP acted as a shield for the unacceptable behaviour of the Irish leadership.

We tried to persuade them otherwise and then were accused of 'heavy-handedness' towards both the Irish leadership and the Greeks and AP in telephone calls. It is a complete fiction that four or five people at one go attempted to systematically bombard AP into supporting the position of the IS. Prior to the IEC I spoke to AP once, in a joint telephone call along with Tony Saunois and Niall Mulholland, who is responsible for Greece on the IS, and also had short conversations with him at the beginning of the IEC.

After this phone call a new Greek legend took flight. AP claims that he proposed a "liaison committee" to handle the crisis over Ireland. This is not true. What was proposed by him but not agreed to by us was a commission. We said that we will go back and discuss it with comrades, which we did, and then I explained to him at the beginning of the IEC that we had met opposition to this proposal, not just from the Spanish but from others who remembered the experience of Scotland and the ill-fated "commission" on that occasion. But this did not prevent him from declaring in another bombastic outburst that the IS had 'betrayed him' by not automatically acceding to his suggestion, shouting at the IS as he walked back to his seat: 'Tell the truth! Tell the truth!' The clear implication was that we lied when we disputed his version.

This says everything about the method of AP, which we have noted on other occasions when we have disagreed with him on an issue. Unless you immediately jump to attention and agree with him you can expect an outburst and usually a distortion of the position which we have attempted to put forward. In particular, on this and other political issues in which there has been a conflict with him and the Greek EC in the past, it raises questions about his handling of differences within the Greek organisation. In effect his approach is that if you do not immediately agree with his proposal you are betraying him! This is no way to conduct a healthy discussion and the handling of inevitable differences, including misunderstandings, which will come up in any large organisations like the CWI. We have had many differences in the British organisation, including the formation of tendencies and factions, and intense discussions over issues of perspectives, programme and orientation. We cannot remember any such discussions and similar differences within the Greek organisation. Perhaps this says something about the internal regime in Greece under AP's leadership.

We had many occasions when we disagreed with AP and we think we were in the right. One such difference arose not just with the Greeks, but with others such as the German comrades over their approach towards the largely petty bourgeois anti-capitalist movements in the 1990s. Of course we orientated towards this movement as we have done and will continue to do so in movements of women, on trans issues, the environment, etc. The evidence of our discussion and differences over the tactics for the anti-capitalist movement is dealt with in abundance in my books on the history of our party which also covers the activity of the CWI.

Our differences with the Greek comrades arose not because they were intervening in the anti-capitalist movement but how they intervened, their exaggerated expectations of the gains to be made from what was essentially a very confused student/middle-class layer with a smattering of workers. Moreover, they had an incorrect definition of the social role of radicalised students at that time. After clashes with them at an IEC, I was subsequently in Greece discussing this question with AP and particularly the late Nikos Remoundos, the founder with me of the Greek organisation, and other comrades on the Greek EC. AP advanced the novel theory that so impoverished were students today, and particularly in Greece, that in effect they were 'now like workers'. We begged to differ and were vocal in our opposition to this false categorisation of even the most impoverished working-class students as 'workers'.

Students socially and in the place they occupy in society are not the same as workers who are organised by big industry with a collective consciousness that flows from this. This does not mean that we don't try and win the best of the students to a Marxist, Trotskyist position. But we do not leave it at that; we seek to develop them as Marxist cadres who can play a role in assisting the working class and in the process can learn from them in the struggle, on condition that they approach this work not seeking to lecture workers.

Trotsky in the 1930s, in the middle of the dispute with the petty bourgeois opposition in the American SWP, made the apt comment that they had in the US "many good middle-class young men and women" but these had not immersed themselves sufficiently in the struggles of the working class, thereby learning from them and in the process hopefully taking a big step along the road to becoming effective Marxist cadres. He advised that these student comrades should be "wet by the rain and dried by the wind".

He was so alarmed at the social composition of the SWP – particularly the opposition of Shachtman and co – that he proposed that unless these students linked themselves to circles of workers and recruited some of them to the revolutionary party in six months, they should be reduced to the level of sympathisers.

Of course it would be artificial to apply this in a blanket fashion today but nevertheless this general approach of Trotsky retains its full force in this complicated period facing the workers' movement and ourselves. In recent times we have recruited comrades from a petty bourgeois milieu and background but have been forced to promote some of them prematurely to leading positions, including on leading bodies of the party, when their record and activity – particularly in the workers' movement – did not justify such rapid promotion. We have to adopt a much more demanding approach towards these new recruits ensuring that their promotion to positions of authority only after they are tested out in actively assisting in the struggles of the working class. Above all they should be set the task of winning workers.

This does not in any way denote a 'prejudice' against students per se. On the contrary, some of the best comrades we have won, including at the level of the present leaderships of our sections, have come from the student field but have been first tested out in the workers' struggles before they are promoted to positions of leadership.

AP claims, as have others in other sections, consistently throughout his document that they – the 'Non-Faction Faction' – had the majority at the last IEC. That is not true and will be shown to be false as the course of this political battle unfolds. Even at the IEC the real 'minority resolution' – which was, as we have explained, an open cover-up by the Irish leadership of their own members – was passed by a majority of 3! This was only achieved because comrades who would have supported the IS were not present. Moreover, some comrades and sections who were present and did not vote or abstained did so because they were not clear on the issues but have since indicated support for the IS and many have declared support for the 'Trotskyist' faction. It has to be said that we have been considerably assisted in building our support by the general revulsion and opposition to AP's document and his unprincipled support for the Irish.

At the same time, the voting rights at the IEC do not fully or accurately recognise the current weight and membership of each section. For instance England and Wales has four IEC members; Greece has four full members and Israel has two. Between 2015 and today the Greek membership has declined, which includes a period of mass upheaval in Greece. There is also the weight given to relatively small sections in terms of membership but who are nevertheless considered as important for the long-term development of the CWI.

Despite his convoluted language AP clearly blames the IS for the dispute breaking out at this time. He writes: "The crisis is a result of the IS's mistake of escalating the attack whenever it met resistance, instead of taking a step back to reconsider its tactics and approach." This is a travesty of the truth. I explained to AP in the infamous 'phone call' prior to the IEC that we and others have attempted, not over months but for years to try and persuade the Irish comrades of the incorrectness of their ideas on identity politics, on the programme in elections, including the transitional programme, on the party profile, etc. And not just the IS; Bryan Koulouris in the US and Danny Byrne are on record attacking the Irish in very strong language. We met with a brick wall as we had done earlier in Scotland, Liverpool and many other examples of former comrades who were breaking from the revolutionary project and particularly the CWI.

The Irish IEC members' refusal to criticise their own members – even in private and sensitively – over the crass comments made by some of them at the CWI school in Barcelona provoked a new discussion in the IS. AP advocates we should wear a blindfold and pass over what we considered was a breach with a Trotskyist position on these issues. 'Back away' – hide the differences – is the cry; take them up on a more propitious occasion in the future. This is, in effect, the approach of AP which is an abdication of real revolutionary leadership. Trotsky consistently advocated "say what needs to be said and do what needs to be done come what may".

AP conveniently forgets that we were drawn into this discussion on the 'hack' months after the Irish leadership discovered this. When we did not automatically comply with their proposals they 'escalated' this into an attack on the IS. We acted in a responsible fashion to defend the reputation of the Irish organisation and the CWI, which provoked even more hostility from the Irish comrades and the mobilisation of their primarily full-time machine to 'crush' the IS delegation at the subsequent meetings that took place in Dublin, following the fractious meeting in London when they remained obdurate. The counter-measures taken by a small group within the Irish NEC, without the agreement of the full Irish NEC or discussed with the IS for nearly two months, was a breach in the methods of democratic centralism and the democratic functioning of the party structures. AP does not even comment on these events. Therefore we are right to conclude that all that the Irish and, it seems, AP want is a passive international leadership that just accepts what we consider are potentially huge dangers to the reputation of the CWI and the Irish leadership, which could put in jeopardy the great achievements of the past. Belatedly, AP came to the same conclusion as us; that is why he persuaded the Irish to now accept their 'mistakes' – which are a lot more than this – because of the severe potential legal dangers that they faced. We stressed the potential danger of this, particularly to the elected representatives in Ireland and elsewhere.

A further travesty of the truth is also attempted by AP over the history of the Greek organisation and its relations with the IS. He effectively attempts to rewrite history on issues such as the dispute over the euro and China. It is true that one IS member, Lynn Walsh, raised questions about whether or not the euro would actually be implemented but this was connected to the economic perspectives, which were widely discussed at this time by the bourgeois, of a possible economic meltdown. If such a downturn had taken place this could have shipwrecked the euro before it was even launched. With the onset of the crisis of 2007-08 and its enduring effects even during the so-called 'boom' the euro could yet collapse.

There is nothing surprising in this which is in line with Trotsky's analysis of the ultimate incapacity of capitalism to overcome the limits not just of private ownership but of the nation state. AP passes over the even greater mistakes of his new friends in the Swedish leadership, some of whom argued not only that the euro could be implemented but that the nation state could be overcome and a new 'European bourgeoisie' could be formed! Moreover, Greece itself could have come out of the euro in 2015 if the Tsipras leadership had been pushed by mass pressure into opposing the Troika and its savage programme of austerity. Britain was stopped from joining the euro by the pressure exerted in Britain, both from sections of the bourgeois and the labour movement correctly seeing it as a vehicle for implementing savage austerity. In the new situation that we confront, the euro could yet collapse, triggered by any number of countries: in Italy, in Germany even, the countries of Eastern Europe and also the fallout from the crisis that has been generated by Brexit in Britain. The cheap attempt at point scoring made by AP on this issue – which we repeat is an attempt at rewriting history – may indicate that he and the Greek EC think that the capitalists will be able to unify the productive forces in Europe and overcome the insuperable barriers of the nation state. Such a perspective is utopian on the basis of capitalism, as we have consistently pointed out in our material particularly in opposition to the Mandelites and now, it seems, to some in our own ranks.

AP also applies the same method to the question of China – its class characteristics – and how it will evolve in the next period. It is not possible to give a full explanation here of how our position has developed. We opposed the Swedish leadership who approached the phenomena of China in a one-sided and dogmatic fashion, characterising it at one stage as already arrived as a capitalist regime – and crudely playing up the 'Communist Party dictatorship' – without any qualifications whatsoever. We oppose this crude over-simplification of the complex processes that have unfolded in China. We said that it was clearly moving in a capitalist direction but when we were debating this issue it was more of a hybrid with a clear capitalist sector but the retention of a huge state sector. Therefore it was not a simple repeat of the processes that had developed in Russia and Eastern Europe following the collapse of Stalinism.

The endless debates at IEC meetings – over the precise details and therefore the character of China – led the IS on my initiative to propose a compromise which would recognise the clear process of a movement towards capitalism while at the same time not yet clearly arriving at the completion of this process. I proposed, not AP or anybody else, that we should describe China as a "state capitalist regime with peculiar features". This was accepted by all sides in the IEC but now AP wants to reopen this question in order for him and his allies to once again hopefully score points to the detriment of the IS and those who support us. In reality China remains as a very peculiar 'hybrid' regime. The most farsighted thinkers of the bourgeois internationally have come to the same conclusion as us and have used belatedly our terminology of 'state capitalism' to give some kind of description of what is a highly complex process which is still in a state of flux. Most of the bourgeois refuse to describe China as a 'fully developed market economy' and one of the factors explaining this is the huge retention of the state sector – including the banks and finance houses – which has allowed China, to some extent, to escape the ravages of the rest of the capitalist world following the crisis of 2007-08 through massive state-led spending which has resulted in the accumulation of huge debts.

In reality China's class character is a continuation of the 'hybrid' described by us in the past. It has managed to escape serious economic crisis up to now because of the huge injection of state finance, which has in turn led to a colossal debt for China and threatens the continuation of its growth. But the artificial injection of this issue into this debate is an example of the shallow and incorrect approach of AP, the Greek EC and their allies. We look forward to further robust exchanges and discussions on this issue in the CWI and in the public domain.

Let us also remind AP of the perspective of the Swedish leadership which was that capitalist globalisation was 'irreversible'. He says absolutely nothing about this. The Swedish leadership – at least, one of them – did have the good grace subsequently to admit at the IEC that they had been wrong and the IS was correct about the inevitable interruption of this process, leading plausibly at a certain stage to 'de-globalisation'. This prognosis of ours had been dismissed by the Swedish leadership and I do not know what the position of AP was on this and other issues.

It would take a book to completely refute all the misconceptions and falsifications of the IS's position over Ireland and many other related questions. However, we are confident that our faction platform, 'In Defence of a Working-Class, Trotskyist CWI', and analysis will be borne out by events and in the support that this will engender in the ranks of the CWI and beyond.

FOR A TROTSKYIST INTERNATIONAL

Tony Saunois for the In Defence of a Working-Class, Trotskyist CWI faction – March 2019

Since the establishment of the International Faction 'In Defence of Working-Class, Trotskyist CWI', at the IEC meeting held in December 2018, the exchanges in the CWI have confirmed our analysis of the development of two main trends. At root, the cause of this crisis has been the objective pressures arising from the contradictory and complex conjuncture bearing down on the relatively small forces of a revolutionary organisation and our respective reactions to it.

We deliberately emphasised two 'main trends' because we were aware that other trends were also present and could emerge in the course of subsequent discussion. The differences between the faction and the Spanish leadership at the London meeting in March 2019 demonstrated this, and is fully analysed below. However, a balance sheet of the discussion, so far, starts from the fact that this is a struggle on our part to defend the CWI's core principles, which are vital to determine its future.

The first main trend, around the international faction, represents the defence of the centrality of the role of the working class, and a Trotskyist method and programme to build a revolutionary party based on the working class. The second, represented by the 'Non-Faction Faction' (NFF), reflects an opportunist trend which has bowed down to the complications of the current objective conjuncture and turned away from an emphasis on building among the organised working class. This has been reflected in an adaptation to the separatist ideas of 'identity politics' and turning away from the trade unions as a central aspect of the work to build a revolutionary party.

Now, a third, ultimatist, ultra-left trend has revealed itself, reflected by the leadership of the Spanish and Portuguese sections. This ultra-leftism is the opposite side of the same coin to the opportunism reflected in the political positions defended by NFF supporters. Moreover, the Spanish leadership never expressed their real position in the lengthy discussions that took place during the negotiations for fusion between our two organisations. They have claimed they were 'deceived'. Yet it is not they who were deceived, but the CWI. Had they clearly revealed their real position, rather than deny the effects of the collapse of the Stalinist regimes and the political consequences for the international working class in terms of the boost that process gave to capitalism – the ideological offensive against socialism and the impact this had on socialist consciousness and the organisations of the working class – the process of fusion would have been put into question. The international faction stands in opposition to both the opportunistic trend of the NFF, and the ultra-left trend represented by the Spanish and Portuguese leaderships. We defend the CWI's genuine Trotskyist methods and traditions, which are necessary to build revolutionary socialist parties based on the working class.

The main leaders of the NFF are united on one thing: opposition to the IS majority. But they mask any criticism some of their members may have of their undeclared faction for opportunistic, factional reasons. In contrast, the international faction has expressed its opposition to the ultra-left approach expressed by the Spanish and Portuguese leaderships.

The powerful opportunistic pressures in this period are one reflection of the turmoil taking place in global capitalism and its reflection in all political spheres of society. It is not an accident that in many countries the main bourgeois political parties are riven with splits and divisions, as are the former bourgeois workers' parties and new left parties like Podemos. The capitalist class is increasingly unable to rule in the old way. As yet, however, the working class has not put itself at the head of the movements that have erupted and there has not yet emerged a more clearly defined socialist consciousness or mass workers' parties embracing socialist ideas. This has complicated the recent period. We are confident that this will change and the CWI must do everything possible to further this process. Massive struggles by the working class are pending which, at a certain stage, will see increased polarisation in society and the crystallisation of a more rounded socialist consciousness and organisation of the working class.

These factors have asserted big opportunistic pressures on revolutionary socialists, even to dissolve the party. The current crisis in the CWI has been reflected in all other organisations claiming to stand on the revolutionary left. This is reflected by the decision by the Irish SWP to dissolve into their broad front, People Before Profit, and to function as a 'network' (a process that the Irish NEC majority comrades seem reluctant to comment on). A similar process by the IST took place previously in Germany. Both represent the abandonment of the idea of building a distinct revolutionary party.

More recently and more starkly, it has been seen in the implosion of the ISO in the USA. This followed a crisis at its convention where the former leadership was removed. It then voted through an online ballot to dissolve the party and disband the website. This is a warning to those in the NFF who argue that the international faction is exaggerating the political differences and trends. The crisis in the ISO mirrors some of the debates taking place in the CWI. It involves the issues of identity politics, the holding of public positions and how we deal with this in a principled fashion, and how sources of finance can affect the revolutionary party. The recruitment of a large layer of middle-class youth who are infected with the disease of identity politics, together with other opportunistic pressures, has led to the rapid implosion of the ISO. They have incorporated identity politics into their organisation, established a 'MeToo' caucus and adopted #IBelieveHer, rejecting any due process to investigate accusations of abuse.

This is a stark warning for our US co-thinkers and others if the issue of identity politics is not approached correctly. Other organisations, like the PSTU in Brazil, experienced splits arising from the pressures of the objective situation – in that case, as a result of the sectarian attitude of the leadership towards the impeachment of the PT president Dilma Rousseff.

Identity politics is a massive issue in the US and internationally. It poses a major challenge for Marxists: how to oppose the separatist and divisive ideas contained within it, and which have penetrated beyond bourgeois and petty-bourgeois academic circles into sections of the labour movement. All left and revolutionary socialist organisations have been affected. Even the Woods-led IMT sect has been forced to confront it. The IMT – which, predictably, has attacked the CWI leadership personally – has been forced, a few months ago, to respond in a lengthy polemic against the ideas of identity politics that clearly infected their ranks. However, Woods argued in a crude way, opposing even the use of the term 'socialist or Marxist feminists', on the grounds that being a Marxist automatically means we are opposed to the exploitation of women. Unfortunately, the Irish section has adapted to the pressures of separatist identity politics, and this is echoed in some other sections, like Greece and Brazil. In Brazil, of course we should combat the vicious attacks against women, LGBTQ+, the working class and others, especially since Jair Bolsonaro came to power. Yet, like in the US, identity politics has permeated throughout society including into the PT and PSOL. We need to resist this, opposing separatist trends and fighting for a unified movement of the working class and others exploited and repressed by capitalism. The NFF accuses us of being 'conservative' or 'hesitant' about intervening in movements against women's oppression. It can find no examples of this, however, because we are strongly in favour of energetic interventions in movements and potential movements on these issues.

In reality, the misrepresentation of our position is based on our insistence on a Marxist analysis of these movements, and the need to intervene with a clear programme. This contrasts with the growing tendency in the leadership of the NFF sections, who claim to oppose identity politics but in practise bow to the approach and slogans of the petty-bourgeois leaderships of movements against women's and other specific oppressions. For example, fighting against victim blaming in the courts is very important, but it does not require us to adopt wholesale the current 'popular' slogans, such as #IBelieveHer, without taking into account the need to fight for democratic rights, including the right to a fair trial. Instead, we should be raising demands which point towards the capitalist nature of the legal system and the need for the working class to fight for it to be brought under democratic working-class control.

The NFF suggests that we are downplaying the movements because we point out their 'cross-class' character. Yet this class composition was clearly the case, for example, in Ireland, where wide sections of the capitalist class supported a vote for abortion rights in the referendum. By pointing out this objective fact we are not downplaying the importance of the movement. Mass movements against women's oppression have our support regardless of whether they are led by bourgeois or petty-bourgeois forces. The CWI has always clearly explained that, while working-class and poor women suffer most as a result of their double oppression, all women are oppressed because of their gender in a class society. In this we have a difference with the IR (Spanish section), which tends to put the emphasis exclusively on the oppression of working-class women.

Nor do we argue, as the IR comrades do, that past women's movements have played no role in the gains won by working-class women. On the contrary, it is clear that in a number of struggles predominantly middle-class women's movements have helped give confidence to working-class women to fight on both social and economic issues. To do this, they have usually turned to class-based organisations and struggle. The key issue for us is that the working class is the only force capable of transforming society and, when intervening in cross-class movements, we have to put to the fore the role of the organised working class in the movement to achieve its aims.

The opportunistic pressures – or 'Mandelism' as we have referred to it in previous documents – are reflected in the ideas and positions adopted by supporters of the NFF. While this may not always have been a conscious process, it is the reality of what has taken place in a number of CWI sections, to varying degrees. Prior to this crisis, the IS majority had underestimated the degree to which these pressures had corroded the theoretical foundations of some sections.

Our charge of Mandelism has provoked some leaders of the NFF, like Bryan Koulouris (USA) and others, to develop the novel theory that this cannot be possible because Mandelism was a product of the 1960s – an entirely different era. But Mandelism is an expression of a form of opportunism. Are the comrades seriously arguing that opportunist adaptations could only apply in an era like the 1960s? What of the capitulation of the SPD in Germany in 1914! Pressures of opportunism and ultra-leftism arise in all periods, in varying degrees. The issue is how to resist them. In the future, we will also need to be prepared to combat left-reformist, centrist and left-centrist ideas and organisations.

The crisis began in Ireland, where the section has adapted to the pressures of separatism reflected in identity politics, turned away from organised, systematic and consistent work in the trade unions, and where consciousness to build the revolutionary party has significantly diminished. This has been admitted by the Irish leadership, especially in their document, 'Setting the Record Straight, Part Two', in paragraph after paragraph. In paragraph 85, they state: "The diminishing of party building consciousness has affected the whole of the party, including the leadership. The development of the leadership has also been impacted upon, because there hasn't enough been an upward pressure on the leading bodies from a stronger political and experienced cadre throughout the party." The question, therefore, is posed, why the Irish leadership failed to address these issues and change the situation?

Should the current trajectory of the party in Ireland continue it would unfortunately face the same fate as the Irish SWP and ISO, and following our former Scottish section, heading towards disintegration and disappearance as a distinct Marxist organisation.

Recently, in the debate, some comrades have argued that the Irish party has taken steps to correct the weaknesses that have developed. We do not agree that verbal acknowledgements or an abrupt new turn to intervene in current industrial disputes, like the nurses' and midwives' strike, for instance, represents a qualitative change in the approach of the Irish leadership. We would welcome, of course, a genuine return to systematic, patient union work, like that carried out by the leading Siptu comrade over years. But just twelve days before the nurses' and midwives' strike the Irish NEC majority argued that "there isn't really an active layer in the unions that could be mobilised". They justified an "element of an open turn" away from the trade unions as a necessary "detour away from the obstacles of the unions". The failure of the Irish NEC majority to really change their position was also reflected on the issue of the hack, which triggered the crisis. They played down defending their actions following the IEC meeting. But at the recent debate in the Australian NC, Kevin McLoughlin (Ireland) returned to defend what they had done and claimed that they had uncovered a "factional battle plan" because of it.

The Irish NEC majority and their international supporters make occasional references to some (usually unspecified) 'mistakes' they have made. Yet, in debate after debate and throughout their voluminous documents, they attempt to defend, justify and rationalise their political and organisational mistakes. This double-bookkeeping method has nothing in common with genuine discussion and debate. This should include openly accepting mistakes in front of the membership to try to arrive at principled conclusions, to collectively learn from debates and to politically strengthen the entire CWI.

The NFF has also argued that the comrades' successful work in Nipsa, in Northern Ireland, is a refutation of the Irish section turning its back on systematic trade union work. In the first place, Nipsa work is carried out in the north, while the mistaken "Open Turn" away from union work was carried out in the south. In reality, the gains made by the Nipsa comrades are due to their tireless, systematic work, in often difficult circumstances. Other consistent union work is carried out, for example in Unite, involving youth comrades, but again this is, by and large, in the North.

Since the debate began, similar opportunistic pressures have been more clearly revealed to have affected other sections and are reflected in the political material published both in the documents and publicly. NFF supporters say no evidence has been produced to prove this. When it is, however, they simply deny it as evidence. On the Greek website, for instance, in most articles there is a lack of consistent transitional demands. Occasionally, socialism is mentioned but as a formulaic addition. Many of the NFF sections seem to be falling into the trap of adopting a minimum and maximum approach to programme, whereby socialism is tagged on to some articles without using a transitional method that leads to this conclusion or explains what it is. In Greece, the article for International Women's Day 2018, while condemning the rise in domestic violence, makes no reference to the class struggle, capitalism or socialism. This omission is present in many other articles, such as one carried on 1 September 2018, titled 'Sexism under the Knife', dealing with plastic surgery. Other articles on the environment lack concrete demands. The material on the Eldorado gold company in Chalkidiki, in general, lacks clear transitional demands. The article carried on 25 December 2018, while correctly attacking the mining company, makes no appeal to the local population or the mine workers but limits itself to how things will get worse. It attacks the local trade union leadership but makes no demands on the unions regarding what they should do. This is in line with the wrong arguments advocated by Andros Payiatsos (AP), that it is not possible to place demands on the Greek TUC!

The lack of a transitional approach towards the working class was reflected in the article on the same issue carried on 18 February 2019. The comrades wrote: "The workers though, that are defending the interests of the company, need to ask themselves if their own health and that of their kids, the very future of their land, should come before their wage packet, which they have today and will not have tomorrow." There was no attempt to raise alternative employment or the rights of those working in the industry. This contemptuous attitude towards the miners had echoes of the attitude adopted at last year's UN climate talks by the environmentalist David Attenborough, who has become popular through his TV nature documentaries. When questioned about the fate of Polish coal miners Attenborough shrugged his shoulders and had no answer regarding their employment or livelihoods!

While cosmetic improvements may have been made in some recent articles, these and other examples clearly reflect the opportunistic approach adopted by the leadership and the dilution of our distinct transitional and revolutionary socialist demands.

This trend has been reflected more recently by the leadership of our US co-thinkers, as the 2020 presidential campaign begins, in the approach towards Bernie Sanders and other left Democrats, like Alexandria Ocasio-Cortez (AOC), a member of the Democratic Socialists of America, in New York, who was recently elected to the House of Representatives. It is correct, as the IS has consistently argued, to intervene in these developments in a skilful manner. In our opinion, however, comrades have recently gone too far and are not sufficiently critical of Sanders or Democratic Party lefts like AOC. The 2020 election will not be a mere repeat of 2016.

The slogan comrades have used when intervening in Sanders events, 'Trump out, Bernie in – Build a mass movement', does not strike the right note. We should be raising the demand, 'Trump out – Bernie in, on a socialist programme', as we have with Jeremy Corbyn. In the material, the demand for Sanders to break from the Democrats, run independently and form a new party is given less emphasis. We think this is a mistake. The proposal from leading US EC members, that we make a token financial contribution to the Sanders campaign, which was rejected by the US NC, illustrates the weakness in the comrades' approach. Similarly, the criticism we make of AOC is extremely weak. While the call for a new party was included in the public financial appeal by Kshama S, in January, for the Seattle re-election campaign, the headline was: "Why I stand with AOC against the corporate Democratic Party establishment." This was an opportunistic attempt to ride on the back of AOC's current 'notoriety' and popularity. The weakness of our criticism of AOC and her programme is reflected in the slogan, 'A Green New Deal'. Although an article has recently been published explaining that this would only be possible with the implementation of a socialist programme, comrades are still putting forward the slogan of a Green New Deal in isolation. The poster at the Seattle election launch read, 'Seattle needs a Green New Deal', rather than raising the demand for a 'Workers' Green New Deal' or a 'Socialist Green New Deal'.

The dilution of the programme and demands are a reflection of the opportunistic pressures that are present. Our task is to resist them, albeit skilfully, and not to buckle to them. If we do not do this we will not build a solid basis for Trotskyism in the US.

A crucial aspect of the debate has been centred on the issue of the trade unions. Despite the howls of protest from the NFF, the Irish section – and now apparently some others – abandoned systematic and consistent trade union work. The Irish leadership justified this because of the high degree of bureaucratisation of the trade unions, their role in social partnership and the relatively low level of trade unionisation. AP, from Greece, argued in his document that it was impossible to place demands on the Greek TUC because of its treacherous role. In the subsequent paragraph of his document, however, he proceeded to place demands on the TUC, thereby facing both ways. Significantly, AP makes no reference to the KKE (communist party) -led trade union federation, PAME.

Andy Moxley (USA) in his letter, which was replied to by Peter Taaffe, [see page 164] underlines the real attitude of many leaders of the NFF much more clearly. He accused the faction of "retreating into a reactive, mechanical approach towards is an incredibly complicated period for the working class". Yet what did he mean by this statement? He went on to argue that some unions are "so thoroughly bureaucratised in many instances they have ceased to have the characteristics of a workers' organisation ..." This is an entirely wrong perception of even the most right-wing bureaucratised trade unions, which still retain a working-class base despite the treacherous role of the leadership.

Leon Trotsky answered this point in his unfinished work, 'Trade Unions in the Epoch of Imperialist Decay'. There he dealt with the trade unions even being integrated into the capitalist state and work in the unions in fascist states. He argued clearly: "In the absence of workers' democracy there cannot be any free struggle for the influence over the trade union membership. And because of this, the chief arena of work for revolutionists within trade unions disappears. Such a position, however, would be false to the core. We cannot select the arena and the conditions for our activity to suit our own likes and dislikes … All the less so, can we renounce internal systematic work in the trade unions of totalitarian and semi-totalitarian type … or because the bureaucracy deprives the revolutionists of the possibility of working freely within these trade unions."

In the same article, he wrote: "In spite of the progressive degeneration of trade unions and their growing together with the imperialist state, the work within the trade unions not only does not lose any of its importance but remains as before and becomes, in a certain sense, even more important work than ever for every revolutionary party."

This was written in 1940 at a time when the level of unionisation was relatively low in most countries compared to the massive strengthening of the trade unions that took place in the post-war upswing. This does not mean that we should be imprisoned within the official trade union apparatus or only orientate towards the already unionised layers of the working class. In particular, we need to take initiatives to reach the new layers of the working class which are as yet unorganised. We need also to recognise the positive developments of the radicalisation of a section of the middle class which is becoming increasingly 'proletarianised', such as medical doctors and others. Some of these layers have begun to take up working-class methods of struggle. This process has not yet been completed and is at an initial stage of development, politically and organisationally. However, this does not mean we should turn away from intervening in the organised sections of the working class and building a strong base there to confront and challenge the most entrenched bureaucracies.

Unfortunately, the opportunistic, rightward collapse that has taken place in the CWI has now been mirrored by the ultra-left approach adopted by the Spanish leadership, with the support of the Portuguese leadership. Our opponents in the NFF, and others, are trying to make hay out of this development. But we make no apologies for what has taken place. We have acted in a transparent and politically principled manner. The process of unification with the IR has now obviously not been successful and is disappointing. However, we ask our opponents, do they think it was correct to attempt to carry it through? No comrade at the IEC or in the international opposed the unification when it was proposed. It is not the first time such efforts have failed and it will not be the last. Woods and the IMT, in an open letter to CWI members (which is full of personal bile) mocking us for the "splits" and "divisions" that are taking place in the CWI. We would ask, how many splits has the IMT suffered in Spain, Pakistan, Venezuela and other countries? Factional struggles, regrettable though they may be, and sometimes even splits, are necessary in order to clarify programme, perspectives and the forces that will carry out the tasks facing Marxists.

The NFF appeal for "principled revolutionary unity". This is the summation of their platform! Their appeal for unity is done on a totally unprincipled basis, as they use it to mask and avoid debate on the central political issues involved. In the recent debates, they are reduced to gossip, innuendo and protests about the conduct and tone of the debate, and to making false charges of how their supporters are dealt with at the international centre. This is to evade dealing with the central political and theoretical issues posed by the international faction. This unprincipled grouping refuses to declare itself as a faction. Yet it produces documents, co-ordinates its activities and convenes an international meeting – ie it is an undeclared un-principled faction.

In their latest 'Open Letter' to the CWI membership, which fails to deal with any political issues, they claim they have a majority of the CWI and the IEC. A majority for what? Most of the sections with NFF leaderships have not taken a position on the political positions put forward by the international faction. In their latest letter, they talk of rights for the "minority". What do they mean by this? If they are intending to propose a regime change and remove the current IS majority, they should openly say so. While formally they may have a majority on the IEC, this is not a full representation of the balance of forces in the CWI. The IEC is not a full reflection of the strength, class composition or social weight of the different sections. Some groups were made sections and given IEC membership in recognition of the potential which existed for them to develop. The memberships of the sections in Poland, Cyprus and others are smaller than some of the branches in other sections. The composition of the IEC is not, therefore, an accurate reflection of the CWI.

We make no apology for attempting unity, on principled basis, with the Spanish comrades and others. Trotsky undoubtedly was disappointed that his attempts to convince Andres Nin, in Spain, and Diego Rivera, in Mexico, eventually failed. However was it correct for Trotsky to attempt it? In 1933-34, Trotsky also attempted to form a 'Block of four', as a step towards building a new international. Yet this collapsed after a few months. Was he correct to attempt this? We believe so, and have applied his method in our attempts to build the international. Following the collapse of Stalinism we explored discussions with other organisations, such as the USFI, UIT, and the DSP in Australia, to see if it was possible to reach agreement in the new world situation following the collapse of Stalinism. These efforts eventually also failed. Yet was it correct to attempt to see if agreement was possible? We answer yes. Other efforts to reach agreement with other organisations will emerge again in the future and will need to be explored. In the future, powerful new parties will emerge with which it will be necessary to enter into discussion and explore the prospect of fusion. The new forces will comprise the main components for the building of a powerful revolutionary international. Yet this process will also involve fusions and splits, and may involve other existing revolutionary forces, as well. There is no other road in a struggle to build a revolutionary international organisation.

The Spanish leadership failed to fully reveal its position, especially on the political conse-quences and confusion which arose from the collapse of Stalinism. The differences raised by the Spanish leadership centred on the assessment of socialist political consciousness amongst the working class and masses, at this stage, and the world situation. The CWI was the first to recognise the consequences of the collapse of the former Stalinist regimes and that capitalist restoration was taking place (something that the IMT, in which the IR was affiliated, denied until 1997). The Morenites, in Latin America, took even longer to recognise the reality of capi-talist restoration. There was an economic and political counter-revolution in the former USSR and Eastern Europe. The consequences of this were not confined to the former Stalinist states.

Flowing from this was the launching of a massive ideological offensive by the capitalist class, a throwing back of political socialist consciousness, collapse of the former workers' parties and increasing bureaucratisation and swing to the right amongst the trade union leadership. It resulted not only in a throwing back of political consciousness but also a crisis of organisation of the working class in most countries.

The consequences of this process are still being felt today. They are reflected in the current complex conjuncture which exists. Following the global crisis of 2007-08, a wave of struggle and a political radicalisation took place. There was the outbreak of revolutions and revolts in the Middle East and North Africa. In Greece, the elements of a pre-revolutionary situation which erupted reflected the stagnation and potential collapse of capitalist rule. However, it was not reflected in the emergence of a clear socialist consciousness and organisations of the working class. Elements of these were present but not in a rounded out manner. The radicalisation was also reflected in the indignados movement, and the upheavals that unfolded in many countries. The growth of Syriza in Greece, the formation of Podemos in Spain, and later, the election of Corbyn to lead the Labour Party in Britain, were all a product of the consequences of the capitalist crisis, and elements of political and social radicalisation that existed. We recognised the significance of these developments and positively attempted to intervene in them.

However, these developments also had important weaknesses reflecting the enduring impact of the collapse of the former Stalinist regimes and that the working class has not yet consciously put itself at the head of the movements that have erupted. This is reflected, as we have explained in many documents and at meetings, in the extremely weak programme advocated by the 'new left', which is not even left reformist. These programmes are to the right of the left reformist policies of the 1970s and 80s. It is also reflected in the character of the new parties, which are not yet workers' parties but often comprise elements of 'two parties in one' and lack active participation by the working class. The class composition and methods of organisation (for example, 'horizontal' structures, including online ballots) of parties like Syriza, Podemos, the Left Bloc and Momentum, are mainly a reflection of the layers involved - semi-working class, petty bourgeois and semi-petty bourgeois - which have been radicalised by the capitalist crisis.

The leadership of IR ignore these weaknesses and prettify the situation. In discussions they drew the conclusion that the IS was, at least, partly responsible for the crisis in the CWI because of the emphasis we have placed on the issue of the throwing back of socialist consciousness and working class organisation. This, they allege, gave the justification for the opportunistic turn taken by the NFF leadership. But Trotskyists cannot refuse to identify a problem because some may react to it opportunistically. The task of the leadership is to diagnose the problem and then deal with it in a principled manner.

Revolutionary socialists are optimistic but it is also essential that a realistic assessment of the objective situation and subjective strengths and weaknesses, are made, in order to accurately assess and effectively intervene in the class struggle. We cannot bury our heads in the sand and be in denial about the objective and subjective conditions which currently exist. To re-discuss these questions is returning to the polemics we had with the Grant/Woods group, which denied the process of capitalist restoration until 1997 and continue to deny its effects on the working class and its former parties and organisations. To deny these developments is the response of a sect incubated from reality. The leadership of IR revealed, to our surprise, that they were still agreeing with the IMT approach on these questions.

Reflecting this denial, the leadership of IR refuse to accept that there was any hint of "anti-party" consciousness at the time of the indignados movement in the Spanish state. This was a feature of the situation not only in Spain but it was also present, for a period, in Greece, Brazil, Chile and many other countries. This was a temporary mood and changed quite rapidly, giving rise to the growth of Podemos at a later stage. However, to deny this was a problem, at the time, is to bury one's head in the sand in an attempt to prettify the situation. The conclusion of the IR leadership on this question is totally one-sided. We need to support and participate in a struggle to build genuine mass parties of the working class, with an active working class membership, which function as instruments of struggle and as a forum to fight for a socialist programme. Such parties can emerge through a series of struggles, with many false starts. However, the new left parties which have emerged are not yet of this character. The future of the existing left parties is far from secure, as the example of Syriza demonstrates.

The same approach was reflected in the arguments of the IR leadership in relation to the process of revolution and counter-revolution in Venezuela. The leadership of IR attack the IS majority for drawing a distinction between the Chilean revolution in 1970-3 and Venezuela. This allegedly was a "theoretical mistake" – although they never explained where the theoretical error was to be found. However, as we have explained in the CWI's analysis on Venezuela, the top-down, bureaucratic, idealisation of Chávez, in the manner of the Latin American 'caudillo' tradition, was a weakness. This was quite distinct from Chile, where a higher consciousness existed, in part due to the more powerful and lengthy tradition of independent workers' parties and organisations. Allende was, of course, revered by the Chilean masses but he was never viewed in the same manner as Chávez. He was subject to criticism by the working class and by the different mass parties which existed, including the Communist Party, the different factions of the Socialist Party and the MIR. We should not forget that the formation of the Cordones Industriales – embryonic soviet-type organisations - were in opposition to the Communist Party, the right-wing of the Socialist Party and the trade union federation, the CUT. The consequences of the collapse of the former Stalinist states, was reflected in Castro's statement that it "was as if the sun had gone out". He, of course, meant it from the stand point of Cuba losing its material support from the USSR but his comments also reflected the scale of the political consequences this has had for the working class and its organisations internationally. To deny this is to bury your head in the sand.

These issues were all discussed during the process of unification with the IR, and some of the issues were debated at international meetings following the unification process. The leadership of IR, at that stage, indicated they were in agreement with the general analysis of the CWI on these questions – with the exception of the existence of an anti-party mood at the time of the indignados movement. What is now clear is that the IR masked their real positions, which they have now returned to. They have returned to the approach of the IMT on these major issues.

For the leadership of IR the issue is simply reduced to the subjective question of the crisis of leadership of the working class and the need for mass revolutionary socialist parties. The CWI has always recognised the decisive question of leadership and the need for building revolutionary parties, generally, for a successful revolution. Even should the working class manage to seize power without a party, which is a theoretical possibility, a party would need to be rapidly built afterwards. However, the question of the political consciousness of the working class, which is a subjective factor, is also related to the question of resolving the crisis of leadership and to become part of the objective situation. If it is only a question of the crisis of leadership and the lack of a mass revolutionary party then why has no revolutionary party or organisation, anywhere in the recent period, experienced substantial growth and development?

If it only a question of the party then why has the IR only experienced minimal growth, with approximately 350 members, in total, after leading such massive youth mobilisations? At the time of the British miners' strike, 500 miners joined the Militant. In the Liverpool struggle, we recruited nearly 100 in one night! This and the explosive growth of the POUM, which grew to 70,000 in six weeks during the Spanish revolution or the Bolsheviks (who grew from seven thousand to hundreds of thousands during the Russian revolution), all illustrate that the subjective factors of party and political consciousness, and the objective situation, are interconnected. Differences on all of these issues resulted in the IR leadership indicating they would leave the faction, as they subsequently did, and stating that it would therefore make no sense for them to remain in the CWI.

We have fought this internal political struggle on a principled basis, against the NFF and now also the Spanish and Portuguese leaderships. The struggle erupted on questions pertaining to the Irish section. While sharply disagreeing with the Irish leadership, we were not prepared to re-write the history of the CWI and repudiate what the Irish or other sections have achieved in conducting important struggles. Peter Taaffe recently wrote an introduction to 'In Defence of Marxism', in which he recognised the role of the Irish section in past struggles, including the water charges campaign, the Jobstown trials, and the recent abortion campaign. The Spanish leadership wanted these references removed. But we were not prepared to go along with re-writing our history due to the current factional struggle.

The CWI is currently passing through a testing time. This has been echoed in all organisations claiming to be of the revolutionary left. The difference with them is that we will emerge stronger politically, steeling and developing youth cadres in the process who will play a key role in developing and growing our forces at a later stage. At root, what lies behind this crisis are objective factors and a political and theoretical atrophy which affects the leadership of many sections. This is reflected in an opportunist trend. This trend has adapted to the current conjuncture and, in varying degrees, succumbed to the pressures of identity politics.

The international faction rejects the claim that this is a dispute between an old, conservative, out-of-touch leadership, and those who are supposedly prepared to face up to the "new movements". On the contrary, it is a struggle to defend the methods and ideas of Trotskyism – of the centrality of the working class and an orientation to intervene in its organisations – as opposed to an opportunistic searching for short cuts. This is a crucial struggle for the future of the CWI and Trotskyism. The international faction will, therefore, convene an international conference of its members and supporters to assess the debate and determine the next steps necessary to defend the policy, programme and methods on which the CWI was founded in 1974. But let there be no doubt, this crisis will result in a stronger, battle-hardened CWI, well-placed to face the revolutionary storms to come.

Conciousness, Class Struggle and the Revolutionary Party

Tony Saunois, on behalf of the IS Majority – May 2019

Six months after the November IEC meeting, the 'Non-Faction Faction' (NFF) finally managed to assemble together a political platform ('The world at a crucial conjuncture: new phenomena and tasks – the crisis in the CWI'). The document is, in part, a combination of truisms and generalisations. Taken, as a whole, it confirms, as we have consistently argued; the NFF represents an opportunist right-ward departure from a Trotskyist method and programme. Like those from a 'Mandelite' trajectory, it includes insurance clauses of correct points but then defends opposing or contradictory ideas.

The first five pages of this 'platform' attempt to give a political summary of the current political conjuncture, most of which has been plagiarised from previous CWI documents that were prepared by the International Secretariat (IS). As we will comment on, the few additional points they have inserted are wrong or one sided, especially when dealing with issues relating to consciousness and the current stage of the class struggle. The platform falls far short of the alternative 'perspectives' that we were promised by the leaders of the NFF. They accuse the IS majority of not facing up to the new period but bring nothing new themselves to the table.

At the November 2018 IEC, and immediately following it, the leaders of the NFF denied that any fundamental differences existed. Now, at last, they recognise that, "The debate has revealed important differences on how to respond to the new period" (para 4). At the recent meeting of the England and Wales NC, Stephen Boyd (Ireland), went further and admitted that "fundamental" differences exist". We are also told that these important differences are "not so crucial or so fundamental as to raise the prospect of a split of the CWI as the faction claims". But it is the degree of political divergence away from the political foundations of the CWI and Trotskyism, on the part of the leadership of the NFF, which is the cause of a threatened split.

They argue the differences relate to "perspectives and methods of work" (para 34). In paragraph 36, they list the differences which have emerged concerning the trade unions, the women's movement, the national question, the united front, the youth and environmental movements, and the transitional programme and method. They go on to claim, "It is beyond doubt in our opinion that the IS has not been able to respond, in recent years, in a satisfactory manner in relation to the challenges of the epoch which we live through" (para 38). They continue with the assertion that the IS "has been slow in capturing the mood and the needs of the new phase in the class struggle internationally." (para 40) Comrades will search in vain for any alternative documents that have been presented by the leaders of the NFF to the analysis produced by the IS in "recent years". The leaders of the NFF have supported all of these documents, with some minor amendments. They allege "top down methods" have been applied, without giving any specific examples. For a Trotskyist revolutionary organisation, all the differences listed by the NFF are on fundamental questions. If there is not agreement on these crucial issues it is clear a political rupture has occurred. The NFF talks wildly about "threatened expulsions" but the IS majority/faction is making a political judgement; the current trajectory of the NFF sees them turning away from the fundamental ideas, programme and methods of the CWI.

The NFF wants it both ways. They list a catalogue of fundamental differences which they say have developed with the CWI leadership, over a period of time. They then argue that, in reality, they are not so different fundamentally, as to justify a split. Yet they do want a change in leadership of the CWI – regime change! This is the right of all comrades to propose. However, what is the political motive for such a change? Is it because they have embraced "ageism" and think some of the IS members are too old! If so, at what age do they propose the leaders of a revolutionary party should be compelled to retire? Will some of the NFF leaders meet the age criteria they seem to want to lay down? Would they also apply the same criteria to Bernie Sanders or Jeremy Corbyn?

The NFF have tried to portray the faction as "old" and out of touch. Yet, unlike the NFF, we have sent not only more experienced, older comrades to the debates but also younger comrades, especially from England and Wales and Scotland. The spokespersons for the Faction in the debates have included many female comrades, along with comrades who are from an Asian background, and also comrades who are LGBTQ+. It is not the question of "age" which is the issue. It is, as we have argued, a change in leadership, as proposed by the NFF, with the political aim to alter the course of the CWI on the issues listed above, in a more opportunist, rightward direction. The NFF are dishonest in not clearly stating that this is their real objective.

The ideas defended by the Irish leadership, and then other NFF sections, cover 'Identity Politics', how we intervene in the social movements (such as, the environmental movement, the women's movement and LGBTQ+), the trade unions, the transitional programme, and the methods needed to build the revolutionary party, and some other issues. This all represents an opportunist turn away from the principles, programme and perspectives that the CWI was founded on. As a cover for this historic retreat by the NFF, they accuse us in their platform of moving in the direction of an "abstract, even economistic approach to the class struggle".

In their latest document, new differences have emerged from the NFF leaders, particularly over the question of the political consciousness of the working class and the role of the revolutionary party. At some of the debates, for example, during the recent England and Wales NC, we were falsely accused of arguing that this period is now "reactionary" and of explaining the question of political consciousness in a one-sided manner. We have never argued that this period is dominated by reaction, in general. There are elements of both revolution and counter-revolution present. However, we cannot simply dismiss the complications which exist, as the former Spanish section does, and bury our heads in the sand. As we have explained in other material, these complicating factors relate to the political consciousness of the working class and the character of the new left, which has emerged in some countries. This is largely the result of the legacy of the collapse of the former Stalinist regimes and the throwing back of socialist consciousness - the legacy of which we still have to confront today.

The NFF leadership appears to have been infected with the same virus as the former Spanish section. They claim that we do not take into account the "radicalisation to the left of tens of millions of workers and youth in the wake of the economic collapse in 2008-9...This has included the re- emergence of a basic level of class consciousness". In fact, we laid great stress on the radicalisation which took place following the economic crisis in 2007/8, and all of its political consequences. Yet we also pointed to some of the limitations and weaknesses which existed in the movements that erupted at the time. Initially, we hoped that the 2007/8 crisis would result in the emergence of a more pronounced socialist consciousness. However, this did not happen, and we have acknowledged this at numerous international meetings. We explained how, with the onset of a new crisis, there will be the emergence of a more pronounced anti-capitalist, socialist consciousness amongst layers of workers and youth.

Following the crash in 2007/8, there were complications in the movements which did develop, as we analysed, at the time. During the movement of the 'Indignados' a pronounced "anti-party" mood was present. This involved some positive features, including a hatred of the existing political parties but also present was a reaction, sometimes violently, against the very idea of building a new party. The same sentiment developed in many other countries, including in Brazil and Chile. This eventually gave way to a new mood. We saw the emergence of Podemos, in Spain - a new party, but with big weaknesses and limitations. The former Spanish section argued against the idea that an anti-party mood had existed in Spain during the 'Indignados' movement. One of the leading NFF supporters, DB, echoed, at the time, the ideas defended by the Spanish leadership. Yet comrades who were present on some of these protests were literally chased away by some anti-party elements!

We heralded the tremendous combatively of the Greek working class, reflected in more than thirty general strikes against the austerity package of the Troika. However, we also commented on the character of these strikes – they were more "protest" actions rather than a challenge for power by the working class, as was the case in other countries, notably France in 1968. Of course, with a revolutionary leadership, they could have developed in this direction. However they did not. In Greece, during the economic crisis etc., the political consciousness of the working class was not sufficiently developed to enable it to go over the heads of the reformist leadership. Of course, the question of political consciousness is not totally separated from the question of the leadership – the two are related. However, it is necessary to have an accurate assessment of it, at each stage.

It was very different during the revolutionary events in Barcelona, in July 1936. The working class went over the heads of the leadership, took matters into their own hands, armed themselves with hunting rifles and chair legs, and stormed the military barracks. In Chile, 1970-73, the working class formed the Cordones Industriales, and neighbourhood committees or 'JAPS'. This was in opposition to the CUT (TUC), the Communist Party and the right-wing of the Socialist Party (PSch). At the same time, large left reformist and centrist parties and groupings developed in the PSch, MAPU and Isquierda Christiana (the latter two of which split) along with the growth of the Movimiento Isquierda Revolucionaria (MIR). These two revolutionary movements were a measure of how much further advanced the political consciousness and confidence of the working class was in these situations, compared with the movement which erupted in Greece, and elsewhere, following the crisis in 2007/8.

It is important to discuss these features. This does not mean challenging the need for a revolutionary party but in order to have an accurate estimation of the situation, which is crucial. How else can we avoid confusing the first month of pregnancy with the ninth, as Lenin warned against?

The NFF leadership have caught the Spanish virus and seem to dismiss the importance of estimating the political consciousness of the masses. However, in adopting this mistaken premise, the NFF have turned in the opposite direction to the ex-Spanish comrades. The former Spanish section has drawn sectarian conclusions from their denial that political consciousness is a problem. They reduce everything to the absence of a revolutionary party and leadership. The NFF leadership diminish the importance of political consciousness, reducing everything to the absence of a revolutionary party but then draw opportunist conclusions.

Everything is reduced to the question of the "party". The absence of a revolutionary party is crucial but is not the only issue. The question is posed – why have revolutionary parties not grown or developed in the recent period? Why is it that in Spain the IR remains with approximately 360 members after such massive mobilisations, some of which they help initiate? This is reflection of some of the obstacles which still exist, and need to be overcome, in the next period of time, through a combination of workers' and youth experiences in struggle and by the intervention of revolutionary socialists. To assist workers and young people overcome these obstacles, revolutionary socialists need to recognise that they exist in the first place!

In paragraph 38 of their document, the NFF say revolutionary upheavals in Egypt, Syria and Libya "turned into open counter-revolutions, due to the absence of the subjective factor – i.e. the lack of a mass revolutionary party". They continue, "In the past 10 years, the weakness of the subjective factor, i.e., the lack of mass revolutionary parties, enabled the ruling class to go on a counter-offensive, on a global scale, after the 2007-8 crisis and make the working masses of the planet pay for the crisis that the capitalist system itself created."

The subjective factor for us has two main components: the revolutionary party and also the question of the political consciousness of the working class. The weakness or absence of these, in turn, inevitably becomes a part of the objective situation. They are interlinked, as we have explained many times in the analysis of the CWI. It was not just mass revolutionary socialist parties that were absent during the movements in Egypt, Syria and Libya. There were no mass workers' parties, at all, and only in Egypt did some unions exist outside the official state organisations. In Tunisia, a different situation existed with the UGTT, where we formulated demands to take this into account, which CG (IS Alternate) initially opposed in the IS. In Egypt, the vacuum which existed allowed the Muslim brotherhood to step in for a period. The absence of the creation of mass parties was itself a reflection of the consciousness which existed.

As we explained, the radicalisation which did take place after 2007-8 represented as step forward but it had limitations. The question of political consciousness is not static and neither are the political consequences or organisations that flow from this. The situation in many countries has changed since the movements which developed post 2007/8, largely due to the limited character of the 'new left' that emerged. The NFF leadership seem blind to this development. In paragraph 17, the NFF argue that the traditional social democratic parties are increasingly rejected by wide sections of the working class and middle class. They argue that there has been a growth in support for the new left parties. This was the situation post 2007/8. However, now it has become more complicated because of the weakness of the new left. The former social democracy, in some countries, has recently experienced an electoral revival, such as in Spain, Finland and Portugal, and opinions polls point to a likely similar development in Denmark. This has been mirrored by a decline and stagnation in the "new left", including Podemos and the Left Block. There has been an ebbing in the enthusiasm for Corbyn, in Britain, which may damage the electoral recovery the British Labour Party had experienced under his leadership. The growth of Salvini's support, in Italy, and right-populist forces in other countries, all point to a more complicated situation due to the failure or limitations of the new left radicalisation that followed the crisis in 2007/8. Since then, amongst significant layers, political consciousness has taken a step back. In Britain, this is reflected in the current rapid growth of the newly-formed 'Brexit Party' led by Nigel Farage.

This, of course, is not uniform amongst all layers, in all countries. A layer of youth have been radicalised on the environment, taking part in movements in which we have successfully intervened. However, the situation is not the same as the radicalisation that followed the crash of 2007/8. This, of course, will change and can be very rapidly, given the underlying social and economic situation of capitalism. This is demonstrated by the mass protests in Brazil, at the present time, against Bolsonaro's policies, like his pension 'reform', and in defence of education.

Political consciousness is not static. It can take leaps forward but also steps back, if it is not channelled into a real alternative for the working class. The onset of a new crisis is certain to lead to even deeper polarisation and will include the emergence of a more pronounced anti-capitalist socialist consciousness amongst crucial layers of the working class and young people. Mass struggle in a number of countries can also help to speed up political consciousness in a left and socialist direction.

This raises the question of the revolutionary party and the absurd allegation, made by the Spanish and now repeated by the NFF, that PT (IS) argued that a revolutionary party was not necessary during the Spanish revolution. This point has been answered by PT (IS) in his reply to BK from the US. The supporters of the faction, including PT, fully defend the essential need for a revolutionary party. We have been working for decades to build one!

Yet, as we have explained, theoretically it could not be excluded that in some specific situations the working class could take power prior to a mass revolutionary party being created. This is not a new issue for Trotskyism or the CWI. This point was raised by Lenin in relation to the 1918 German revolution. We commented on this in an article by BL (IS) on the centenary of the 1918 revolution, which was recently republished on the Socialist Alternative website. Trotsky, as we have explained, also dealt with this issue. The CWI echoed this point in the past, in relation to Hungary during the uprising against the Stalinist regime, and in some other specific situations. However, to consolidate power and develop the revolution, the crystallisation of a party would become essential.

In a certain sense, the completion of the social revolution, albeit in a distorted form, without a party being formed beforehand, did take place in Cuba. Castro took the power with a small band of guerrillas, as the former Batista regime collapsed. A party, although in a bureaucratic form, was only established a considerably long time after the revolution.

Differences on these issues, together with the other central questions of the transitional programme and method, 'Identity Politics' and the need for a systematic, consistent orientation to the trades unions, represent a fundamental point of departure by the leadership of the NFF from the ideas that the CWI was built upon. To pretend that these questions are of secondary importance, as the NFF leadership do in their statement, is to deny reality.

The question of the trade unions has been a central part of the debate which has opened up. In their platform document the NFF authors insert an insurance clause, proclaiming they agree with the importance of work in the trade unions. They argue, in paragraph 59, that Marxists should have an "ongoing flexible orientation towards union work. What we are discussing is adopting flexible tactics in relation to the trade unions, depending on the differences in the objective situation from country to country".

The debate is not about adopting flexible tactics, taking into account the specific situation in each country. Our specific tactics to intervene in the trade unions have always been flexible. The difference is over whether always to conduct systematic, consistent work in the trade unions or if it is justified to turn away from them, for a period, as the Irish and some other sections have done. One of the conditions for affiliation to the Comintern was that Communist Parties "must *systematically and persistently* develop communist activities in the trade unions …." [our emphasis] This 'condition', of course, was aimed at mass or large Communist Parties but it is relevant to our work today.

The NFF has given extensive quotes from Trotsky regarding the question of the trade unions, none of which refute what we have argued. Where have we ever adopted an approach that means "passively to tolerate subordination of the revolutionary mass movement to the control of openly reactionary or disguised conservative (progressive) bureaucratic cliques"? (From The Transitional Programme, 1938). The NFF omit to quote Trotsky in the same Transitional Programme document: "It is necessary to establish a firm rule: self-isolation of the capitulationist variety from mass trade unions, which is tantamount to betrayal of the revolution, is incompatible with membership in the Fourth International".

The position of the Irish leadership was justified by them because of the rightward shift in the unions after the Croke Park deal and the lack of a militant rank and file. Then they rejected a proposal made by the IS, during a visit by TS (IS), that they launch an opposition trade union platform in the trade unions. They have subsequently argued that it is correct to temporarily turn away from the unions to win radicalised layers, especially of young women and LGBTQ+ people who could then be re-orientated towards the unions, at a later stage. This classic Mandelite approach has been defended by the leadership of Socialist Alternative, the Greek, Swedish, Russian and other NFF sections leadership. The NFF seem to argue we only undertake union work when a favourable situation exists within the unions. But a solid base of support for us cannot be built within the trade unions and work places with such an approach.

The Irish leadership began by making appeals to Irish 'exceptionalism' – the low level of unionisation and activity in unions. As the debate has progressed, we have now heard of American exceptionalism, Greek exceptionalism, Swedish exceptionalism and more. AM (USA) justified a turn away from systematic trade union work citing the SEIU as an example of how rotten the trade unions have become. Yet the SEIU local in Seattle has recently endorsed Kshama Sawant's election campaign!

The current low level of unionisation and lack of a large active base, like that of the 1970s and 1980s, is part of an international problem which exists. This is something the IS has explained in many documents in recent years, before the crisis erupted in the CWI, and during this internal crisis. Yet recognising that this problem exists is not a justification for turning away from the trade unions or not placing demands on the union leaderships. Neither is it a reason to abandon doing consistent, systematic trade union work. This does not mean that we identify the "official trade union structures with the whole of the 'working class'", as the NFF accuse us of. This absurd argument is a strawman put up to mask turning away from systematic, persistent work in union branches and structures.

It is not a question of having a "fetish" about the trade unions, as the NFF states. It is recognising that, despite the difficulties which exist, the trade unions still are vitally important as mass organisations of the working class, even if a minority of workers are organised within them. For Trotskyists, it is a matter of principle that we undertake persistent work within unions, and challenge the leadership of them.

The relatively low level of unionisation reflects the set-backs which have taken place since the collapse of the former Stalinist regimes, the increased bureaucratisation and swing to the right by the union leadership, and also changes in the economy and the decline in manufacturing industry that has occurred in many capitalist countries. Yet the low level of trade union density is not a new issue. Trotsky pointed out in the Transitional Programme that trade unions, even the most powerful, usually organise no more than 20-25% of the working class. The high levels of unionisation in the post-world war two-era, especially in the industrialised countries, were the exception rather than the rule.

In their latest statement, the NFF justify the Greek section not placing demands on the Greek TUC (GSEE). Initially, they denied this was the case, despite Andros P having made exactly that point in his document. Now they add the rider that they called on the GSEE to call a plan of strikes, culminating in an all-out general strike. After 2015, they argue, it would have been "out of touch with reality" to do so. The call for an all-out general strike after 2015 may not have been correct, however this does not mean it was correct not to place any demands on the union leadership. Given the betrayal which took place, the demands should surely have been sharper, denouncing the leadership for not calling the necessary action.

There is no contradiction in doing this and also demanding workers take the necessary steps to organise action themselves, if the leaders are not prepared to do so. Following the betrayal of the 1926 general strike, in Britain, Trotsky still raised the issue of placing demands – very critical demands – on the trade union leadership. The approach of the Irish and Greek leadership, now justified by the NFF, has been to turn away from the struggles inside the trade unions following a betrayal and/or defeat of the working class, when the situation inside the trade unions has become more, and sometimes, extremely, difficult. This approach has echoes of the British SWP and their counterparts. But we must work in the trade unions even in the most difficult conditions.

The lack of understanding of the leadership of the NFF in how we place demands on the trade union leadership is reflected in paragraph 54 of their document. Referring to the Indignados movement, the 'Occupy' movement and the Water Charges campaign, in Ireland, they say that none of our sections, when intervening in these movements, "simply called for the existing trade union and left leadership to assume the leadership of these movements, as we would have done in past decades, when big active left currents and a sizeable layer of militant and combative shop stewards were present". We never approached the issue in this way! We never demanded the union bureaucracy, left or right, "assume the leadership" of movements. We made specific demands on the leadership to take action, in order to expose them and, in some cases, this was done to push them to take action. This was also done to assist workers reaching the conclusions themselves of what was necessary to take the movement forward and to build a new leadership, if necessary.

The question of our approach to the women's and LGBTQ+ movements, and the necessity to combat identity politics, has been a central aspect of this debate. Numerous documents have been produced on this issue where we have explained our position. It is necessary that we intervene in these movements. The difference between the two diverging trends is how this is to be done. We have argued that we need to intervene, defending our revolutionary socialist ideas, and to resist separatist ideas and pressures to buckle under the influence of identity politics, which threatens the unity of the working class and the centrality of the role of the working class. The leadership of the NFF have bent to these pressures.

The NFF, in their latest statement, accept that maybe mistakes have been made and they should be discussed further. However, they also say in the next sentence that "we do not accept that any mistakes that were made in this work were crucial". In their usual manner, they do not say what mistakes were made or when and where. We remind the NFF that these "mistakes" in Ireland include the failure to put forward a socialist programme in the 2016 election campaign; taking an "open turn" away from the trade unions; and intervening in the 2018 Repeal campaign without raising any wider class or socialist ideas in the mass material we produced. Are these not crucial mistakes? Do the NFF support the main election slogan of the Irish section in the European Union elections, for a "socialist feminist voice for Europe"? In writing, the NFF make no comment on this election slogan but verbally the NFF fully defend and refer to it as a "model campaign".

The NFF protest that there has been a "consistent under-coverage of women's movements in our international material, including our key political documents". Yet the CWI website has a section on women's struggles and issues. In their latest document, the NFF extensively quote from the "significant" 2016 World Congress document on women [see page 223] but fail to point out that it was prepared by the International Secretariat. Comrades will search, in vain, for alternative documents from these comrades in recent years. Did any of the NFF comrades raise their voices in opposition to the positions of the IS at numerous CWI schools and IEC meetings, when these issues were discussed? Did NFF supporters DB and GG ever raise concrete proposals concerning women's struggles at IS meetings or provide a coherent alternative analysis? The answer is no!

However, a different approach was being adopted by the Irish leadership on this question. Following the 2018 CWI school, it was the IS who proposed, in August 2018, to the Irish leadership that a meeting take place to discuss these and other issues before the current crisis erupted. It is the Irish leadership, and now apparently the NFF leadership, who are departing from the CWI approach towards dealing with these and other issues.

We have explained that we, of course, support an intervention into the women's movement, the environmental movements, LGBTQ+ struggles, and movements to combat racism etc. but with our class orientation and socialist policies. The NFF pushed for us to call for an "international strike" on International women's day despite there not being a uniform situation on this question in many countries and a multiplicity of issues emerging. A few weeks later, there was the outbreak of big youth protests, in many countries, on climate change and the environment. We have organised a combative and audacious intervention in the environmental movements which developed. In many areas of the neo-colonial world, the struggle on environmental issues is assuming an extremely sharp character and includes a big class polarisation. The issues involved over water supply, deforestation, fishing and other issues, directly affect the working class and poor, which brings them into conflict with the big multinational companies.

We need to be aware of the opposition we will encounter in these movements from a layer of petty bourgeois and even bourgeois element that are also involved in them. The NFF diminish the importance and threat these obstacles pose. Yet we need to confront them. The US leadership go into contortions in documents trying to justify their approach on this issue. Despite claims to the contrary, the main point is that the chief slogan on posters, placards etc. produced by the US section have mainly called for a "Green New Deal" rather than a "Socialist Green New Deal" or a "Workers' Green New Deal". The poster produced by comrades prominent at Kshama Sawant's election launch carried the slogan, "Seattle needs a Green New Deal". But slogans including 'socialist' or 'workers' are necessary to distinguish us from those layers of the petty bourgeois and bourgeois, who are beginning to support the Green Deal idea.

Articles in the sections' newspapers or the websites are not, at this stage, aimed at a mass audience, but the posters, especially election posters, are aimed directly at broader masses. The position adopted by the US leadership on this question points towards a form of the "maximum" /"minimum" approach to programme and propaganda, rather than the use of the transitional method. Amongst the ideas we need to combat are the demands of some sections of the petty bourgeois involved in this movement who argue that production and consumption must be reduced for all rather than developing production on a planned socialist, eco-compatible basis.

We note the silence of the leadership of the US on our criticism of the opportunistic slogan they have used: 'Trump Out; Bernie In – Build a mass movement'. As the IS majority/faction argued, we should have demanded: 'Trump Out- Bernie In, with a socialist programme' or 'Trump out – Bernie In, and fight for a socialist programme'. In the material produced by the US leadership, the weaknesses of Sanders' programme are evaded. Some US comrades have even argued we should wait until a movement has been built before we raise criticism of Sanders.

While it is necessary to pose the need for socialism and the impossibility of fully resolving the climatic and environmental crisis on a capitalist basis, we also need to develop a transitional approach to this question. This includes a transitional approach to the workers employed in polluting sectors of the economy, like the gold miners in Greece. Amazingly, the Greek section now defends the dismissive approach they took towards the gold miners and the unions involved. They argue that they did take up the demand for alternative work for the workers, but, when this got no response, they simply dropped it! This approach is a departure from the approach of the CWI. It underlines the lack of a consistent intervention and orientation towards different sections of the working class using a transitional approach and trying to open a dialogue with the workers concerned.

In the latest NFF statement, it is clear that the leadership of this opportunist trend have lost the transitional method and understanding of how the transitional approach needs to be applied. Our criticism of them is not just that they have not raised the issue of socialism. In some material they have but it is simply tagged onto the end of their articles and texts. There are no transitional demands or proposals that link the immediate demands or struggles to the conclusion that socialism is needed.

The NFF make the absurd allegation that we are re-writing CWI history. They draw on the debates that took place over the Youth against Racism in Europe (YRE) programme, and the later youth initiative we attempted, International Resistance/International Socialist Resistance (IR/ISR). The NFF lump together the YRE and IR/ISR. In the 1990s, the YRE did develop and take off, and captured the mood, at that time, and we gained a lot from it. The IR/ISR, in the main, did not get an echo and failed to develop.

In relation to the issue of the YRE programme, there was extensive debate in the CWI on this question. The IS was clear that as a broad organisation, it would be preferable but not essential to include the question of socialism in the YRE programme. This was particularly an issue in Germany following the collapse of Stalinism and reunification of the two states. The IS produced a resolution on this question for the IEC, at the time, explaining that while the YRE did not have to include a full socialist programme, the CWI sections would argue, in a united front method, for socialist ideas and programme. We were bitterly opposed by the Swedish leadership and Vincent Kolo (VK) on this. They argued in a rigid, dogmatic way that it was essential to include socialism. The Belgian leadership and others, at that time, agreed with the position of the IS. The IEC Swedish comrades, and VK, are now signatories to the recent NFF platform and we may assume they have modified their position on this question. The same issue applied to the debate on the IR/ISR.

We also stressed that, while it was not necessary to have our full programme in the YRE or IR/ISR, we, as an organisation and as individual comrades, had an obligation to raise our socialist ideas and programme in the publications of the party and in discussions.

The issue we have raised regarding Rosa, in Ireland, and other campaigns, was not that our full programme was not raised. It was that Rosa lacked a working class orientation, was limited to only demands on abortion, and there was a total, or near total, absence of our own party profile - programmatically and as a party. It is not us who are re-writing CWI history. It is the NFF who are mixing up what we said about the YRE, a broad organisation, and what we emphasised regarding our own revolutionary party.

The IS has always been open to discussing new international campaigns, as the CWI has done in the past - very successfully in the case of the YRE - where it is agreed that there is the basis and resources for it. But now, the NFF lambast us for not taking Rosa-type initiatives on women's oppression across sections (not that the leaders of the NFF formally proposed any such concrete initiative, at the time). But the situation was not comparable on an all-European basis. Likewise, the Greek section's 'Green Attack', was launched, by the comrades' own admission, "in a previous period", when there was not the same strong mood internationally amongst the youth on the environment/climate change, as has developed more recently.

It is true that it would be a serious mistake to be "afraid of engaging with large sections of radical young people (including when they come from a middle class background) ...." But this should include when they are influenced by petty bourgeois ideas like 'identity politics'. A revolutionary party needs to conquer a base amongst the students in the universities and other sections of the middle class. The task is to engage with them and confront petty bourgeois ideas, not adapt to them. If we succeed in convincing students and young people of revolutionary socialist ideas, we need them to adopt the standpoint of the working class.

To say the IS/faction have evaded these tasks is answered by the growth of our work in the universities in England and Wales, where we are now the largest organisation on the revolutionary socialist left. As a point of historical accuracy, what marked the early days of Militant, in Britain, was that it was rooted amongst young workers. In the early 1960s, the growth that took place was mainly amongst young workers, especially in Liverpool, with a thin layer of students in other areas, mainly Brighton, who did place themselves on the standpoint of the working class.

The NFF have conducted a global campaign claiming they are defending "democracy". They demand the COC [Conference Organising Committee - see page 236] resumes its role and functions. They falsely claim both Danny Byrne (DB) and Cédric Gerome (CG) were "banned from the centre". The NFF leadership has tried to use the COC as a replacement for the International Secretariat. We are not prepared to accept this attempted political coup. DB and CG were never banned from the centre. It was agreed by all concerned, including DB and CG, that they should work from home and come into the centre when they needed to or to attend meetings. They were given full access to the resources at the CWI centre. Then having consulted the leaders of the NFF they conducted a global campaign trying to present themselves as the victims.

The NFF protest in their latest document about PT's comments regarding the existence of "propaganda groups" in the CWI. This only reveals their lack of a sense of proportion about what real forces the CWI has, at this stage. The term "propagandist" groups, was not an insult but an accurate assessment of what we have in most CWI sections. We have some sections which have undertaken mass or semi-mass work. But we also have small groups which have, in some cases, intervened very energetically in a number of movements. However, with 10, 20 or 50 members, they are not parties but propaganda groups.

The NFF demand an IEC in August. They claim they will not remove the IS "in August" but have made clear they will do this at a subsequent world congress. It is the democratic right of any member to challenge the leadership and, if necessary, propose it is changed. Yet, if this is to be done, it must be on a political basis, with a clear political alternative, programme, perspective, method and orientation put forward to justify such a change.

The leadership of the NFF do not admit in writing that there are fundamental political differences. Yet clearly a political rupture has occurred in the CWI. The alternative leadership sought by the NFF signifies a right-ward turn, in an opportunist direction, which would shift the political axis of the CWI away from the principles it has defended since its foundation in 1974. We will not be a party to such a political breach of method and orientation. We will continue to struggle for building a working class, Trotskyist CWI in the coming years. We confidently look forward to the impending class battles that are already beginning to unfold. They will offer big opportunities to build revolutionary socialist parties and a Trotskyist international, based amongst the working class and youth.

ON THE GREEK
RESOLUTION

Weizmann Hamilton and Shaun Arendse, IEC member and IEC alternate (South Africa) – February 2019

This comment is being made in the context of learning that the Greek EC resolution of 4 January was unanimously adopted by the Greek NC over the weekend of 19-20 January. What this indicates about the political trajectory of the Greek section is extremely worrying and justifies the concerns of the faction. We fully endorse the 14 January statement by Peter Taaffe on behalf of the IS majority [see page 11] answering the Greek resolution and wish to make some additional points in support.

Distorting events

The Greek resolution repeats a false narrative on the origins of the current crisis. In the run-up to the IEC there was a tendency by some IEC members to substitute their own shock – at the sharp divisions that existed between the IS and the majority of the Irish leadership at the time these divisions were brought to IEC members' attention – for the 'start' of the dispute, discounting what had unfolded over the previous months. Unfortunately, for some, this developed into a position of 'shooting the messenger', ie the IS, which exploded at the IEC into a wholesale rejection of the IS's handling of the issue. The baseless accusation that the IS majority is alone to blame for the current crisis is forcefully maintained and repeated in the Greek resolution.

But the crisis clearly originated in the response of the Irish NEC majority to the universally condemned actions of the hack. It was escalated into an 'all encompassing' international crisis, not by the IS, but by those IEC members who refused to defend – and still refuse to defend – the approach of the IS, from the moment they were belatedly informed of the situation that had developed in Ireland, as fundamentally correct and principled. The basic approach of the IS must be resolutely defended. Secondary questions of 'tone' must not distract from this. Unfortunately, this has not been the case and is developed to an extreme in the Greek resolution.

There is no excuse for this. The IEC was sent a large amount of documentation regarding the crisis on 6 November. Contained in this was a resolution that the IS proposed to the Irish NEC in September which was, if anything, too mild. After praising the work of the Irish section and condemning the hack, it simply says: "However, the IS is also of the view, that mistakes were made by the Irish leadership in handling this issue". [see page 230] When the Irish NEC majority objected to this sentence the IS proposed "that an additional clause be inserted stating that the Irish leadership does not agree that it made mistakes in handling this issue."

In tabling the original resolution, and then being willing to amend it further, the IS was clearly bending over backwards to try and create the conditions for a calm and principled discussion, not just on the hack but the wider political issues the IS was already raising. Indeed, the hack would most likely never have been 'escalated' to the IEC if this resolution had been accepted by the Irish NEC majority. After it was rejected, the IS then correctly took the issue to the Irish NC. When the Irish NC comrades took the unfortunate decision to retrospectively endorse the actions of the Irish NEC majority the IS then took the issue to the IEC. This was entirely correct in the circumstances if they believed a fundamental breach of the democratic norms of the CWI had not only been committed, but was now being more widely endorsed.

There is not a serious word on any of this in the Greek resolution. Instead the correct steps of the IS are given a very different 'spin'. The Greek account states that:

"The crisis is a result of the IS's mistake of *escalating the attack whenever it met resistance*, instead of taking a step back to reconsider its tactics and approach. Refusing to accept the result of the vote in the Irish NC, *they tried to use the international leadership against the Irish leadership*." (emphasis added)

And later:

"It is the first time in the history of the CWI that the IS meets the opposition of the majority of comrades in the IEC and is voted down. *As a result of the opposition they met, they reacted in a panicked manner, feeling that the authority of the IS was being put into question.* The authority of the IS, however, should not be based on pretentions that the IS makes no mistakes. It is natural to make mistakes and mistakes should simply be corrected through collective efforts. *This is the real cause of the crisis and the threat to the unity of the CWI.*" (emphasis added)

There are serious political implications to the characterisation the Greek resolution gives to the IS's conduct which will be developed below.

But if the supporters of the Greek resolution seriously believe that this is a true account of the motivation and conduct of the IS how can there be any talk of 'unity'? This IS must surely be removed! However, this was not proposed in the IEC meeting by any of the IEC members sharing this view of the IS's conduct, and it is still not being proposed. But the strident and fantastical criticisms of the IS are nevertheless being maintained and repeated.

Invented differences?

To support the narrative that the crisis has been 'manufactured' because the majority of the IS cannot stand opposition, the Greek resolution says that:

"When in the course of the IEC one section's leadership after another stood up in protest, the IS discovered "crucial differences of principle", on nearly every political and organisational issue and, also, two diverging trends in the CWI …"

To say "one section's leadership after another" is an exaggeration at best. The same could be said about those section leaderships defending the IS. They also "stood up in protest" – at the conduct of the Irish NEC majority and those IEC members shielding them.

The clear implication of the Greek resolution is that broader political differences were invented to justify the bureaucratic intransigence of the IS and later the cynical formation of a faction to disguise this. This assertion is false and a convenient justification for minimising the serious and fundamental political issues raised by the faction.

The documentation sent to IEC members on 6 November contained material clearly showing that differences with the Irish comrades on the application of the transitional method had been raised as far back as the 2016 general election campaign – raised at the time in a letter by Philip Stott. This was already formally disputed is writing by the Irish NEC majority in an accompanying reply also circulated to the IEC. An IS document criticising aspects of the Irish section's women's work was included [see page 91]. Shortly after, the IEC received a reply from the Irish NEC majority, which, in addition to challenging the IS's criticisms, clearly indicated further differences on our orientation to the trade unions. Later, a document written by Paul Murphy (Ireland) drawing attention to differences on the application of the united front method was sent to the IEC.

All of this material was available to IEC members in advance of the IEC meeting. It was not invented on the floor of the IEC as the Greek resolution implies. If anything the differences were only more clearly exposed on the floor of the IEC. The IS was raising political differences with the Irish leadership long before – years before! – the crisis around the [hack] even existed.

A dangerous method

The Greek resolution attempts to further clarify Andros Payiatsos' (AP) now 'infamous' IEC contribution to show that he was not advocating for a 'federal CWI'. But the reproduction of the transcript of AP's speech in the Greek resolution simply draws attention to the even more alarming comments that 'sandwich' the point they are attempting to reassure us on. Comrades can read the full quote the Greek comrades chose to select in their resolution. It includes:

"…the IS, in its relations with the sections, whenever they come to a minority, whenever they are defeated, then they start a procedure to *overthrow the national leadership* and try to find points of support for a new leadership. *Because this what happened in Ireland – and everybody knows this*. (emphasis added)

And later:

"…it doesn't mean that they will not continue to disagree with it [a structure where an IS position is voted down], but it does not mean that they *start a process of overthrowing the leadership, i.e. crush the majority in order to build on the basis of a certain minority…*" (emphasis added)

Already in this debate, a number of comrades have raised that considered written contributions should be given decisive weight over semi-improvised verbal contributions. This is generally correct. Now we find ourselves in a position where the entire essence of the Greek resolution – a 'considered written contribution' endorsed by the broader Greek leadership – reaffirms the position AP put forward verbally at the IEC. Unfortunately, it indicates a method completely alien to the CWI.

The method of the Greek resolution reveals the consolidation of a step that can lead to an eventual full retreat from democratic centralism. The basic and correct approach of the IS described above – attempting to correct the mistake of the Irish NEC majority directly with those comrades in the first instance, then via the Irish NC, and finally taking the matter to the IEC – is blamed as the source of the crisis. Further, the IS's correct 'progression' of differences through the structures, up to the IEC, is presented as an attempt to "use the international leadership against the Irish leadership"!

But how should the basic outline of the IS's approach fundamentally differ in future disputes? The simple answer is that it couldn't be any different because the basic approach of the IS was correct. At no point did the IS stray outside of the democratic structures of the international. The same cannot be said of the Irish NEC majority. The IS stated every opinion and assessment that they developed of the crisis openly and honestly at each stage. Again, this cannot be said of the Irish NEC majority. The IS accounted to the IEC for its handling of the crisis, including in detailed documentation circulated ahead of the IEC.

The Greek accusation that the IS was engaged in an attempt to "use the international leadership against the Irish leadership" creates a starkly different impression and displays a fundamentally wrong attitude to democratic centralism. If the Greek comrades are genuinely not retreating from a central plank of democratic centralism – the right of the IS to intervene in sections – as they claim, but want to maintain their (over the top) 'outrage' at the IS's 'tone' or the (disputed) informal comments of some IS members about the possibility of a split (answered by the faction elsewhere) this should not stop them from explicitly defending the basic outline of the IS's handling of the crisis. This would be the way to correct the supporters of the faction, that on this issue at least, there are no fundamental political differences.

Of course, this is not what the Greek resolution does. It puts forward no alternative for how concretely the IS should have handled the crisis differently beyond entirely subjective criteria. For example, opposition to a "heavy handed way", a search for "alternative ways to argue for its [the IS's] positions and opinions", "avoiding unnecessary polarisation". The Greek proposal for a 'liaison committee' was an exceptional proposal to try and mend relations between the IS majority and the Irish NEC majority after they had already broken down – it surely was not a proposal for a new 'standard' procedure whenever the IS raises differences or finds itself in opposition to a section's leadership.

In effect, the Greek resolution only defends the right of an abstract IS to intervene in sections in a general way – not the right of this IS to have intervened in this specific situation in the concrete manner in which it did. This is a clear example of why it is correct for supporters of the faction to raise 'Mandelism' as a characterisation of a developing and dangerous trend, whereby correct formal (or abstract) positions are then contradicted in practice.

Unless it is explicitly stated how the IS should fundamentally alter its approach next time, what future framework is being set up by the Greek resolution? The generalised attack on the IS, accompanied only by an abstract 'reaffirmation' of the principles of democratic centralism, clearly points down a road where degeneration on this fundamental political principle can develop.

The Greek resolution sets up an environment where it is legitimate to dismiss as a hostile attempt at 'regime change', future efforts by the IS to correct what they believe to be mistakes when they are 'rejected' by a section and the matter is 'escalated' to the IEC. Because, on the basis of the Greek resolution's arguments, how are we ever to determine otherwise? Whilst formally defending the right of the IS to intervene, its intervention can end up being rejected in every specific case. If this trend is allowed to develop it will lead to the liquidation in practice of democratic centralism.

To allow this to pass unchallenged poses the collapse of the CWI as a democratic centralist revolutionary international, precluding the possibility of coming to united positions on perspectives, and the strategy and tactics necessary for the victory of the socialist revolution on a world scale. The faction has organised and openly declared itself to oppose this.

Appeal

The Greek resolution should be rejected for its distortions and for the wrong method it is based on. If those IEC members currently opposing the IS majority and the faction – for example those from Ireland, Sweden, Belgium, and their co-thinkers in the US – maintain a silence and do not condemn this resolution out of expediency to maintain a 'united front', this would indeed indicate the existence of an unprincipled and undeclared faction. The comrades should not lose time in condemning the Greek resolution.

SOCIALISMO REVOLUCIONARIO DECLARATION

Socialismo Revolucionario, CWI in Chile

*I*n the face of the crisis which has developed in the CWI we wish to declare the following:

For us the central task continues – and will continue being – the defense of a revolutionary Marxist programme, based on Trotskyist methods, to build the revolutionary party.

Also for our section, the working class continues to be the central agent for the revolutionary movement necessary to defeat capitalism.

For this reason our orientation must be to build among the organised working class. This means we need to orientate to the basic organisations of the working class, the trades unions, despite the actual leadership of them.

We believe in the need for one party of revolution at world level – which is not a confederation of national parties – with one centralised leadership based on democratic centralism. At the same time we understand that a world organisation – in which different political situations exist, different traditions and national sensibilities – international democratic centralism cannot function in the same way as it does in a national section, even when steps are taken to bring together the methods of each section of the international. Open discussion, time to debate fraternally to arrive at a necessary concensus, and an atmosphere to reflect and interchange ideas are necessary.

All of these points have to be seen as the defense of the founding basis of the CWI, which is why we joined this organisation more than 30 years ago, and what we wish to defend in the next period. We are sure the working class will begin to move to defend its fundamental rights, which today are being sharply curtailed.

In relation to the 'emerging issues' like feminism, the ecological movement, LGBT, the national question (the indigenas movement in Latin America) we believe that it is fundamental to intervene in them in an energetic manner – each generation arrives at the struggle for socialism through its own road – but this intervention must be with our class programme and as part of the class struggle, not by making fundamental concessions to petty-bourgeois and bourgeois ideas.

Having said this, we wish to make clear that this does not mean that we are supporting an opportunist (reformist) or sectarian (ultra-left) position – two roads which are a dead end for the building of a revolutionary alternative of the workers.

It is difficult for us to understand why some argue that we cannot participate or orientate to the trade unions because they have a reformist leadership; but we are prepared to orientate, for example, to the feminist movement which often is led by sections of the petty-bourgeois and even bourgeois.

After seeing the sharp exchanges between leaders of different sections and comrades from the IS, it is difficult to see how it is possible to rebuild confidence. New developments, turns and movements of the class could facilitate the road towards re-unification, and we should avoid closing bridges of dialogue in the future, even if the split definitively takes place.

We face a collapse between some comrades and sections, and the more we speak of the need for unity, in concrete acts we are divided; although this final collapse has not yet happened.

For the other side [ie the opponents of the faction], despite the massive interchange of declarations, accusations and attacks, still we don't see – "what are the political differences that exist?" Seeing the declarations of the different sections, many say that political differences don't exist and that everyone defends the principles of the CWI – therefore we ask ourselves; "What is the political basis which today you are questioning the IS? What is the basis upon which you wish to remove the Secretariat?" For us, a section on the periphery and without the material conditions to judge accusations and counter-accusations which have been made in the course of this factional struggle, it is difficult to establish the veracity of many assertions.

We believe that we face a false political debate, where the sections which oppose the majority of the IS are not showing their real political position; until now they have not shown the real political programme they defend. If deep political differences really don't exist it would be totally irresponsible to unleash a split in the CWI. For its part, the IS has not played the role of moderating and facilitating the corresponding political debate. We think that it has kept internally, within the IS, important differences with sections like the Irish or the Brazilians. This was an important failure on the part of the IS. The IEC members should be kept informed of these debates on a regular basis. Between each World Congress, it is the IEC which is the leadership of the international, and should clearly play this role.

What we see is that there are elements within the CWI that are positioning themselves for a split, but are attempting to pass the responsibility to others; a very old political tactic. We do not want a split but we need to recognise that this division is in reality already done. This is reflected in the meetings that have been organised by each block, independent of the others.

Until now the only ones who have put forward a programme and policy which they defend are the comrades and sections that are part of the faction.

Based on this the Chilean section, following a series of discussions that have taken place, has taken the decision to join and become a part of the faction. We support the programme that has been defended by the faction comrades, as we have tried to explain in the previous points made in this declaration.

With this decision we are not signing a blank cheque to any leader of the international; we are adhering to a revolutionary Marxist programme, in the tradition of Trotskyism and the working class. In this sense, it is fundamental to view the discussion with the lens of the historic writings of Marxists and Trotskyists, which can guide us to improving and strengthening our interventions at different conjunctures.

As we have already said, we have criticism of the comrades of the IS, of how they have developed the discussion about Ireland. We would have liked for the criticisms which existed to have been taken openly to the IEC before, so that we would not have been taken by surprise by these developments. The same applies to the criticisms that have been raised about our Brazilian comrades and other sections.

To end, we need to state that despite this hard blow for our international, we will continue to work hard for the construction of a revolutionary political alternative of the working class. Our convictions remain in defence of the revolutionary ideas and the necessary task of building a revolutionary international of the working class.

On Democratic Centralism and the IEC – A Reply

by Angelika Teweleit, Michael Koschitzki, René Arnsburg, Sascha Staničić and Tom Hoffmann, Germany

Once again, a supporter of the Non-faction faction, in this case Claus, with his paper "DZ, IEK, Formalitäten und eine Gretchenfrage" (DC, the IEC, Formalities and a 'Crucial Question'), has presented a text which does not deal with the crucial political questions of the debate in the CWI and leaves the reader helpless.

He does not tell us what the author's stance is on the dilution of our programme in Ireland and Greece, on the task of a systematic orientation towards the trade unions, on the yielding to identity politics, on the demand to Greek miners to give up their jobs for the sake of the environment and on the blatant breach of democratic norms in the Irish section. All Claus writes is: "The coordinating sections... draw different conclusions from the criticism of the Irish and Greek sections. Both camps have also published political texts in which different attitudes to different issues become clear. In this respect, all members can judge the camps."

Unfortunately, Claus does not share with us the conclusions he draws from the faction's criticism. He does not tell us whether he also has criticisms, how he evaluates them and whether he considers it necessary to correct the policy of the Irish and Greek sections. We have no choice but to assume that in this case the motto 'silence is consent' applies. The NFF's political declaration published on 7 May ['The world at a crucial conjuncture: new phenomena and tasks – the crisis in the CWI'] also largely abstains from the concrete points of criticism raised by the faction or tries to disqualify this criticism as slander. This confirms our assessment that our criticism is not recognised and that no corrections are being made.

At the same time, Claus is using heavy artillery to pass a devastating verdict on the IS majority and the faction: "This is a toxic method which, if further reproduced, would make any qualitative extension of the international impossible... Such methods damage the CWI - and if they were midwives of a secession around the IS, they would also infect it from the beginning with an incurable political genetic defect through an excess of centralism, regime and cult, and condemn it to infirmity."

This is on the one hand a transparent attempt to unsettle comrades, but on the other hand a clear statement that from his point of view irreconcilable differences have developed. However, this does not quite fit in with the NFF's statement that these are not fundamental differences and with Claus' statement at the end of his text that he sees only "sectarian elements" in the faction's politics and would be prepared to fight against them as a minority. He justifies this with the principle of hope: "In this respect, we can only hope that the IS and the faction have only run themselves off, see themselves pushed into a corner and have developed the undemocratic and unbolshevik ideas as a reflex. In this case there would still be a chance that they would come out of their corner again."

We would suggest to Claus that he should be less concerned with psychological explanations than with a clear political stance and ask him: What is your assessment of the line of development of the Irish section? Do you support the programmatic intervention in the abortion campaign? Do you support the one-sided "socialist-feminist" orientation of the current election campaign in Dublin? Do you think there have been dangerous structural changes in the Irish section (overweight of full-time staff, financial dependence on state funds, informal and bureaucratic structures) that need to be corrected? Do you support the attitude of the Greek section towards the miners? Do you share the comments of the Greek EC on the trade union question and do you think that their "What we fight for" programme in their newspaper expresses an orientation towards the organised parts of the working class and the trade unions? The list of questions could be continued.

Political basis of CWI endangered

We too had hope at the beginning of this debate. The hope that a real debate will take place, in which our criticism will at least be taken up and in which positions will converge in order to maintain a common basis for the construction of the CWI. The opposite has happened. We have pointed to dangerous opportunist adjustment processes and a majority of IEC members reject this assessment and have stood up protectively to the critics. In the process it has become clear that similar developments exist in other sections as well. We see this as a development that threatens the political and programmatic basis of the CWI and are not prepared to let this happen.

On five pages Claus tries to pin bureaucratic and undemocratic methods on the IS majority and the faction and to disassemble the argumentation of Sascha in his answer to the Belgian comrades – only to agree with the political logic of Sascha's argumentation on the last page of his text!

Claus seems not to understand or not to want to understand that, due to the quality of the political differences, it is not an abstract question of the legitimacy of the IEC that he tries to defend long and broadly. It is about the question: which forces represent the political continuity of the CWI? All comrades must answer this question on the basis of the political positions that are clearly and unequivocally represented by the faction and far less clearly and unequivocally represented by the NFF.

The dispute over the IEC date has developed into a proxy dispute over this actual question. All we say is: the IEC is not a mirror of the relationship of forces among the members of the CWI. That is undeniable. The IS had set an IEC date for November because it wanted more time for the debate before decisions can be made and because the faction will hold a conference in July to discuss and decide on how to proceed. The NFF has declared that it will nevertheless convene an IEC meeting in August. We have come to the conclusion that an IEC meeting under the given circumstances will be tantamount to an attempt to shift the political foundations of the CWI in an opportunistic direction.

There is also no reason to assume that there will be a real debate at an IEC meeting, but that blocks will face each other. For whether we like it or not, the IEC has ceased to exist as a collective leadership of the CWI and the CWI is in fact already two organisations in one. From our point of view, this is made clear by the behaviour of the IS minority and the character of the NFF declaration. The two representatives of the IS minority did not participate in the last two meetings of the International Bureau (IB), partly without excuse. During the same period, they prepared a paper which, among other things, questions the CWI's analyses, which we have all carried out together in the past (eg on the question of consciousness). They have, however, refrained from discussing these issues in the IB. This is an expression of the real situation in the international and of the fact that NFF comrades are in fact no longer interested in cooperation (for example, the Swedish leadership repeatedly did not respond to requests from us). Claus himself has documented his cynical attitude to the current conflict by making fun of the splitting of the Spanish and Hamburg comrades on Facebook several times.

An IEC meeting in August serves the NFF to document its majority position in this body and to set the course for qualitative political and personnel changes in the leadership of the International, not to find compromises, as Claus implies. The most revolutionary act is to say what is. And so it is.

Claus accuses us of claiming that the IEC is only good for peacetime. He does not seem to be aware of what he is expressing. Debates and conflicts about content in a revolutionary organisation do not lift the "state of peace" because different parts struggle for the best way together and on the basis of principled programmatic agreement. Peace is over when different parts fight against each other and one part wants to give the organisation a new political basis. The sad truth is: this state has been reached. And from our point of view it was brought about by the NFF from the first day of the IEC meeting. So yes: an IEC which brings together two consolidated currents deviating in fundamental questions cannot and will not unite our international.

Generation change?

That this is the point becomes clear when Claus casually asks: "Is it not conceivable for the IS members that a generation change does not always take place under the control of the old generation, but takes place at times and opportunities that were not previously on one's radar, especially if all those involved in the IS and the IEC have delayed it for too long?"

To discuss the question of generational change so detached from an assessment of political differences has nothing to do with a Marxist approach to such questions. We are not a football team where there is a physical boundary at some point to be on the team. We are a revolutionary organisation that also represents the memory of the workers' movement and is dependent on having a leadership that is politically up to date.

Why doesn't Claus make it concrete? Who is no longer able to fulfill the task in the IS for reasons of age? Our experience is that the formally oldest comrade in the IS, Peter Taaffe, belongs to the (mentally) younger comrades in the CWI in his thinking, his tactical flexibility and his ability to make suggestions for new situations. Especially in recent years he has made a decisive contribution to ensuring that the section in England and Wales and the entire International have correctly positioned themselves on new issues such as the Corbyn phenomenon, the Sanders candidacy in 2016 and Brexit.

Our experience is that – even if there were sometimes differences of opinion – we could always discuss the situation in Germany and the development of the German section very profitably with Bob, the third oldest in the IS, and received a lot of help. We are of the opinion that Hannah and Judy (both of whom belong to the generation that also leads the NFF) have made an excellent contribution to the work of the IS in recent years. And there was the attempt to initiate a rejuvenation process with the admission of three younger alternate members to the IS – TU Senan, Danny Byrne (DB) and Cédric Gerome (CG) – in the last years. The fact that this does not automatically mean, however, that a committee is strengthened politically as a result, can be seen from the role played by DB and CG as supporters of the NFF.

Yes, the question of the future personnel composition of the IS arises, but it is hypocritical when NFF comrades try to turn the current political conflict into a generational conflict. It is about a conflict of fundamentally different approaches to the question of programme, orientation and also internal democracy in the organisation.

'Anything goes'?

It is about what political and ideological coherence a revolutionary international must have. Apparently the NFF takes the attitude of 'anything goes' as long as there is a general commitment to Marxism. This contradicts our understanding of a Marxist international that is a world party based on democratic centralism. Claus had sent reflections on the crisis in the CWI to the German EC in December, which expressed a similar misconception of the character of a revolutionary Marxist international: "We must clarify to what extent Bolshevism must be modernised. The CWI's claim to have a line remains correct. Mandelistic arbitrariness leads to reformism. The question, however, is whether the line must not be drawn with a broader pencil, so that structurally more experiments and parallel different approaches are possible... Ideological firmness and hardness have kept the CWI intact. However, if the pressure becomes too strong and the direction from which the pressure comes, becomes unpredictable, hardness can also become a problem because fractures become more likely. It needs to be clarified whether the organisation can become more flexible in the sense of allowing more dissent and not claiming to clarify all questions conclusively, perhaps more 'trial and error' and 'best practice' than 'we have always known it'".

We are not of the opinion that the CWI represents an attitude of "we have always known it" and we are of the opinion that in recent years too much rather than too little "trial and error" has been possible in the International. We would have liked Peter Taaffe to have insisted in 2006-07 that his concerns about our tactics of not joining Die Linke in the East and in Berlin should have been expressed more decisively and that he should have insisted on a comprehensive debate instead of trusting us too much (to explain for newer members: at the time of the merger of WASG and PDS we had decided to join the new party only in West Germany. We corrected that a year later). But we also think it's right that the IS doesn't pursue a micromanagement policy and doesn't try to lead sections out of London. In practice, this has led to a certain "trial and error", which may have gone too far. But also this question cannot be discussed separately from the evaluation of the "errors". And the leaders of the national sections themselves are responsible for these.

Breaking democratic centralism in Ireland

We find it breathtaking that Claus has managed to write a contribution on the subject of democratic centralism for this debate without a single word on the rupture of democratic centralism that took place in the Irish section. The NFF's approach to this question says a lot about the unprincipled nature of this trend.

Let us recall that, in the summer of last year, four members of the Irish leadership disregarded all democratically elected bodies of the organisation and made decisions that exposed the organisation to great dangers and violated the personal rights of many members. The reason was that they suspected an opposition grouping in the party (which was admitted at the beginning of the debate, then denied and now in fact admitted again). The IS was not willing to support this undemocratic approach and called for a discussion within the organisation. As a result, the Irish NC described this procedure as "democratic and principled" in a resolution of October 2018. This decision continues to apply. While the Irish participants in the IEC defended their approach in principle in the discussion, supported by a number of other IEC members, they then – quite surprisingly – agreed at the end to a resolution criticising their approach. This was, in our view, a manoeuvre to gain a majority in the IEC for their draft resolution and thus to push through and win a vote at the meeting that put the IS in a minority position. From the beginning, we didn't take the comrades seriously on this self-criticism and in the course of the debate it became clear that they were increasingly defending their actions. It's a scandal that other IEC members and NFF supporters have joined in. For us, the balancesheet is clear: if anyone has broken democratic norms and acted bureaucratically, it is the majority of the Irish leadership; and if anyone has defended democracy in the CWI, it is the IS majority and the faction.

All comrades must be clear: the NFF wants to build an organisation in which such undemocratic methods are explicitly accepted. The example has been set and there is no other way to interpret the complete silence on this incident in the NFF's policy statement. We are far from using the same terminology – "incurable genetic defect", "infirmity" – as Claus does, but we are sure that an NFF-led organisation would be burdened with a heavy mortgage that would take revenge at the next opportunity.

The Crucial Question!

In the section 'A Crucial Question' Claus removes his argumentation that the faction is undemocratic, centralist and infested by a "non-healable genetic defect" and explains that our action is justified "if for a minority it is certain that a situation threatens in which the international could fall into the hands of non-reformable opportunists who would use the names, traditions, and resources of the organisation to pursue entirely different goals".

Claus then tries to emotionally charge this question by addressing the question to us: "Are the members of the SAV [Socialist Alternative, at the time of writing the German section of the CWI] who signed the letter 'For the revolutionary unity of the CWI' organic opportunists for the faction members? Or useful idiots of forces in Ireland, Greece and elsewhere who would inevitably destroy the CWI if they had more influence internationally in the leadership?"

For us, the categories "non-reformable", "organic" and "inevitable" are secondary. We certainly donnot call comrades idiots. Nor is it a question of whether slipping into an opportunistic attitude is a conscious or unconscious process. It is about whether there is this sliding towards opportunism and whether there is a willingness to reflect on it, to acknowledge criticism and to initiate corrections. From our point of view there is this slippage and unfortunately there is no recognition of our critique, no self-reflection and no corrections. The conclusion we draw from this is that the CWI is at risk as a revolutionary Marxist organisation based on a programme and method that we have developed over decades. We all know that mistakes that are not corrected become a tendency. That is what has happened. The fact that the NFF has a majority at the IEC level (and this is also to be expected at a World Congress, since the number of delegates for a section is limited to a maximum of five and the weight of the section in England and Wales would not be reflected at a World Congress) means that this dangerous development would spread to the whole international. Once the leadership of the international falls into the hands of members who have embarked on an opportunist course, this process will accelerate and affect and discredit the whole International. We cannot accept this and it would be negligent to proceed according to the "principle of hope" and, contrary to all the experiences of the last six months, to bet that there will still be a correction.

This is all the more true because it is clear that the NFF considers the use of undemocratic methods to counter political opposition within the organisation to be acceptable. The breach of democratic norms in the Irish leadership was used to gather information about and combat a suspected opposition group in the organisation.

We consider this development tragic, especially for the German section, because we do not believe that the signatories of the declaration "For the revolutionary unity of the CWI" are organic opportunists, most of them not even non-organic. But unfortunately they have chosen to support in this struggle those forces that have embarked on an opportunist course. We assume that the motives of most comrades were to want to prevent a split at all costs, because they do not recognise the significance of the differences or assess them differently than we do. We know that some of the comrades see themselves closer to the faction than to the Irish or Greek section in the concrete questions of content. We call upon these and all comrades to position themselves politically in this conflict. The concrete question is: on what political, programmatic and methodical basis can we build a revolutionary organisation? Which leaders of the CWI embody these political foundations?

The political declaration of the NFF, but also its other papers and contributions in debates, makes it clear that they have decided to change the majority relations in the International and to realign the organisation. Their statement makes it clear that there is no recognition of the criticism of the faction and that the course taken in Ireland and Greece is not only to be accepted, but also to become formative for the whole international. The fact that they are sticking to a convocation of the IEC in August, although they know that for many members of the faction this means the 'point of no return,' makes it clear that they have opted for a separation of ways. In this case, we call on all comrades to continue the successful work of the SAV as part of the CWI together with us and to adhere to its programmatic and methodological principles.

ON AN AUGUST IEC

Tony Saunois, for the IS Majority

The recent declaration from the Non-Faction Faction (NFF) IEC members demands that the IS majority convene a meeting of the IEC in August 2019. This declaration follows a meeting of the NFF which took place in London between 28 and 29 May. Once again, the hypocritical dishonesty of this grouping is revealed. Having protested for six months that they are not a faction, they now issue a demand signed by NFF full members of the IEC, based on a 'resolution' agreed at an international secret meeting of their leading members. For six months this opposition grouping to the IS majority has been 'co-ordinating' their activity and production of documents, holding at least two international meetings. Yet they still try and maintain the pretence they are not an organised faction. This totally dishonest approach is a reflection of the politically unprincipled opportunist nature of this grouping.

They claim to invoke the CWI constitution by demanding that the IS majority convene an IEC in August but completely ignore the fundamental political differences which have been revealed in the debate over the last six months. As we have argued since the outbreak of this crisis in November 2018, there are decisive political differences of a fundamental character, relating to perspectives, programme, orientation, the trades unions and the centrality of the working class, how to intervene in the movements relating to women, LGBTQ+ and the environment, the transitional method and methods of building the revolutionary party.

These issues have been debated in numerous meetings and the production of over 100 documents. However, in the proposed agenda the NFF have circulated for an IEC meeting in August, these central questions are absent. This dispute in the CWI began on the question of the method of work and political orientation and programme of the Irish section. The recent election results in Ireland represent a severe electoral set-back for the Socialist Party. Again this is omitted from inclusion on the NFF proposed agenda. Once again the NFF, as it has throughout this dispute, proposes to evade political debate and discussion on these and related questions.

Now, after six months of debate the NFF have now finally admitted that important and fundamental differences exist on these issues. This was made clear in recent debates by their spokespersons and in their factional platform produced six months into the debate (The world at a crucial conjuncture: new phenomena and tasks – the crisis in the CWI). This we have replied to in our statement 'Mass political consciousness, the current stage of the class struggle and the revolutionary party' [page 32]. Now towards the end of the debate, the NFF supporters in England and Wales have publicly declared a faction.

It is evident a political rupture has taken place in the CWI. The leadership of the NFF have broken from the political orientation and methods that the CWI was originally founded on. They have moved in a right-ward opportunist direction.

The NFF deny this and hide behind the mask that they represent the 'IEC majority.' This 'majority' in no way represents the overall balance of the CWI membership, as a whole, in which the NFF is clearly in a minority. The NFF argue they are in a 'majority' on an IEC in which the Russian section has two full members with a claimed membership of only 25; the Israeli section has two full members and 45 members, and the Cypriot section has 1 full IEC member with a claimed membership of 21. The Polish section has 1 alternate IEC member, yet 5 members attended the recent debate on the CWI crisis! To claim a 'majority' of such a gathering brushes aside the real balance of forces of the CWI membership.

The NFF have a clear political objective - to shift the CWI and its leadership, including the International Secretariat, in a right-ward opportunist direction. It is for this reason they are demanding that an IEC be held in August. Generously, some of them have stated in the debates and some documents that they will not make any changes to the IS at an August IEC meeting. Their intention is clear however. An August IEC meeting would be used to politically shift the CWI in the opportunist direction defended by the NFF leadership. They would then either remove or change the political balance of the current IS majority at a World Congress in January 2020. It is clear the current, unrepresentative IEC is split into two political blocks which have already ruptured on a political basis. There are currently two international organisations functioning in one with diverging political analysis and method.

The political rupture is now also reflected organisationally by NFF-led sections. Socialist Alternative in the US is currently $30,000 behind on their regular political donations. The Belgian subs are being paid into an account in Belgium which the IS has no access to. The Australian section has failed to pay subs for the current quarter and the latest subs from Sweden have not arrived. This breaches the CWI constitution and clearly indicates that the NFF is in the process of breaking from the CWI not only politically but organisationally. In such a situation, the IS majority is not prepared to convene a meeting of an IEC as it is currently constituted.

It is not justified to convene such a meeting, at the cost of thousands of pounds, where no political agreement exists on the fundamental issues that have been debated and when a political rupture has already occurred. The convening of a meeting on the basis of a reconstituted IEC and CWI congress, which reflect the real balance of the CWI membership and viable sections, where there is the prospect of genuine debate and discussion, and the prospect of reaching political agreement on the fundamental issues under debate, is the only basis such a meeting could be justified.

An international meeting of the faction has been convened by the IS majority for July 22-25, with the sponsorship of the sections in England and Wales, and Scotland, the support of the German NC and others, to debate all of these issues and decide on the next steps to go forward and build the CWI, on the basis of the Trotskyist methods and principles it was founded on in 1974.

Declaration in Support of the International Faction

Carah Daniel (Branch Committee member – Dublin Fingal Branch), Billy Flynn (Dublin South West Branch), Olaf Hoch (Branch Committee member – Dublin Fingal Branch), Ciaran McKenna (Branch Secretary – Dublin Fingal, SIPTU Section Organiser DCU, SIPTU Education Sector Committee member), Councillor Donal O'Cofaigh (Fermanagh and Omagh Branch, National Committee member), Fiona O'Loughlin (Dublin Fingal Branch, Regional Executive Committee and National Committee member), Sarah Zanchetta (Dublin Fingal Branch)

*I*t is now a little over six months since an unprecedented crisis broke out in our international. In this time the debate in the Irish section has been largely confined to the NC, with the exception of branch discussions on (elements of) the workers' united front tactic and one all members' meeting in February. The discussion in the NC has focused on the leadership's actions in response to the 'breach', the orientation towards cross-class, identity politics movements, and what the NEC majority has called the 'open turn' away from the trade unions.

The experience over this period has demonstrated that on their present path our section's leadership are on course to break with the revolutionary traditions of Trotskyism, as well as the theoretical and organisational foundations of the CWI forged over more than 45 years. This political and organisational retreat is rooted in the complex and contradictory objective situation facing Marxists over the past period. It is clear from the course of the international debate that it is not just the leadership of our section, but also sections supporting the undeclared 'opposition faction', who are on a profoundly opportunist trajectory.

The weight of objective pressures has resulted in a rightward move away from Marxism, with the situation in our section more advanced because of the disproportionate number of elected representatives; the greater dependency on the income from those positions; the ratio of full-timers to active comrades in the south; and the weight of the mass work relative to the small size of the party's cadre base. In the context of a relatively low level of socialist consciousness and the absence of mass workers' struggles, in order to sustain electoral positions a mistaken opportunist approach has been adopted and the leadership have failed to consistently defend a fully Trotskyist programme.

The debate in our party has confirmed the crystallisation of a tendency, under the banner of the undeclared opposition faction, which has abandoned use of the transitional programme and method, conducted an 'open turn' away from the mass workers' organisations and adapted to alien class ideas, including identity politics.

The discussion at the most recent NC meeting – to which representatives of the IS majority were excluded – confirmed the advanced state of political backsliding on a number of points. This process of crystallisation and its reflection on an international scale, confirms the correctness and necessity of the decision by the IS majority to establish an international faction in defence of the legacy, orientation and organisational traditions of the CWI.

The most recent Irish NC meeting confirmed that there are now effectively two internationals operating in parallel, but in shadow form. The indefensible decision to withhold our section's affiliation fees to the CWI demonstrates clearly that a decision has been reached by the undeclared opposition faction for a split. Comments made by some of the NEC majority comrades revealed advanced plans for the establishment of structures in an international led by themselves. This includes 'permanent standing commissions,' apparently allowing them to intervene into the 'second and third tiers' of activists in sections, over the heads of their national leaderships. It is far from clear how these plans are coherent with the principles of a democratic centralist international.

As such, we the undersigned declare ourselves in support of:

1. The platform and documents produced by the In Defence of a Working-Class, Trotskyist CWI faction, which provide the clearest and most consistent expression of the CWI and its founding ideals; and,
2. The stance taken by the IS majority which represents the orientation, programme and methods that underpin a principled revolutionary international.

We welcome the meeting in July that is being organised by the international faction and will participate in this event. We will support all efforts to ensure the safeguarding of a principled revolutionary international. A prerequisite for this is defending and building on the theoretical and organisational foundations conquered by the CWI over the last 45 years.

We wish to reinforce our commitment to the rich legacy of CWI practice and theory developed through decades of struggle for a principled, socialist approach to the national question; in particular, we stand in defence of a strategic orientation to the mass workers' organisations, striving to win workers to a Marxist programme, as key to overcoming the sectarian divisions within the working class in Northern Ireland and resolving the national question on this island on a socialist basis, in solidarity with the working class in England, Scotland, Wales and the whole of Europe.

In making this declaration, we recognise that many within our section are only now beginning to question the road the NEC majority are taking them down. We appeal to them, as revolutionaries, to place the root political questions primary, as opposed to making decisions based on personal friendships, animus, misplaced party loyalties or misinformation.

We appeal to all those who hold dear to the principles and legacy of the CWI, who agree with the main political analysis and conclusions in the documents of the international faction, to engage with us and to join with us in defence of a working-class and Trotskyist CWI. At a time of mounting crisis in global capitalism and imperialism, the necessity of building a healthy, democratic centralist international demands nothing less.

PROGRAMME, METHOD AND POLITICAL CLARITY

French National Committee resolution, July

The dispute that is shaking the CWI should have made it possible to have substantive debates, real confrontations of analyses and the will to discuss. Even if it is each point of the programme that must be discussed, it is normally very educational for members and leading comrades. It is therefore with a certain weariness that we see that in most of the texts sent by NFF supporters, it is always the same – emotional reactions, putting in question the very right to criticise.

It should be remembered that everything started from the way the Irish leadership treated the hack, which reflects both a method which is not acceptable, but also represents a refusal to solve political problems by democratic and transparent means. Being in the same international organisation means that the functioning of each section concerns each member regardless of the country he or she is in. Without an immediate condemnation of these methods we cannot have confidence and, beyond that, we cannot trust leaderships who do not firmly condemn the Irish majority methods.

We can only therefore disapprove of the key document that the NFF published in May which they called a resolution of the majority of the IEC ('The world at a crucial conjuncture: new phenomena and tasks – the crisis in the CWI'). It does not even mention this case, let alone condemn it. The Greek leadership asserts in another document that this is a "secondary issue" compared with the rest.

The duty of criticism

With each criticism, the comrades stubbornly refuse any correction to their policies. Even though there may be some blunders here, we see this approach as a serious danger, which we described in the resolution adopted by our National Committee (NC) in March. There has been a "national falling back" of the leaderships of sections who no longer behave as part of the same global party, unified by its international programme but who consider that they conduct their politics without worrying about those of the other sections. In the above-mentioned NFF document, there is no expression of disagreement on the important differences that exist between one section and another within the nff – on trade unionism, on the programme of campaigns like Rosa or on election campaigns. Whether the comrades do it consciously or not, it is a federalist way of functioning that they express in their document: elements of a global analysis but then each section conducts its own politics. The text even justifies the Greek leadership's theses on the uselessness of putting demands on trade union leaderships.

This functioning is not that of a Marxist international which, as a world revolutionary party, must have a unified programme as developed by Marx but especially by Lenin and Trotsky. How is it a problem to criticise mistakes, even sometimes with harsh words? This is the second aspect that not only disappoints us but also wearies us, reading extremely long documents that only combine generalities, emotional reactions and statistics. It is not by adding up the numbers that policy is decided.

Although they may have been shaken by the initial tone of some of the exchanges, the NFF comrades (the self-styled 'coordinating sections') never sought to discuss the substance. They spent their time saying that the criticisms raised by the IS majority and the faction were unjustified and exaggerated. The main problem is that by saying this, the comrades consider there would be no need to raise criticisms. In this kind of debate, the tone is secondary for those who really want to debate. It is the substance that is primary, rather than debate remaining on the level of emotional and barely political reactions.

Restoring a Marxist debate

In fact, in the last decade or so, we have not had enough discussion about the programme and work of each of the sections. We have limited ourselves to more general agreements, or have delegated dealing with disagreements to the IS. We must now break with this and return to having a greater focus on exchanges between sections and a critical reading of their publications. For us, what has bothered us in recent years is that while within the French section we often discuss the programme of other sections, there was no opportunity internationally to make it a broad and substantive debate. Obviously, we cannot spend a great deal of time on this and it is primarily the role of the IS to do so. But precisely when the IS opens this debate in the international and comrades simply refuse to engage in the debate and acknowledge errors or even mistakes, this is this the way a blockage is created and the crisis is exacerbated. If a faction was created, it was precisely because the comrades of the NFF considered that the points raised by the IS were minor and that, in their opinion, we should carry on the same way. If there had not been a faction, other errors would have gone on without us really having the means to discuss and correct them as it is now part of the NFF's way of functioning such that each section's leadership can do whatever it wants, without being prepared to stand corrected or to be criticised too harshly.

The comrades of the NFF should think about this in depth because these are the methods which flow from their May document. And for us, not only is this way of functioning wrong, but it makes further crises inevitable. Disagreements become so pronounced that the political campaigns become incompatible between one section and another.

Anyway, whatever the comrades of the NFF might say, this debate will have allowed us to see that some so-called sections no longer regularly publish newspapers, do not get involved in the immediate struggles of the workers and do not even seek to establish themselves in the unions. Yet these are the very foundations for the construction of a revolutionary Marxist party.

What has become clear is that our disagreements with some NFF sections' leaderships are deep. This is certainly in part due to a lack of discussion, but there is also a growing divergence in the political work of the comrades. On issues such as the environmental movements, women's rights, on electoral campaigns such as that of Sanders or the Socialist Party campaigns in Ireland, the analysis of mass struggles such as the yellow vests in France, the mobilisation of the Algerian people etc., we say these disagreements are enormous. This is because on all these issues, as we wrote in our March resolution, it is not that the comrades completely eliminate the working class. It is quite simply that for them, it does not have a central role - it is not the class that must lead the struggle and then the revolution. It is one thing to talk formally about socialism, workers' control etc.; it is another thing to train the members – the cadres – to raise class issues wherever they intervene with the aim of highlighting the working class' central role. Demanding, for example, a global climate strike, or a global women's strike, may be a way of doing some agitation but it is by no means the way to reach the majority of the working class.

The working class is not only an instrument capable of hindering the capitalists, it is the only class that, in order to emancipate itself, must take power and thus emancipate all humanity by breaking the dictatorship of exploitation through the building of socialism.

This is precisely the most important point of disagreement and will not be resolved by quoting articles with the words "workers' control" in them. Because the real issue is what the sections do in practice, including in relation to the trade unions, but also in the daily class struggle. This is where our programme is most important, not only when we produce analyses or general slogans. On women's rights, for example, it seems equally important to us, if not more so, to get involved as we do in France, in strikes by women workers, to encourage them to take a leading role, to join a union and to lead trade union branches.

On the environment: the current movement allows for general ideas against capitalism, with perhaps a little on socialism, but the general tenor of this movement is to blame the way things are produced and therefore even workers themselves, and not capitalism as a whole. While some sections of Europe's youth are mobilising, the majority of workers in the neo-colonial world are still barely scraping together a living. While the demonstrations in March were important – and there will be other important days of mobilisation – they are in essence no different from the big anti-war mobilisations of 2003 and so far they have been smaller. At that time there were also strikes (of railway workers and dockers in Italy, school students in Germany), but nevertheless, we did not say that this movement was objectively leading to revolutionary conclusions. At that time we all agreed that the main problem of anti-war campaigns such as those organised by the swp was the lack of class content they gave to the movement and their refusal to develop socialist propaganda. Why should we not point out the same weaknesses today of campaigns on the environment, or women's rights? Why, moreover, is there not as much material produced around the fight against racism, imperialism and the terrible devastation of the neo-colonial world, which are certainly linked to these other subjects: because it is not fashionable?

Why discuss in detail

In reality, the global situation has become both more explosive and unstable. This means that we have to pay much more attention to the slogans and the programme we put forward. There can be no one slogan. We must be able to address different layers of the working class and to start where they are, to include them in a programme that does not divide, but on the contrary mobilises the broadest possible layers of workers. The forces leading movements like the ones on women's rights or the environment (and others) on the contrary, in practice, divide and set sections of workers against each other. At the heart of our intervention in these phenomena must be the need to unify the working class, on the basis of a programme that includes specific democratic issues, on the environment and other questions. This requires more precise discussions on the consciousness of the masses, the social composition of different struggles, the issues and necessary slogans for them. We cannot, when the whole debate is about whether our sections intervene correctly in situations and put forward the correct programme, spend time replying that the criticisms are exaggerated, that this debate is only there to create divisions, etc. Comrades who react in this way are mis-educating their members, teaching them that all criticism is bad and diminishing their ability to take a critical approach.

The comrades of the US NC (so not new members who are taking their first steps grappling with developing slogans) write in their document that they do not understand the criticism of the slogan "Trump out; Bernie in!" and see no difference with the slogan of the British comrades "Tories out; general election now." This shows how dangerous this decline in critical thinking is. We have never campaigned with the slogan "Mélenchon for president!" because we must not encourage illusions. Mélenchon as president would carry out capitalist politics, just as Sanders would. The issue is one of mobilising the masses and how workers could use an electoral victory. The slogan of the us comrades does not dispel this illusion. On the contrary. And it is nothing like the slogan of the British comrades which basically consists of advocating a deepening of the political crisis of the Tory government. In one case, a slogan traces a path towards calming down the political crisis, in the other it seeks to accentuate it. If the comrades don't see the fundamental difference, there is a serious problem.

At the present stage, and for years to come, we have above all to make propaganda and develop our members to know how to use each slogan, how to apply and adjust them, precisely to avoid confusion. To believe that at this stage we are able to play a decisive role on a very large range of subjects is wrong, because it depends on the consciousness of the masses on the one hand and, on the other hand and in a crucial way, on the roots that we have developed among the masses and in particular among workers, in the workplaces etc.

On consciousness

It is finally quite logical that the NFF, just like the leaderships of the former Spanish (IR) and Portuguese sections, should agree on this point i.e. not to admit that one of the current obstacles is the confusion that reigns in the working class. IR have even preferred to leave the debate rather than engage with this question in depth, simply because the leadership of ir are not concerned with the actual level of consciousness of the masses; they focus only on an advanced layer, receptive to the dominant themes in the struggles. IR seem to consider it a crime to analyse consciousness, including its limits, in order to see what perspectives and possibilities flow from it. The Bolsheviks did precisely this in July 1917, by correctly analysing that the masses were not ready to take power. Marx understood that the Paris Commune of 1871 was premature – which did not prevent him from supporting it and developing a programme to extend it to all of France. It is not so much the understanding of socialism that characterises the crucial level of consciousness of workers, but their understanding that they can and must take power. It is then that the question of leadership becomes the most crucial question - the one that determines whether or not workers do take power. In the past, Stalinist or social-democratic bureaucrats had to use very elaborate tactics to pass off a few social gains as a victory, during major periods of struggle that raised the question of power. Today, the immediate question is much more to convince workers to organise themselves, to go further than one-day strikes or demonstrations. A few timid steps are taken in this direction, but we are still far from a widespread development of struggle committees in factories and neighbourhoods, even in a country with a widespread movement like Algeria, even though this remains a key point of our programme.

These are crucial points. We have had long and absolutely indispensable discussions in the French section on the yellow vest movement, to understand how it is not a movement of the working class as a class, to understand and to know what attitude the unions should have taken, what slogans and demands to develop in such a movement. And this does not only apply to France, because this kind of movement, in one form or another, is expressed everywhere: a rejection of politicians, the government etc., but with few slogans and demands aimed at the capitalists, the ultra-rich, or exploitation. Most of the yellow vests are workers, but most of these workers are not striking and therefore are not building the movement in a way that challenges the capitalists. Still, the same issues remain: it is a question of the leadership of the struggle, the programme which is put forward, and whether it is the working class that must lead the struggle, on its class basis and not in a partial way as a simple component of 'the people.'

In general: environmental movements are not demanding the end of capitalism, they are demanding that capitalism does not pollute. Against racist, sexist or gender oppression, they demand equal rights but without putting capitalism in question, which amounts to demanding equal exploitation. This assessment does not mean that these movements are not important, but establishes the overall level of consciousness of the movement. This means that our transitional approach must not lose sight of the essential point: that is that our whole activity must be orientated towards the aim of reaching the working class and making sure it takes a leading role.

This concern is not to the fore in the NFF documents and this is the clearest statement of our divergences, after months of documents being circulated (which, in itself, is a demonstration of the democratic vitality of the CWI).

In conclusion

The NFF comrades used an unfortunate approach. They began by denouncing the fact that a faction was formed and appealed to all those who feared a split. Then they whipped up the fear of a split, paralysing the critical thinking of a whole layer of members. They increased the emotional pressure by saying that a faction leads to splitting and that being in a faction is negative. Stupefied by this fear, comrades reduced their criticisms and differences and, for the moment, there is a false unanimity in the NFF, a mere façade, to present a block. But it will have a negative impact when real political debates arise, and that will come quickly. It took the comrades six months to put together a document that has only one objective: to blame the IS for all the problems and carefully avoid criticising each other.

Once the fact of being in a faction was presented as negative and dangerous, it was enough to accuse the IS of all the wrong-doing. Thus the beautiful union is made on a single policy; to be against the IS which is the cause of everything. In doing so, once again, the comrades are preparing for a painful future, because from now on the members who will follow them will reject even the very idea of a leadership for the party and will consider – as we can already read in some documents – that it is the national context that determines the programme and not the development of an international programme, that we then try to translate for each particular situation. With each criticism or tension, these comrades will no longer look for political issues but simply see 'bureaucratic' mistakes in this or that structure. By not starting from the discussion on the programme and accusing the IS of all the wrongs, the NFF is making a concession to the petty-bourgeois habit of looking for culprits rather than finding solutions.

And since it is also said that the IS is bureaucratic, it is even suggested that bureaucracy is not a social and political phenomenon, but the fault of a handful of leaders who are greedy for who-knows-what. However, even if the IS does make mistakes, the current debate could have been used to correct them, starting from the right position: namely on our international programme and on the centrality of the working class. This is what the NFF comrades avoid in all their documents: they would have no problem on the basis of the programme they are putting forward and therefore all the blame is on the IS alone. Summarising the CWI's problems with "It's the IS' fault" is not only childish but, in fact, hardly political.

But this prepares us for the last argument: "We are the majority of the IEC, so we are right. Our problem is just a handful of old leaders" (without saying, of course, that the main leaders of the nff have also been at the head of their sections for 25 years or more). Thus, no political programme is proved right and the debate is now so depoliticised that it is enough to say, "We are the biggest so we are right". However, this kind of argument is politically false. What matters are the ideas and the programme, not the result of a vote or the number of signatories to a document left deliberately vague to ensure a significant number of signatures.

If the comrades think they will face the coming period in this way – the explosive nature of movements but also their extreme complexity due to the confusion in the consciousness of the working class – they have not taken the path which will educate their members correctly.

For our part, six months of debates discussing nothing no longer interests us. The French section does not recognise itself in the theses of the NFF leaders. Comrades do not need an IEC to see disagreements that are written on hundreds of pages. In any case, we will now only give an extremely limited amount of time to further discussions in this debate and we will discuss with the faction the perspectives for our international current. We will see if the discussions resume some day but, for now, let each current carry out its work with its policies and genuine members must frankly and honestly assess the balance sheets of these experiences. With those comrades who wish to discuss again on this basis, the door will remain open.

The NC of the French section, at its meeting of July 7, therefore unanimously adopted the following resolution: "Given the state of the discussions, the debate has come to an end and we consider that it is no longer possible to be together, the level of political agreement is no longer sufficient; we are no longer building the same organisation".

ON OUR FOUNDING PRINCIPLES

Statement from the Nigerian supporters of IDWCTCWI

In England and Wales, the process of the debate culminated in July 2019.
However, internationally this developed at different paces.
The following statement was written in October 2019, after the re-foundation of the CWI,
and after the non-faction faction had launched World Socialist Alternative (WSA).

After about 7 months of debate in the Democratic Socialist Movement (DSM) – the Nigerian section of the Committee for a Workers International (CWI) – and about 11 months of debate internationally, it has become quite clear that this is not simply a 'foreign dispute' which is of secondary importance to the work of the Nigerian section. Rather, it is a disagreement over fundamental ideas, programmes and methods of Marxism, especially in a difficult period. We therefore have a duty to take a clear, scientific and bold position that correlates with the founding principle of the DSM.

At the core of this debate is the question of how Marxists can preserve, strengthen and attempt to build revolutionary forces in the current conjuncture where, despite the over-ripe objective conditions for a successful socialist revolution, the subjective conditions – the existence of mass workers parties with clear programme and a fighting leadership – remain largely weak and, in many countries, non-existent. Social democracy and the old reform-ist parties have moved further to the right, helped by the collapse of the Soviet Union. The labour aristocracy has become ever more tied to the capitalist state machinery; evermore cut off from the reality of the rank-and-file; and ever-more incapable to lead even the most basic struggle for improvement in livelihood and working conditions, except where pushed by a great upsurge from below. This sharply poses the task of rebuilding combative workers' organisations. It is like all the obstacles towards a successful socialist revolution analysed in Leon Trotsky's "Death Agony of Capitalism and the Task of the Fourth International" [the Transitional Programme] have become magnified and multiplied a thousand fold.

The resulting situation is that, over a decade on from the global economic crisis, capital-ism remains in existence in all countries, even though weak and tottering on the brink. In the intervening decade, the working class both in the advanced capitalist world (US, Britain, Greece etc) and in the neo-colonial and Arab world (Tunisia, Egypt, Libya, Algeria, South Africa, Nigeria, Sudan etc) made numerous advances, many of which were defeated or rolled back before achieving fundamental change of society. In some cases (Arab spring, Greece etc) defeats were immediately followed by a ruthless counter-revolution which further deci-mated the activist layers and set the movement back years.

In this difficult situation, not only can the most revolutionary of organisations falter but under the right conditions, a reformist trend can also begin to grow within it. Under the impact of a difficult objective situation, beginning with looking for a different way to apply programme and methods – under the guise of making the revolutionary organisation more attractive to a new generation, or new movements – in reality this has led to the watering down of the revolutionary essence of the party, in order to opportunistically adapt to the new situation. We believe that this development had already begun to take place within the CWI, and is at the root of the present crisis.

Consequently, two international organisations representing two distinct ideological tendencies have emerged. One trend, represented by IDWCTCWI faction/re-founded CWI defends the working-class and Trotskyist character of the CWI. The other, represented by the 'co-ordinating sections'/World Socialist Alternative (WSA) increasingly deviate from the fundamentals the CWI, lowering the banner of socialism, inconsistently orientating to the working class and its mass organisations, supporting or shielding mistakes in Ireland or elsewhere, and an adaptation to identity politics and petty-bourgeois ideas.

While this debate was set off in the Irish section of the former CWI, as the debate unfolded it has become clear that the basic lines of differences on the fundamental questions are replicated in all countries and sections. In the Nigerian section, the main lines of differences between the supporters of the IDWCTCWI faction and the WSA are not only about the international debate. It would be fatal to ignore the reality that, as the debate progressed, disputes concerning how to build a revolutionary party in Nigeria have equally been thrown up. Therefore, it is not surprising that SO, writing on behalf of supporters of the WSA said "a federalist revolutionary international can develop better, on its own pace under the full force of democratic centralism, but a bureaucratic organisation has no future than to face disintegration with the rule of tyranny in the near future". This quote, which speaks warmly of a federalist international, reveals the real political character of some supporters of WSA and how they are moving rightward – not only on political questions, but organisationally as well.

So, what is also at stake in this debate is the character and nature of the DSM as a revolutionary organisation. The logical consequence of the position of SO is a federal DSM which is loosely organised, with individuals and branches doing as they wish, and the centre simply monitoring. A bold leadership – which follows and maintains lively connections with all sections and layers of the organisation, point out errors, tries to correct them through discussion and does not flinch at voicing it's criticism – is seen as 'bureaucratic centralist' or lacking 'revolutionary patience'. The supporters of the re-founded CWI reject this opportunistic organisational formula and defend the democratic centralist character of the DSM.

Going forward, a discussion has to take place on what kind of revolutionary organisation we want to build. A revolutionary organisation is a combat party of the working class, not a committee of friends. To be able to play that role, ideological clarity, fidelity to the programmes and organisational discipline are indispensable requirements. Loose arrangements in which different branches or FTs do as they wish, while the centre looks on under the guise of 'revolutionary patience', cannot be acceptable. This can also be said in relation to attitudes to subs, political development, recruitment, paper sales, interventions in mass struggle etc. Especially because of the character of the period we are in, where the idea of a revolutionary party with a democratic centralist internal regime can sometimes be widely, but wrongly, seen by the new generation as akin to dictatorship, Marxists cannot be indifferent to the slightest indication of similar mood emerging or thriving in its fold. Full and democratic discussion and debate at all levels, and unity in action in implementing agreed resolutions, are the two most important attributes of democratic centralism. The third is a bold and capable leadership able to offer political leadership for the work. Unless the DSM is built in this manner, we will not be able to play an appropriate role in the class struggle, despite any abundance of opportunities that may come our way.

The fundamental issues

The fundamental political questions that are involved in this debate are: 1) the centrality of, and attitude towards, the organised working class, 2) trade union work, 3) womens struggles and identity politics and 4) democratic centralism. In our opinion, the political questions posed by this debate are fundamental, given the fact that they touch on the very foundations and traditions of the CWI.

The IS majority/re-founded CWI criticism of WSA trade union work is about inconsistent intervention in the trade unions, and the inconsistent recognition of the centrality of the working class, lacking a systematic approach pointing all movements in the direction of the working class and its mass organisations. Therefore, the usual response of WSA supporters – which consist in listing trade union interventions – does not suffice. The IS majority is not saying the Irish or other sections do not intervene in trade union struggles. What we are saying is that this is being done inconsistently and in some sections, there is a refusal to place demands on the labour movement because of the fear, as the Greek comrades bluntly put it, that the CWI comrades would be seen as people "from another planet".

No doubt, internationally, trade unions have often become bureaucratised, lacking internal democracy and with the leadership completely cut off from the reality of the rank and file. In Nigeria, trade union officials act as the unofficial police of the capitalist system to monitor workers and prevent revolt. This notwithstanding, Marxists have to develop a consistent programme of intervention in the trade unions and rank-and-file workers over and above the head of the bureaucracy. Without this, we renounce the struggle for influence and leadership of the working class regardless of whatever success we make in other interventions in social movements.

The struggle of women, students and oppressed layers can provide an important theatre for Marxists to intervene. Under the right conditions, these struggles can help to increase the radicalisation in society, and even inspire the working class to act. But however these movements grow, given their cross-class character they cannot replace the movement of the working class nor prove as decisive. While intervening in these movements, the role of Marxists is not to adapt, but to develop a transitional approach to help raise consciousness of the need for socialist transformation, through a working class-led revolutionary overthrow of capitalism. Not doing this consistently amounts to lowering of the socialist banner and adaptation to petty-bourgeois influences, which sometimes dominates these movements.

In our view, consciousness continues to lag behind. This is true both of the world situation since the 2007-08 world economic crisis and in Nigeria, since the economic recession of 2015 – Nigeria's worst recession in 25 years. Despite the severity of this crisis which shows the limits of capitalism, socialist consciousness has not yet developed, and the working class in many countries has not yet put itself at the head of the struggle. Of course, the exact correlation of forces is not the same in all countries, and there are important features in some countries (US, Britain etc) which could lead to a more decisive breakthrough in future. But a general feature is that there is anger everywhere but there is as yet no clear mass understanding of what is behind the crisis and what needs to be done. In Nigeria, the highpoint of class struggle was January 2012. Since then, struggle has taken a nose dive under the management of the bureaucratic apparatus of the labour movement. In having a clear understanding of the stage of consciousness, a revolutionary party is able to develop a clear vision and prepare for the next stage of struggle that will inevitably arrive, while insulating itself from opportunism and preventing demoralisation of its ranks.

The Nigerian section, even before it became a full section of the CWI in 1987, was built on the core principles of recognition of the historical role of the working class in the struggle for socialist transformation of society and the consistent orientation of Marxists to the class and its mass organisations. The history of the DSM over the past three decades is a history of consistent struggle to defend this programme against all manner of revisionism.

Therefore for us in the Nigerian section, the debate in the international is not an academic exercise. We consider it a fundamental struggle to preserve the revolutionary character of the international, upon the principles and foundations which led to our initial founding as a CWI group in 1985, and our affiliation in 1987. To this extent, we are in political agreement with the IDWCTCWI faction. A DSM built on the programmes and practice being put forward and defended by the WSA will be one which has deviated from its founding principles. In effect, this will mean a DSM that does not orientate consistently to the working class and its organisations, that adapts to the current, undeveloped, consciousness of the working class and broad masses and that comes under the influence of identity politics and other petty-bourgeois ideas under the guise of intervening in the struggle of women and oppressed people. This is not the CWI the Nigerian section formally affiliated to in 1987.

Between unity and defence of principles

Unable to respond to the fundamental political questions, supporters of WSA have inundated us with pious call for unity since this debate started. We fully agree with the need for unity, but on a principled basis. A unified revolutionary party on the basis of the opportunistic and reformist programmes being canvassed by the WSA will be as useless to the working class as not having a revolutionary party at all. More so, these disagreements touch on the very fundamentals of the DSM's own founding principles with which it began to gather and build its forces against the mainstream Stalinists, Pan-Africanists and other pseudo-Marxist/Socialist/anti-imperialist forces which dominated the students and workers movements in the 80s.

Indeed, the concrete essence of DSM's growth through the 1990s is the firm and uncompromising sharpening of its ideological and political character against all kinds of reformist tendencies within the workers and mass movements. As a result ,we suffered a minor split in the 1990s over the question of how we intervene in the struggle against the annulment of June 12, 1993 elections, with the departure of a layer which became the CWA and aligned with the International Marxist Tendency, which had split from the international on questions concerning the British Labour party. This is to demonstrate how the founding generation of the DSA, following the examples of Lenin and Trotsky, have never flinched from taking bold decisions against opportunism and ultra-leftism when it became necessary to do so.

WSA supporters have ransacked the stores of history in a frantic search for historical reference points to support their current trajectory. In the process, Trotsky has become a casualty. Truly, unlike Lenin, Trotsky pursued a conciliatory course of action during and after the 1903 split in the RSDLP which he later regretted, seeing the roles Menshevism and Bolshevism both played later, in 1905 and 1917. Writing about this later in his autobiography Trotsky said "After 1904 I stood outside of both the Social Democratic factions. I went through the revolution of 1905-1907 arm-in-arm with the Bolsheviks. During the years of the reaction, I defended revolutionary methods in the international Marxist publications against the Mensheviks. I still hoped, however, that the Mensheviks would move farther to the left, and I made several attempts to bring about a union in the party. It was not until the war that I became finally convinced of the utter hopelessness of the Mensheviks" (Leon Trotsky, My Life, chapter 28 – "Trotskyism" in 1917).

Subsequently, especially in the work of the Left Opposition and afterwards in the initial work building the Fourth International, Trotsky had a firmer approach towards ideological disputes, fighting for the unity of revolutionary forces but not being afraid of a separation of ways when politically necessary. Therefore, the attempt by WSA supporters to enrol Trotsky in their school of historical falsification is completely outrageous. Contrawise, Trotsky laboured hard in his polemics with the Stalinists to admit and explain his mistakes in this regard, while praising Lenin to have been proved right over the impossibility of any reconciliation between Menshevism and Bolshevism. "On November 1, 1917, at the meeting of the Petrograd committee (the minutes of this historical meeting – historical in every sense of the word – are still kept secret) Lenin said that after Trotsky had become convinced of the impossibility of union with the Mensheviks 'there has been no better Bolshevik'. And in this he proved very clearly and not for the first time, either that it had not been the theory of permanent revolution that had separated us, but the narrower, though very important question of the attitude toward Menshevism" (Leon Trotsky, My Life, chapter 28 – "Trotskyism" in 1917). Nearly a century after Trotsky wrote these lines, WSA supporters want to repeat exactly the same mistake by ignoring all of the benefits that history now provides – a benefit Trotsky did not possess at the time.

Pious wishes will not necessarily keep the revolutionary movement united. Only ideas and programmes can. According to the first programmatic document of the Labour Militant, predecessor of the DSM, "an organisation is first of all an idea, programme and perspectives. On the basis of a Marxist perspectives should the most conscious and disciplined fighters in the working class be organised for the task of political mobilisation of the mass of the workers for socialist transformation of society. Only when there is agreement among members of an organisation on a programme and perspectives can we ensure unity at critical moments which demand concrete action. Lack of an agreed programme and perspective will mean the disintegration of the forces of any organisation (due to fundamental difference of opinions) as urgent practical issues arise in the movement. Only on a **principled** basis of sharing similar ideas, programme and method of work can a united socialist organization be built among left organisations which are in grouplets. At the same time however, we are prepared to cooperate with other forces to **act** on **particular** issues" (Programmes and Perspectives for the Nigerian revolution, 1987).

Conclusion

We stand on the resolution of the Special National Committee of June 2019, and the DSM

NEC majority document, which politically conclude that the IS majority/IDWCTCWI/re-founded CWI contain the constellation of ideas and programmes which best correlates to those upon which the DSM was formally founded. For this reason, the Nigerian section should affiliate to the re-founded CWI. Therefore, we call on all comrades who are committed to retaining and building the section as a principled Trotskyist revolutionary organisation to support this position.

By affiliating to the re-founded CWI, this does not mean we agree one hundred percent with every action of the group or tendency or every section affiliated to it. Indeed, as part of the process of affiliation, we will enter into discussion with the leadership of the international over such issues as 1) democratic centralism and how it functions, 2) The role and functions of the International Secretariat and the IEC, 3) lessons of the CWI dispute and how to move forward building a revolutionary international. We believe this discussion can help to improve the work of the re-founded CWI and, most importantly, ensure that we move on from this dispute stronger, more united and more successful in seizing the enormous revolutionary opportunities on the horizon.

2. WOMEN *and* IDENTITY POLITICS

IN DEFENCE OF
SOCIALIST FEMINISM

*Christine Thomas, Socialism Today
224, December-January 18/19*

*F*eminism is back. All over the globe women have been taking to the streets and speaking out about gender oppression. Mass protests against violence against women have erupted in response to horrific rapes and murders of women in India and Argentina. On 14 November, more than 1.5 million students answered the strike call of the Sindicato de Estudiantes (SE) and Libres y Combativas, the socialist feminist platform of SE and Izquierda Revolucionaria (CWI) against sexism in schools and in the legal system of the Spanish state. In Ireland, Poland and Argentina women have organised to defeat new and existing reactionary constraints on their reproductive rights, challenging the stranglehold of the Catholic church over social issues.

#MeToo has spread around the world raising awareness of the scourge of sexual harassment, while the elections of Donald Trump in the US and Jair Bolsonaro in Brazil have provoked massive movements against the sexism of both presidents and in defence of hard-won rights for women against anticipated attacks. In Scotland over 8,000 low-paid women working for Glasgow city council have taken historic strike action to demand equal pay.

Although these are mainly disparate movements, and not all countries have been affected in the same way, it would probably not be an exaggeration to say that a third feminist wave is on the move. This follows in the wake of the 19th century first wave and the second, which mainly spanned the late 1960s and 1970s. Each has been marked by its own characteristics, shaped by prevailing economic and social conditions. However, it is also possible to trace recurrent strands of thought and practice running through them, which socialist feminists need to address.

The 19th century women's rights movement emerged in the US from the struggle for the abolition of slavery. If black people had the right to equality then so did women. The leadership of the first wave internationally rested overwhelmingly with middle-class women who principally emphasised their rights to legal and political equality with men of their own class. This included the right to vote, but also equal access to the public spheres of higher education, professional employment and politics which were considered male preserves in contradistinction to the female domestic sphere. In many countries, however, the late 19th century was also marked by a growing confidence among industrial workers, explosive struggles by sections of super-exploited workers, including many women, and the consequent rise of new forms of trade union organisation and the development of socialist and Marxist organisations.

Increased access to higher education and work outside the home spurred a questioning of wider gender inequality by women involved in the second wave. The women's liberation movement, although never numerically large in an organised form, succeeded in bringing questions concerning sexuality, gender violence and women's control of their own bodies into popular consciousness. It developed against the backdrop of social radicalisation and mass movements: international protests against the Vietnam war, the powerful US civil rights movement, the fight for national liberation in the colonial countries. Widespread strikes and industrial struggles were also breaking out in many countries, at times assuming a revolutionary potential.

In the US, the relationship with the workers' movement was quite weak. In Italy, on the other hand, it emerged directly from the mass workers' struggles and they were closely linked. In other countries such as Britain, the workers' movement also exercised an important influence on the feminist movement. This was a time when the potential of the organised working class as a viable agency for fundamental social change was evident. Yet those struggles and strikes show how, even at times of mass struggle, the relationship between the working class, revolutionary political leadership and system change needs to be consciously drawn out. This was highlighted by the events in France in 1968, when the working class was prevented from overthrowing capitalism by the lack of leadership by the powerful Communist Party.

The new wave

The current wave of protest has developed in the context of the biggest post-war economic crisis and the devastating consequences of a decade of austerity in many countries. On the one side, the severity of the crisis has had a radicalising effect on consciousness, resulting in a growing rejection of many of the institutions and instruments which capitalism has relied upon historically, such as the media, church and, most dramatically, the traditional political parties. As the movements of women testify, this changing consciousness is also giving rise to a challenging of the sexist and divisive ideology capitalism has used to back up its economic and social control.

At the same time, however, consciousness is still being shaped by the legacy of the pre-crisis period, when workers' organisations were weakened by neoliberal attacks and an acceptance of the dominant capitalist ideology following the collapse of the Stalinist Soviet Union. Although there have been some important workers' struggles, particularly in Greece, Portugal and some other European countries immediately after the crisis, collective struggle has been at a historically low level in many of the more developed capitalist countries. The inability or unwillingness of leaders to fight back against neoliberalism, austerity and the effects of globalisation have often led to a rejection of all political parties and a scepticism about the ability of the working class to act as a collective force for change.

The present global movement of women combines elements of a new consciousness with vestiges of the old. The fact that women, and other oppressed groups, are combining to struggle against their shared oppression is a very positive development, especially when contrasted with the previous two decades when the emphasis was on individual rather than collective struggle. 'Post-feminist' ideas reached their peak in the 1990s and the turn of the century. One of the main messages relayed through the media, popular culture and politicians was that, by transforming their own attitudes, shaking off victimhood and adopting sufficient determination, many of the existing obstacles to gender equality could be overcome. As a consequence, issues such as sexual harassment came to be increasingly viewed as individual problems.

Today, collective struggles involving a new generation of young women are once again raising awareness of gender violence, sexism and inequality. Although #MeToo developed initially as a mainly social media 'movement' dominated by highly-paid women in the entertainment industry, it has found a huge echo, lifting the lid on widespread sexual harassment and abuse by men in positions of power and control. With the confirmation of Brett Kavanaugh as a supreme court judge in the US, the movement took to the streets. Its impact beyond the realms of entertainment and politics could clearly be seen when McDonald's workers went on strike in ten US cities in September to protest against workplace sexual harassment and in the global walkout by thousands of Google workers.

Just like the previous waves, the new movement is a contradictory one, with competing ideas and strategies. These throw up theoretical and strategical challenges for socialist feminists. During the first feminist wave, the major debate for Marxist and socialist feminists revolved around how to relate to the 'bourgeois' women's movement, as it became known, especially when demands for the right to vote and legal equality with men were gaining an echo among working-class women.

Many socialists, male and female, felt it was not possible to campaign around issues of specific concern to women related to their gender without this leading to the division of male and female workers. There were fears that engaging with the bourgeois women's movement and its demand for legal changes within the existing system would result in those ideas being absorbed by the workers' organisations, undermining the struggle for fundamental economic and social change for the benefit of the whole working class. These ideas were successfully resisted by women such as Alexandra Kollontai in Russia and Sylvia Pankhurst in Britain.

Radical feminisms

The dangers of adaptation are present in any movement in which different ideological trends emerge. The main strands of thought competing in the second wave were bourgeois, or liberal feminism, radical feminism and socialist feminism. It would be more correct to speak of radical 'feminisms' as there were differing ideas over the basis of male dominance. For some it was located in men's control over women's sexuality. For others it was rooted in male violence.

However, unlike liberal feminists, for whom women's inequality is caused by discrimination and prejudice, radical feminism attempted to elaborate a social structure theory of women's oppression. This located gender inequality in a patriarchal system in which men as a group dominate women as a group. For most radical feminists, patriarchy was considered a social system separate from capitalism and other systems of economic and social inequality.

This theory of 'the patriarchy' has been opposed by Marxist and socialist feminists. Basing ourselves in particular on Friedrich Engels' work, The Origin of the Family Private Property and the State,* we have argued that institutionalised male dominance is not universal, that societies have existed in which egalitarian social relations have prevailed. Women's oppression is rooted in the emergence of societies based on class divisions. It is so intrinsically intertwined with class society – including today's dominant form, capitalism – that it cannot be analysed separately or ended without eliminating class society itself.

It is not always easy to stay ideologically firm in the face of a new radicalised and enthusiastic movement. Some socialist organisations, even some who defined themselves as 'Marxist', allowed themselves to be swept away by the second wave, adapting to the movement and accepting its ideas and strategy uncritically. Even the use of terminology is very important, as it reflects underlying ideas. A loose use of the term patriarchy, for example, adopted uncritically from the radical feminists, would have given credence not just to the idea of two separate systems, but also to the erroneous strategy flowing from this – a struggle against patriarchy separate from the struggle against capitalism.

The second women's movement contributed to achieving important gains in many countries, including the right to divorce, access to abortion and contraception, and legislation outlawing unequal pay and discrimination. The more extreme separatism of radical feminism, however, failed to provide a viable strategy for ending women's oppression and its influence has since waned.

In fact, another positive characteristic of the current movements has been precisely the openness of a new generation of women to involving men in their struggle, as well as forming alliances with other oppressed groups. The idea that different oppressions 'intersect' is in some ways a step forward from the cruder strands of radical feminist ideas which tended to see women as an undifferentiated social category, ignoring or downplaying differences based on race, class, etc. 'Intersectionality', however, tends to see class as just one form of oppression among many, without understanding how all oppressions are rooted in the structure of class society.

The effects of austerity

The economic crisis has led to a certain undermining of the liberal feminist notion of securing gender equality through gradual improvements within the capitalist system. Even before the crisis, the much vaunted economic gains and career advancements for women were mainly confined to the middle classes and the inequality gap between women widened. Nevertheless, the idea that continual progress was possible gained a certain currency even among many working-class women. The crisis and its effects have destroyed many of those expectations, strangling at birth the hopes and aspirations of a younger generation of women.

While there has been no conscious master plan to turn back the clock and force women out of the workforce and into the home, private sector job cuts, and particularly the austerity axe wielded by governments on the public sector, have destroyed many women's jobs and increased the precariousness of those which remain. At the same time, through the slashing of public services such as nurseries, elder and respite care, working-class families in particular

---

* *Although some of the facts on which Engels based his ideas have been refuted by subsequent scientific and anthropological developments, the general theory of the interconnectedness of class and gender oppression retains all its validity (see: Engels and Women's Liberation, Socialism Today 181, September 2014).*

are often left with no choice but to shoulder the extra burden themselves. Most of this, along with the harmful consequences it can wreak on finances, health and personal relations, falls to women.

With women still predominantly responsible for the care of children within the family, especially at pre-school age, lack of affordable childcare is often the main reason so many working-class women are still confined to low-paid, female-dominated and part-time jobs, and a major factor contributing to the gender pay and pension gap. Low pay means that working-class women and families are unable to pay privately for childcare from their own wages, while the structural economic crisis means that state spending on public childcare or financial subsidies to cover the cost of private care is strongly resisted or cut back.

Inherent, therefore, in the huge movements of women is not only the rejection of certain capitalist institutions and sexist ideology, but also the potential for the maturing of a broader anti-capitalist and socialist outlook. However, this will not be an automatic process. The inability of capitalism to deliver the material interests of working-class women – jobs, pay, benefits, pensions, etc – can be seen clearly during a crisis. The link between class society and other aspects of gender oppression, such as violence, sexual harassment and sexism, is less clear.

In the recent movements there is often a tendency to consider these problems as deriving from the behaviour or misogyny of individual men, or of a vague 'culture' which encourages rape or sexism, without seeing how attitudes, behaviour and culture are shaped by the capitalist society we live in and the ideology carried over from previous class societies. The emphasis has therefore been on raising awareness, educating men and changing attitudes and behaviour without any of this being linked to broader economic and structural change – much in the way that liberal feminists have argued in past movements.

Class-based society

Socialist feminists believe that all of these things are important. Violent and sexist behaviour carried out by individual men should be challenged wherever it occurs. The cwi has always severely criticised those who have tried to ignore or minimise such behaviour in the name of 'unity' between working-class women and men. We have initiated broad campaigns which have raised awareness about domestic violence (in Britain) and sexism in schools (Sweden). Both of these campaigns had an effect in changing attitudes and behaviour and, in the case of the Campaign Against Domestic Violence, in securing changes in the law. But because of the nature of capitalist society, legal reform, awareness raising, changing individual men's behaviour or changing ourselves can only go so far.

Violence against women, sexual harassment, restrictions on women's sexuality and bodily autonomy, sexism and gender stereotyping are all rooted in unequal relations of power and control. As part of the process of the formation of the first class societies based on private property relations, women became the property of individual men within the family unit – a social institution which organised and controlled both production and reproduction in the interests of the dominant economic class. Men within the family, fathers or husbands, controlled women's bodies with regards to their sexuality and reproduction, often with the socially sanctioned or encouraged use of violence. Women's inferior status and social role became enshrined in the legal system, backed by the church and other institutions of class rule. Rape was considered a crime against the male of the family whose property had been defiled.

Thousands of years later we face a contradictory situation. Capitalism inherited the gender ideology of previous societies as well as the institution of the family which it then fashioned to suit its own economic interests. As economic and social conditions have changed, however, the family and social attitudes have undergone a sea-change in the more developed capitalist countries, particularly over the past few decades. Rigid gender norms and the idea of the traditional family unit have been undermined in many countries by the influx of women into the workforce, the increase in single-parent households, recognition of same-sex marriage and the growing acceptance of transgender people. The victory of the movement for legal abortion in Ireland, and the near victory in Argentina, has shown how it is possible to defeat the reactionary ideas still promoted by the Catholic church regarding women's reproductive rights.

Nonetheless, backward attitudes and behaviour can continue to flourish long after the initial material basis for those ideas has disappeared. The capitalist system, for example, no longer directly promotes violence against women in most advanced capitalist countries. On the contrary, important laws have been passed around this issue and it is generally viewed as a social problem which should not be tolerated.

However, capitalism is based on unequal economic and social relations in the workplace, the family and in wider society. The segregation of women in low paying sectors of the economy and the transfer of the burden of public services to the family make it more difficult for women to leave violent relationships. Moreover, they sustain the inequality and inferior status from which gender violence derives.

Norms of gender roles, behaviour, dress and imagery are perpetuated and shaped from cradle to grave, reinforced by capitalist institutions like the media, the education system, the judiciary, etc, as well as the beauty, leisure and fashion industries. Capitalism is a system in which commodities are sold on the market to make a profit. That commodification is extended to the bodies of women, both directly through the sex 'industry' and indirectly through images and text. The internet and social media have merely expanded the instruments through which sexist gender norms can be diffused. Bringing an end to rape, sexual harassment, domestic violence, sexism and gender discrimination cannot, therefore, be achieved without fundamental structural change – eradicating the capitalist system and the network of unequal economic and power relations on which it is based.

The role of the working class

One of the challenges for socialist feminists is to explain the centrality of the working class in the process of changing society – because of its role in the capitalist production process and its potential collective consciousness – and to orient the new generation of female fighters towards the working-class movement. One of the strengths of the Campaign Against Domestic Violence, which was launched in the early 1990s and rapidly became a broad-based campaign, was its ability to orient towards the working class.

For the first time, it established domestic violence as a workplace and trade union issue. It explained how the violence experienced by women in the home also impacts on their working life and the role that unions could play in securing economic and social change to enable women to leave violent relationships and lead independent lives. This was achieved despite the fact that the link between domestic violence and the workplace was not immediately clear and despite the opposition of radical feminists who were opposed to any link with 'male-dom-inated' trade unions.

At a time of low level workplace and industrial struggle, explaining the central role of the working class is not necessarily a straightforward issue. A positive aspect of the current in-ternational movement, however, has been its adoption of the strike as a weapon of struggle (on 8 March, International Women's Day, for instance) and the turning to male workers for solidarity. The two-day strike of Glasgow council workers was extremely significant. Thou-sands of women workers stopped work to battle for equal pay, while male refuse workers and others took illegal secondary action and refused to cross picket lines to support them. The McDonald's and Google strikes against sexual harassment and unequal pay were also vivid examples of the potential of forging unity between female and male workers around an aspect of gender oppression, in this case in predominantly unorganised sections of the working class.

Challenging right-wing populism

The other challenge is the need to create and build the political instruments which system change requires. On the one hand, capitalism's economic and political crisis has fuelled a re-jection of capitalist institutions and ideology. On the other, the bankruptcy of the traditional parties of the working class and the absence of viable anti-capitalist political alternatives have resulted in the anti-establishment mood being electorally channelled towards right-wing populism in a number of countries.

Trump, Bolsonaro, and Matteo Salvini and the Lega in Italy, have openly expressed sexist opinions or behaviour and espoused socially reactionary ideas. Even though these ideas are not necessarily supported by the majority of the population, or even a majority of those who voted for them, they pose a real danger to the social rights of women and other oppressed groups. Trump, in particular, has been able to create a social base among a layer of white men who feel alienated and undermined by economic crisis and social change, and are receptive to prejudice and backward ideas about women and other social groups.

In the US, the ground is being prepared for a further undermining of abortion rights and attacks on transgender rights. In Poland, an offensive has been launched against wom-en's already very limited abortion rights. In Italy, the government is discussing a law in the name of 'parental equality' which would actually make divorce more difficult for women with children and increase domestic violence. The mass demonstrations on Trump's in-auguration day, and the outpouring of women onto the streets in the #NotHim protests against Bolsonaro before and after his election, give an indication of the scale of resistance that future attacks could unleash.

In Italy, Non Una di Meno, which was inspired by the movement in Argentina, has become one of the most organised and influential women's groups internationally, capable of mobilising tens of thousands of women and men. Victories can be won, as we have seen in several countries, but those gains will always be vulnerable to further attacks, as the renewed offensive in Poland has demonstrated, unless a political alternative is created to challenge the root causes of the problems women face.

With all their contradictions, the new women's movements represent the first stirrings of a potentially broader working-class and anti-capitalist struggle. A new generation of young women fighters are being radicalised and mobilised, and could be won to the fight for socialist change. There will be attempts to orient these movements towards existing capitalist political parties – towards the Democrats in the US, for example – or to remain completely independent from all political parties, regardless of their orientation, as with Non Una di Meno. The challenge for socialist feminists is to participate in the movements, engage with the ideas and strategies which emerge, while maintaining ideological clarity. To explain how the struggle to end gender oppression in all its forms is only possible in the framework of a broader struggle by the working class against the capitalist system itself.

Identity politics and the struggle against oppression

Hannah Sell, Socialism Today
192, October 2015

Over recent years there has been a growth in support for what can broadly be described as 'identity politics' among many, mainly young, people who are rightly angry about and radicalised by their experience of sexism, racism, homophobia, prejudice against disabled people and other forms of oppression. In one sense, identity politics is an inevitable part of the political awakening of many members of oppressed groups within society. Recognising that you are oppressed, and that you can fight against your oppression through a common struggle with others who share the same oppression, is a vital first step.

However, the history of struggle against oppression shows that, on the basis of experience, those participating tend to go beyond identity politics as they recognise the root cause of their oppression lies in the structure of society. The highest point of the vast rebellion against racism in the US in the 1950s and 1960s, for example, was reached by the Black Panthers, who were founded in 1966 with the magnificent concept: "We do not fight racism with racism. We fight racism with solidarity. We do not fight exploitative capitalism with black capitalism. We fight capitalism with basic socialism".

Today, both the #Black Lives Matter rebellion and the movement for $15 Now are the first stages of a new mass uprising against poverty and racism in the US. However, the pushing back of consciousness globally over the decades following the collapse of Stalinism in the late 1980s and the capitalist triumphalism that accompanied it, mean that the new movements did not begin where the Panthers left off, with a socialist outlook. Nonetheless, there is a growing anti-capitalist mood among young people in the US, which is a first step to drawing socialist conclusions.

At the same time, identity politics is many activists' starting point. While those involved in struggle may see this mainly as a means to fight back, the form of identity politics that has emanated from the universities and has dominated over recent decades concentrates overwhelmingly on discussing personal experience of oppression rather than trying to find the means to end it.

This includes all the strands of identity politics that have become more prominent in recent years, such as intersectionality and privilege theory. In Britain these concepts remain little known in wider society, but have become commonplace in, for example, university feminist societies. Intersectionalists argue that different oppressions 'intersect'. Indeed, they do: a black working-class woman is triply oppressed, for example. But intersectionalists often see their role as cataloguing and describing oppressions and their intersections rather than abolishing them.

Supporters of 'privilege theory' are best known for telling people to 'check their privilege' during (often online) debates. The founder of privilege theory, Peggy McIntosh, argued that a white, upper-class, heterosexual man, for example, is carrying around an 'invisible knapsack' full of unearned privileges. The argument goes that power is not concentrated in the hands of one class, or in the state, but is spread throughout society and therefore exists in all social and interpersonal relationships. Privilege theory states that every individual is part of a multiplicity of oppressive relationships. It concentrates overwhelmingly on exhortations to individuals to change, to check their privilege.

But it is not possible to eliminate either oppressions or privileges merely by exhorting individuals to change their behaviour. In fact, in many countries there have been significant improvements in social attitudes to different forms of oppression in recent decades, but they have not resulted in the ending of the oppressions concerned.

Racism ingrained

In Britain, for example, while racist prejudices are still widespread, crude racist ideas are far less socially acceptable than they were 30 years ago. This has come about for a number of reasons, above all the determination and increased confidence of black and Asian people to fight discrimination and racism. Another important factor was the widespread involvement of black and Asian workers in the trade unions in a common struggle alongside white workers. Both of these factors helped to foster a strong feeling among a large section of the white population, especially youth, that racism is wrong and should be combated.

Nonetheless, racism remains deeply ingrained in British society. The police are up to 28 times more likely to stop and search you if you are black or Asian. The gap between average pay for white workers and those from ethnic minorities has actually increased over recent years despite an improvement in social attitudes. Over half of young black men are unemployed, more than double the unemployment rate for young white men.

In the US the situation is even starker. While deep-rooted racism remains, there has also been an improvement in social attitudes. There has been the development of a black middle class and even a small black elite. Both processes are reflected in the election of a black man as US president. The vast majority of the black population, however, remain among the poorest and most oppressed in society, facing violent state repression. One hundred and thirty five African Americans were killed by the police in the first half of 2015 alone.

Racism does not just stem from individual prejudices, but from something more fundamental: the nature of capitalism as it has actually developed. Malcolm X correctly declared that, "you can't have capitalism without racism". Capitalism, as Karl Marx famously said, came into being "dripping from head to foot, from every pore, with blood and dirt". (Capital, Volume 1, Chapter 31) He was referring, particularly, to the role of slavery in the accumulation of capital. With slavery came the development of all kinds of pseudo-scientific racist theories designed to justify the enslavement of African peoples. Racist ideas were then adapted to justify the colonial oppression of large parts of the world.

Capitalism was forced to abandon direct colonial rule as a result of the magnificent revolutionary movements that took place against it. Economic exploitation, however, is more brutal than ever. Two hundred and fifty years ago the gap between the richest and poorest countries was around five to one. Today it is 400 to one. Racism is used to justify this vast gulf and also that black workers are usually among the poorest and most oppressed sections of the working class even in the 'rich' countries.

Women's oppression

Similarly, blatant sexism is no longer acceptable in the way it would have been in the past, particularly in the economically advanced capitalist countries. Women have won greater rights in recent decades. There are different factors that have led to this, including the development of improved and widely available contraception. However, many of these gains can be traced back to the growing confidence of women as a result of many more women working rather than being isolated in the home.

Nonetheless, women continue to be oppressed. This oppression stems, not merely from the attitudes of men, but from the role of women and the family in capitalist and earlier class societies. Most of us think of 'the family' as the individuals who make up our own family, who are often the people who are closest to us. Historically, however, the family as an institution has also acted within class societies as an agent of social control with the father as 'head of the household' having responsibility for disciplining women and children. While this concept has been weakened in the modern era by the growing confidence of women, it is far from eliminated. The idea remains deeply ingrained that women are possessions of men and that we need to be loyal and obedient to our partners, and that violence and coercion are acceptable means for men to achieve that, both towards 'their' women and 'their' children.

At the same time, women continue to bear the brunt of domestic responsibilities despite increasingly also going out to work. In many cases women are still, as the Russian revolutionary Leon Trotsky put it, the 'slaves of slaves'. While in Britain, for example, most studies show men accepting that they should do an equal amount of domestic chores as women, there is still a considerable gap between intentions and reality. One survey showed that on average women did 17 hours a week of domestic chores (excluding childcare) whereas men did less than six.

It is true, therefore, that men get some gain from women's disproportionate bearing of the domestic burden, in having a few more hours leisure time. The main gain, however, is for capitalism. By putting the main burden of domestic life, the bringing up of the next generation (from which the future workforce is drawn) and caring for the sick and elderly on women, they are removed from the responsibility of society as a whole.

Power concentrated in the capitalist class

To suggest that power is not concentrated in one class is to completely misunderstand the nature of capitalism. Today, wealth and power is concentrated in fewer hands – the owners of the major banks and corporations – even than when Marx was writing. According to Oxfam, the richest 85 people on earth – a double-decker bus full – have as much wealth as the poorest half of the world's population. The richest 85 include five women and one African, although white men predominate. Their role in society, however, does not stem primarily from their colour or gender, but that they are part of a tiny super-wealthy ruling elite.

The world's 100 biggest companies now control 70% of global trade. Even if their boards of directors included many more black people or women it would not make any material difference to the exploitation suffered by the working class and poor worldwide, not least black women. Look at South Africa, where the incorporation of a tiny minority of blacks into the capitalist class has made no difference to the dire poverty suffered by the majority. And capitalism is increasingly incapable of taking society forward. Many of the rights partially taken for granted by previous generations in Europe, like a relatively secure job, home and pension, are now things of the past.

To say that social relations in modern society are capitalist relations is not to take an 'economic determinist' view of society: arguing that every aspect of the 'superstructure' of society – the state, politics, culture, social attitudes and so on – are rigidly determined by the character of the economy. On the contrary, there is an inter-relationship between the two. At the same time, politics and social attitudes reflect not only the current character of capitalism but also remnants of the past and – particularly in mass struggles of the working class and the oppressed – the seeds of a potential better future. Nonetheless, it is clear that as long as we live in a capitalist society, where wealth and power rests with the tiny elite who own and control industry, science and technology, then the superstructure of that society will also ultimately reflect and act in the interests of that ruling elite.

No amount of demanding that people 'check their privilege' will eliminate social attitudes generated and sustained by capitalism. While determined mass struggle can force capitalism to adapt to a certain extent – as has been the case with LGBT rights, equal pay legislation and other measures – permanent and deep-rooted change, particularly where it threatens the functioning of capitalism, will only be achieved by the socialist transformation of society.

The horrific bureaucratic degeneration and then collapse of the Soviet Union have obscured the importance of the Russian Revolution in giving a glimpse of what socialism would mean for those suffering oppression. In Russia in 1917 the working class led a movement of the oppressed which successfully overthrew capitalism for the first, and so far, the only time. Russia's extreme poverty and the isolation of the new workers' state led to its degeneration. Nonetheless, in the early days it gave a glimpse of how a new society could overcome oppressions that had existed for millennia.

In 'backward' Russia, legal changes were introduced very quickly which were many decades ahead of any capitalist country. These included universal suffrage, civil marriage and divorce when requested by either partner, equal pay, paid maternity leave, the right to abortion and the legalisation of homosexuality. Oppressed nationalities were given the genuine right to self-determination. Measures were taken to encourage nationalities and cultures oppressed under tsarism, including the development of a written form of some languages for the first time.

Of course, legal or formal measures do not in themselves end oppression. Decades after the passing of equal pay legislation in Britain, for example, women still earn an average of £5,000 a year less than men. Addressing women's oppression in the Soviet Union, Trotsky described how legal equality was a step forward, but actual equality in social relations required a far more "deep-going plough", capable of providing real economic equality and lifting the domestic burden from women, and transforming social attitudes ingrained over millennia. A whole number of measures began to be introduced in the aftermath of the

Russian revolution (including free childcare, communal restaurants and public laundries) which, while never fully implemented due to the degeneration of the Soviet Union, gave a glimpse of how the domestic burden could be lifted. That, in turn, could have laid the foundations for the building of a society based on women's equality.

Many intersectionalists put very little emphasis on campaigning for economic and practical measures to lift the burden on women, instead concentrating overwhelmingly on social attitudes and trying to create spaces within society that are free of oppression. Yet freeing women from the heavy load of being the carers, cooks and cleaners for the whole of society is an essential prerequisite for ending women's oppression. Twenty-first century capitalism, far from taking steps towards this, is driving in the opposite direction.

Austerity affects women severely. It includes huge cuts in public services that partially lifted some of the responsibilities that fall on women. David Cameron's big society could be summed up as demanding that women compensate for the cuts to health, child and elderly care by taking the burden on themselves. This is a demonstration that, under capitalism, even where oppressed groups make gains, they are never guaranteed to be permanent. This also applies to the devastating, sometimes life-threatening, consequences of austerity for disabled people.

Combating prejudice

Pointing out the need for fundamental change in society does not in any way downgrade the importance of combating oppressive and reactionary ideas and practices while we live in this society, including within the workers' movement. However, this will by necessity be a constant battle. Intersectionalists call for 'safe spaces' with zero tolerance for anything considered an oppressive view. But it is utopian to try and create a safe space which is sealed off from the society in which we all live and are affected by. Turning inwards in order to concentrate on doing so – rather than turning out to build a movement capable of winning real change – is doomed to frustration and failure. Far from creating safe spaces, this can often lead to an undemocratic environment, where the individuals dominant in a particular 'space' assert that they feel oppressed by ideas and opinions they disagree with.

There is also a dangerous tendency to suggest that the value of someone's contribution to a discussion should be based primarily on what oppressions they as an individual suffer from. This is completely false. Britain's first and only female prime minister, Margaret Thatcher, undoubtedly suffered individual oppression as a woman, but the neo-liberal programme she drove through was completely against the interests of working-class women. Recently, Jeremy Corbyn, the new left leader of the Labour Party, has been attacked supposedly for not having enough women in his shadow cabinet, although his front bench is the first that has been majority women. More women voted for Corbyn than for the other right-wing candidates (two of whom were women) in the leadership election because he stood against austerity. Had he chosen a pro-austerity woman as shadow chancellor rather than the left MP, John McDonnell, most of the women who voted for him would have correctly been deeply disappointed.

The issue of safe spaces also relates to intersectionalists' views on gender: that the concept of two genders is a social construct and, in reality, gender is more like a spectrum. Emphasis is often put on supporting transgender people and all those who rebel against societal gender constraints. This includes some who do not identify as either male or female but as 'gender-non-conforming'. This reflects a positive rejection of current gender relations and homophobia by a growing number of young people. Socialists, of course, support the democratic right of individuals to define both their own gender and sexuality. However, while there is radicalisation among an important layer on this issue, that does not mean it is possible to create, as some intersectionalists attempt, spaces within capitalist society completely free from societal pressures regarding gender.

Capitalism shapes the outlook of all of us from the time we are born, with all of the distortions of the human personality that creates. This includes how we are expected to behave appropriately for our given gender. It is not possible to fully escape this; in this society capitalist gender roles are an objective reality. Even rejecting capitalist gender norms means reacting to, and therefore being affected by, those norms. It is not possible to prescribe exactly how human relations, including the role of gender, would flower in the future when freed from the rigid straitjackets imposed by capitalism.

The role of the working class

The crucial issue for anyone determined to end oppression, therefore, is how to end capitalism and begin to build a world that is free of oppression: a 'safe space' for all. Today, just as when Marx described the working class as the 'grave digger of capitalism', it is the key force on the planet capable of ridding us of this bankrupt system. Both privilege theory and intersectionality would list social class – what they would describe as 'classism' – as one form of oppression. However, it features as one item on a list and is often discussed in terms of the prejudice people face because of having a working-class accent or postcode. The centrality of class in the structure of society is not recognised. The basic idea that a Nigerian worker would have more in common with a worker in Britain or the US than they would with Aliko Dangote, the only African to make it on to the list of the richest 85 on the planet, would not be understood. The fact that it is the working class that is ultimately responsible for the creation of the capitalists' profits and that by collective action it is capable of bringing capitalist society to a halt is discounted as outmoded.

Yet the working class is not 'disappearing'. In fact, it is potentially stronger today than it was at the time of the Russian revolution. Many countries where workers were a tiny minority of society a century ago now have large and powerful working classes. In the economically advanced countries, like Britain, deindustrialisation has meant that the industrial working class is much smaller. However, there still remain groups of workers with enormous power to bring society to a halt when they strike – anyone who lives in London and witnessed the recent London Underground strikes knows that. Deindustrialisation has not led to young people becoming 'middle class', but has forced them into low paid, temporary work, often in the service sector. At the same time, large sections of the population – including teachers and civil servants – who would have previously considered themselves middle class have been driven down into the ranks of the working class in their living conditions and social outlook.

The history of the 20th century repeatedly demonstrated the preparedness of working-class people to fight for socialism. However, it also demonstrated that the capitalist class does all it can to cling to power, not least by attempting to divide and rule by turning different sections of the working class against each other.

In recent years there has been increasing radicalisation and struggle globally, including revolutionary movements. Out of these, largely unsuccessful, struggles conclusions will begin to be drawn about what is necessary to change society. That requires a mass revolutionary movement, bringing together different sections of the working class – with different experiences and outlooks – in a mass party with a clear programme and a determined and accountable leadership.

Such a party would not be a model of a new society, but a tool to bring it about. Nonetheless, it is crucial that such a mass party would include in its ranks all of the most oppressed sections of the working class and that it is a vibrant and democratic force in which all participants feel able to express their views. Its programme, as was the case with the Bolsheviks in Russia, has to fight for the rights not just of the working class in general but also for different specifically oppressed groups.

Undoubtedly, such a movement would also win the support of wide sections of the middle class and even individuals from the capitalist class who saw the need for a break with capitalism. This would particularly include those who suffer oppression under capitalism and who recognise that the only way to end homophobia, racism or women's oppression is to join the struggle for a new society.

Struggle itself unifies
It would be ludicrous and deplorable to argue that those fighting their particular oppression should hold back and 'wait' for a unified struggle of the whole working class. Mass struggle is a thousand times more effective than exhortations to individuals to change their attitudes in winning social progress. It is always the case that a movement has a greater chance of success if it is able to reach out to other sections of the working class, and that therefore it is important that the programme put forward by a particular movement attempts to do this. However, that is in no way to suggest that any group should artificially delay fighting back until they, for example, convince more white or male workers of their cause.

Nonetheless, to permanently end racism in the US, for instance, will require ending capitalism and will therefore have to involve a struggle uniting different sections of the working class – black, Hispanic, Asian and white. This is a practical question. The African American population, who suffer the worst police racism, are 13% of the population and will not be able to win alone. The capitalist class will try to increase divisions between different sections of the oppressed, particularly at times of heightened struggle. The oppressed need to increase their strength by trying to maximise unity. The $15 Now movement in the US and the election of Socialist Alternative member Kshama Sawant in Seattle give a glimpse of the growing possibilities in the US to build a united workers' movement.

Achieving unity does not mean downplaying the importance of combating the specific oppressions different groups in society face. On the contrary, it is vital that socialists campaign for the workers' movement to fight to take up every aspect of oppression. The Socialist Party has a proud history of doing this – for example, spearheading the Campaign Against Domestic Violence in the 1990s which was central to getting the trade unions to take the issue up.

Intersectionality on university campuses in Britain has had a tendency to turn campus feminist societies inwards, focusing on a fruitless attempt to grade degrees of oppression rather than fighting to end it. However, many of those initially attracted to these ideas are searching for a way to change society and will quickly come up against the limits of identity politics in all its forms.

One small indication of this is the popularity among young people of the film Pride, which tells the true story of Lesbians and Gays Support the Miners (LGSM). LGSM recognised the common ground between their struggle against the Tories and that of the 1984/85 miners' strike. Their attempt to support the miners was not without difficulties – with prejudices on both sides – but ultimately forged a real unity. LGSM understood that a victory for the miners would have been a massive defeat for Thatcher, the Tories and the capitalist class – and that was in the interests of LGSM people. They never once responded to white, straight miners, who were often initially homophobic, by telling them to 'check their privilege'. One result of their heroic efforts was big parts of the workers' movement wholeheartedly taking up the struggle for LGSM liberation, including National Union of Mineworkers lodges from across the country leading the 1985 Pride demonstration.

The miners' strike was a major event in the class struggle in Britain, but it will be dwarfed by events that will take place in the future against the background of a crisis-ridden capitalism trying to drive the living standards of the majority into the dirt. For some intersectionalists it will require witnessing the power of the working class in action in order for them to draw the conclusion that the route to ending their specific oppression is not as part of fragmented separate groupings, but by throwing their lot in with the class struggle. However, growing numbers of young people, particularly when they become active in concrete struggles, are already being attracted to socialist ideas as the only way to achieve real liberation for all humanity.

WOMEN'S OPPRESSION AND IDENTITY POLITICS - THE CWI'S APPROACH

Hannah Sell, for the International Secretariat

This document was written as a contribution to the discussion in Ireland, prior to the IEC. It is based on notes for an introduction at the October Irish NC meeting; and subsequently developed into a written contribution at the request of the Irish NEC majority after the October NC meeting ran out of time to start the discussion on identity politics.

This brief document is dealing specifically with issues relating to how we take up identity politics in Ireland and internationally, which the IS thinks needs to be discussed. It does not attempt to give an overview of our general position on a Marxist approach to the oppression of women. Most recently this was summarised in the resolution unanimously agreed at the 2016 World Congress, which can be found on page 223.

The CWI has a proud history of campaigning for the rights of all oppressed sections of society. In many countries we have intervened and played a leading role in movements against racism, including via Youth against Racism in Europe in the early 1990s on a continent-wide basis. In Britain we also initiated Panther in the early 1990s, aimed specifically at young black workers. We have also led numerous campaigns against women's and gender-based oppression including the Campaign Against Domestic Violence in Britain and now Rosa in Ireland, Libres y Combativas in the Spanish state and many more. At every stage we have correctly fought to try and make sure the most oppressed in society are fully represented at every level of the CWI.

Today, as we go on to outline, there is an important radicalisation taking place around issues relating to women's and gender-based oppression on a global basis. In some countries radicalisation has resulted in mass movements. This is particularly where the ruling class, significant sections of it, or individuals like Trump, have a more openly reactionary attitude towards the rights of women, which has inevitably come into sharp conflict with women's aspirations for equality.

Clearly, where movements relating to women's oppression are posed, it is vital that we turn to them, intervening and, where possible, playing a leading role as the comrades have in Ireland North and South, and in the Spanish state. Such movements can represent the first steps towards collective struggle by previously unorganised layers of women and can be an important step forward. In many cases, initially, their leadership is dominated by bourgeois and petty-bourgeois feminists who try and divert the movement, for example as a means to win support for big-business Democrats in the US.

Our task is to skilfully link the immediate demands of the struggle to the need for a united struggle of the working class for socialism, as the only means by which genuine liberation can be achieved. Historically and today, our record on this is second to none. Other Trotskyist organisations have tended either to ignore movements against women's oppression or, more often, to have acted as uncritical supporters for them, without any attempt to win them to a working-class standpoint. Attempts to find a short cut to winning mass support have resulted in the wrecking of many organisations.

In recent movements against gender-based oppression the weaknesses of the workers' movement, along with a relatively low level of consciousness, has meant identity politics has often had considerable influence. In one sense identity politics can be an inevitable part of the political awakening of many members of oppressed groups within society. Recognising that you are oppressed, and that you can fight against your oppression through a common struggle with others who share the same oppression, is a vital first step.

However, the identity politics that currently has influence emanated from the capitalists via the universities over recent decades. At bottom these ideas are used by the ruling class to obscure class divisions, and play a divisive role. They have also seeped into the workers' movement in many countries. They put an overwhelming emphasis on cataloguing and describing different forms of oppression, tending to emphasise differences rather than common interests. The toxic discussion on trans rights currently taking place in the British trade unions, with sections of feminists wrongly arguing that improving trans rights undermines the rights of women, is an example of the consequences of seeing different oppressed groups as in competition with each other rather than campaigning for a united struggle against all oppression. We have consistently intervened in the debate defending trans rights, while fighting for a class approach.

Identity politics also tends to lay the blame for oppression on the behaviour of individuals rather than fighting for changes in the structure of society. Whenever we are intervening in a milieu where such alien class ideas are widespread it is inevitable we will come under pressure to make concessions in that direction. The answer, of course, is not to step back from intervening, but to guard consciously against the dangers, patiently explaining the central role of the working class in the fight to transform society. We are concerned that the comrades in Ireland have not done this sufficiently.

It is our duty, as the elected leadership of the CWI, to raise our concerns in order to strengthen the work of the whole international, particularly as these issues and pressures are arising in many sections of our international. This has always been the approach of the CWI. We are striving to build the embryo of a world revolutionary international, not a series of national organisations linked together in name only. We should welcome all comrades – including the Irish comrades – feeling free to raise doubts and differences about any aspect of our international's work.

In order to engage in a discussion on these issues the IS wrote to the Irish IEC comrades on 31 August 2018 proposing a meeting to discuss a series of issues, starting with the question of Identity Politics. Unfortunately, the discussion on this crucial issue has not yet begun, although it is now scheduled to do so at an Irish NC meeting on 17 and 18 November. However, given, in our view, the urgency of starting to discuss these issues – with the aim of reaching principled agreement – the IS has here outlined our central concerns. We would ask that this is circulated to the Irish NC and we also propose to circulate it to the IEC. We propose comrades respond in writing which we will also circulate.

Before we come to outlining our concerns it is necessary that we reiterate our recognition of the tremendous victory that was scored in the Repeal Referendum, the important role the Irish section played in achieving it and, in particular, the section's role in helping to ensure the referendum resulted not only in the repeal of the eighth amendment, but in the winning of abortion on demand up until twelve weeks. The referendum was an important victory for women and for the Irish working class, and inflicted a serious blow on the Irish state and the Catholic Church. Kevin McLoughlin said at the recent NC that in his opinion we were hesitant about the work the Irish comrades have done among women, giving as an indication that there had only been one article on it on the CWI website between Savita's death and the end of 2017. As Tony Saunois explained to the October Irish NC, we are keen to give prominence to the comrades' role in this work, as was shown at the CWI school and would happily have published more articles had they been submitted. In fact, at the time of the Irish NC there were eight articles and videos on the CWI site relating to the comrades in Ireland's work on women.

How we respond to radicalisation of women

Kevin McLoughlin has argued that the IS has not "engaged in a serious way with the women's movement as it has emerged over the last two years" and has been "hesitant" about it. We reject this and ask what concrete measures the comrades think we have failed to take. At the last World Congress we had a discussion on women's oppression and unanimously agreed a document. We have considerably stepped up our coverage on the CWI site of issues relating to women's oppression, particularly, but not only, linked to International Women's Day (IWD) when we have always carried special material.

However, we think there is a difference in how we assess the movements that have and will take place, and how we see them in relation to other struggles which are likely to develop. As part of this we think the comrades could be in danger of overstating the importance of the victory on abortion rights. At the recent CWI school for example, Laura Fitzgerald, replying in the commission on the issue, said, "There will never be an issue like this again which poses so clearly the kind of society we want in people's minds." The referendum victory is a real step forward for women and is very important, but it will nonetheless be dwarfed by the experience of collective action in the class battles that will develop in the coming years, let alone a conscious struggle for socialism.

In our view a tendency has also developed of some leading Irish comrades seeing all struggles through the prism of the women's movement, rather than seeing how it interconnects with other struggles. It is important that we have a balanced approach, recognising that working-class women can also move into action on many other issues as well as those directly related to their specific oppression, and that moves towards 'sectional' struggle are not, always, in all circumstances, a step forward. If, as we are concerned there could be a tendency to do in Ireland, comrades put the issue of a movement against women's oppression above all other trends, there is a real danger we could miss important opportunities to win the most thinking layers now, but particularly in the future when mass movements develop on other issues.

For example, we understand that the public meeting advertised on the recent very important 10,000-strong housing demo was a Rosa public meeting entitled 'Why Housing is a Feminist Issue'. We know that party meetings have now been organised, but think it was a mistake to make a Rosa public meeting the cutting edge of the intervention in the demonstration and, if you did decide to do so, to have that meeting title. Surely any good young people who had been attracted to Rosa during the referendum campaign would have seen the need to campaign on housing without us highlighting it as 'a feminist issue', when in reality it is a much broader issue.

In addition, in 2018, every one of the monthly public meetings advertised on the Socialist Party Ireland Facebook Page has been related to women's or LGBTQ+ oppression. Clearly these have been important issues over the last period and should have been give prominence, but we think that is going too far. In Ireland due to our long record of struggle and the relatively high public profile the party has as a result of the TDs' (Teachtaí Dála - MPs) positions, we have been able to win a base among important sections of the working class. There is a danger that – as a result of the overwhelming turn that has been made to issues relating to women and gender oppression – we could become perceived by a layer of workers for whom that is not the only or primary concern as 'not for them'. This can obviously include layers of male workers and older women, but also young women and non-binary people who – while partly radicalised by their specific oppression – do not consider it to be the most central issue for them.

Global radicalisation of women

The radicalisation that has taken place is primarily, but not exclusively, of young women. In Britain, to give one example, only 36% of women would describe themselves as feminist, but among 18-24 year olds a majority (54%) do so and among younger teenage girls and women the figure is even higher – around 70%. We would also agree that the younger generation who are radicalised by women's oppression tend to reject the rigid gender norms imposed by capitalism.

In our view, while of course there were struggles prior to 2007, this radicalisation flows from the experience of a generation who have grown up in the age of austerity. Prior to then, at least in the economically-advanced countries, capitalist propaganda peddled the ideas of 'post-feminism' – suggesting women were on the verge of winning equality. While this was never true, there was a grain of truth in it in many countries. Over the previous decades women had been drawn into the workforce in many countries on an unprecedented scale. This was a central factor in the increased confidence of women and the improvements in social attitudes that resulted.

Under pressure from the workers' movement, and from women's struggles, women had taken significant steps to equality in law, although reality lagged far behind. At the same time the hollowing out of manufacturing industry in much of Europe and the US, and the overall driving down of workers' wages, meant that it was no longer so clearly 'the norm' that men had better-paid work than women and, increasingly, it was vital for both parents to work in order to make ends meet. All of these factors meant that – before the economic crisis – young working-class women were, in general, more confident of their prospects than young working-class men.

That confidence then came up sharply against the effects of the economic crisis which, of course, has hit women particularly hard. At the same time, all the problems of sexual harassment and violence remained and were in sharp conflict with the propaganda of women's equality. It is therefore no surprise to us that young women have been to the fore of the general radicalisation that has taken place, and also feel strongly on issues relating to their own specific oppression. Nor should it be a surprise to us, given the block created by the right-wing trade union leaders, that there is sometimes more confidence to struggle on social questions than on economic issues. In Ireland, for example, the accumulated anger at austerity has had very limited outlets as a result of the role of the trade union leaders, but could be expressed via the referendum.

The #metoo phenomenon has, on a global basis, highlighted an increased determination by women to refuse to accept sexual harassment and abuse. While in many countries it has, so far, remained mainly at the level of a social media campaign, in others it has led to movements on the streets. In a whole series of countries, from Ireland to Argentina to Spain and now India, very important movements against different aspects of women's oppression have taken place and are still taking place.

However, in our view, it is not the case that movements relating to women's oppression will be central to struggle in every country in the next period. In addition, in many countries where such movements occur, the working-class elements within them can quite quickly become part of broader struggles of the working class (although of course the demands specifically relating to women's oppression would remain an important aspect of those movements).

Varying approaches of the capitalists
We should expect movements to take place wherever significant sections of the capitalist class attack women's rights or have an openly reactionary approach to gender-related oppression. In the US for example, following the Supreme Court appointment of Kavanaugh, it is very clear that there is the speeding up of the development of a mass movement against the blatant sexism of Trump and his allies, and in defence of abortion rights which face attack. Trump is also attempting to unravel all the gains made by trans people over the last period, which will also inevitably trigger a movement on the streets.

In Spain the remnants of Francoism, with its brutal repression of women and dominance of the Catholic church, means that the issues of women's oppression are particularly strongly felt. In that sense there is a similarity with Ireland, where the state has since its inception been intertwined with the Catholic church, meaning that movements on these issues were inevitable and fuelled by the deep-seated anger with the capitalist establishment. The response to the Pope's visit, in the wake of the referendum, showed the deep-rooted revolt against the Catholic church. At this year's CWI School the comrades vividly described how young people had convinced their families to vote for Repeal. The contrast with the Brexit referendum was striking – there the majority of young people tried to convince their parents to vote for Remain, and largely failed. Clearly there are many differences between the two referendums, but one factor is surely that in Ireland young people were convincing their parents to strike a blow against the Irish 'establishment' – which they were happy to do, whereas in Britain, the way to strike a blow against the existing order was to vote for Brexit.

In Britain, by contrast, while clearly there is a radicalisation around women's oppression – which it is important we respond to – it is not automatic that this mood becomes a movement. If the government was to launch an attack on abortion rights – for example – it would ignite mass struggle. However, at this stage Theresa May continues to pose as a defender of women's and LGBTQ+ rights – making speeches against domestic violence, wearing 'I'm a feminist t-shirts' on International Women's Day, proposing changes to make it easier for trans people to self-identify and so on. All these are cynical – and cheap – ways in which she can try to make the Tory party appear more socially liberal, whilst at the same time slashing expenditure on refuges for women fleeing domestic violence, along with other public services. The England and Wales section has initiated a new campaign on this important issue. In the past comrades in Britain led the successful Campaign Against Domestic Violence, which succeeded in winning legal changes and getting policies in opposition to domestic violence adopted by the trade union movement. Today, however, the economic difficulties facing women fleeing violence are worse than ever. It was the devastating cuts to domestic violence services, often implemented by Labour councils, which pushed even a Labour shadow minister, Dawn Butler, to make positive comments about the record of Militant-led Liverpool City Council at this year's Labour Women's conference.

Nonetheless, in Britain and a number of other countries, the lack of a social base at this stage for launching new attacks on women's or LGBTQ+ rights means that the major capitalist parties are unlikely to move in this direction in the short term. Even the far right in Britain is forced to dress up its reactionary ideas in the clothes of falsely claiming to defend women and LGBTQ+ people against the supposed threat of Islam. In Ireland the capitalist parties have also been forced to bend to the mood in society. Irish PM Varadkar's calling of the recent referendum to remove the blasphemy laws from the statute books is part of his pose as socially liberal. Of course, the continued role of the church in education and the health service are real obstacles to Irish capitalist parties' ability to bend on these issues, but we should still not underestimate how far they can go under pressure. Ultimately, while capitalism can never provide real equality for women or LGBTQ+ people, it can nonetheless be pushed a considerable distance in terms of legal changes, while continuing to attack the living conditions of every section of the working class.

What is a transitional approach to the struggle against women's oppression?

In every struggle in which we intervene, we aim to have a transitional approach, linking current demands to the need for socialist revolution led by the working class. The decade-long capitalist crisis has led to enormous accumulated anger against the existing order. Nonetheless, the legacy of the preceding period has not yet been fully overcome. Globally the working class entered the era of austerity ill-prepared, with a low level of socialist consciousness and of organisation. While this is changing, under the hammer blows of brutal experience, aided by our intervention, the scissors – the gap between the objective crisis of capitalism and the consciousness of the working class – remains wide. Nonetheless, we have to strive to connect with existing day-to-day struggles in the way we formulate our programme. However, the starting point when deciding what programme to advance is obviously not existing consciousness, but objective reality and then how we engage with it. If we were starting programmatically from existing consciousness we would not be putting forward a programme for the socialist transformation of society.

We are concerned that the Socialist Party recruitment leaflet the comrades have produced, aimed at those who were involved in the referendum campaign, talks about a "grass roots movement from below with young people at its beating heart" and "anti-capitalist struggle", but does not make even the briefest attempt to explain what socialism means or the role of the working class. The final page of that leaflet, which puts the case for joining, entitled "organised for change", states:

"Repeal was not an isolated event. It was part of a global revolt against sexism and misogyny. This has given rise to the #metoo phenomenon; the thousands who took to the streets of Ireland to say, 'I believe her' after the acquittal of Paddy Jackson and other Ulster rugby players in April; the six million-strong feminist strike in the Spanish State on International Women's Day; the #NiUnaMenos movement against gender-based violence in Latin America.

"This global revolt is a new generation of young people saying 'enough is enough'. Opposition to sexism, racism, homophobia and transphobia is linked to an aspiration for a truly equal society and a growing opposition to a society run in the interests of the super-rich elite.

"We can be truly proud of what we achieved in May, but we should register that if we organise together we can defeat the status quo. We can make real change. We can end all of the injustices and inequality in an anti-capitalist struggle.

"That is why you should be a socialist and this is why you should join us in organising for socialist change."

Of course there is nothing wrong with referring to important movements that have taken place against gender-related oppression, but it is wrong in a Socialist Party recruitment leaflet to make no attempt to link them with other struggles of the working class or, in fact, to raise the role of the working class at all.

We are concerned that it could be the comrades' approach to initially limits themselves, when discussing with this layer, to anti-capitalist propaganda. We recognise that many workers and young people would consider themselves anti-capitalist, but have not yet drawn all the conclusions that we have. This is never our goal, however. Our aim is to win workers to the full programme of the CWI. In some cases – particularly on the basis of the experience of struggle – workers who had not previously drawn anti-capitalist conclusions can be drawn very quickly into our ranks.

What measures were necessary, when intervening in the struggle for abortion rights, to win the best layers to the CWI? Clearly, the militant and campaigning stance taken by the comrades – for which they were attacked by a layer of bourgeois and petit-bourgeois feminists – was an important positive factor. It was also necessary, however, to combat the ideas of petit-bourgeois feminism. Central to this is arguing that the organised working class could play a potentially decisive role in fighting for the right to abortion and other women's rights.

An essential part of doing this would be pointing to the significant mass working-class movements that we have led in Ireland – on the bin and water charges. In addition we should point to the potential power of the trade union movement which, despite their overwhelmingly rotten leadership and having being weakened, continue to be the largest working-class organisations in Ireland. Many, probably a big majority, of the young people who became politically active for the first time during the Repeal movement would not have seen the trade unions as relevant to their struggle. Nonetheless, as part of educating them about the role of the organised working class we think it would have been important to have had a concerted campaign to put demands on the trade union leaders to organise campaigns and action for the right to abortion, along with campaigning in the workplaces. We could, for example, have used the positive work on this done by the NIPSA comrades in the North as an example of how to put pressure on the union leaders in the South. This approach could also have helped us reaching a wider layer of working-class women.

Obviously, the comrades in Ireland do not have the valuable political weapon of the students' union (SE) which the comrades in the Spanish state were able to use so effectively as a lever to force significant sections of the trade unions to take strike action on 8 March 2018. Nonetheless, we ask the comrades, were measures taken to put demands on the tops of the trade unions, combined with direct appeals to the rank and file? Appeals to anti-capitalism or even socialism in general, if not linked to the role of the working class in achieving it, are of limited value in winning radicalised young people to our approach.

Of course, comrades may argue that they did take this approach and received no response. Either way we think more should have been done to explain our approach in our public material. Rosa, as far as we can see, did not make any demands on the trade union leaders in its #timefor-choice campaign. We fear that this is because such initiatives were not seriously pursued and that this reflects a wrong approach to the trade unions, where the rottenness of the leaders is wrongly used as a reason not to put demands on them, or to sufficiently orientate to the ranks of the trade unions.

When Ruth Coppinger spoke at the England and Wales Socialism 2014 event, the comrades who had organised it asked for any comments on the workshop on women she addressed. Ruth responded:

"I thought the session was very trade union focused and probably not aimed enough at young women. I know Britain is different to Ireland but I thought even for England it would be imbalanced. Most women wouldn't be in unions. Most young women wouldn't have seen unions doing much for women. I thought a lot of the contributions were from middle-aged women and were economic. Think the social issues, rape culture, sexism are now massive issues in society and could have gotten more coverage."

As it happens, the workshop that year had a particular trade union focus that had not been the case in many other years. However, in our view Ruth's comments also reveal a misunderstanding about the necessity of us explaining how economic and social change can be won and the role of the organised working class in achieving that, as well as an underestimation of the importance of economic issues for working-class women, including young women. This generation of petty-bourgeois feminists put very little focus on winning material gains for women, concentrating overwhelmingly on individuals' experience of sexism. In that sense their ideas are a retreat from at least some of the feminist struggles of the 1970s.

We, however, while of course combating sexist attitudes in society, should continue to put central the issues of equal pay, freedom from sexual harassment at work, the right to free childcare, decent housing and so on. For the big majority of working-class women these are crucial issues around which they can be mobilised into action. This has been graphically demonstrated by the fantastic Glasgow mass strike of women council workers fighting for equal pay, with CWI members playing a leading role. More than 700 women joined the union to take part in the strike, showing the pole of attraction the unions become when they organise action. What better example of workers' unity in action than the predominantly male Glasgow bin workers coming out in unofficial solidarity action with them, showing that they understood that the fight for equal pay is in the interest of the whole working class.

Comrades may argue, as Ruth does in her comments, that Ireland is different to England, Scotland and perhaps other countries, with a lower level of trade union participation and struggle. Even if this is the case we don't think it should alter our basic approach. We would accept that the role of social partnership in Ireland has meant that the trade union leaders have, overall, played a particularly bad role. Nonetheless, we do not think there is a fundamental difference between Southern Ireland and other countries. In recent years Southern Ireland has seen a number of important strikes such as the 2017 transport workers', Ryanair and the mainly female Lloyd's Pharmacy workers. The fact that ICTU was forced to back the recent 10,000-strong housing demonstration, at least in name, is also an indication they can be forced to act under pressure from below. Overall, trade union density is actually higher in Southern Ireland – at around a third – than it is in Britain – where it is now only a quarter. Union density – in Ireland and Britain – is also actually higher among women workers than among men. Of course, in both countries trade union membership among the young is very low.

However, as a new generation begins to get organised to fight for its rights at work, it is inevitable that they will look to some form of trade union organisation. It is a debatable issue whether, as greater numbers of young people begin to see the possibility of fighting back in their workplace, they will found new unions or join existing ones. In our view, the general trend, at least in Northern Europe, is likely to be that workers first try and use the ready-made tools of the existing unions, only turning to found new ones if they are blocked by the union bureaucracies. This is the dominant trend in Britain, for example, although there are also some small 'new' unions, predominantly involving migrant workers. These can start to coalesce with the existing unions on the basis of a struggle for their democratisation. Regardless of what form such developments take, however, we have to explain to the young people we can reach the potential power of the organised working class. The US McDonalds strike against sexual harassment is a graphic illustration of how young women workers can see the unions as a means to fight back against the oppression they face as women. The same is true of the Google strike, which also represents the start of a new section of the working class, tech workers, entering the field of battle. While our approach will be instinctively understood more easily by working-class women, who are our main priority, we can also win some women from middle-class backgrounds, by convincing them that the only road to which they can win liberation is via the struggles of the working class. We will not do this, however, if we do not put our arguments clearly and firmly.

Of course, we are in no sense suggesting that we should have pulled back from organising independent action in the referendum campaign and instead 'waited' for the trade union leaders. This has never been the approach of the CWI. For example, in the poll tax movement in Britain, we put demands on the trade union leaders while at the same time organising a mass campaign of non-payment from below. In explaining to the young people we have met in the referendum the potential role of the working class, we should not only use the example of the trade unions but also the magnificent mass campaigns we have led in Ireland. It is surprising, therefore, that so little use is made of the water charges victory, which demonstrates graphically how united working-class struggle can win and, crucially, our role in leading it. The pamphlet that comrades have put together on socialist feminism to use as a recruitment tool from the referendum campaign does not, for example, include a single reference to the water charges movement.

In addition to specific demands on the trade unions to take action for abortion rights, in our view, the propaganda of the comrades on the issue would have been strengthened by a greater weight being given to the link between a woman's right to choose when and whether to have children, and winning economic improvements for working-class women. These points are included in Rosa's 15-point programme, but seem to have been given little emphasis in day-to-day campaigning. We should always stress that – unlike the reactionary anti-abortion campaigners who do nothing to improve the lives of women and children – we are fighting for a real right to choose, meaning not only the right to high-quality safe contraception and to abortion, but also the right to decent housing, pay, fertility treatment, parental leave and childcare. In this way we can have an effect on sections of working-class women and men who remain unsure about the question of abortion. This is also a way of drawing out that capitalism is increasingly unable to offer any real right to choose because, even when abortion on demand is granted, the economic and social gains made in the past are under relentless attack.

How do we recruit and politically consolidate the layer we have reached in the referendum campaign?

It is absolutely correct that we have turned to, and attempted to win, the layer of young people who have been radicalised by the referendum campaign. It is also correct that in doing so we have an open and welcoming approach, and attempt to use language which does not put up unnecessary barriers to them. We do not agree with the abstract 'purist' approach of the small groups like the IMT, for example, who refuse to use the terms 'Marxist feminist' or 'socialist feminist', both because, "nowadays the concept of feminism has become so broad as to become virtually meaningless" and because "feminists often blame 'patriarchy' for most of the problems of society". We agree that feminism has become such a broad term that Theresa May can adopt it and also that feminist theorists usually consider patriarchy and not class to be the central division in society. Nonetheless, the vast majority of people who consider themselves as feminists see it as meaning simply supporting equal rights for women. It is therefore not incorrect to use the term, provided it is not on its own, but we also give an indication of our class approach with the addition of terms like socialist or Marxist.

However, even here we have to be clear ourselves and with our periphery, what we mean by the term. There is a certain comparison with the decision in the 1990s of a number of our sections, including Britain and Ireland, to change our name to 'Socialist Party' or similar 'broad' names. We did so because at that stage the reformist and social-democratic formations which previously would have claimed the word had capitulated wholesale to neo-liberalism leaving us able in some countries to use the world socialist, but give it a clear Marxist content. We had to guard, however, against the tendency of some comrades to think that in changing our name we were also 'blurring' our ideas. In claiming to be socialist feminists we are not therefore agreeing with the forces collected under that banner in the 1970s and 1980s that represented various strands of reformism. We should be careful about uncritically quoting left feminist academics who, while they may in some cases describe themselves as socialist feminists, do not have a rounded-out position on how to end women's oppression. Hester Eisenstein, to give one example, an academic who has worked for the government of New South Wales, is quoted uncritically in the 'Socialist Feminism' pamphlet.

We think it is a mistake to suggest that young people who are rebelling against the rigid gender norms of capitalism are automatically or generally the most radical section of society, thereby downgrading the role of other sections of the working class and miseducating those young people. Of course, at this point of time, in Ireland, a layer has been radicalised around these issues. However, in general there is no automatic connection between individual rebellion on these issues and drawing conclusions about the need for collective struggle for a new society. To give an example from Britain, it would generally have been true in the 1980s, when the Tory government was implementing specifically anti-gay legislation, that LGBTQ+ campaigners were often anti-Tory and even looked to the workers' movement for support. Today, however, after capitalism has adapted to pressure from below and all the major capitalist parties formally stand for equal rights, being LGBTQ+ in itself is no indicator of political views. In the 2015 UK general election LGBTQ+ voters supported the Tories and Labour in equal numbers.

At the 2018 CWI School, comrades in the leadership of the Irish section emphasised that young women and non-binary people are the most radical in Ireland at this point in time and that we will cut ourselves off from the most radical young people if we didn't put issues of bodily-autonomy central. At the same time, they did not, in our view, counter the views put by a young Irish comrade in a commission that a rejection of gender norms is a rejection of the system itself. Nor, when a new young comrade argued that, as a Solidarity TD candidate, she would be representing "young queer women", was any attempt made by the three Irish NEC members who spoke afterwards to gently correct her mistaken approach by, at least, pointing out that she would be representing not only young queer women but all sections of the working class. Taken as a whole, we were concerned that a trend could be developing in the leadership of the Irish section of not adequately dealing with the issue of identity politics.

The use of language

If we adopt wholesale the language of petit-bourgeois feminism it will not help us in this vital task. We should use terms like misogyny and patriarchy with care because they do not aid us in a theoretical understanding of the root causes of women's oppression. Misogyny – meaning hatred or contempt of women and girls – can be an accurate description in some circumstances, but it does not point towards the reason such hatred exists or where it stems from, so does not help to raise the level of understanding of the layer we are trying to reach. The term patriarchy also has limited use. We live in a patriarchal society, in the sense that men have more power than women. Nonetheless, as Marxists, we understand that the oppression of women developed alongside and intertwined with the development of class society and it is class, not gender, which is the most fundamental division in society. Our language has to help the radicalised young women we can reach to draw that conclusion, not reinforce wrong ideas. Sometimes material produced by the comrades in Ireland seems to slip into calling for movements of, "young people, of women, of LGBT people, of workers", which goes too far towards the identity politics approach of listing 'class' as one in a series of oppressions without explaining its centrality. It is true comrades often emphasise in speeches that it is poor and working-class women who suffer most from the abortion ban, but this is not the same as explaining the potential power of the working class as an agent of change.

We also have to patiently explain to new members that it would be a mistake to use language in a way that put up unnecessary barriers to reaching out to other sections of the working class and is unnecessarily inaccessible to them. To state the obvious, an essential part of the role of a revolutionary party is to aim to unite – via its programme – all the heterogeneous layers of the working class with their different needs and experiences. Of course, at this stage, we can only reach a minority of the most thinking layers, but still aim to instil in them an approach which will allow us to reach the mass of the working class in the future.

Clearly, what language we use is not fixed. At every stage we have to attempt to use language which is scientifically correct and which takes the consciousness of our audience forward, which reaches out to a layer who are radicalised on a particular issue, but does not exclude sections of workers for whom that issue is not central. This is a difficult balance which changes over time. When, for example, in the 1970s we proposed including 'housewives' in committees to plan nationalised industries it was a correct attempt to reach out to working-class women who were not in the workplace, but it would obviously not be correct today!

We also recognise that the best language to use will vary between countries. Nonetheless, we are concerned that it seems to have become commonplace to use terms which, while they might be understood among young feminist activists, can be off-putting or easily misinterpreted by broader sections of the working class such as 'cis-normative', 'toxic masculinity' and even 'rape culture'. The first is not understood beyond a narrow audience, and while the second is a description of a narrow, repressive idea of masculinity which most men reject, to those who don't know that, it can sound like being male is, in and of itself, 'toxic'. We should also, in our view, have some caution about how we use the term 'rape culture' so as not to be seen to be implying that all, or a majority, of men are potential rapists.

While we have to welcome all that is positive in current moods, we should be careful not to uncritically follow them and thereby make mistakes. For example, it is enormously positive that more women are beginning to feel confident to speak out against sexual abuse. We shouldn't, of course, exaggerate the extent of the progress that has been made. The accusations of sexual harassment and abuse are still far outnumbered by the number of incidents which go unreported because of a justified lack of confidence on the part of women that they will be taken seriously. We have to stand in clear opposition to the sexist character of the capitalist state and in support of the rights of all victims. The turnout of thousands of mainly young women in opposition to the Ulster Rugby rape trial, shows the mood of burning anger that exists amongst an important layer against the blatant sexism of the court proceedings, as does the hundred thousand who marched under the banner of the SE in Spain against the court's treatment of the victim of the 'wolfpack' rapists.

However, as we have discussed previously, in welcoming these movements, and understanding why slogans like 'I believe her' are used, we have to be careful not to go along with the conclusion of many petit-bourgeois feminists that every accusation of sexual assault made by a woman against a man has to be accepted as proven regardless of evidence. Our approach is one of sympathy and solidarity with the person making the accusation, but at the same time we support the right to a fair hearing and the right of the accused to a fair trial. Underlying the conclusion of those feminists who insist that the woman is always right, regardless of evidence, is a belief that the fundamental division in society is between men and women, with men responsible for all the ills of the world. That is not our starting point. We recognise that sexual abuse of women by men is extremely widespread, and often goes unreported, but we cannot draw a conclusion in each individual case from that. Aside from anything else, were we to do so we would be handing a weapon to the capitalist class, who would only have to make accusations against any effective male leader of the class struggle in order to discredit them. To be clear, that is not in any way to suggest we try to brush sexual abuse in the workers' movement under the carpet. On the contrary, it is vital we tackle it wherever it occurs if we are to effectively make the case for the workers' movement being the best vehicle to fight for women's rights.

Our attitude towards 'separate' organisations

In general, the attitude of the CWI towards organisations or parties of particular sections of the oppressed – whether black, women, LGBTQ+ or others – is not fixed, but depends on the concrete circumstances. We have to have a flexible approach, basing our position on the political direction of travel. Where a new formation is a step towards raising the consciousness and cohesion of the working class we should support it, but not if it is a step in the opposite direction. In Britain, for example, we did not support the foundation of black sections in the Labour Party in the past, as it mainly represented a section of black careerists furthering their own interests, who emphasised separation from the rest of the labour movement. The opposition of Lenin and Trotsky to the Bund, which organised among Jewish workers in Russia, to give another example, was not based on its existence, but its programme of 'cultural autonomy' which tended to emphasise the divisions in the working class. Of course, there is a difference between our approach to broader organisations and to a revolutionary party where, although sometimes transitional structures are necessary on a temporary basis, we always aim to organise all sections of our membership together in common structures.

Nonetheless, as well as sometimes participating in and supporting 'sectional' broader organisations, we can in certain circumstances initiate them. The prominence Rosa has achieved during the referendum campaign has been enthusiastically greeted throughout the CWI. Inevitably, as a result, a number of other sections have launched versions of Rosa as a means to intervene among radicalised young women. Others have used different banners, particularly Libres y Combativas in the Spanish state.

As we said at the start, the CWI has a long history of initiating numerous campaigns, organisations and banners which are aimed at reaching out to a specific section of society that have been radicalised on an issue and winning them to Marxism. Nonetheless, we have to weigh up at each stage 'what we give' and 'what we get'. For example, comrades in Britain were involved in initiating Panther in the early 1990s, with the goal of winning black youth who were attracted to black nationalist ideas. Panther had considerable success, mobilising large numbers on demonstrations and to meetings for a period. Bobby Seale spoke at a Panther meeting in Brixton, London with around 2,000 mainly young black people present. It was the biggest ever meeting of its kind in Britain. He also met with the leaders of Panther and the party. However, for a combination of reasons, primarily the very difficult period after the collapse of Stalinism, and the weakness of our black and Asian cadre, the end result was that we lost people to black nationalism rather than winning new people from it.

At this stage we do not think there is one international model we can use as a banner for our work against women's oppression. Rosa, however, can continue to play a useful role in

Ireland as can similar banners in other sections. However, we think it is vitally important that comrades adopt a clear, working-class orientated approach, if we are to win people from it.

We would also have questions about whether, during the referendum, the profile of the party lost out too much to the profile of Rosa. For example, we understand that the big majority of posters we produced for the referendum were in the name of Rosa, with a minority in the name of Solidarity and none by the Socialist Party. Obviously the TDs were known as Solidarity and/or Socialist Party members and had a high-profile in the referendum campaign, particularly Ruth. Nonetheless, in order to fully capitalise on that, we think it would have been better to have consciously had a higher party profile.

We also believe it is important now to draw a balance sheet of what we have achieved via our Rosa work and what role we think it is going to play in the future. During the referendum we know that hundreds attended meetings called by Rosa and around 1,000 people gave their details to campaign with Rosa. Inevitably there has been a lull since the referendum result. However, it would be useful to get figures on how many are actively involved in Rosa at the moment. Our understanding is that it is does not have any elected structure and has relatively small numbers – maybe around twenty – attending its all-Dublin fortnightly meetings. We in no way suggest that Rosa therefore has no value, but if that information is accurate it is currently in reality a banner or campaign, rather than a more developed organisation with its own structures and life. Of course Rosa could fill out again, on the basis of the future struggles that will develop over the separation of church and state. However, in our view that is likely to be only one of numerous fields of struggle that will develop in Ireland and may not be the most central in the immediate period. We therefore think that Rosa should not be the centre of the comrades' work to the extent it appears to be and what resources are dedicated to it should be discussed accordingly.

Conclusion

In summary we are concerned that, in their anxiety to recruit as many as possible from a layer who have been radicalised by issues related to gender oppression, comrades in Ireland are in danger of making too many concessions to the consciousness of that layer. To do so would be to attempt to take a short cut which would have negative consequences.

This is a road that many revolutionary organisations have gone down at different times, with disastrous results. Famously USFI leader Ernest Mandel, prior to May 1968, wrote off for decades the prospect of mass working-class struggle in the advanced capitalist countries and instead focused on 'liberation movements'. The US SWP also, in their desperation to give uncritical support to the Black Power movement, ended up lagging behind the most advanced elements within it, even criticising the Black Panthers for arguing it was possible to be black and racist and to be black and a capitalist.

We are not suggesting that the Irish comrades have taken this profoundly mistaken path, but we are worried that some errors could have been made in that direction which need to be corrected. We hope by raising our fears openly it will enable an honest and constructive debate from which we can reach principled agreement.

For a Marxist Approach

Peter Taaffe, Hannah Sell, Judy Beishon
(England and Wales IEC members)

This document briefly summarises the CWI's analysis of and approach to movements against women's oppression. Unfortunately, the dispute that erupted at the 2018 IEC meeting revealed a retreat from this approach, which is based on the need to build a revolutionary party with a programme centred on the role of the working class as the key agent for the socialist transformation of society as the only means to lay the basis for the ending of gender oppression. The clearest and most developed example of this retreat is in Ireland, where, as we will explain, the majority of the leadership of the section have moved towards seeing struggles around gender oppression as central to the struggle for the transformation of society. Linked to this, their interventions into concrete struggles for women's rights – in particular the abortion referendum – have not used the transitional method, raised a socialist programme or pointed to the role of the working class in fighting for women's rights. At the IEC and since, however, a number of IEC members have uncritically defended the erroneous stance taken by the Irish majority to movements on women's oppression.

If the IS was to allow this retreat from a class approach to develop unchallenged it would threaten the political foundations of the CWI, leaving us unprepared for the mighty class struggles ahead. This alone, aside from the other vital issues that arose at the IEC, necessitated the formation of a faction.

The IS's approach to movements against women's oppression

At the recent IEC meeting, and since, the theme of those who oppose the approach of our faction has been to argue that we have underestimated the scale and importance of the women's movements that have taken place internationally. The Irish NEC majority's reply to the IS on the issue sums it up saying: "A tendency to understate the significance of this development inevitably had an impact on concrete initiatives and interventions or lack thereof." This is also suggested in the document by IEC members Andros Payiatsos (AP), Vincent Kolo (VK) and their co-thinker Bryan Koulouris (BK) on why they disagree with our faction. They say: "The position of the IS, in putting its main emphasis on 'future class battles' in contrast to this historic battle taking place today, runs a certain risk of overlooking important opportunities round newly radicalized layers present or developing into today's situation." We will deal with the crucial issue of our approach to 'future class battles' later in this reply, but we entirely refute the allegation that we underestimate the importance of the many struggles against women's oppression that have developed internationally. At the last World Congress we had a special document and discussion on the struggle against women's oppression [see page 223], rather than on youth work, trade union work or any of the other vital issues we might have discussed, exactly because we recognised the importance of the struggles that have and will develop. For IWD 2018 we had a special drive for the socialist world website, with twelve special articles on the site, again because we saw the importance of orientating towards the growing radicalisation on women's oppression.

Linked to this we also refute the argument in the Irish document that: "The IS seem to imply a rigid distinction between those who are radicalised on economic questions and those who are radicalised on social questions." This has been repeated ad-infinitum – that we believe there is a 'Chinese wall' between economic and social issues, are only interested in battles on economic issues and so on. Our international has a long history of campaigning on social questions, including against violence against women. Of course, in doing so, we have linked them with economic issues, with which they are intertwined, especially for the working class and poor.

In their document the Irish NEC majority comrades belittle our reference to the Campaign Against Domestic Violence (CADV), on the grounds that it is "from a quarter of a century ago". The point, however, is that the CADV is an illustration of the long and proud history of the CWI on these issues and of a correct method of orientation. In Britain, the CADV successfully fought for the trade union movement to take up the issue of domestic violence, at a time when many – including supposed Marxists – were arguing that it was divisive to take the issue up in the workplaces. It also successfully fought for changes in the law, particularly relating to women who had killed their violent partners. In a very difficult period after the collapse of Stalinism, we were nonetheless able to use CADV to raise the level of the workers' movement about how the oppression of women is an intrinsic part of class society. We explained that it affects all women, including those from the ruling class, but that the working class were the only possible agency of overthrowing capitalism and therefore laying the basis for the ending of women's oppression. At the same time the CADV always linked the campaign against domestic violence to 'economic demands' such as the provision of refuges, grants for women fleeing violence, and mass council housebuilding, which for working class women were and are vital to successfully leaving violent relationships.

We ask the comrades: do you think the CADV showed an international that puts a 'rigid distinction' between those who are radicalised on 'economic' and 'social' questions? Or is it that you think we have since abandoned that stance?

The document on women, put by the IS to the 2016 World Congress which the comrades voted for and raise no criticism of, puts a central emphasis on issues relating to violence against women, saying for example: "Even then sexism remains ingrained into the fabric of capitalism. It is now less socially acceptable in many countries to openly state that women are the possessions of men, but this idea – and that it is acceptable to enforce it with violence or the threat of violence – remains deeply embedded and was enshrined in law until relatively recently. Marital rape only became illegal in Britain in 1991, Spain in 1992, and Germany in 1997. While no longer legal or openly acceptable, marital rape is still widespread and rarely punished. Nor is rape in general. It is estimated that in Britain only 15% of all rapes are reported to the police, and only 7% of those result in conviction. According to the UN, of all the women killed globally in 2012 almost half were killed by their partners or family members. In contrast, only 6% of killings with male victims were committed by intimate partners or family members."

In many sections the CWI has intervened in, and some cases led, campaigns relating to 'social' questions on the specific oppression of women. Prominent among these is, of course, the tremendous role that the comrades in Ireland played in fighting for abortion rights, a historic blow against the Catholic establishment and victory for the working class. (Incidentally, the document by AP, VK and BK claims that we challenged the use of the term 'historic' in reference to the referendum victory. This is nonsense. The Irish majority tried to suggest that there was some meaning behind our document using the adjective 'tremendous' rather than 'historic'. There was no such meaning.) The comrades in the Spanish state, supporters of the faction, have been able to use the lever of the student union (SE) to organise magnificent student action, across all states with two hundred thousand on the streets in more than 50 towns and cities, on IWD and against the Spanish courts' shameful light sentencing of the 'wolfpack' rapists. We are wholly in favour of playing this role in movements on these vital questions wherever possible.

CWI's proud traditions on analysing women's oppression

The CWI has developed a worked-out Marxist approach to women's oppression over many decades, as outlined in Christine Thomas' book, 'It doesn't have to be like this' and numerous other materials. Violence against women, gender stereotyping and all the discrimination suffered by women are all rooted in the existence of class society. As part of the formation of the first class societies – based on private property relations – women became the property of individual men within the family unit. Today, thousands of years later, capitalism has created a contradictory situation. It has inherited the institution of the family from previous societies and fashioned it to suit its own interests. At the same time, capitalism itself, particularly in the recent period in the economically developed countries, has tended to undermine the traditional family unit as a result of women being drawn into the workforce. In many countries, women have won large elements of legal equality, and violence against women is no longer openly tolerated. While huge prejudice and discrimination still exists there is nonetheless greater acceptance of LGBTQ+ rights. Nonetheless, capitalism is incapable of ending the oppression of women or rigid gender norms. Violence against women remains endemic, reflecting deeply ingrained attitudes that women are the possessions of men. In general women remain concentrated in the lowest paying sectors of the economy and take the majority of the burden of caring for children, the elderly and the sick – a burden that is increasing considerably as a result of austerity.

Of course, it is vital that – at each stage – we analyse new developments relating to women's oppression and the struggle against it. Nonetheless, we do not accept that there is something fundamentally new in the current wave of radicalisation which invalidates our previous analysis. The reply to the IS by the Irish majority makes repeated and general assertions about the scale and depth of what they describe as 'the global women's movement' which they describe as a 'fundamental shift in consciousness'. However, they give no coherent explanation of what has caused this fundamental shift in consciousness. Points are raised about 'an unwillingness to accept inequality or any further vestiges of sexism' and 'a new generation of young women are being radicalised by continued women's and LGBTQ oppression'. Women's oppression has, of course, existed in different forms since the dawn of class society, but that does not explain why movements are taking place now.

There is a danger in the Irish majority's approach of idealism, with no serious attempt to draw out the material basis for the current radicalisation. On the contrary, when the IS pointed to, among other factors, the undermining of all the institutions of capitalism as a result of the capitalist crisis, we were ridiculed. Incredibly Kevin McLoughlin, Irish IEC member, said to the Irish NC regarding the referendum that, "when comrades say surely there is an anti-austerity anti-establishment element to the vote in Ireland it really wasn't the case." This spurious argument is partially backed up by AP, VK and BK when they say: "IS speakers stressed austerity as a main factor behind the victory in the Irish referendum. While this was an important factor, movements for political change and revolution do not only stem from economic issues. Most that voted for the change did so for the issue itself, the right to abortion."

This completely misunderstands the point we were making. As we explained at the IEC, of course, people voted for abortion rights in the referendum because they supported the right to abortion. We were attempting to discuss why social attitudes have changed so dramatically on the issue. In 1983, when the vicious anti-abortion eighth amendment was introduced in Southern Ireland, almost 67% of voters voted in favour of it. Today a sea change has taken place. Clearly, there are many reasons behind this. This is the case with all movements against women's oppression. In reality there is not one global women's movement, but a worldwide radicalisation, with different movements – all with their own features – taking place in different countries.

Nonetheless, in our view it is indisputable – both in Ireland and globally – that an important aspect of radicalisation of young women is the crisis of capitalism, which has undermined the hopes that existed in the previous generation that capitalism offered young working and middle class women better prospects than their mothers and grandmothers - with improved education, jobs and opportunities. Today they are more likely to have higher education, but face harder lives in other respects. This has profoundly undermined the authority of all institutions of capitalism – including the media, the church and capitalist parties - leaving them less able to influence social attitudes and events.

The reality of life for working class women in this era contrasts sharply with their expectations. Improved educational opportunities and the large increase in the number of women in the workforce in many countries – a particularly steep increase in Ireland – have given women more confidence. At the same time, the gains won by the workers' and women's movement in the previous era have raised women's expectations of equality. The fact that, under the pressure of those movements, large sections of the capitalist classes worldwide proclaim that they stand for equality also gives more confidence to challenge the very different reality.

The Irish reply to the IS asserts that we argue: "there could be more movements of women, but particularly where existing rights are attacked or in countries with a particular legacy of oppression. In conversation IS comrades have indicated that the movements seem to have mainly been in Catholic countries." It is clear in Ireland that the openly reactionary backward character of the Irish capitalist state, intertwined with the Catholic Church is an important factor. The deep felt accumulated anger at the Catholic Church for its crimes against working class women and children in particular is undoubtedly a major radicalising factor in Irish society. The IS does not, however, suggest that movements on women's oppression are likely only in Catholic countries. On the contrary, in the many countries where regimes implement openly reactionary politics towards women, often on religious grounds, mass movements of women are on the cards. So too will we see movements in countries where new attacks on women are being launched, as capitalist politicians try to increase their social base, as with Trump's attacks on abortion in the US. And, of course, significant movements can also develop in other countries around aspects of women's oppression, as indicated, for example, by the google walkouts.

The Irish majority argues that the current women's movement has 'deeper roots than previous women's/feminist movements'. In some senses – particularly the depth of anger against the existing order – it could be argued that this is deeper than previous 'feminist waves'. However, the general difficulties of the period, the still-low level of working-class consciousness and organisation, obviously also effect movements against women's oppression. The Russian revolution came within the time frame of the first wave of feminism and France 1968 in the second. We do not accept the argument of petit-bourgeois left feminists like Hester Eisenstein who is uncritically quoted in the Irish comrades 'Socialist Feminism' pamphlet as saying that: "it took the nineteenth and twentieth centuries' women's movements to claim the rights of women as full citizens". The women's movements which, while predominantly from the upper layers of society did also involve working class women, played a role; but so did the workers' movements, war and revolutions.

Moreover while the huge, accumulated anger against the existing order is reflecting in movements against women's oppression, it is not the case that a majority of those participating put the blame for their oppression at capitalism's door. This is bound to be the case when a section of the capitalist class claims to be fighters for women's equality. Even among the most radical layers of such movements, who see themselves as anti-capitalist, the need to overthrow capitalism, never mind the central role of the working class in achieving that, is not generally understood. This is inevitable given, at this stage, the still low level of independent working class organisation and struggle.

Our role, in intervening in these struggles, is to support the fight against gender oppression, but to skilfully link that to demands which point towards the necessity of the socialist transformation of society and the central role of the working class in achieving that. Unfortunately, rather than do that, the Irish majority have made serious mistaken concessions to existing consciousness.

Differences not on whether to intervene – but how

Our differences with the Irish majority lie not in whether it is correct to instigate, to intervene in and to fight for the leadership of movements against gender oppression, but in how we intervene in them, particularly how we use a transitional approach to raise the consciousness of those we can reach. In addition we believe, on the basis of the Irish NEC majority's reply to us, and the discussion that took place at the IEC, that we have a different estimation of the role of women's movements in the transformation of society. As we explain later this is a crucial issue from which other issues flow.

At every stage the IS majority has attempted to pursue discussion on these issues with the

Irish leadership. This proved difficult prior to the IEC, as they have repeatedly prioritised the discussion on the hack, to the exclusion of starting the debate on women and identity politics. The IS first wrote to the comrades asking for a meeting that included discussion on women and identity politics on 31 August, 2018. The IS majority finally had an initial discussion at the Irish NC on 17 November 2018, just one week before the IEC.

In our view it is not only the Irish majority who have tried to avoid a serious discussion on these issues, but also the comrades who have organised in their support. Within the IS, the dispute with Danny Byrne (DB) on these issues began with his reluctance to agree that the IS should write to the Irish NEC to ask for discussion on their approach. In AP, VK, and BK's document disagreeing with the faction, they say of the IEC that, regarding movements against women's oppression, "The need for a bold working class, socialist approach in our work in these movements, distinguishing our class struggle feminism from the bourgeois and petty-bourgeois leadership of these movements, and emphasising the united struggle of the working class for socialist change, was not questioned by any comrade in the discussion." This, to put it mildly, is not accurate.

The Irish NEC majority reply shows that this is not the approach the comrades took to the referendum campaign, or are defending in its aftermath. In part one of their reply 'The Irish Section and Identity Politics' the comrades described how they clashed with supporters of identity politics in the abortion referendum campaign, but they can only give one single example of this: the clashes that took place over our tactics on the abortion pill. We accept that those tactics played a role in the campaign. However, tactics of this kind do not in themselves do anything to politically challenge the ideas of the petit-bourgeois feminists.

Nor does this type of militant tactic, which inevitably is only carried out by a small minority, act to encourage mass participation in the struggle for abortion rights. A referendum, which is an electoral campaign, is inevitably quite a low level of struggle compared, for example, to mass strikes or even demonstrations. This does not make it less important for us to participate in referendum campaigns, but it does make it vital that we raise demands that go beyond voting and point towards the need for mass working-class action. The abortion pill tactic does nothing to encourage this. Such a tactic can be a useful adjunct to our central tasks, but not more than that. It certainly did not – and how could it? - 'emphasise the united struggle of the working class for socialist change'.

Nor did the comrades do this in the material they produced during the referendum campaign, particularly in the mass produced material that was used to campaign for a 'yes' vote. In their reply to the IS the comrades explain that: "Substantial resources and the party itself was only directed into Rosa in the first six months of 2018, in the run up to the referendum itself", but it is particularly what the comrades did and didn't do during this period, in the run up to and during the referendum campaign, which alarmed the IS and led to it asking for discussion with the comrades on the issues.

In their reply to the IS the comrades give quotes from material they have produced from as far back as 2013, but only one from a 2018 leaflet, which is not related to the abortion referendum. They do not quote from any of the Rosa material produced for the referendum campaign because it would not have backed up their assertion that they raised socialist ideas during the campaign. There may have been individual Socialist Party leaflets produced at local level during the campaign. However, it is indisputable that all of the mass produced material during the campaign was in the name of Rosa. Prior to the referendum there were also mass produced Solidarity newsletters, delivered to households in our constituencies, which dealt with the referendum, but this went no further programmatically than the Rosa material.

The point we are making is that huge layers of workers and young people were politicised around the issue of abortion during the referendum campaign and we – particularly as a result of the TD's profile, but also to some extent Rosa's – had an opportunity to intervene, using a transitional approach, to raise the class consciousness of those we could reach. In our view the comrades failed to do that. It does not answer our charge that a major opportunity was missed in the mass work done around the referendum campaign to point out that some longer, more rounded, material was produced in pamphlets or websites, because this was only aimed at a much smaller layer. We would argue that at least some of the mass material should have been produced in the name of the Socialist Party, but the central question for us is the programmatic weakness of the material that was produced. As you will see it talks about how 'young people, in particular, have the power to determine the outcome of this referendum and really make history' and it talks about how winning abortion rights 'will empower all those who are fighting economic and social inequality'. It does not, however, make any reference to the working class, to socialism (other than in the name of Rosa), or link the right to abortion to any economic demands. This was the case in all of the mass material. Rosa is a banner which we initiated and lead, with a limited layer consistently active beyond our ranks. There was nothing to prevent us putting a fuller programme in Rosa material.

The Greek EC resolution on the crisis says that, "Rosa's 15 point programme is a clear class-oriented programme". In fact, it falls far short of this. It is quite limited, talking of how "people power movements are key to social change". The furthest it goes is in the final demand which concludes, "For a mass movement of women, workers and all the oppressed to challenge capitalism's rule of the 1% super-rich". However, even this limited programme was not included in the mass-produced Rosa material during the referendum.

In paragraph 127 of their reply, the comrades justify their approach in not raising economic demands, not even guaranteed free healthcare for all, linked to giving women a real choice when and whether to have children, saying:

"We've consistently raised the need for public childcare, housing etc, to ensure working-class families can make the choice to have children and not subsist in poverty, in relation to abortion. The comrades' assessment that this would have been helpful in convincing people unsure of abortion, misses the main point. Once we were in the actual referendum campaign, it was necessary to focus and openly deal with abortion, and not to be seen to avoid it. The real situation people face and why this right is a necessity – these questions and the points of the pro-lifers, needed to be answered directly and this was our focus."

Verbally in debate at the Irish NC Laura Fitzgerald was more explicit, arguing it would have been wrong to raise those demands during the referendum.

It is clear that it was essential to argue for the right to abortion as the central point in our referendum propaganda. However, we think it is completely wrong to refuse to link this to demands on pay, housing, childcare, family leave etc. Not only could this have helped to win some who were unsure on abortion, demonstrating that it is us – and not the reactionary anti-abortion campaigners – who actually fight to give children a decent life, it would also have played a vital role in exposing the pro-capitalist politicians who had cynically come behind the call for abortion rights, but were and are presiding over a devastating housing crisis, low pay and astronomical childcare costs (an average of over €1000 a month in Dublin for example). By limiting themselves to issues directly related to abortion alone, the comrades were tending to reflect the existing mood of a radicalised layer, rather than connecting with it, but then – via our programme – going further. Of course, we understand that during a referendum campaign for a measure that could make a real difference to millions of women's lives there was bound to be considerable pressure to limit ourselves just to the immediate question on the ballot paper. Our role, however, is not to concede to that, but to explain how, by raising broader demands, we could not only improve the prospects of winning the referendum, but prepare the ground for future struggles.

Anti-capitalist propaganda and a transitional approach

In the Belgian IEC members document, written to defend the Irish majority, they suggest that the IS has no evidence that the Irish comrades are not sufficiently using a transitional approach in their work, arguing that one leaflet is not evidence of this. That of course is true but, unfortunately, it is clear from the Irish comrades reply, from their argumentation in the debates and from numerous material, that our concerns were fully justified. We agree that every section will have produced poor leaflets and articles at different points which they would not wish to stand over. The problem is when it is not a question of this or that individual mistake, but when individual mistakes cohere into a trend, which the comrades are not prepared to honestly assess and correct, but instead defend. This is the approach taken in the Irish comrades' reply. In paragraph 81, for example, the Irish majority say: "We engage in a lot of anti-capitalist argumentation consciously as a key way to raise the need for socialist change and the centrality of class. The more convincing an argument is made as to why it will be impossible to deal with the issues people face, the more the material necessity of each person getting involved in a collective struggle is clarified. This not only exposes reformist ideas, but raises the urgent need for an organised working-class movement."

In fact, the mass produced material for the referendum campaign certainly did not include 'a lot of anti-capitalist argumentation'. The most that was included was in the Rosa leaflet pro- duced prior to the referendum campaign saying that there needed to be "a socialist feminist chal- lenge to the capitalist establishment and this inherently unjust system". This reflects a tendency to limit even anti-capitalist agitation to leaflets aimed more at the activist layer, rather than the mass. In addition, even in the comrades' anti-capitalist agitation there is a worrying tendency to pose issues in a diffuse way which does not sufficiently point in the direction of the socialist transformation of society. In the quotes the comrades give in their reply as positive examples of their material, for example, they four times refer to 'challenging' the capitalist system, a phrase that is open to the interpretation of 'standing up to' or 'reforming' capitalism rather than replac- ing it. There is also a tendency to talk about neo-liberal capitalism, or even just neo-liberalism (although this is not evident in the quotes given in the comrades' reply) which again can be interpreted to mean that it is only neo-liberal capitalism we are opposed to.

However, even if the anti-capitalist argumentation of the comrades had been more ex- tensive and better, it is simply not true that it would constitute, "a key way to raise the need for socialist change and the centrality of class". Many of those involved in the anti-abortion struggle, including some petit-bourgeois feminists, would consider themselves 'anti-capitalist' in a broad sense, but would either have no conception of, or would disagree with, "the need for socialist change and the centrality of class".

What is a transitional approach?

The CWI has an excellent record of adopting a transitional approach unlike many other supposedly Trotskyist forces. Such forces have either continued to repeat, as if by rote, demands from the programme put forward by Trotsky in 1938, without taking into account the concrete situation we face today, or – in the case of the SWP and their international followers in particular – arguing that it is not relevant today and instead putting forward a 'minimum and maximum' approach – with minimum day to day demands reflecting today's consciousness and then, separately - when appealing to a narrow audience – calls for revolution: with no link between the two. Unfortunately, in the Irish comrades' material there seems to be a drift, perhaps not consciously, towards the latter approach. They put forward a very limited programme, as our platform explains [see page 3] in the 2016 election campaign and in much of the Solidarity material produced since. It is significant that the Southern Irish paper has no 'what we stand for' section, or similar list of demands.

In this reply, however, we want to deal in particular with the comrades' failure to apply a transitional method in the abortion referendum and in other work relating to gender oppression. We recognise that on social issues relating to women's and other oppressions this can be a difficult task, not only because of the generally low level of consciousness, but also because while the inability of capitalism to deliver the material interests of working-class women – decent pay, housing etc – can be seen clearly in the current era of capitalist crisis, the responsibility of class society for other aspects of women's oppression can be less obvious to those we are trying to reach. On issues including violence, but also the lack of reproductive and abortion rights, blame can tend to be limited to a vague 'backward culture' or specific backward institutions, such as the Catholic church, particularly when a section of the capitalist class claim to be fighting for women's rights in these fields. Of course this does not make it less vital to take these important issues up, but it does mean we have to work out demands that help those who are listening to us to draw conclusions about capitalism's responsibility for these ills, and the need for socialism. Vague statements about anti-capitalism or socialism, with no programmatic link to the immediate issues, do not in themselves achieve this.

For example, in November 2018 the Irish comrades received widespread publicity following Ruth Coppinger's underwear protest in the Dáil (Irish parliament) against victim blaming in the courts. This was an important opportunity to raise aspects of our programme on the capitalist state. However, in the article published on the issue on the Irish party website (15 November, 2018) only one demand relating to the justice system was raised: "This movement must absolutely demand and fight for changes such as compulsory training for judges and juries in cases of sexual violence and education about consent in schools." We are, of course, not opposed to training or education, but do we think any amount of training would change the class character of the legal system, or the role of judges in representing the interests of the ruling elite? And training by whom? More representatives of the ruling class? There is nothing in this demand to clearly differentiate our approach from that of the Blairite Labour MPs in Britain, for example, who are also campaigning against victim blaming in the courts, but whose solution is to abolish juries because they are 'prejudiced'. Far better to raise demands about the election of judges, and democratic working class control of the legal system (and the education system) to at least point towards what social force offers a solution. The article does have a general sentence concluding it: "We need to build a movement of women, young and LGBTQ people and all sections of the working class around an anti-capitalist and socialist-feminist programme which challenges this system and all the injustices it perpetuates." This in no way, however, compensates for the lack of transitional demands on the concrete issues posed.

Some comrades have suggested there is no difference between the approach taken on this issue by comrades in the Spanish state and in Ireland. This is not the case. For example Libras y Combativas' (LYC) website article on the Wolfpack judgement: "This case is not an isolated case of the guilt of a judge or judge who does not have enough gender training as they pretend to make us believe. It is one more example of how justice is contingent on the interests of the capitalists." And LYC demands call for the dismissal of all judges and police officers responsible for such victim blaming judgements.

This links to the questions the IS raised in our initial statement on language and terminology. Of course we fully support trying to reach young people who are radicalised by their anger against sexism and sexist violence, but in doing so our role is to point them towards the responsibility of class society and the central role of the working class in ending it. To support the essence of a movement does not mean we have to take up and repeat all of its slogans. That is why we argued that, "We should use terms like misogyny and patriarchy with care because they do not aid us in a theoretical understanding of the roots of women's oppression". We went on to say that, in general, we recognise that what language we use is not fixed, but "at every stage we have to use language which is scientifically correct and takes the consciousness of our audience forward, which reaches out to a layer who are radicalised on a particular issue, but does not exclude sections for whom that issue is not central." Clearly this is a difficult task and, as we explained, is bound to vary from country to country. What is central for us is not what specific phrases we use, but that we do not simply reflect the demands of those currently radicalised, and aim to develop them further.

Regarding Ireland, we explained that we were concerned that "it seems to have become commonplace to use terms which, while they might be understood among young feminist activists, can be off-putting or easily misinterpreted by broader sections of the working class such as 'cis-normative', 'toxic masculinity' and even 'rape culture'." On the latter, we did not say it should not be used in any circumstances, but made the point that we should be careful how we use it "so as not to be seen to be implying that all, or a majority of men are potential rapists" or putting the blame for sexual violence on a vague 'culture' rather than capitalism. There is a danger of this, for example, in the Rosa leaflet the comrades produced for intervening in the March 2018 rape trial protests which says: "new generation of women and young people will not stand for victim blaming or a toxic macho culture that perpetuates sexism and gender based violence." Our job is to draw out how 'macho culture' is a reflection of class society. At the IEC the comrades played down the degree they use the kind of language we criticised. However, the experience of the IS comrades who attended the Irish NC, which discussed identity politics, was of leading NC members defending the need to use language like 'toxic masculinity' and 'hetero-normative'. When one NC member argued that anyone who was put off by the language should not be considered a potential party member no one disagreed. However, if we commonly use language of this kind which is not used or accepted by large sections of the working class we will certainly alienate potential members, not necessarily because they disagree, but because our organisation feels like it is 'not for them'.

Transitional demands, the abortion movement and the trade unions

In the comrades reply they show a total lack of understanding of the points the IS made relating to the need to raise demands on the organised working class. It is incredible that AP, VK and BK can state in their document that the "Irish comrades replied to these specific points, showing the work that had been done in these respects in the campaign". The Irish comrades give some, limited, examples of trade union work done, including moving some resolutions during the referendum campaign, but their reply to the IS tries to put a political case against orientation to the trade unions.

The faction has already made the central points on the trade unions in our platform and will write further material on it elsewhere. In this document we think it is necessary to highlight the response the comrades gave to our raising the potential role of the organised working class. They said:

"Such a campaign would have gotten bogged down in bureaucracy, and opposition by some to a Yes stance and in demands to tone down discussion on the use of abortion pills and the demand for full abortion rights. Both of these were crucial if we were to force acceptance of 12 weeks on request and in winning the Yes vote in the referendum. Put simply, the unions were not a mechanism to have a broad impact around a strong pro-choice position as they were behind the general population on the issue. Such an approach would have used up a lot of energy and resources needed for the main lines of battle."

What does this mean? The IS was not suggesting that we retreat one iota from our programme on abortion rights, but that we put demands on the union leaders to also fight for full abortion rights. As the IS explained, this was our approach in Britain in the anti-poll tax movement, where we combined building an 18 million strong non-payment campaign completely outside of the official structures, along with putting demands on the trade unions to take a fighting stance. The comrades say that "the unions" were "way behind the general population on the issue" of abortion rights. We assume they mean the union leaders rather than their members. We understand that the Irish trade union federation ICTU, and many trade unions, did have a position in favour of repealing the eighth amendment, but were not clear on standing for, and certainly not on campaigning for, full abortion rights. Surely then this was an important opportunity to expose the rottenness of the union leaders and to exert pressure on them. This would have allowed us to raise a programme which pointed the way towards the working class playing a greater and more collective role than voting, as individuals, in the referendum. It would have educated the radical youth we have around us on the potential role of the working class. This was the approach of the comrades in the Spanish state, who were able to use their role in the SE to call strike action on IWD and then use it as a lever to demand union leaders to do the same. This could have been done by raising demands on the unions and then taking them to the workers. The lack of union structures would not have prevented workplace petitions and meetings, for example.

The Irish majority criticise the IS, saying our implication is that putting demands on the trade unions, "should have been an important part of the campaign". How much time is spent doing such work is primarily a tactical question, which we had formed no definite judgement on. We did, however, think it should have been a politically important part of the campaign. For Marxists the central role of the working class in changing society is fundamental. Central to the role and the outlook of the working class is its relationship to the means of production. It is in the workplace – first and foremost – that the working class comes into conflict with the capitalists. This does not mean that other forms of protest – including elections and community struggles – are not also very important, but it is vital that a revolutionary party has an orientation towards the workplaces. It is essential that even small CWI sections, that are assembling the initial cadre by concentrating almost entirely on youth work, still put demands on the trade unions to educate the youth we are winning, as well as beginning to give those youth a vital practical education in intervening in workers' struggles and building in the workplaces.

Even where the unions appear completely empty we have to attempt work to bring around us the most fighting elements in a struggle to transform the unions. This can, in this period, involve all kinds of flexible tactics. Our general approach is to fight to transform the existing unions because, despite the huge obstacle at the top, they remain in most countries the biggest mass workers' organisations and are based in workplaces. As part of that general approach, however, there can be circumstances where we – along with others – fight to found new unions. What is excluded is that we have no serious or consistent orientation towards the workplaces. This, however, has been the approach of the leadership in Southern Ireland over a whole period. What they have described as an element of an 'open turn' away from the unions at this stage is a serious mistake.

However rotten the leaders of the unions, in Ireland as in many countries, the unions can be forced to organise action – as is being shown by the nurses' and midwives' strike due to take place in Ireland. Previous to that there have also been important strikes in transport, retail and other sectors. We cannot stand aside and wait for a change to take place in the unions, but have to work to organise the most militant and determined elements in the workplaces in order to prepare for future battles. We believe the failure to do this systematically, particularly in Southern Ireland where we have no organised union caucuses, with, at most, occasional limited meetings of comrades in the unions, is miseducating our younger cadre, not least about their role in their own workplaces. The call for lunchtime walkouts on IWD this year could play a useful role, but only if it is combined with a serious orientation towards the workplaces.

The obstacle created by the trade union leaders and the relative absence of democratic structures and activists are not peculiar to Ireland, but exist to one degree or another in many countries. The unions in the Spanish state, for example, are among the worst in Europe, but the comrades still put demands on them, without the advantage of three TDs whose authority could be used to aid this task. Even if in Ireland there are very limited numbers of workers active in the union structures, there are clearly larger numbers who get active during strikes. Not only is union density in Southern Ireland slightly higher than Britain, but over the last five years around twice as many workers (per head of population) have been involved in strike action.

What was the character of the movement for abortion rights?

AP, VK and BK's statement in defence of the Irish majority says that the IS "described the struggle for abortion rights as a 'cross-class' movement in contrast to a working class movement, which formally speaking is correct. However, other comrades replied showing similarities with other movements and phenomena: climate, anti-war, opposition to the European Union, LGBT+, democracy, anti-racism, refugees and more." There is an implication here that, by making the very obvious point that the movement for abortion rights was a cross-class movement, we were diminishing its importance. This was not at all the case. Speaking for the IS Hannah Sell made the point that no movement under capitalism is a chemically-pure working class movement, there are always, to a greater or lesser extent, different class pressures exerted on a movement. Nonetheless, she argued, whereas the anti-poll tax movement in Britain, or the anti-water charges movement in Ireland, were predominantly working class movements, other movements like the abortion rights movement in Ireland, or the global anti-war movement in 2003, are very clearly cross class movements, with sections of the bourgeois attempting to put themselves in the leadership of them. A number of the self-appointed leaders of the abortion movement, for example, are now standing as candidates for Fine Gael, and Taoiseach (PM) Varadkar is attempting to pose as a champion of women's rights. By the time of the referendum, even Fianna Fáil was forced to formally support Repeal, although a majority of its TDs did not. The Irish comrades own initial balance sheet of the referendum campaign, "The 8th repealed – how yes won," pointed out that: "The vote was very high among the middle class and working class. The figures point to it being higher among the former, though in the campaign it was clear that the depth of feeling on the issue was strongest in the working class."

We raised the cross-class character of the movement not to lessen its importance but to emphasise the need to put a clear class programme and to attempt to expose the role of the capitalist elements of the leadership. It was necessary for us to make these self-evident points because the Irish majority reply to the IS stated: "The abortion rights struggle in Ireland also took place outside the union structures, but that doesn't mean it was not a working class struggle." Clearly it was a struggle which was of vital importance to working-class people who voted for abortion rights, but it was a struggle which involved sections of all classes. An objective and realistic assessment of the character of a movement is a vital prerequisite for intervening in it effectively. The Irish majority comrades repeatedly talk about the working class being the 'beating heart of the referendum campaign', but have not put forward demands which raise the level of that 'beating heart' about their role or the character of others involved in the movement.

Will women's movements be 'central'?
In the concluding section of the Irish comrades reply, under the heading, 'conclusions and some questions for the IS' they say that our view on women's movements that it, "tends to pose them as secondary or support acts to greater events. Women's rights or struggles can be seen as sectional issues, but we must remind ourselves that women are half the population and a huge proportion of the overall working class". They then quote part of paragraph 22 from our document. The whole of the paragraph stated:

"However, in our view it is not the case that movements relating to women's oppression will be central to struggle in every country in the next period. In addition in many countries where such movements occur the working-class elements within them can quite quickly become part of broader struggles of the working class (although of course the demands specifically relating to women's oppression would remain an important aspect of those movements)."

The Irish majority responded by saying:

"It is difficult to know what is being said here. Generally the paragraph seems to be cautioning, raising that women's movements won't be central or primary. If that is the main point we'd like to ask the IS to outline its rationale for such an assessment? Given the reality of recent events; wouldn't a more open attitude to the potential be more appropriate?"

In the following paragraph they then conclude that, "the radicalisation among women seems to be more universal, global and interconnected. It is not a temporary phase, but a more fundamental shift in consciousness and is deeper, in that it is not the preserve of middle class layers, but is also reflective of a change amongst working class women". They then go on to say that "more discussion is needed on these issues including about the possibility that these issues of equality could be quite central."

This is alarming. It confirms the concern originally raised by the IS that there could be a tendency in Ireland, "to put the issue of a movement against women's oppression above all other trends."

In our view it was clear what we meant when we said that working-class elements within women's movements can quite quickly become part of broader movements of the working class. An important radicalisation of women has taken place on a worldwide scale, which has and will result in mass movements in numerous countries. At this stage, there is a low level of general class struggle in many of the countries where movements against women's oppression are taking place. However, this will not remain the case. That is what we meant by saying the movements against women's oppression will become part of broader movements of the working class, not that movements against women's oppression will cease but they will be joined by other struggles and that, particularly as mass workers' struggles develop, there will be a tendency for women's movements to polarise on class lines. Implicit in the argument of the Irish majority that "issues of equality could be quite central" is that there will not be mass struggles on other issues in the next period. Of course, we have to intervene in movements taking place today, not sit and wait for 'future class battles' as AP, VK and BK suggest we are proposing. However, our intervention in today's battles is always attempting to prepare for the future, by raising the consciousness of those we can reach and winning the best layers to our party.

Our international is preparing for the mass workers' struggles and revolutionary movements of the future, in which the working class will have opportunities to take power. Could such movements be 'sectional' rather than more general? We don't believe that a Marxist analysis can lead to the conclusion that is how events will develop. In the revolutionary movements of the future, struggles against women's oppression will not be 'central' or 'primary' unless comrades are arguing that it is women or LGBTQ+ who are the social force that can overthrow capitalism. Doubtless comrades will express outrage at the suggestion they could think such a thing – but it is the logical conclusion of some of their arguments. Of course, women and LGBTQ+ people will play an important part in overthrowing capitalism, but as part of the working class as a whole. To achieve this requires a party with a programme that can unite the different layers of the working class in a common struggle. It is vital to fight to ensure demands against women's and gender oppression are emblazoned on its banner, but alongside all the other issues that affect different layers of the working class.

In the IS' original document on these issues we raised the danger of repeating the mistakes made by the Mandelites who, prior to May 1968, "wrote off for decades the prospect of mass working-class struggle in the advanced capitalist countries and instead focused on 'liberation movements'. At the time we argued that, "we are not suggesting the Irish comrades have taken this profoundly mistaken path, but we are worried that some errors could have been made in that direction which need to be corrected." Unfortunately, in the period since, far from openly discussing and attempting to correct those errors, the comrades are standing over them and attempting to justify them. The fact that a number of IEC members – as typified by AP, VK and BK's document – are acting to defend the stance the Irish majority have taken is a fundamental political error, which, if had not been challenged by the IS majority and the faction, would have endangered the political foundations of the CWI.

Women's Oppression and the Global Women's Movements

Christine Thomas, IEC member, Italy

*T*he current international debate taking place in the CWI has raised points about the character of the global women's movements and perspectives for their future development. In particular, the IS majority has been heavily criticised by those who oppose the faction for its stance on these movements.

In the Irish NEC's reply to the IS document on women's oppression and identity politics the IS is accused of "understating the significance of the global feminist movement" with a consequent impact on "concrete initiatives and interventions and a lack thereof". The Belgian IEC members in their document criticise the IS for not taking a leading role in this work and not taking "this new and massive mood sufficiently into account."

In her speech in the debate at the Greek NC, Ruth Coppinger went even further. Not only did she accuse the IS majority of turning the transitional approach into a "fetish" but also of "sitting looking," of "not intervening," of "being critical and only pointing out the dangers of the movement." In 13 years, she said, the IS has taken no initiatives on the question of women. The initiatives which have taken place have only come from the sections themselves.

These attacks have been launched primarily as a diversion from the sharp political criticisms that the IS and the faction have made of the Irish majority, including the incorrect orientation of Rosa and the Irish section in the abortion referendum campaign. At root, however, are two fundamentally different analyses of the global women's movements and two contrasting perspectives about what form future struggles will take.

Materialist vs idealist analysis

At no time during the debate have the Irish comrades and their supporters attempted to explain the material roots of the current global movements, either in writing or in speeches. Why are these movements taking place now and not 15 or 20 years ago when issues such as violence against women and sexual harassment – two of the main questions around which women have been mobilising internationally – were just as prevalent? The unifying factor is clearly the global economic crisis which broke out in 2008 and the affect that it, and subsequent policies of austerity and rising inequality, have had on consciousness. Through its economic effects – attacks on jobs, public services, working conditions and the welfare state

– the crisis has destroyed expectations amongst many working-class and middle-class women, that things could get materially better. At the same time, the crisis has eroded confidence in capitalist institutions, the traditional political parties, the legal system, the church etc, as well as a rejection of the sexist ideology which the system and its institutions have fostered. This has led to an increased challenging of all forms of inequality, injustice and oppression, especially – but not exclusively – by a younger generation of women and men.

The crisis has also resulted in the election of right-wing populist governments in the USA, in Brazil, in Poland, in Italy etc, which have to varying degrees provoked significant movements against current or future attacks on the social gains that women, the working class and other oppressed groups have won as the result of struggle and changing social attitudes. The fact that women make up a large part of the workforce in many countries will also have been an important factor in increasing confidence and changing attitudes, but in most cases this has been a long-term process taking place over decades and is not alone sufficient to explain why these movements have erupted precisely at this time.

Diverse and heterogeneous movements

This is the general backdrop to the current movements. In reality, the Irish majority comrades have taken an idealist rather than a materialist approach to explaining their emergence. At the same time, they have attempted to generalise from their own experiences in Ireland, experiences that are not necessarily applicable to other countries or movements internationally. We need to be very clear. There is not a single, homogeneous global women's movement but many different and varied women's movements and protests. Any analysis has to take account of the specific characteristics.

The abortion referendum campaign in Ireland was an offensive struggle to remove a reactionary amendment to the constitution inserted under pressure from the Catholic church in 1983 and to secure the legal right to abortion. The Irish experience is almost unique in the European Union where similar severe abortion restrictions exist only in the north of Ireland and in Malta. We have seen an offensive battle in Argentina, which almost won the right to abortion, and other movements in Latin America around the question of reproductive rights. In Europe and the advanced capitalist countries, however, most of the movements around abortion rights have been defensive struggles against attacks by right-wing bourgeois and populist governments on existing rights, as was the case in Spain under the Rajoy government in 2014 and in Poland more recently. Or, in the case of the USA, mass protests which erupted in anticipation of a further undermining of abortion rights and even a legal assault on Roe v Wade following the election of Trump. There were specific factors in Ireland which contributed to the 'yes' vote in the referendum campaign, most notably the outrage following the death of Savita Halappanavar in 2012, but also the irreparable damage done to the authority of the Catholic church by the widespread child sex abuse scandals.

The control and influence of the Catholic church is still significant in countries such as Poland, the Spanish State, Italy, as well Latin America, and has been a factor in many of the movements that have taken place. In the case of Brazil, the Evangelical churches played a significant role in the election of Bolsonaro. In Italy, 70% of hospital doctors and anaethetists are conscientious objectors, rising to 90% in some regions, seriously undermining the legal right to abortion for many women. In many cases this is due to the control and influence of the church over hospitals and the career prospects of hospital staff. It is also the case that the Catholic fundamentalist wing of the Lega, which forms part of the governing coalition in Italy, has been pushing pro-life legislation at a local level. This is in addition to proposing counter-reforms to the divorce laws, which would make separation more difficult for poorer women and seriously endanger women experiencing domestic violence. These attacks have mobilised hundreds of thousands of women and men. Italy has also seen some of the biggest movements internationally – outside of Latin America – against violence against women, which initially exploded in response to the horrific rape and killing of a young girl in Argentina in 2016.

In Ireland, north and south, as well as in the Spanish State, it has been outrageous judgements and comments in rape trials that have been the trigger for huge protests challenging the reactionary and sexist character of the legal system. But while our comrades in the Spanish State have skilfully put forward demands which link those protests to a critique – not just of the sexism, but also of the class basis of the capitalist legal system – the Irish comrades have limited themselves to demanding the training of judges and juries, which does not bring into question capitalist control of the judiciary. In the same way, while the demand for the separation of church and state is undoubtedly an important democratic demand to raise in Ireland – and other countries where the Catholic church's grip on state institutions such as schools is still strong – we need to go further and raise the transitional demand of democratic working-class control of the education system. Incredibly, when this was raised in the debate at the NC in Greece, Ruth Coppinger replied that no section of the CWI puts forward this demand! This comment shows just how far the Irish comrades have moved away from the transitional method. The transitional programme is not a "fetish" but a fundamental part of the approach of genuine Trotskyists in bridging today's consciousness with the task of the socialist transformation of society.

It is clearly not possible to analyse here all of the many protests which have taken place around aspects of women's oppression, protests that have affected almost every continent of the globe. However, it is important to point out that there are still many countries where a radicalisation around women's oppression may exist but has not as yet expressed itself in significant protests, or indeed in any movements at all. Where movements have arisen, in some cases they have done so spontaneously around single issues and then disappeared again when the protest or movement has finished. In other instances, more lasting structures have been formed, sometimes – as in the case of Argentina and Italy – growing into a broad feminist movement with permanent (horizontal) structures, with a detailed programme and capable of mobilising hundreds of thousands of women and men.

Politically arming the CWI

With such heterogeneous movements and moods it is precisely the task of each section of the CWI to analyse and evaluate the character and perspectives of the movements in their particular countries and on that basis to determine the level and means of intervention or initiatives that can be made, taking into consideration of course the forces we have and the other work we are involved in. The role of the IS is that of providing the sections with the theoretical tools to intervene, not to draw up a one-size fits all blue print that can be applied to every section regardless of the specific conditions in each country.

At the same time, however, the IS has the responsibility and duty to criticise a section when a serious deviation from the basic orientation and method of Marxism has occurred, as is the case in Ireland, and to organise to ensure that such an incorrect method does not become generalised throughout the CWI. The unanimous vote by the Greek NC, in favour of the Irish NEC's document on women's oppression, is a political endorsement of the serious errors that this document contains, errors which have already been outlined in the document "For a Marxist approach to struggles against women's oppression" [see page 105]. Together with the political support for the Irish comrades expressed in the debates in Sweden, Belgium and the USA, it is clear that an incorrect approach and orientation extends well beyond the Irish section, and totally justifies the formation of the IS majority faction.

We have to pose the question to the critics of the IS: what is it about the character of the current global women's movements that negates the IS's and the CWI's previous theoretical analysis of women's oppression? What is it that renders invalid our analysis of how women's struggles are likely to emerge, and what our general orientation and approach to those struggles should be? Although it is never completely spelt out, implicit in the criticisms made of the IS by the Irish majority, and the leaderships of other sections who support them, is the idea that a qualitative change has taken place that requires a fundamental reappraisal of what has gone before. Why is the document, which was unanimously voted on at the plenary session on women's oppression at the 2016 world conference, no longer relevant to the current situation? [see page 223] Although published by the England and Wales section, the book 'It Doesn't Have to be Like This' has been translated into several languages and extensively used as a basis for discussion on women's oppression throughout the CWI. Is there a fundamental difference in these global movements which means that the analysis and general approach to cross-class movements on issues concerning women's oppression outlined in the book is no longer adequate?

This is not year zero. The CWI has years of experience of intervening on the question of women's oppression, experience that we can and should draw on in the current movements. And yet in their document the Irish comrades dismiss those experiences as if they were irrelevant to the present situation. The creation of broad women's organisations or platforms in not something new to the CWI. Initiated by our comrades in England and Wales, the Campaign Against Domestic Violence (CADV) was a broad, structured campaign with conferences and a democratically elected national committee. It had the affiliation of 5 national trade unions and 400 union branches, with many union delegates participating in the national committee. CADV was cited in the IS majority document precisely because of its ability to orientate to the workplaces and trade unions, and therefore raise consciousness about the centrality of the organised working class in changing society and ending oppression. Rosa failed to do this during the abortion referendum campaign.

The basic ideas, strategy and orientation of the CWI regarding women's oppression, as outlined in our international material, retain all their validity for today's struggles. The IS and the IEC have provided the comrades with the theoretical, programmatic and practical tools for intervening in the new women's movements. Unfortunately those tools were not employed in the abortion referendum campaign in Ireland. In the most important and significant struggle that the Irish section has been involved in on the question of women's oppression, a campaign with a potential mass audience for our ideas, the comrades abandoned the transitional method, consciously decided in their main mass produced material to not link the question of abortion to the broader economic and class demands, which would have brought into question the capitalist system and the need for socialism, and made no systematic and organised orientation towards the trade unions or to the key workplaces. As a consequence they missed a vital opportunity to politically challenge the ideas of petty-bourgeois feminism and to raise mass consciousness about what would be necessary to end women's oppression and prepare for the much bigger class battles to come. These were not isolated mistakes but a continuation of previous incorrect approaches; a mistaken method, which not only has not been repudiated, but is politically justified in the Irish NEC's response to the IS document on women's oppression and identity politics.

Cross-class alliances

In their document on women's oppression, and in their verbal contributions in the debate, the Irish majority comrades have placed a lot of emphasis on the working-class composition of the abortion referendum campaign. Generalising once more from their own specific experience,s the comrades write that the global radicalisation of young women "is not a temporary phase, but a more fundamental shift in consciousness and is deeper, in that it is not the preserve of middle-class layers, but is also reflective of a change amongst working-class women." Again we have to be quite clear. All of these movements taking place internationally around the questions of violence against women, reproductive rights, sexism etc, are cross-class movements involving women from both working-class and middle-class backgrounds. Working-class women may be more active in some movements than in others, but it is still the case that in many instances middle-class women are in the leadership. Inevitably these movements will contain competing and conflicting analyses of the causes of the economic, social and cultural oppression that women face, and differing strategies regarding how that oppression can be ended.

There is no doubt that support for repealing the 8th amendment and for the right to abortion in the first 12 weeks of pregnancy was strong in the working-class areas of the south, just as support had been strong in the marriage equality referendum. The vote in both referendums reflected a significant shift in social attitudes and dealt a serious blow to the authority of the Catholic church. But even where the support or participation of women (and men) from a working-class background is quite high, that does not in itself automatically equate with a class consciousness, of an awareness of how oppression is intrinsically linked to class society, or to an understanding of the primacy of the organised working class in overthrowing capitalism and creating a socialist society that could lay the basis for ending exploitation and all forms of oppression.

The conditions unleashed by the economic crisis have created a radicalisation that could potentially lead to the development of a broad anti-capitalist and socialist consciousness, particularily amongst a new generation of young women. But this is far from automatic. There are many positives in these movements, including, of course, the turn towards collective struggle and away from the ideas of individual self-improvement advocated by post-feminism. But the ideas of petty-bourgeois feminism, which locate violence against women in the behaviour and misogyny of individual men or in a macho culture with no understanding of how that culture is intrinsically linked to capitalism and class society, are still very prominent. As are their limited strategies for change, advocating changing behaviour, attitudes, culture and the law, but without challenging the existing system.

Although there are signs of the beginning of change in some countries, these global movements around aspects of women's oppression have mainly been taking place in a period in which the level of collective workplace and industrial struggle has been at an historically low level. As a consequence the importance and centrality of the organised working class in changing society is understandably far from clear.

That is why it has been so necessary to firmly criticise the incorrect method and orientation of the Irish comrades in the abortion referendum campaign, and the uncritical backing given to these from other sections of the CWI. An historic victory was achieved – in that women in Ireland have secured the right to abortion – but in the process the comrades missed a huge opportunity to politically challenge the ideas of petty-bourgeois feminism, and to raise the consciousness of a mass audience.

Working-class women

The participation of working-class women is not unique to the current global women's movement. It is true that middle-class women predominated in the women's liberation movement of the late 60s and 70s, especially in the USA. Like today, this was a diffuse movement that spread from the US to Europe and elsewhere but without any global or, in many cases, national structures. Participation in the conscious raising groups was often quite limited. Women's liberation was a sentiment rather than a mass, unified movement, but one that had a huge effect on consciousness in society, raising awareness about sexism, violence against women, reproduction, the family, the gendered division of labour and sexuality. Whilst riven with significant ideological and strategic divisions, it nonetheless contributed to the passing of important legislation on equal pay, sex discrimination, abortion, divorce etc, and to the setting up of refuges, rape crisis centres, women's health clinics and in some cases local child care facilities.

In countries like Britain the role of the organised working class was very significant in this process. The women's liberation movement developed in parallel with a growing radicalisation and militancy by women in the workplaces and the trade unions around gender inequality, particularily with regards to unequal pay. The historic strike that was begun by female sewing machinists in Fords in Dagenham, Essex, demanding re-grading from unskilled to the equivalent of the (predominantly male) semi-skilled production workers had a seminal effect. This led to further strikes and protests by women over equal pay, and the formation by a group of trade unionists of the National Joint Action Campaign for Women's Rights. Working-class and socialist women participated in the women's liberation meetings and conferences. Strikes and trade union action by women workers had a strong influence on the women's movement and vice-versa. In Italy too, the initial base of the women's movement was middle-class but it rapidly spread to become a large popular movement involving radicalised women workers organised in the trade unions against the general backdrop of mass industrial, social and political unrest.

Working-class women and their organisations also played an important role in many countries in the struggle for women's suffrage, especially in the latter period. Unfortunately in many cases their contribution to the struggle has been hidden from history, leading to the misconception that this was purely a movement of middle-class women. In the North of England, working-class women in the textile industries in particular did not just fight against poverty pay and exploitation at work, but enthusiastically organised to campaign for the vote. They canvassed workplaces collecting signatures and went to the homes of workers after factory hours. In the same way Sylvia Pankhurst attempted to build a mass base for women's suffrage amongst women in the sweatshop industries of London's East End. We should remember that the origin of International Women's Day was the march of women garment workers through New York City's Lower East Side protesting against sweatshop conditions but also demanding the vote. The Congressional Union, one of the most radical suffrage organisations in the US, particularily orientated towards working women.

Cross-class alliances and worker's struggles

Of course, with women making up a much larger part of the workforce in many countries today (over 60% in the EU, for example) they will inevitably play a central role in future struggles of the organised working class. But that is very different from arguing, as the Irish comrades have, that the women's movements – that is, cross-class movements – will be central. Our perspective is one in which mass workers' struggles will once more be to the fore; of huge class battles involving both working women and working men.

Does this perspective mean that when mass workplace and class struggles develop women's movements organised across class lines will disappear? Not at all. Because of the structural, economic and power inequalities on which capitalism is based it will continue to reproduce and reinforce aspects of oppression such as violence against women. More ideological and concrete attacks by right-wing populist governments are likely in the future with the potential for class-class alliances to be formed to resist them. This may not only be against the 'cultural' oppression women face but also against attacks on public services from which middle-class women benefit as well as working-class women. As long as capitalism continues as an economic and social system then the basis for the development of cross-class movements against oppression will always exist.

Today the women's movements and other social movements can appear more significant than they actually are in some countries precisely because of the absence or low level of workplace struggles. This was not the case in the past, where women's movements took place in the context of general industrial and social ferment. In Britain, to give just one example from the 'first wave', between 1910-1914 the women's suffrage protests were taking place during 'the great unrest'. This was a period in which the Liberal government was under siege; civil war looming in Ireland over Home Rule; strikes amongst miners, railworkers and dockers which spread to other sections including tens of thousands of previously unorganised women in the sweated industries. In the words of Trotsky "a shadow of revolution" was hanging over Britain. And of course revolution did break out in 1917 in Russia with international reverberations affecting all aspects of society, including the campaign for the vote.

The 'women's liberation movement' emerged and evolved against the backdrop of the civil rights and black liberation movements and the radicalisation of students against the war in Vietnam. But it was also a period that included the revolutionary strikes of May '68 in France and significant workers' struggles in other European countries such as Italy. Although we cannot give an exact timetable, our perspective is that similar struggles will erupt, notwithstanding the bureaucratisation of the trade union leaders and the failure of new left organisations. In that sense the current global women's movements are an anticipation, a precursor, of much greater future class battles.

In the future we would expect to see an interconnection between cross-class women's movements and mass workers' struggles as in past; the dovetailing of movements against oppression with working-class action in the workplaces, especially given the much higher level of participation of women in the workforce compared to before. Historically cross-class women's movements have always experienced internal ideological and strategical tensions and divisions arising from the class differences within them. The middle-class suffragists wanted to secure the vote to be equal with men of their own class. The working-class suffragists wanted to secure the vote so that they could transform their economic and social conditions through political change. Socialist feminists emphasised the importance of uniting with working-class men to fight capitalism and end oppression, radical feminists moved increasingly in the direction of separatism. Splits along class lines have always been inherent in cross-class social movements and that is likely to continue to be the case now and in the future.

But working-class women have generally moved to take issues regarding gender oppression into their own organisations. The working-class suffragists raised the question of women's suffrage in their trade unions and in the burgeoning socialist organisations. They demanded, with some success (but also facing some resistance), that those organisations support the campaign for the vote. Women trade unionists in the '2nd wave' fought for issues such as abortion and sexual harassment to become trade union issues in the same way that the CADV was able to make domestic violence a trade union issue in the 1990s.

More recently we have seen the extremely important strike by female Glasgow council workers who successfully achieved equal pay through militant strike action, securing the solidarity of male workers in other sections of the council. In the MacDonald's strike in the US and in the international Google walk outs, #MeToo moved from social media to the workplaces. Of course, both equal pay and sexual harassment are clearly workplace issues. Our role has to be to ensure that the current movements around issues of women's oppression that are less workplace related – such as gender violence and abortion – are nonetheless orientated to the workplaces and the trade unions, precisely because it is the organised working class which will be central in future struggles to change society. The way in which we were able to use Libres y Combativas and the School Students Union in the Spanish State to put pressure on the unions to call for general strike action on 8th March is an indication of what is possible.

The current international women's movements are taking place in a different objective situation from past movements. The economic crisis has lead to an important radicalisation amongst some sections of society, which has been reflected in an increase in social movements, most notably around the question of women's oppression. But, with some exceptions, we have not seen mass strike action and struggles by the organised working class in most countries. There are already signs that this is beginning to change but we cannot say how long the present situation will continue. There is however, nothing in the movements today, no qualitative or fundamental change that invalidates our previous analysis of women's oppression, of cross-class women's movements and how we should relate and orientate to them. While cross-class movements around women's oppression will undoubtedly continue to develop in the future, the central role in future struggles will be that of the working class.

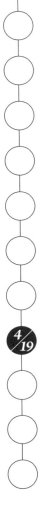

NEW MOVEMENTS VS OLD TRUTHS?

Hannah Sell, for the IS majority

The debate that has taken place in the CWI over recent months has been unprecedented both for the enormous number of words produced by the 'Non-Faction Faction' (NFF) and by their complete failure to seriously engage with the political arguments that we, the 'In Defence of a Working-Class, Trotskyist CWI' faction (IDWCTCWI), have put forward.

The starting point of the CWI, as with all serious revolutionary organisations, is our ideas; our programme and our method. When a major faction fight develops, as is the case now, the roots of it are always to be found in political errors. Every member of our international who wants to defend and strengthen our party has a duty to try to draw out the underlying political issues, taking the arguments of the opposition seriously and trying to follow them through to their conclusions in order to raise the level of understanding of the whole organisation. Instead the NFF endlessly evade doing so, concentrating on arguments about the premature establishment of a faction, or a 'bad method' or undemocratic regime. We do not accept their arguments on any of these issues, but they are a diversion from the real questions at stake. A bad regime always has as its starting point a wrong political approach.

What does the NFF consider our wrong political approach to consist of? They think that we are conservative regarding struggles against women's oppression, that we are 'retreating to safe ground' and we are incapable of measuring up to the 'new period'. Of course, no matter what its historical record, there is no guarantee that any revolutionary party will be able to measure up to new challenges. We face a constant need to develop our programme on the basis of experience, above all of the class struggle. However, a serious opposition is duty bound not to just throw out accusations but to justify them and point towards how the mistakes can be corrected. So far the NFF have been utterly incapable of this because to clearly state their disagreements would expose their real political trajectory.

After more than five months of debate the NFF have proved themselves to be, as Trotsky said of the 1938 opposition in the US SWP, "a typical petty-bourgeois tendency". His description of that opposition sums up the NFF particularly in its "disdainful attitude towards theory and an inclination towards eclecticism" and "disrespect for the tradition of their own organisation."

This is shown again in Socialist Feminism and Class Struggle by NFF supporters Elin Gauffin (EG – IEC member for Sweden) and Cédric Gerome (CG – alternate IS member).

This reply is a response to the central points in that dishonest document. It also takes up some of the points raised by Women and the Struggle for Socialism Today, the document by Jess Spears, Diana O'Dwyer and Aprille Scully (JS/DO'D/AS), three members of the Transform the Party (TTP) faction in Ireland.

Nothing is stated clearly in the NFF document by EG/CG. They hint that there are new questions which the theoretical arsenal of the CWI is not equipped to deal with, arguing that "New questions are being raised and discussed in the current movements and among the youth that can't simply be answered by referring to the past legacy of the CWI, however precious and valuable this legacy is". Unfortunately JS/DO'D/AS (TTP) argue along the same lines that we need to do far more "adapting and sharpening that fundamental Marxist analysis to apply it most effectively to today's events" and there is a "danger of Marxists resting on an old analysis and defending old truths".

However, nowhere do either of these documents explain clearly what the new phenomena are, never mind how the CWI's analysis should be corrected. In our view, while there are important developments relating to radicalisation around gender oppression which we have turned to and addressed, none of them require a fundamental reassessment of our analysis. If the authors of either document disagree, they are duty bound to say so openly and to specify where and in what way, drawing conclusions about what this means for our programme and approach in concrete struggles. Neither document does this.

In the case of the EG/CGs (NFF) document, we draw the conclusion from the limited arguments they put and their uncritical defence of the approach of the Irish majority that they believe the IS should lead the whole of the CWI down the road taken by the Irish section.

EG/CGs (NFF) document does exactly what we raised there was a danger of in the first document, seeing "all struggles through the prism of the women's movement". Why else does it have a section entitled, "the current period of women's movements" which lists a whole host of movements in which women have played an important role including the "mass revolutionary struggle" in Algeria and the "women workers' strikes on wages and other conditions" such as "the US teachers, the Irish nurses/midwives, the strike against wage discrimination in Glasgow, the hospital strikes in Germany, the textile workers in Bangladesh"?

We agree that women workers have played a vital role in all these struggles, and that in some cases they were overwhelmingly dominant. Nonetheless, none of these struggles can be defined primarily as being "women's movements". Women played an important role in the Russian revolution, more recently in the 'Arab Spring', and in numerous other revolutionary movements. Nonetheless, we would never have characterised any of them as 'women's movements'. The participants' aspirations have usually included an ending of different aspects of women's oppression, but combined with other demands. Had the Bolsheviks treated the 1917 revolution as a women's movement they would never have been able to lead the working class – of all genders – to take power.

Nor are the strikes listed actually 'women's movements'. To categorise them in this way is both mistaken and divisive. It is our role to fight for the maximum unity of the working class around a fighting programme. We have to be the hardest fighters against every aspect of oppression, and strive to ensure every struggle features the demands of all sections of workers involved. We also have to be very sensitive to groups of strikers who see their struggle primarily as a fight of women or black workers, rather than as a more general struggle of the working class. For a Marxist organisation to act to emphasis or deepen divisions or separatist tendencies is, however, criminal.

We should laud the role played by militant women workers in these strikes, but without ignoring the role played by male strikers who are also taking part. Nor should we suggest that the primary reason that the strikers are having to take action is because they are exploited as women, rather than the reality – that they are exploited as workers but suffer double-oppression as women. This disastrous approach was taken by the SWP in Birmingham in England, where they made the central issue in a strike of low paid, mainly female, home care workers the question of their gender, including stunts where the women dressed as men to point towards their work being low paid because they were women. This was combined with a failure to make solidarity appeals to other, mainly male, local authority workers – like the refuse collectors – who had recently been involved in militant and successful strike action. It is correct to point out that work that is traditionally done by women tends to be lower paid as a result of women workers' double oppression, but not in a way that suggests that it is male workers, rather than the employers, who are responsible for this.

Why does it matter if workers' strikes or even revolutionary movements are wrongly categorised as women's struggles? Firstly, because it leads to wrong conclusions about the nature of struggle in this period, secondly because it will leave us facing in the wrong direction when future mass struggles of the working class erupt, and finally because it leads to the kind of fundamental programmatic mistakes that are now being made by the Irish section and others. EG/CG (NFF) ask in paragraph 61 if the logic of the IS majority position is that, "the fight against sexism and gender oppression should take a back seat" so as not to "put off workers"? They draw this inference from the IS document from November [Women's Oppression and Identity Politics - the CWI's approach; see page 91] that warns of the danger in the Irish section, that "as a result of the overwhelming turn that has been made to issues relating to women and gender oppression – we could become perceived by a layer of workers for whom that is not the only or primary concern as 'not for them'".

At the time the Irish majority acted with outrage that they could be perceived in such a way. Yet look at their current campaign in the European elections. The comrades have used the fact they are standing with a higher Socialist Party profile to argue that they are correcting their mistakes. This does not help at all if the programme they are standing on is not that of the CWI. The candidate Rita Harrold, is standing as a 'socialist feminist voice for Europe'. Her programme, as described on the Irish Socialist Party's website consists of the following headlines, (each headline is followed by a brief paragraph of text which are commented on, but not included in full, here):

• Opposition to gender-based violence
• Public services. The accompanying paragraph does correctly call for free childcare and the development of a national health service, but there are no other concrete demands. The whole paragraph is written with a focus on women. The second sentence, for example reads: "Sexist ideas about caring roles, parenting and "women's work" means that the needs of parents, especially lone mothers, and the important work of childcare professionals are criminally undervalued."

• System change not climate change
• A rigged system. The brief paragraph here correctly talks about the need to break with 'a rigged capitalist system' which has caused a housing crisis and low pay. The emphasis, however, is not on how it exploits the working-class majority but on how it is a "system that promotes sexism, racism, homophobia and transphobia".
• For a socialist Europe. This concludes by with a call "to build the socialist feminist movement".

This programme is wholly inadequate. It is very clearly aimed exclusively at a section of mainly young people who are radicalised around gender issues and on the question of the environment. We are fully in favour of raising demands to appeal to this layer, but not above all others. Rita's programme is not designed to appeal to workers of any gender whose main concerns are housing, wages, pensions, or austerity in general. Nor does it give any pointers towards the role of the working class in fighting for social change.

EG/CG (NFF) suggest that we are arguing to downplay the need to fight against sexism so as not to put off 'sexist workers', but this is a complete misunderstanding of our position. We were arguing that our programme has to aim to unify all the heterogeneous layers of the working class, taking up the issues that are important to different sections. This does not in any way mean 'soft-peddling' on issues of oppression because of conservative or reactionary ideas that inevitably exist among sections of the working class, but it does mean putting forward a programme that is not exclusively aimed at the layer who are radicalised primarily on issues of oppression.

In doing so we are also educating the layer who are radicalised on issues of oppression about how to reach out to other sections of the working class, even including a layer with some reactionary ideas. As Marxists we understand that consciousness is not fixed. Workers who have swallowed some of the reactionary 'muck' of capitalism – racism, sexism and homophobia – can change their approach on the basis of workers' struggle. The gilet jaunes movement in France, despite its confused character, demonstrated this with groups of white workers started rejecting racism as they experienced organising alongside migrants. Putting a programme that has the potential to unify the working class should be automatic for the CWI. Even though we are not yet a big enough force to have, in general, an effect on the mass of the working class, we are still aiming to educate the minority we can reach on the approach needed to do so.

Clearly, however, the Irish majority have completely retreated from the CWI's approach. Unfortunately, the fact that the Irish European election programme has been praised in the US and elsewhere is an indication that others in the NFF are on the same road. In EG/CG's (NFF) document, the comrades suggest that our approach, "can create the danger of dismissing a layer of mainly young women radicalised by gender oppression as something bad that can destroy the revolutionary programme rather than be part of it". We agree with reaching out to, and attempting to win to our revolutionary party, young people radicalised by gender oppression, but we do not agree with uncritically adopting their ideas rather than convincing them of ours. That, however, unfortunately is now clearly the approach of large elements of the NFF.

Reflecting petit-bourgeois academic feminism
The comrades are reflecting the approach of a layer of petit-bourgeois academic feminists.

Unfortunately, the document Women and the Struggle for Socialism Today by JS/DO'D/ AS, from the Irish TTP faction, while it makes useful points on the abortion referendum, also reflects this approach. While they agree with some of our criticisms of the Irish majority they go on to say our position, "contains a danger of a workerist approach to intervening in the women's movement, eg putting a heavy focus on economic demands, and seems to lack recognition of the new challenges we face in a landscape dominated by identity politics". They argue that "a third approach is necessary: one that starts with a more comprehensive analysis of the material and cultural changes that have taken place in the last 40 years, including the ideas that have become prominent". They criticise our analysis of identity politics saying there is a "big gap in our understanding of how identity politics (and the class interests it represents) have gained a foothold in this new wave in the context of a fundamentally different objective situation, of ongoing capitalist crisis and a historically weakened labour movement".

We think we have analysed and drawn the main conclusions that are necessary on the central issues that JS/DO'D/AS (TTP) raise. There is not space here to give more than a thumbnail sketch of why support for identity politics has grown. The central reasons are the general features that define the current era. Firstly, the crisis of capitalism and the decades of attacks on workers living standards in many countries, which have intensified enormously since the start of the 2007-08 crisis. This, as we have repeatedly explained, has fuelled enormous anger against 'the existing order' which is leading the capitalist class to fear for their future, leading the founder of the world's biggest hedge fund to declare that capitalism created such inequality it had to "evolve or die" because otherwise they would face "some kind of revolution".

That they have not already faced revolution reflects the legacy of the previous era. While consciousness about the need for an alternative to capitalism has increased under the impact of the crisis, levels of working class organisation and socialist consciousness have not recovered from the consequences of the collapse of Stalinism. It is therefore no surprise that, while important struggles have developed in different countries against different oppressions, the mass of participants in them do not clearly see the necessity, never mind the possibility, of overthrowing capitalism to achieve their goals. Nor do they easily see the need to look to the working class as a force for social change, as they have not yet experienced even a glimpse of its potential power.

In its broadest sense 'identity politics' is not new at all. We've been arguing against it in different forms since our inception, as did our predecessors. What was Lenin's opposition to the programme of the Bund, with its elements of bourgeois nationalism and claims to be the sole representative of the Jewish proletariat in Russia, if not opposition to a form of identity politics? When we argued, ultimately unsuccessfully, against 'black sections' in the Labour Party in the 1980s, we were arguing against a form of identity politics. As we warned, the setting up of black sections did not increase participation of black and Asian workers in the Labour Party, but did act to promote a layer of petty-bourgeois careerists. When we had the opportunity, we demonstrated our approach in practise. In Liverpool City Council we were able to create thousands of jobs and gave particular priority to black youth who suffered the highest levels of unemployment.

The difficulties in combatting identity politics in this period are not primarily to do with its special characteristics, but with the general problems of relatively low working class consciousness and organisation. Further experience of events will lead to leaps forward in consciousness. We can play an important role, however, in speeding that process up by raising demands that link the struggle against specific oppressions to the need for mass working class struggle for socialism. The most important thing we need to do to win layers who are radicalised, but influenced by identity politics, is not to study the detail of the latest academic theories of identity politics, but to put forward a fighting programme which expresses the aspirations of those radicalised layers and to strive to convince them, in practise where we can, of the need for united working class struggle to achieve it. JS/DO'D/AS (TTP) quote Lenin on winning women making exactly this vital point, that we need to raise, "demands that are no more than practical conclusions, drawn by us from the crying needs and disgraceful humiliations that weak and underprivileged women must bear under the bourgeois system".

Trotsky wrote in 1937 about how "reactionary epochs [act to] lower the general ideological level of the movement and throw political thinking back to stages long since passed through". He went on to explain how the task of a revolutionary party in such conditions is, "not to let itself be carried along by the backward flow: it must swim against the current". He concluded, "Fools will consider this policy 'sectarian'. Actually it is the only means of preparing for a new tremendous surge forward with the coming historical tide". Today we face different conditions. As we have explained elsewhere, under the impact of the global economic crisis we have seen a general undermining of the authority of capitalist institutions and radicalisation taking place. Nonetheless, the legacy of the previous epoch remains, and means that there is not yet, in general, the development of mass workers' parties, and the new formations which do exist have very limited programmes and often a predominately petty-bourgeois character. The CWI successfully swam against the current in the 'reactionary epoch' which followed the collapse of Stalinism. It would be criminal if we were now to throw away our programme and methods in favour of reflecting the ideas of the first hesitant and inexperienced waves of radicalisation, instead of intervening in them with a clear programme in order to prepare for a 'new tremendous surge forward'.

The biggest problem with JS/DO'D/AS's (TTP) document is not that it poses many unanswered questions but where it looks for answers. One of the key paragraphs in the document is point 70 which states, in relation to social reproduction theory specifically, and "contemporary anti-capitalist and socialist feminist theories explaining women's oppression" in general: "The lack of open debate around these ideas illustrates how their needs to be a cultural shift in the party and the international towards more open discussion of new ideas and theories on the left to see what is useful and what is not rather than largely limiting ourselves to historical materials we overwhelmingly agree with but which may have limited applicability to current political questions, in particular developing a Marxist approach towards identity politics".

There is a good reason we focus on "historical materials", and in our view declaring their "limited applicability" today is an indication of a lack of understanding, or even agreement with, their central tenets. In the key works of Marx, Engels, Lenin and Trotsky the central lessons of the struggle for socialism up until their deaths is summed up. Of course much has taken place since, but we apply the same method; it is not for nothing that the CWI's statutes start by saying: "The Committee for a Workers' International stands on the foundations of the ideas of Marx, Engels, Lenin and Trotsky; of the main decisions of the first four Congresses of the Communist International; of the Founding Conference of the Fourth International; and the documents of the Marxist movement since 1938."

We have to constantly update our analysis on the basis of events but in doing so we learn primarily from the real struggles of the working class. We never assume that we are the only ones that have drawn the same conclusions as us on the tasks facing the working class. On the contrary we are sure that others will do so, if not yet on the basis of experience. Their ranks will not include, however, academic Marxists who have not put themselves on the standpoint of the working class, and who do not accept the most basic lessons of the struggle so far: on the need to break with capitalism, the central role of the working class, and the vital role of a revolutionary party.

Social reproduction theory

The specific example of 'contemporary socialist feminist theory' that Women and Socialism focus on is social reproduction theory. This is not actually contemporary; it was developed by Italian 'autonomist' Marxist feminists and others in the 1970s. Nonetheless, its resurgence in a slightly different form among a layer of feminists, including the authors of the 'Feminism for the 99%' manifesto, does reflect a turn to the left among many of the new generation of feminists. We should therefore take it up sympathetically, as Christine Thomas has done in the May 2019 edition of Socialism Today. Nonetheless, it does not offer new insights into the oppression of women. The original advocates of social reproduction theory attempted to 'improve' Marx by arguing that unpaid domestic labour does not just have a use value but also an exchange value and therefore forms part of capitalist economic relations. This was not only theoretically wrong but led to wrong demands – particularly wages for housework which reinforced traditional gender divisions.

Today, most advocates of social reproduction theory do not take this theoretical stance. They have varied views, and endless debates, on exactly how to define their theory. Their general approach, however, is to argue that the creation and maintenance of labour power (ie giving birth to, bringing up and caring for future and current workers) is central to the functioning of capitalism and that therefore those – mainly women – who are responsible for this have considerable power to challenge capitalism. Commonly they also include women workers in fields such as paid domestic work, childcare and healthcare as part of the sphere of social reproduction. Some include all social struggles – such as the struggle against climate change – as part of this sphere.

Capitalism created, for the first time, a division between paid work outside the home and unpaid work within it. It is true of course that this unpaid work is vital for capitalism and an enormous burden on working class families, primarily women. Capitalism's drive to commodify every aspect of human existence has meant a tendency in one sense to shrink the sphere of unpaid work at home. The first and second generation of workers uprooted from a past as poor peasants would still tend to grow some vegetables, keep chickens etc. Today, a least in the advanced capitalist countries, with all adults in most families forced to take waged work outside the home to make ends meet - many barely get to cook never mind grow their own produce. At the same time the burden placed on the family is increasing. The shrinking of the 'social wage' means that tasks previously carried out by the public sector, such as care for the elderly and the sick, have been thrust back onto the family, primarily onto women. On the one hand this has increased the commodification of those tasks – carried out either by domestic servants at home or outsourced to private care homes – but for working class families who cannot afford to pay, it has enormously added to their burden.

The double burden therefore suffered by working class women is absolutely clear. This does not mean, however, that women in the home are in a powerful position to challenge capitalism. On the contrary, going on strike from domestic tasks in the home – as social reproduction theorists have proposed - can only ever have a limited symbolic effect. It does not offer a means to fight for the only effective way to lift the burden on women - socialisation of unpaid work in the home via the provision of public services and living benefits for those not in work.

That is not to suggest that that the only battle that matters is between capital and labour in manufacturing workplaces. Most social reproduction theorists would accuse 'traditional' Marxists of having this approach. In doing so they are reacting – understandably – to the approach of Stalinism, but are grossly caricaturing genuinely 'traditional' Marxism. While it is true that workers in manufacturing workplaces are in a particularly powerful position due to the highly productive character of their labour it has never been the case that this is the only arena of struggle that matters. Struggles of workers in the public sector – who, however socially-useful their jobs – are not productive from the point of view of capitalism, can nonetheless have a major effect including, indirectly, on the profits of the capitalist class. Public sector teachers' strikes, for example, in the modern era, often mean parents working for private companies have to stay at home thereby hitting the capitalists' profits. In addition struggles outside of the workplace – such as rent strikes, campaigns for affordable food, or for public services – have also been an important element of working class struggle since the dawn of capitalism, and have often been led by women.

We have never taken the approach that only those who work – never mind only those who work in manufacturing – make up the ranks of the working class. In the past a big proportion of workers – whatever their gender – was likely to sell their ability to work in a factory. Today particularly in the advanced capitalist countries, millions still work in factories but there are others working in different fields who, nonetheless, produce new value. Others again work in the public sector or don't work but are part of the working class because of their social outlook and their economic situation – their wage level and standard of living, etc. Working class women who labour in the home to bring up children, care for the elderly etc but do not have paid employment would come into this category.

However, the conclusions drawn by social reproduction theorists do not offer any clear way forward. They tend to argue for a turn to a 'new form' of class struggle – such as the 8 March women strikes – which combine both strikes in the home and of women in paid work. How such action could be effective and what its exact goals should be is not made clear but implicit is that women's struggle is the central factor in this new era. They often also echo the intersectionalists by listing other struggles of migrant workers, LGBTQ+, environmentalists and others who should be linked up with. Unfortunately it is clear that the Irish majority have also moved in this direction. We, of course, agree that these struggles should link up, but point to the need to break with capitalism, and the central role of the working class in achieving this because of its role in production and therefore potential collective power.

JS/DO'D/AS criticise the IS for not "emphasising the huge change forced upon capitalism over the last decades in relation to LGBTQ+ people" and similarly that "the IS assertion that identity politics are 'at bottom'… used by the ruling class to obscure class divisions, is raised in an extremely one-sided way" and that this "does not help us understand why 'capitalism has adapted' to any of their demands in the dark period that lies behind us". It seems that in these sections the comrades are arguing that identity politics has, up to a point, played a positive role in winning improved rights for women, LGBTQ+ people and others, and that we do not recognise this.

Why have women and LGBTQ+ people been able to win greater rights in recent decades? A central factor is the mass struggles that have taken place which have forced concessions from the capitalist class. We have always recognised the importance of such struggles. That is why we said in the November 2018 document [page 91] that, "in one sense, identity politics can be an inevitable part of the political awakening of many members of oppressed groups within society. Recognising that you are oppressed, and that you can fight against oppression through a common struggle with others who share the same oppression is a vital first step". To take up mistaken ideas in a struggle, and to argue that past battles would have been far stronger had they had a clear programme and orientation to the working class, is not to suggest that they were unimportant. The US civil rights movement, for example, was a mass struggle which clearly had seismic effects, but that never prevented us pointing out its programmatic limitations. The women's liberation movement in the 1970s was dominated by the petty bourgeois and was of a limited size in organised form, but we rightly credit it with having helped give women, including working class women, confidence to fight on a number of issues.

In reality, the struggles which helped win the gains of women in particular were not, in fact, mainly in the current era. It was the second 'feminist wave', and crucially in many countries working-class action, which was central to winning the big elements of legal equality in many countries which were a factor in paving the way for the situation today. The single biggest reason for the changes that have taken place though is the increased drawing of women into the workforce which has given women more confidence to demand equality. JS/DO'D/AS (TtP) refer to needing more analysis of the "material and cultural changes that have taken place in the last 40 years" but those decades cover very different periods. It was the post-war upswing, with its changed class balance of forces, and then the structural changes to capitalism which took place in the subsequent decades which saw the steepest increase in women working in the advanced capitalist countries. This laid the basis for 'post-feminism' – the idea that women were on the verge of winning equality, which has been shattered by the capitalist economic crisis.

The increase in women working also inevitably tended to undermine the capitalist institution of the family with the development of more varied living arrangements, including single parent families, acceptance of LGBTQ+ rights and so on. This is not, in itself, a threat to the capitalist class, who, provided they can still offload the responsibility for bringing up the next generation onto working class households, can cope with their more varied character, and, of course, attempt to profit from them via the 'pink pound' etc. Women, however, continue to bear the brunt of responsibility for domestic tasks and to suffer lower pay. Nor is capitalism capable of overcoming the reactionary ideas that have been ingrained over millennia, even though positive legal changes have taken place. On the contrary, sections of the capitalist class can consciously use such backward ideas to try and shore up their social base.

All of these points are part of the political arsenal of the leadership of the CWI which the NFF are trying to distort beyond all recognition. That doesn't stop them plagiarising it, however! The leadership of the US section, for example, have a new book on women which lifts wholesale a series of chapters explaining women's oppression from 'It doesn't have to be like this', the book on the issue produced by the England and Wales section and written by Christine Thomas, a supporter of the IDWCTCWI faction. Unfortunately, while the NFF avoid theorising their move away from the approach of the CWI, instead reprinting it for lack of a worked out alternative, their constant attacks on it – the claims of the IS majority's conservatism, hesitancy and dismissal of movements against women's oppression – reflect their real political trajectory towards identity politics.

Answering the distortions in the Socialist Feminism document

They attempt to disguise this with false attacks on our position. Unfortunately, we feel it is necessary to answer the central distortions raised in the final part of this document. For example, EG/CG (NFF) correctly say we have repeatedly pointed to the 2016 World Congress discussion on women, and the document unanimously agreed at it, to demonstrate that the IS takes struggles against women's oppression very seriously, and had a longstanding worked-out theoretical approach which was briefly summarised in that document. We have asked the NFF to show in what way it is 'conservative' and they have been unable to do so. Instead EG/CG (NFF) resort to saying that, "in reality there were many amendments and changes to that text. The outcome was a collective product that showed the strength of the CWI". This is a transparent attempt to claim that the document did not represent the views of the IS majority. Of course, as is very often the case with documents agreed at world congresses, there were a number of amendments from different sections on which agreement was reached with the IS in a process of discussion. Nonetheless, of the 4,343 words in the final document only 673 were additions to the original IS draft, none of them on the central points. The document was agreed by the whole of the IS, including CG who did not make any amendments to it.

EG/CG (NFF) argue that, "In fact, the control of women's sexuality is central to the origins of women's oppression, as first analysed by Engels. We think that the IS majority does not appreciate enough the importance of these issues." Yet this point is ABC for our organisation and was briefly summarised in the IS draft of the world congress document which deals with the origins of women's oppression and situation today, stating: "the idea remains deeply ingrained that women are the possessions of men who need to be loyal and obedient to their partners. The whole of society is permeated with propaganda endlessly re-emphasising the 'proper' role of women – as home-makers, mothers, sexual objects, peacemakers and so on". It goes on to describe how violence against women, and the threat of violence, "remains deeply embedded".

What concrete examples do they give to show that we do not take the suppression of women's sexuality seriously? They say, "the most striking example of the IS majority's downplaying of the issues of sexual oppression is the rather dismissive approach adopted to the #metoo wave, so rarely mentioned in the faction's speeches or writings." The only concrete example they can give is one article by a US comrades which, when it was published in the England and Wales paper, was edited, apparently to "carefully cut out any mention of #metoo". The edit of this one article has been used numerous times in the debate, showing the paucity of other examples. Never mind the articles the Socialist has carried taking up the questions of sexual harassment and abuse. For example, in its material for IWD this year, where the Socialist called for campaigns and mass action on the campuses and in the workplaces to stop sexual harassment. Nor is comment made on what we said on #metoo in the November IS document [page 91], for example: "The #metoo phenomenon has, on a global basis, highlighted an increased determination by women to refuse to accept sexual harassment and abuse. While in many countries it has, so far, remained mainly at the level of a social media campaign, in others it has led to movements on the streets. In a whole series of countries, from Ireland to Argentina to Spain and now India, very important movements against different aspects of women's oppression have taken place and are still taking place." Do the comrades think this is an unbalanced approach?

On the edited article, we do not think it is reasonable to draw conclusions from the edit of one article, carried out under the pressure of producing a weekly paper. Nonetheless, the edits that were made were not to "cut out any mention of #metoo" but to rebalance the descriptions of its 'power' as a 'movement', when it still remained more of a mood than an active movement on the streets, as it still is in most countries. We also made other changes, for example pointing to the undemocratic role of the US Senate and Supreme Court which was not mentioned in the original. This twisting of the facts is comparable to the dirty attempts to claim that a suggestion made by an IS member with responsibility for the international website that a 1,675 word article on the Belfast rugby rape trial should have one sentence about the accused's high profile 'apology' – not to give it validity but to expose it – has been used outrageously to try and claim we downplay the importance of sexual violence.

To justify their accusations of conservatism they resort to ripping partial quotes out of context and giving them meanings that they never had. The November IS document [page 91] was written, at the invitation of the Irish majority, to outline in writing our initial concerns about the approach that the Irish majority were taking to movements against women's oppression. It was not, and was never meant to be, a rounded-out summary of our overall position, hence it including a link to the world congress document in the first paragraph. Nonetheless, EG/CG (NFF) make completely inaccurate assertions about its content.

For example, in paragraph 9 EG/CG (NFF) state: "The first IS majority document emphasised the 'lack of a social base at this stage for launching attacks on women's or LBGTQ+ rights in a number of countries'. This has to be nuanced." It does, and it was! The full quote was in a section sub-titled, "varying approaches of the capitalists" which spent three paragraphs describing how "we should expect movements [against women's oppression] to take place wherever significant sections of the capitalist class attacks women's rights or have an openly reactionary approach to gender-related oppression." It then made a contrast with Britain pointing out that "there is clearly a radicalisation around women's oppression – which it is important we respond to" but that "it is not automatic [HS emphasis] that the mood becomes a movement". In other words movements were possible, even likely, but not guaranteed. It went on to state that, "Nonetheless, in Britain and other countries, the lack of a social base at this stage for launching new attacks on women's or LGBTQ+ rights means that the major capitalist parties are unlikely to move in this direction in the short term." Only by ripping half a sentence out of context have the authors been able to find a point which needs 'more nuance'.

The same method is used throughout the document. To give another example, it quotes the November IS document [page 91] as saying that the radicalisation on gender issues, "flows from the experience of a generation who have grown up in the age of austerity" and comments that, "This is true to a large extent, but insufficient". In this they appear to differ from the Irish majority. Kevin McLoughlin, national organiser of the Irish section, has said that we were "completely wrong" to suggest there was an "anti-austerity element to the referendum vote", yet EG/CG (NFF) make no criticism of the Irish comrades approach, instead pointing to our 'insufficiency' on the basis of half a sentence as if that was all the document said! They then suggest we have belatedly rounded out our position, pointing out we referred to the "'current economic, social and political crisis of capitalism' and the undermining of the ruling class institutions, including the Catholic church" in our second document [For a Marxist Approach; see page 105].

They proudly proclaim that, "this latter point has been emphasised by the Irish comrades from the beginning". In fact the Irish comrades have rightly pointed to the role of the Catholic church but have denied the connection between economic crisis and the undermining of the institutions of capitalism. By contrast we gave an accurate explanation of the current wave of radicalisation even in that first brief document, explaining how legal gains in many countries came into sharp conflict with, "the effects of the economic crisis which, of course, has hit women particularly hard. At the same time, all the problems of sexual harassment and violence remained and were in sharp conflict with women's equality". We went onto explain that: "In Spain, the remnants of Francoism, with its brutal repression of women and dominance of the Catholic Church, means that issues of women's oppression are particularly strongly felt. In that sense there is a similarity with Ireland, where the state has since its inception been intertwined with the Catholic church, meaning that movements on these issues are inevitable and fuelled by the deep-seated anger with the capitalist establishment." Of course these points could be developed further, as they were in the second IS document, but it is ridiculous to try and build a case on our failure to understand the role of the Catholic church from the first document.

The dirtiest 'red herring' in EG/CG's (NFF) document is in paragraph 83, where they try to equate the IDWCTCWI, and Peter Taaffe in particular, with the Stalinist tradition to "see men as the real workers and women as the supplemental earners. Counterposing these 'groups' to the working class could give the impression that we stand for the caricatural image of the working class as being male, white, heterosexual and unconcerned by issues of gender oppression and race." And on what basis is this sweeping assertion made, which flies in the face of the approach of the CWI? Because of an alleged "recurrent reductionism to describe women as a 'group'". In fact neither of the two documents written by the IS majority and the IDWCTCWI on women's oppression say any such thing. This entire edifice is based on a verbal contribution by Peter Taaffe, where they quote him as saying: "the struggles of these discontented groups like the gays, the blacks, the women, but who do not have the power of the working class". EG/CG (NFF) then respond to this quote by saying, "How can half the population be a group? Men are not described as a group" This is juvenile stuff. The phrase 'group' does not automatically refer to a minority, but in any case what point are EG/CG (NFF) making? Peter was referring to sections of society who are oppressed under capitalism (as clearly men are not on the basis of their gender) but who do not have the power to overthrow it through their efforts alone. For that they have to align themselves with the collective power of the working class. To suggest that stating this basic truth is to argue that these 'discontented groups' are unimportant, or that a majority of them are not also members of the working class, suffering as Marx described it double or even triple oppression, is laughable.

Unfortunately, however, it reflects the descent into identity politics that has taken place in the NFF. Many activists in the CWI have experienced the attempt by our political opponents to use identity politics to prevent debate on our ideas on the grounds that a Marxist analysis and programme equals an attempt to oppress them. These methods are used not only against us but others on the left. What else is the attempt to use false claims of both anti-Semitism and sexism against Jeremy Corbyn by the right-wing of the Labour Party? Unfortunately the NFF documents are full of smears that use the same method. Only uncritical adulation of the movements against women's oppression is acceptable. This bears no resemblance to Marxism!

Any attempt to give an objective, scientific description of the movements that have taken place against women's oppression is given as an example of us not taking them seriously. Ludicrously, in the Irish majority 'setting the record straight part one' for example, a list of quotes from the IS majority are given to show how, had they been adopted "it is likely that now there wouldn't be abortion on request up to 12 weeks free through the health service" in Ireland. Among the various spurious quotes they give is our description of the movement for abortion rights, and other similar movements, being "cross-class". This statement of a basic material fact is used to suggest we are somehow demeaning the importance of the movement.

Now in this latest document the authors attack us for apparently suggesting that the repeal referendum in Ireland, "qualified as a bourgeois-democratic plebiscite". We can't find anywhere we've used that exact phrase, but it is nonetheless a statement of plain fact. Do we therefore underestimate its importance? Of course not. The winning of abortion rights in Ireland was a significant victory for the working class. Nonetheless, we understand that elections and referendums are – compared to mass movements on the streets, never mind general strikes or revolutions – a low level of class struggle. This is just as true of other very significant referendums – on Scottish independence or Brexit for example. This did not prevent our sections, correctly, devoting considerable energies to them.

In conclusion, the NFF should stop distorting our approach on the question of women's oppression and instead state clearly and plainly what their own is, describing not just what the 'new questions and issues' are that they currently vaguely refer to, but what their answers are.

ASIA AND IDENTITY POLITICS

Jagadish Chandra (India), Ravi Chandra (Malaysia), Srinath Perera (Sri Lanka), Siri Jayasuriya (Sri Lanka), CWI IEC members

The undersigned IEC members from India, Sri Lanka, and Malaysia fully support the ID-CWTCWI platform, particularly re-emphasising the points made in the fourth and fifth paragraphs [see page 3]. We co-founded the IDWCTCWI faction at the IEC, as we believed that it was neccessary to defend the CWI from an incorrect orientation, strategy and methods.

Even though a number of comrades who are not part of the faction vehemently argued at that time against the formation of a faction – claiming that there is no political basis – now they have been proved wrong. As the new year unfolded, the comrades who oppose the faction are frantically active, with documents being written revealing fundamental differences on a number of political positions.

In the CWI sections in the Asian region, particularly in South Asia, we are numerically small at present, primarily owing to the complex political situations with which we have been dealing for decades – the questions that today have become the central to the debate in our international. Without the sharp political direction and clarity of perspectives that the leadership of the CWI has provided, we would have been lost long ago, either to the easy attractions of liberal bourgeois politics, or to lucrative careers as NGO activists.

But it was the dogged explanations – on the centrality of the working class – that gave us the necessary tools to navigate through the sectarianism, communalism, ultra-right-wing nationalism, religious fanaticism, grotesque racism ie casteism etc. We have faced up to the pernicious influences; Stalinism and Maoism – bought and sold as Marxism; and bourgeois liberalism – camouflaged as secularism and progressivism. This has been in a period of significant ideological retreat, following the collapse of the Soviet Union.

In Sri Lanka, Malaysia and India, the bureaucratic official leaderships of the trade unions have a vice-like grip over the rank-and-file members of these mass organisations. In India, overwhelming numerical strength lies with the Stalinist Communist Party of India – Marxist (CPI(M)) and the Communist Party of India (CPI). Both of them use the phraseology of "democracy" and the "independence of the working class" etc. In areas where we have members such as Karnataka, Chennai and Kolkata, our comrades have been threatened with dire consequences for distributing leaflets putting forward ideas of unity, strike actions and solidarity messages for striking workers.

But, in spite of the life-threatening difficulties they face, our comrades have doggedly kept the orientation towards the working class and its organisations, such as the official trade unions. We continue to maintain our political positions, with a far-sighted perspective of where the new stages of struggle will emerge. Through our demands we continue to fight for influence among organised workers.

It is not our intention to belittle the practical reasons why comrades of some European sections of the CWI have been led to adopt certain tactics and methods of mass work. It would be wrong on our part to draw direct parallels with the situations here. But it would have been a lot easier to gain new members if we had succumbed to the pressure to water down our programme and focus on building 'movements,' rather than a cadre-based Marxist revolutionary organisation.

In India, the Stalinists – who lead some trade unions – have missed several important opportunities. For example, the fiasco of de-monetisation and the rise in GST (Goods and Services Tax) in 2016. For nearly ten weeks, there was seething anger against the Modi regime right across India. Even a feeble call for mass protests would have paved the way to bring down the government. It is this potential that we point towards, and we refuse to turn away from our orientation to the working class just because we are a small force.

There have been eighteen general strikes since 1991, and in all of them the 'Communist'-led unions have played a central role. The numbers participating in these class actions swell by millions each year. And yet not a single tangible reform, let alone a hint of revolution, has resulted from this struggle over the last three decades.

It is not our intention to draw analogies with the excellent work of the CWI European sections, who are horrified at the reference to Mandelite methods. The Stalinists and Maoists in South Asia, however, can be called unconscious Mandelites. Despite leading organisations of tens of thousands of workers, and being engaged in organised strike action, they have frittered away the chances for revolution. They have no understanding of the centrality of the working class and its power to lead the battle to end capitalism.

Perhaps it is the collective theoretical understanding of the CWI that has helped maintain the South Asian sections, as the entire non-'communist' left – including some of our former fellow-travellers – are now fermenting in other sectarian organisations. Many activists have totally abandoned the principled position of genuine Marxism and have adopted the language of Stalinism and Maoism. So-called revolutionaries in Sri Lanka now act subserviently to this or that wing of the bourgeois. The rump of the Nava Sama Samaja Party (NSSP), for example, defends the right-wing United National Party-led (UNP) government; using the bankrupt argument that there is a need to block the road to the "fascist" Rajapakse clan. The Stalinists in India use the same argument to defend their support for the capitalist Congress party, with the rhetoric of opposing the 'fascist' Modi. In Sri Lanka, Vickramabahu, former leader of the Trotskyist NSSP, has zigzagged; first supporting India's Indira Gandhi as an anti-imperialist, 'progressive' bourgeois; before later giving uncritical support to Tamil guerillas. He advocated social democratic measures as the way out of the crisis; then later characterised Rajapakse as representing fascism, and gave all-out support to UNP PM Ranil, claiming it was a strategic political necessity.

The CPI(M) Stalinists in India use Marxist rhetoric, quoting various socialist theoreticians from Gramsci to Trotsky to justify their wrong formulations. They use non-Marxian terminology, and phrases like religious fascism, cultural fascism, neo-colonial fascism etc, to confuse and even derail the struggle against capitalism and landlordism as a whole. This is why these forces are now faced with major crises, including historic splits. We stand firmly opposed to these false methods of Stalinism, and defend the CWI tradition and scientific Marxism.

In Malaysia, in the last general election in May 2018 Barisan Nasional (BN – National Front) and United Malays National Organisation (UMNO) – who together dominated politics for almost 60 years – were kicked out with the overwhelming support of the working people and poor.

The new government – Pakatan Harapan (PH - Coalition of Hope), elected on a populist manifesto – has reneged on one promise after another. In the following five by-elections there has been a decreasing turnout among the working class and poor, showing that the support for PH is deteriorating. Meanwhile, the right wing – UMNO and the Islamic Party (PAS) – are whipping up racial and religious sentiments, especially among the majority Malay and Muslim populations, to regain support. The identity politics of UMNO and PAS means they linked racial and religious sentiments to social and economic situations to influence the Malay working class and rural poor.

The CWI section in Malaysia, although still small in numbers, whenever possible has campaigned for working class unity to fight the 'divide and conquer' politics of the right wing. With the vacuum on the left, we have urged the trade unions to take the lead, to build solidarity among workers, poor and other oppressed in society. We are aware that the trade unions, as in many other countries, are passive and do not organise the majority of the working class (6% of workers are unionised in Malaysia). but they still have significant numbers, and have the authority to unite the working class and poor, to wage struggle against capitalism and right-wing politics.

We have also been careful not to fall into the trap of NGO activism, like the opportunistic and Mandelite leadership of the Socialist Party Malaysia (PSM). The PSM have been uncritically supporting liberal and petty bourgeois politics – especially in relation to democratic demands and identity politics (in LGBT and womens struggles) – for short-term gain, without linking these struggles to the working class. We have been consistent in our working-class approach, bringing these demands into movements such as 'Bersih' ('Clean'); a campaign for 'fair and democratic elections' led by NGOs, but which attracted mostly middle-class and young people. Similarly, in the struggles of women and for LGBT rights, sometimes NGOs put forward formulations such as 'anti-patriarchy,' that can isolate them from the working class. Certain comrades in our ranks, especially from middle class backgrounds, have sometimes been influenced by this petty-bourgeois and NGO approach. We have discussed and clarified with them the need, and importance, of gaining the support and trust of the working class on issues such as democratic rights, environmental degradation and gender discrimination.

We have been involved in organising the 'Atlas Ice' workers in five different factories to establish a union. Although most of our recruits have come from middle class and student backgrounds, our work with Atlas workers plays an important role in linking our members up with the trade unions and workers' struggles in general, as well as to expose our students and middle class recruits to workers' issues, and to increase their awareness of the role of the working class in overthrowing capitalism and achieving socialism.

It has only been the CWI leadership and its forces on the ground that have given thorough, sober explanations; for example, on the limits to which regimes like Modi's in India – or elsewhere in the world – can become full-blooded fascism. We have explained the degeneration of the Stalinists who have been historically wrong, before and after the collapse of the Soviet Union, in abandoning the centrality of the working class. But for us as Marxists, it is our principled analysis that has kept us on a revolutionary course.

What separates us from left apologists in the region is our firm understanding of theory, and the application of united front methods, especially in relation to the crucial national question. No one else on the entire left can match our record in steadfastly defending the rights of religious and national minorities in the region, particularly on the island of Sri Lanka. Our exemplary record on the revolutionary defence of the right to self-determination, up to and including separation, is something which is the envy of various groups on the left.

'Marxism in Today's World,' first published in 2006, has made an invaluable contribution to the ideas of Marxism and their application to the current-day complex realities. It can be a real guide for dealing with various questions, both of today and tomorrow. No-one claims that the CWI has ready-made answers to all the complex problems of the hour. But we have the scientific approach and method to navigate through this difficult period, where our class has not taken the decisive lead.

India has seen big movements so far on various social and democratic issues such as women's rights, environmental rights, on the question of religious chauvinism and on caste-based oppression. There has been a failure, on the one hand of the Stalinist left, both ideologically and organisationally; and on the other hand the failure of the bourgeois system itself; to solve any of the fundamental problems prevalent in the society. This has led to the NGO-isation of politics. Struggle has now entered the neo-colonial countries in a big way. Identity politics is filling the void in these situations, creating enormous confusion and difficulties for genuine Marxist forces, organising the various oppressed sections to draw them behind the banner of the working class.

It is a fact that the movements for various 'rights' are predominantly led either by bourgeois or petty-bourgeois elements who subscribe to identity politics, and are funded by various forces including NGOs. In many neo-colonial countries governments have co-opted the NGOs to run community projects on their behalf. This has invariably given a credibility to these 'agents saboteurs' forces in the eyes of the masses who desperately seek a way out from abject poverty and brutal oppression.

We have never disregarded the importance of these social movements; it is imperative on our part that we engage with these essentially cross-class movements. In a populous country like India, the bourgeois-democratic tasks are so great that any attempt to even scratch the surface of a problem can escalate into a major movement. We have sufficient experience on the ground in engaging in many mass movements such as the anti-POSCO campaign, the Koodankulam anti-nuclear campaign and various caste oppression battles and women's rights campaigns. Even with our small forces, we have played a key role in politically influencing these struggles.

In relation to the struggle against caste oppression, during the periods of Dalit youth upsurge, following the forced suicide of Rohith Vemula – a Dalit student activist – we were at the head of the movement in one state, while Stalinists were isolated because of their sectarian understanding of the caste & class dialectic.

We had to wade through the ideological confusion caused by the Stalinist standpoint on caste. We have held the banner of socialism high and put forward the necessary ideas and programme to show a real way forward. We have tenaciously argued for linking the struggles of the oppressed with the trade unions, including the ones led by the Communist left.

As Marxists, we have swum against the stream, but have steadfastly held on to our fundamental principle of the centrality of the working class. We have an enviable record in raising demands, such as zero tolerance of caste oppression in the unions. Through our modest interventions our comrades have established a reputation as uncompromising fighters.

Our comrades in India have also taken a principled position regarding the recent women's movement that we saw in Kerala. While millions of women formed a human chain demanding entry into one Hindu temple, it remained a fact that millions of men and women from Dalit backgrounds continue to be denied entry to the majority of temples, are refused water etc. Taking a simplified view and restricting ourselves to just marvelling at this latest development would certainly alienate millions of Dalits from our programme. Due to historical experience, our comrades instinctively understood the cross-class nature of the movement.

In India, the forces of the CWI have developed a nuanced approach in battling with the issue of positive discrimination, or 'reservation' as it is called, in relation to the caste issue. Right from the 1980s, we have taken a Marxist transitional approach – as opposed to all the opportunist and sectarian poison put forward by the bourgeois liberals, post-modernists and identity politics dispensers. The Stalinists – who for decades have acted like ostriches, denying the caste realities of Indian society and peddling a mechanical approach to class struggle – have now done a 180 degree turn, arguing that caste is the supreme issue in India.

We steadfastly defend the rights of all oppressed sections, particularly of the Dalits and Adivasi (tribals) who have undergone centuries of social, economic and political oppression of the worst kind, including defending the constitutional guarantee of jobs and education via a quota system. But in the same breath, we vociferously expose the incapacity of the capitalist and landlord system to provide jobs and services. The statistics amply demonstrate that only a miniscule section of Dalits and Adivasis have been assisted by this guarantee, which in effect is re-distributing poverty among the poor, according to their castes.

During the general strike in January 2019, Modi – to shore up his chances in the coming elections – introduced a constitutional amendment of 10% job quotas to the 'Economically Weaker Sections' among the 'forward castes'. No-one would have qualms about unemployed people getting jobs, but the devil is in the detail. Modi's law was to benefit the high income sections of 'forward castes', as an annual income of less than Rs.800,000 ($11,200) is the qualifying threshold. That is to say, anyone among the socially privileged caste elite earning just less than Rs.66,000 income a month would qualify! Needless to say that it is a gross violation of basic human rights, when 900 million are fighting for a mere existence. This clearly shows the oppressing caste bias of the Modi government. We took a principled stand in opposing such 'positive discrimination'. It is nothing but an electioneering ploy to polarise the voters.

One leading comrade in India, when listening to the the points being made in the current debate in the CWI, said: "India is a mine-field of identity politics; without the binding force and guiding principle of the centrality of the working class, we would be hastening a process of Balkanisation."

For decades our comrades in the South Asian region have faced a whole range of pressures exerted on us. We have fought back against all sorts of influences over the years. It is against this background that we found ourselves amazed at the last IEC at some of the positions that have been adopted by leaders of some of our sections. Even while seeing the heartbreaking conditions that exist in countries like India, particularly of the oppressed castes, we have never taken a 'humanitarian' approach and watered down our class approach. While understanding that movements cannot wait for the involvement of the working class, we are amazed that the Irish comrades misunderstand what force has to play a central role in winning lasting democratic rights, let alone defeating capitalism. There is a serious lack of clarity in the phrases used, as well as the formulations in the identity politics document produced by the Irish comrades.

We are further amazed by the fact that it did not occur to some leading comrades that we may have experience in our organisations in battling with these questions over the years. Some comrades at the IEC approached us with the view that we might take decisions not based on our political understanding, but based on personal material gain. We witnessed and experienced – even before the debate started – a barrage of innuendoes and insinuations regarding the financial status of some of the neo-colonial sections.

Yes, it is a well known fact that many sections from the neo-colonial world receive financial assistance from the CWI, which is all recorded, audited and reported to the entire IEC every year. Yes, it is a fact that financial assistance is routed through the IS, which is the administrative body of our international. But if there is a charge against the sections or IEC members who happen to vote with the IS majority that they are being 'bought' by the IS to shore up their influence, nothing can be more disgusting or un-Marxist than that.

Vincent Kolo met us a number of times throughout the IEC, along with other comrades opposed to the faction who tried to influence us to support their stand against the IS. But we said we do not agree with the somewhat opportunist stand they have taken.

We also pointed out that, in the political turmoil that we have had to deal with in Sri Lanka, comrades like Siri – a founding member of the CWI – had not had the chance to have a full discussion with the IS before the IEC. We were completely surprised and taken aback by the details that Vincent talked about. We were not aware of the pre-discussions that had taken place among some of the IEC members.

We also want to note here that it is our experience that we had no effort made from the Chinese/Hong Kong leadership to collaborate in the work in Asia. At times when they intervened, it was with a lecturing attitude on what to do, rather than seeking real collaboration. We were asked by Vincent Kolo about finance and organisational details regularly, but were kept in the dark about details relating to the work of the China/Hong Kong section.

In fact it is vital for all the sections to follow the developments in China, and close collaboration with comrades in Asia-wide discussions and campaigns is also vital. We want to have a say in what is happening there. No attempt was made by the China/Hong Kong comrades, who continue to see themselves as a separate unit.

They also have not made any serious effort to prioritise the attempts to develop an Asia Bureau, with an initial meeting that took place in Sri Lanka last year, with the view of establishing communication among leading comrades in the region. They said they did not have the necessary money at the time as they needed finance for the IEC. Then they complained that we had not kept them informed. Recently, they have managed to fund flights to Taiwan for both Shahar from Israel and Vincent Kolo from Europe.

In Malaysia we have been trying to build contacts and members in Indonesia for some years now because of the links with Malaysia, the similar language and culture. We have been coordinating with the IS in terms of reporting and coordinating the work, especially our discussion with left groups and contacts, and developing political perspectives.

Unfortunately, it has not been the case with Hong Kong/China comrades, specifically Vincent Kolo. On a few occasions he has wanted to instruct us on how to work, but been reluctant to coordinate the work through the international, with the involvement of the IS.

For instance, the Hong Kong comrades work with Indonesian migrant workers, a few of whom have also been connected with a left group that we are discussing with in Malaysia. When we established a website in the Indonesian language, the Hong Kong also built their own seperate website for Indonesian migrant workers, while asking for our help with translation. They knew that, with the assistance of the IS, we have been coordinating this work. Such an example shows the approach of Vincent Kolo in neglecting the democratic centralism of the CWI and the role of the IS.

In our sections, we have consulted the IS on every major political decision we have made. Without exception, we have discussed with the IS before embarking on any significant campaigns, to thoroughly discuss as well as to engage other sections in the region. Despite the problems of resources, and enormity of the land mass we are dealing with, we have made significant progress in bringing together the Indian, Sri Lankan, Malaysian and Australian sections as close as possible. We have also endeavoured to assist with the work in Pakistan and in Kashmir.

In our struggle against the Mandelism of Vickramabahu (a former member of our international in Sri Lanka), it was the clarity provided by the CWI leadership that saw us through, and prevented us from committing hari-kiri by supporting the intervention of the Indian Peace Keeping Force in the island country of Sri Lanka. We can never forget the political and material assistance of the CWI in those times, in protecting the small forces of Marxism to withstand all sorts of life-threatening pressures, both from the authoritarian state regime, from guerrilla fighters and from renegades of Marxism.

Conclusion

We have openly discussed with all the leading comrades in our sections about what happened at last year's IEC, and the developments since. All the comrades unanimously agreed with the position of the faction. This is not an ill-informed decision, but based on the hard experience of defending the methods and programme of the CWI. Comrades in this region know all too well the hard battle and discipline that is necessary to maintain a revolutionary organisation, based on democratic centralism.

We need our international to be clearly based on the principles laid down by Marxism, especially in relation to the tasks of building the forces for international socialism in the neo-colonial world. Trotsky's Permanent Revolution is invaluable for us. Without being part of such an international, there is no chance of holding the banner of socialism high in this part of the world.

We hope comrades in the NFF seriously take on board the experience of the sections in the neo-colonial countries, review their understanding and come to political agreement, to face up to the enormous tasks that are opening up in front of us.

On LGBT+ Rights

Michael Johnson, Leeds Branch and LGBT+ Caucus Convenor

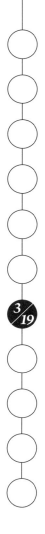

The recent document by Thomas White [titled 'Issues Raised in the Debate on Identity Politics'] raises a number of questions and comments on the current situation around LGBT+ rights internationally and how we respond to them. Thomas also particularly appears to raise criticisms of how the England and Wales section has responded to the ongoing, toxic debate around proposed changes to legislation – the Gender Recognition Act – and self-identification that I feel requires response.

Within the document, the radicalisation of the LGBT+ community – in particular non-binary people – is raised, stating "there is potential for an international movement on trans rights that could be sparked by the rising expectations of young people and LGBTQ+ people in regard to matters of oppression and inequality." Certainly in the last period we have seen growing radicalisation of some members of the LGBT+ community. In recent years we have seen significant protests internationally following the attacks on LGBT+ people in Chechnya, alongside tens of thousands of people in Israel protesting and striking for LGBT+ rights, and the social media protest in China. Even on a smaller scale, we have seen an increasing pushback against the de-politicisation of Pride events around the world, with the fronts of marches hijacked in a number of cities, and the presence of police challenged in cities like Toronto. The England and Wales section have seen an excellent response at the Pride events we have intervened in, selling out of papers, handing out all our leaflets and raising significant amounts of fighting fund for campaigning stalls in some areas.

However, where these protests and even alternative prides have developed, largely they have not turned into any sustained protest or movement; reactions to Chechnya were largely contained to isolated vigils despite our attempts to put forward demands that campaigns could be based around, and that 3 years later action is still required; and Pride events set up as alternatives to the corporatisation of mainstream Pride events have struggled to sustain themselves. This on the whole reflects the same difficulties the wider working class has faced in the recent period and reflects the key issue of leadership.

Thomas rightly points out that "while these layers [of the LGBT+ community] do contain sections of the upper echelons of society, they are in the majority made up of a working-class composition." However, when looking at LGBT+ movements we must reflect that these 'sections of the upper echelons,' by and large make up the leadership of most major LGBT+ organisations, and this has a major impact on the consciousness of the LGBT+ community. The majority of LGBT+ community events are dominated by the petty-bourgeois elements of the community, particularly bar owners. In Leeds, the vigil in response to the Orlando shooting was organised and dominated by the owners of local gay bars and clubs, and Pride events remain focussed on this part of the community. In England and Wales we have the example of Stonewall – one of the largest LGBT+ rights organisations internationally – and Pink News, both of whom have been mainly uncritical supporters of the Tory government, especially in relation to legal reforms. Pink News gave former Tory PM David Cameron an award for being an ally to the LGBT+ community, after years of brutal austerity devastating the LGBT+ community! Stonewall encourages corporations to pay them to be on a list of LGBT-friendly employers, regardless of their actual impact on the LGBT+ community or even having policies against discrimination! And these examples aren't limited to England; in the US the Human Rights Campaign has been a long standing block against left politicians like Bernie Saunders.

This is obviously not a new issue for the LGBT+ community. Issues around leadership and its impact on the development of movements around LGBT+ rights have been ongoing. From the earliest rights organisations such as the Mattachine Society in the US, which was challenged over the number of communists in its leadership, and the Gay Liberation Front's splits over their orientation to class and other oppressed groups. These splits have largely been when those in the LGBT+ community who want to link movements up to broader social issues and demands, come up against the – typically – petty-bourgeois layers in these cross-class movements. For these petty-bourgeois layers, broader demands are unnecessary, with legal, incremental changes being enough. We saw this in the aftermath of Stonewall, when splits broke out over attempts to include work around homelessness, or linking up with the Black Panthers. Section 28 is a particularly illustrative example. Certainly it was a movement that cannot be described as anything but radical; occupations of BBC news rooms in protest, abseiling into the House of Lords and thousands on the streets across England. And while it couldn't defeat Section 28 it certainly won a number of successes; securing funding from local councils for LGBT+ services. However these victories couldn't be sustained into a mass ongoing campaign. Instead, energies were diverted into establishing organisations such as Stonewall who, even when Section 28 was finally repealed, made no demands on positive LGBT+ education to replace it, which still doesn't exist 15 years later. This indicates that even when there is a radicalisation of the LGBT+ community, without a class-based approach this radicalisation can easily be dissipated.

In the document Thomas writes "that specifically people who identify as non-binary by rejecting the binary logic of the bourgeois nuclear family are far more likely to be open to ideas that challenge the system and potentially be some of the most radicalised layers." And yes, LGBT+ people, facing double, triple oppressions are certainly being radicalised by this oppression. However, I feel it is not necessarily the case that these identities predispose people to being open to our ideas.

Currently capitalism is quite happy to turn towards these identities to develop new markets; we have seen major clothing companies and make-up companies like H&M pivot towards developing gender neutral lines in the same way we see major companies stick a rainbow on their logo for Pride season in an attempt to get the 'pink pound' often in a deeply hypocritical way. One year my local Pride was 'proudly' led by Sainsbury's who, within the week of the march, was facing protests for the homophobic treatment of same-sex couples kissing in their stores. As the IS wrote in 'Women's Oppression and identity politics' [See page 91] "ultimately, while capitalism can never provide real equality for women and LGBTQ+ people, it can nonetheless be pushed a considerable distance in terms of legal changes."

Likewise political parties, faced with the growing social acceptance that LGBT+ people have successfully fought for, are happy to pose as LGBT+ friendly to appeal to more people. There is the obvious examples in England of David Cameron and Theresa May's equal marriage and Gender Recognition Act reforms, but even Trump felt the need to pose with a rainbow flag emblazoned with "LGBTs for Trump". In UK reactionary right-wing parties like UKIP are happy to turn up to Pride events and the EDL has boasted of an LGBT division too and try and appeal to the community.

And this has had success, not just from the likes of Pink News giving out awards, but in wider society. It is not the case that, as in the eighties faced with a reactionary Thatcher government, that LGBT+ people voted largely for left-wing parties. One only needs to look to Caitlin Jenner, arguably one of the most famous Trans women internationally, who is also a Republican who for a long period argued that Trump's policies would be good for the LGBT+ community.

It's also worth looking at the ways the sections of the LGBT+ community that are experiencing radicalisation are entering the movement. As written in the IS document "in one sense, identity politics can be an inevitable part of the political awakening of many members of oppressed groups within society… however, the identity politics that currently has influence emanated from the capitalists via the universities over current decades." This has undoubtedly had a massive impact on the LGBT+ community and its potential for developing movements. In my branch our intervention at a Chechnya vigil was challenged by organisers, young Labour Party members, due to the presence of straight comrades! This was obviously a cynical attempt to try and scare comrades away from intervening and why? Because our comrades were putting forward demands that took the vigil from a passive gathering feeling bad about what was happening in another country or even a rally with passive support for the Labour Party to one that called for wider action not just in Chechnya but by the UK government and even local councils. It was not shocking that the three comrades who were able to speak on these issues were among the best received (one comrade was the only speaker that people were asking to hear more from on social media!). This is clearly a massive shift from inspiring struggles the LGBT+ community has faced in the past that emphasised class unity such as in the aftermath of the Stonewall Riots or the work of Lesbians & Gays Support the Miners (LGSM).

Faced with these views it is vital that we ensure that we are able to intervene in a way that challenges these views that could serve to limit our campaigning for united struggle. In Thomas' document, he writes "It has been stated repeatedly that if we orientate towards women or LGBTQ+ people that we run the risk of alienating other sections of the working class particularly older male workers ….Here in Ireland during both the Marriage Equality and Repeal referendums the highest 'Yes' votes came from working class areas. In our experience older or strictly male elements of the working class have been energised and inspired by these social movements which have been led by young people particularly young women and LGBTQ+ people. Instinctive class solidarity played a key role in both referendums."

Of course, that class solidarity that Thomas writes of is definitely a component of a number of movements. We of course saw, in the 1984-85 miners' strike, the fantastic impact that class solidarity had across a number of social groups. Organisations like LGSM formed, due to the understanding of the shared enemies the LGBT+ community and miners had. In turn, this had an impact on the National Union of Mineworkers, who later worked to push forwards the fight for LGBT+ rights within the Labour Party, and challenged Section 28. We of course want to ensure that this inspiring class solidarity continues and develops into a united class movement, beyond action like voting in a referendum, as fantastic as that vote was. To do this we need to ensure our orientation to these struggles is able to situate them into their context to wider battles of the class. And to do this most successfully we need to ensure that we are seen by all workers to be fighting on the key issues that affect them, which includes the struggles of oppressed groups.

All of this is not to downplay the radicalisation of the LGBT+ community or other oppressed groups, which as previously written is certainly occurring. Much like the IS wrote in the document 'Women's oppression and identity politics' [see page 91] in relation to women's oppression, the LGBT+ community, seeing the massive gains around rights in law internationally, was becoming more confident in the direction the movement was going in. However, the effects of the economic collapse hit LGBT+ people hard. In the UK, LGBT+ specialist services are at 'significant risk', and, facing the still-existing issues LGBTphobia in society at large, the ideas presented by 'leading' LGBT+ rights groups – that equality was around the corner, all we have to do is sit patiently and wait – has been tested. And so, a strong mood to fight on issues relating to LGBT+ oppression has grown, though certainly not on the same level as some other social groups internationally, thanks to the limited reforms that have been won. This growing anger has yet to express itself in any mass form in most countries in specific social movements and, due to the current demands around issues like healthcare and housing, is as likely to be expressed in broader struggles of the working class.

This raises the question of our orientation and how we develop our work and programme. Certainly, it is hugely important we continue to ensure that we are visible, fighting wherever struggles take place. However we also need to insure that we do not ignore that we are as likely to meet LGBT+ workers interested in our ideas in workplaces, on picket lines and in broader struggles as we are at Pride events. This also raises the question of the approach of the IS.

In Thomas' document, a quote from the document 'In Defence of a Working-class Orientation for the CWI' [see page 11] is referenced specifically: "We also support the legitimate demands of the LGBTQ+ movement, so long as they do not conflict with the rights of others, and can be resolved by democratic discussion." This quote was also raised by Kshama Sawant amongst others at the recent England and Wales national conference. It was disappointing that Kshama did not stay at the conference to hear my response as an organiser for England and Wales' LGBT+ caucus, but fortunately I am able to respond here. This quote from Peter Taaffe has been used to suggest a 'conservative approach,' a 'lowering of our programme,' and 'making concessions to the right'. Thomas argues Peter Taaffe and the IS majority "are referring to the supposedly conflicting rights of women and trans people in relation to women's only spaces such as refuges and bathrooms" so I feel I did need to clarify to comrades exactly what our position regarding this is.

Firstly, I appreciate that taken out of context the quote from Peter may be confusing and unclear to comrades. It's worth therefore pointing comrades to Peter's very next sentence: "We have championed the demands of all oppressed groups and strata including the LGBTQ+, for instance against the anti-trans position of Mark Serwotka, the leader of the PCS." Again: Peter's next sentence. I would hope comrades see Peter celebrating the work of our comrades, in actively challenging the ideas Thomas rightly writes against, is a far cry from making concessions to the right!

So, what is our actual position if not the conservative one claimed? For context, over the last few years an incredibly toxic debate has emerged in England & Wales around potential changes to the law that would simplify the process of trans people having their gender legally recognised under the Gender Recognition Act (GRA). These changes have been proposed by the Tories in an incredibly cynical manner as they faced growing unpopularity and in turn conducted a public consultation along massively divisive lines that has led to methods including no-platforming, shutting down meetings, threats of violence, intimidation, shaming, and so on being adopted in addressing this issue and centrally the question of whether women's right and trans rights are in competition.

It is in this climate that comrades in England and Wales have skilfully intervened in social movements, trade unions and wider society. We have been very clear putting forward a programme in support of reforms to the GRA but also the need to take the fight beyond the GRA to wider demands for the trans community to push the movement around the GRA into wider struggles for their rights such as calls for vital investment in healthcare and housing to tackle the overrepresentation of LGBT+ in the homelessness population. To quote from one of our most recent articles on the GRA in the February 2019 issue of Socialism Today: "But we do not only seek the legal changes the Tories are consulting on but fight for the services required by trans people, women and all those who suffer under capitalism's inability to provide a decent life for all, such as the NHS, council housing, free education and an end to poverty pay and precarious working."

Crucially, in interventions we have acknowledged that, bearing 86% of austerity and with services like refuges facing massive cuts – in some places more than half of their budget – women have understandable concerns about services and rights. These have been used by the right, and so we ensured that our demands around the GRA are also able to cut across this, and we have challenged the idea that women's rights and trans rights are in competition. This has allowed us to work for a united movement of trans people, women and the wider working class, pointing towards the true causes of the attacks on their services and rights: austerity and capitalism. To again quote from the above Socialism Today article for maximum clarity: "We do not accept that there is a limited pool of resources and rights that working-class people have to fight each other over."

We support all steps forward for the LGBT+ community as victories for the working class, but we must always see that the biggest step forward the LGBT+ community will be in overthrowing capitalism as part of the working class as a whole. History is littered with LGBT+ organisations that lacked that class analysis, thought liberation could be won by the LGBT+ community alone by winning mild reforms piecemeal, or found themselves unable to meet the tasks ahead of them in achieving liberation. The CWI is the organisation with the political foundations and programme that can unite the different layers of the working class in common struggle with demands around issues affecting the wider working class coming alongside demands against LGBT+ oppression. I share Thomas' hopes that through this debate we can develop our analysis and perspectives of LGBT+ struggles across the international, and come out of this even more prepared to intervene in struggles and build the working-class fightback around the world.

3. *The* TRADE UNIONS

MARX AND ENGELS ON THE TRADE UNIONS

Peter Taaffe, Socialism Today 98, February 2006

This was originally written as a review of a new edition of Karl Marx and Friedrich Engels on the Trade Unions, published by International Publishers.

This book is essential reading for all those who wish to understand the role of the trade unions and the tasks of socialists within them. Although first published in 1987, containing the works of Karl Marx and Friedrich Engels on this issue, it has great contemporary relevance.

Written in the 19th century, inevitably parts of the book are dated. However, in the main, the freshness with which Marx and Engels approach the real movement of the working class is evident. What has not dated is the method of analysis of these two great socialist teachers, their almost unerring ability to put their finger on the pulse of the working-class movement at each stage, not just in Britain but internationally.

To read extracts from Engels's classic, The Condition of the Working Class in England (1845), is to marvel once more at how the 24-year-old author illuminated so many aspects of the conditions and the outlook of the working class then and later. Engels knew his way around documents and libraries but this was not enough, as he indicated in his introduction to this book. Addressing the British workers, he writes: "I have not been satisfied with this [study of documents], I wanted more than a mere abstract knowledge of my subject, I wanted to see you in your homes, to observe you in your everyday life, to chat with you on conditions and grievances, to witness your struggles against the social and political power of your oppressors. I have done so ..."

In these few lines is how all socialists, but particularly the new generation entering the struggle for the first time, should proceed in analysing and helping to provide a lever for the more developed sections of the working class in its struggle against capitalism. Not for Marx and Engels the role of 'teachers' from on high. For instance, Marx wrote: "... we do not confront the world in a doctrinaire way with a new principle: Here is the truth, kneel down before it! We develop new principles for the world out of the world's own principles. We do not say to the world: Cease your struggles, they are foolish; we will give you the true slogan of struggle. We merely show the world what it is really fighting for, and consciousness is something that it has to acquire, even if it does not want to". (Letter to Arnold Ruge, September 1843)

It is this approach that runs like a red thread through the analysis of Marx and Engels on the trade unions. In the first section of the book, Trade Unions and Revolution (1844–1848), the inhuman conditions confronting the industrial working class at the time are described and condemned in powerfully written lines by Engels. We learn about the Chartists, the great general strike of 1842, the resort to lock-outs and the vital role and development of the trade unions in confronting the capitalists. He denounces the "absolute power of the lord of the factory in his little state". Things have changed little in Britain, it seems, when the Gate Gourmet 'lords' can treat workers in exactly the same way 160 years later.

In describing the role of the trade unions Engels also touches on the character of the British working class, how it differed at that time, for instance, from the German and American workers. He deals with the general conditions of the working class and how it arrived at a trade union and political consciousness. The different routes and the manner in which it does this is partly conditioned by national factors, differences in the economy, the proportion of workers, etc. He comments: "The incredible frequency of these strikes proves best of all to what extent the social war has broken out over all England".

Striking lessons

On strikes in general and how they develop the working class, he writes: "These strikes, at first skirmishes, sometimes result in weighty struggles; they decide nothing, it is true, but they are the strongest proof that the decisive battle between bourgeoisie and proletariat is approaching. They are the military school of the working-men in which they prepare for the great struggles which cannot be avoided …" Engels was premature in expecting the 'decisive battle' between labour and capital, at that stage, as he later conceded. But his and Marx's analysis of how struggle fuses together the working class retains all its force today.

In relation to the unions, he says they are "schools of war", in which, "the unions are unexcelled. In them is developed the peculiar courage of the English. It is said on the Continent that the English, and especially the working-men, are cowardly, that they cannot carry out a revolution because, unlike the French, they do not riot at intervals, because they apparently accept the bourgeois regime so quietly. This is a complete mistake. The English working-men are second to none in courage; they are quite as restless as the French, but they fight differently".

Engels also describes the cold cruelty of the British ruling class in this 'war'. It uses every device, including eviction from company houses: "This measure was carried out with revolting cruelty. The sick, the feeble, old men and little children, even women in child-birth, were mercilessly turned from their beds and cast into the roadside ditches. One agent dragged by the hair from her bed, and into the street, a woman in the pangs of childbirth".

In the cauldron of the rise of industrial capitalism in England, so too developed trade unions that were blooded in brutal battles with capital. Given that a big layer of the new generation in the workplace does not yet even understand the basic idea of trade unionism, the very simple but profound description by Marx and Engels on the role of the working class and of trade unions bears repetition today. Engels writes: "Large-scale industry concentrates in one place a crowd of people unknown to one another. Competition divides their interests. But the maintenance of wages, this common interest which they have against their boss, unites them in a common thought of resistance – combination".

Of course, because of de-industrialisation, the same conditions do not pertain to the working class en masse as perhaps in the 19th century (although there is still a substantial industrial working class in Britain). Nevertheless, neo-liberalism has ensured the destruction of the conditions of previously 'privileged' layers who perhaps did not even consider themselves part of the working class, such as civil servants, teachers, etc. Marx and Engels also answer the 19th century pro-capitalist arguments – which have been repeated recently, for instance in the miners' strikes of the 1980s – that workers cannot 'afford' to strike or finance trade unions: "… the workers are right to laugh at the clever bourgeois schoolmasters who reckon up to them what this civil war is costing them in fallen, injured, and financial sacrifices. He who wants to beat his adversary will not discuss with him the costs of the war".

On concessions dragged out of the capitalists, Engels writes: "… Messrs the bourgeois and their economists are so gracious as to allow in the minimum wage, that is, in the minimum life … [but] it must in contrast appear to them as shameful as incomprehensible that the workers reckon in this minimum a little of the costs of war against the bourgeoisie and that out of their revolutionary activity they even make the maximum of their enjoyment of life". In the Communist Manifesto, Marx and Engels wrote: "Now and then the workers are victorious, but only for a time. The real fruits of their battles lie, not in their immediate result, but in the ever-expanding union of the workers".

Political struggle

Arising from this struggle inevitably is politics, the generalised struggle of the working class as a whole: "… every class struggle is a political struggle. And that union, to attain which the burghers of the Middle Ages, with their miserable highways, required centuries, the modern proletarians, thanks to railways, achieve in a few years". With modern technology, mobile phones, the internet, etc, what took years in the 19th century can be achieved in a much shorter period today. However, as in the past, this requires leadership and organisation which avoids the pitfalls of opportunism on the one side and sectarianism, a doctrinaire approach, on the other.

The correct method of Marx and Engels is particularly brought out in the sections, Trade Unions and the First International (1859-1872), Socialist Sectarians (1868-1875), on the problems of the us labour movement, as well as the analysis of Engels on the London dock strike of 1888 and the problems of the labour movement at the beginning of the last decade of the 19th century. Marx was the greatest theoretician of the working class but his practical work in the construction of the First International (The International Working Men's Association – iwma) was vital in laying the basis for the rise of the workers' movement both then and after its demise. Engels described the formation of the iwma as Marx's "crowning achievement". What is brought out in the extracts from his and Engels' writings is the necessity for implacable firmness on principled, political and theoretical points while showing the greatest flexibility on trying to facilitate real steps forward both in the trade unions and also politically of the mass of the working class.

There are some very important parallels with the tasks confronting socialists and Marxists today in these pages. The First International, through the work of Marx and Engels, brought together English trade unionists, European socialists and even the anarchists like Mikhail Bakunin. But Marx always tried to point the trade unions towards a generalised struggle against capitalism while supporting all their struggles on a day-to-day basis. For instance, in his fourth annual report to the First International's general council in 1868, he states that the

IWMA, "… has not been hatched by a sect or a theory. It is the spontaneous growth of the proletarian movement, which itself is the offspring of the natural and irrepressible tendencies of modern society". He also states: "If the trade unions are required for the guerrilla fights between capital and labour, they are still more important as organised agencies for superseding the very system of wage labour and capital rule".

But, even while collaborating with the trade union leaders at the time, he also points to their limitations as well as those of the trade unions as a whole: "Too exclusively bent on the local and immediate struggles with capital, the trade unions have not yet fully understood their power of acting against the system of wage slavery itself. They therefore kept too much aloof from general social and political movements". Is this not the characteristic of many of the trade union leaders today? Their members increasingly disillusioned with the Labour Party, they nevertheless refuse to draw the obvious conclusion of seeking and constructing a political alternative. Some may distance themselves from the Labour Party but still retreat into a neutral, so-called 'non-political', stance which ultimately undermines the trade unions and their members' real interests.

International solidarity

In this book, Marx and Engels point to the rise of an aristocracy of labour, particularly amongst skilled workers, whose living standards rose during the economic upswing which followed the collapse of Chartism in the 1840s. This term, 'the aristocracy of labour', was usually associated with the exclusive character of the trade unions – concentrating on the skilled trades to the exclusion of the great mass of unskilled exploited workers – in the late 19th century. But, as this book reveals, the term was in use even by early socialist writers and was familiar to Marx and Engels as early as the 1840s.

Through the first international and subsequently, Marx and Engels attempted to break this down, supporting all strikes, acting as a co-ordinating centre, and trying to persuade the trade unions to broaden their base. In one report to the general council of the IWMA, Marx makes the point, "… it was not the International that threw the workmen into strikes, but, on the contrary, it was the strikes that threw the workmen into the International". Marx showed the vital role played by the First International in solidarity action: "… one of the commonest forms of the movement for emancipation is that of strikes. Formerly, when a strike took place in one country it was defeated by the importation of workmen from another. The International has nearly stopped all that. It receives information of the intended strike, it spreads that information among its members, who at once see that for them the seat of the struggle must be forbidden ground".

How far the trade unions need to travel today to reach the position of the IWMA more than 150 years ago! The Committee for a Workers' International (CWI) does more, it seems, than the 'mighty' trade union apparatus in publicising and eliciting solidarity for strikes in a country, continent and worldwide. The privileged trade union officialdom, in the main, is at home in committees, participating in the drawing up of weighty reports, suggesting pious resolutions for parliaments, but not through class action through picket lines, sympathetic strikes, organising immigrant workers, etc. A typical case was the recent dispute in Irish Ferries, in which East European immigrant labour was used in an attempt to break union conditions and even the unions themselves. The European maritime union leaders did undertake solidarity action.

This was not true of the trade union leaders as a whole who, in the main, are dilatory in organising it. Through solidarity action, especially the efforts of the Socialist Party in Ireland and its MP, Joe Higgins, as well as solidarity action supported by the Socialist Party in England and Wales, the employers did not win a complete victory.

Half a million immigrant workers have entered Britain, Sweden and Ireland in the last 18 months to two years, the overwhelming majority without union organisation and prepared to work for drastically reduced pay and conditions. It is vital that the trade union movement acts like the First International by spreading "information among its members, who at once see that for them the seat of the struggle must be forbidden ground". Polish and other Eastern European workers should be organised, both in their home countries and, when they come to Britain and the rest of Europe, should be recruited immediately into union organisation.

The extracts from Marx's Capital and other works in this book, particularly on the struggle over the working day, have a very topical ring about them. In this era of neo-liberalism, how strikingly contemporary is the following comment? "The general tendency of capitalist production is not to raise, but to sink the average standard of wages … Trade unions work well as centres of resistance against the encroachments of capital [unfortunately, not the case under right-wing leaderships – PT]. They fail partially from an injudicious use of their power. They fail generally from limiting themselves to a guerrilla war against the effects of the existing system, instead of simultaneously trying to change it, instead of using their organised forces as a lever for the final emancipation of the working class …"

Marx correctly described the struggle between labour and capital over the working day as a "civil war" unfolding over 50 years. This resulted in legislation restricting the amount of time workers were forced to spend in the workplace. Even that has been undermined today as Gordon Brown and Tony Blair insist that the European Working Time Directive, limiting the working week to 48 hours, is not applied in Britain! Capitalism is described by Marx as the "vampire [which] will not lose his hold on [the worker] 'so long as there is a muscle, a nerve, a drop of blood to be exploited.'"

Democratic organisation

The chapter on Socialist Sectarians is remarkable for bringing out not just the role of the working class but the different tactics that must be employed in different stages of the struggle if socialists and Marxists are to link up successfully with mass movements of the working class. It must be remembered that when Marx is dealing with 'sects' he is not primarily concerned with the size of such organisations – although this was a factor – but in their abstract, incorrect tactics, their generally denunciatory and lecturing approach towards the working class. People like Ferdinand Lasalle in Germany – who Marx praised for taking the working-class movement forward – had substantial forces behind him but had a false approach to trade unions. The same applied to Pierre Proudhon, the inspiration for anarchism in France, as well as many others.

In relation to the German workers and trade unions, Marx makes the pertinent comment in arguing against over-centralised mass organisations: "… centralist organisation, although very useful for secret societies and sectarian movements, goes against the nature of trade unions. Even if it were possible – I state outright that it is impossible – it would not be desirable, and least of all in Germany. Here where the worker's life is regulated from childhood on by bureaucracy and he himself believes in the authorities, in the bodies appointed over him, he must be taught before all else to walk by himself". Stifling bureaucracy, which is still the hall-mark of trade unions in Britain and throughout the world today, is a barrier to the working class learning to "walk by itself".

Organisation and leadership is vital, but not as a substitute – as some small sectarian organisations in Britain unfortunately believe – for initiative and spontaneity by workers in struggle. The role of socialists and Marxists in the trade unions is to encourage this tendency of workers to act by themselves while helping to provide, where necessary, the ideological and material means for the working class itself to organise and defeat the employers and their system.

Throughout the later writings of Engels is the theme of the opposition of Marx and himself to an ultimatist or one-sided approach to the struggles of the working class. Also the need for political action is a constant theme. Engels, after the death of Marx, pointed towards steps to be taken that would move the mass of the working class into action. He pointed out in 1883: "And – apart from the unexpected – a really general workers' movement will come into existence here only when the workers feel that England's world monopoly is broken".

He denounced the trade union leaders for acting as the tail of the "'great Liberal Party', the party led by the manufacturers". Today, the "manufacturers" are not represented by the Liberal Democrats at least directly, and in any case do not have the clout of their counterparts in the 19th century. But the equivalent of the "great Liberal Party" then is the three main capitalist parties in Britain today, particularly New Labour. Engels constantly writes of the need for the "formation of a workers' party".

Steps forward

While Marx and Engels were meticulous on points of theory – read Marx's criticism of Lasalle for his false idea of an "iron law of wages" – they nevertheless welcomed all genuine steps forward, even of a layer of the working class. For instance, Engels welcomed the formation of the Knights of Labor in the USA following the end of the American civil war. This encompassed 100,000 workers at one stage and Engels fervently hoped it would lead to the development of a US labour party. This did not materialise because, amongst other factors, the expansion of US capitalism towards the west, with land provided for the most energetic, acted as a safety valve for American capitalism and undermined the development of a nationwide labour movement. Only when this came to an end at the end of the 19th century did the labour movement begin to take on national proportions, particularly in the first decade of the 20th century.

While Engels understood that the objective situation was a barrier to the development, in Britain in particular, to a broad-based mass political party of the working class, he never stopped advocating this and supported all steps, limited though they were, towards the achievement of this goal. In relation to the US, he demonstrated the hostility of genuine Marxism to sectarianism of all kinds: "It is far more important that the movement should spread, proceed harmoniously, take root and embrace as much as possible the whole American proletariat than that it should start and proceed, from the beginning, on theoretically perfectly correct lines. There is no better road to theoretical clearness of comprehension than to learn by one's own mistakes". He further adds: "The great thing is to get the working class to move as a class; that once obtained, they will soon find the right direction, and all who resist … will be left out in the cold with small sects of their own".

In relation to England and Britain as a whole, he states at the time of the upsurge of

'New Unionism' that: "A large class, like a great nation, never learns better or quicker than by undergoing the consequence of its own mistakes. And for all the fault committed in past, present and future, the revival of the East End of London remains one of the greatest and most fruitful facts of this ... and glad and proud I am to have lived to see it".

New workers' party

Engels' analysis of this period is rich, detailed, and very useful even today for those who wish to understand strategy and tactics in relation to the working-class movement. It is particularly important in England and Wales today in view of the discussion underway on the need for a new mass workers' party. Writing about the Social Democratic Federation (SDF), formally 'Marxist' but denounced by Marx when he was alive, he writes: "The English Social-Democratic Federation is, and acts, only like a small sect. It is an exclusive body. It has not understood how to take the lead of the working-class movement generally, and to direct it towards socialism. It has turned Marxism into an orthodoxy. Thus it insisted upon John Burns unfurling the red flag at the dock strike, where such an act would have ruined the whole movement, and, instead of gaining over the dockers, would have driven them back into the arms of the capitalists". Engels was fulminating here against the SDF's ultimatumism towards the movement at that stage. This malady eventually led to its shipwreck and collapse.

At the same time, he did not hesitate to criticise the opportunist trade union leaders of the time, denouncing for instance the "bourgeois labour party", as he described the right-wing trade union leaders at the time (how apt this is for those who are still propping up New Labour today), to the exclusivity of the skilled trade unions, as well as the naivety and mistaken tactics of the dockers and gas workers at different stages of their strikes. He also unequivocally welcomed all attempts by the working class, no matter how small, to act independently. For instance, he writes: "The gas workers now have the most powerful organisation in Ireland and will put up their own candidates in the next election ..." He would have been denounced by some of our socialist sectarians today in, for instance, Respect and the Socialist Workers' Party, who insist on a very centralised organisation, controlled by themselves of course, which would exclude trade unionists who see the need, as an initial step, to stand independently against the capitalist parties, particularly New Labour. There are comments like this and many more which make this book invaluable.

Its real relevance, however, is that the conditions observed by Engels which led to the development of the Labour Party in the latter part of the 19th and early part of the 20th centuries are now maturing. New Labour is the equivalent of the Liberal Party then. New Unionism, which paved the way for the formation of the Labour Party, was created by the terrible poverty, the equivalent of neo-liberal capitalism today. The same conditions will produce like results.

Those who may be a bit disconcerted today by the big task of creating a new mass party in Britain only have to read Engels's comments: "One is indeed driven to despair by these English workers with their sense of imaginary national superiority, with their essentially bourgeois ideas and viewpoints, with their 'practical' narrow-mindedness, with the parliamentary corruption which has seriously affected the leaders. But things are moving nonetheless. The only thing is that the 'practical' English will be the last to arrive, but when they do arrive their contribution will weigh quite heavy in the scale".

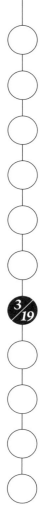

THE NATURE OF THE TRADE UNIONS

Peter Taaffe

Trotsky commented in the 1930s following the defeat of the Spanish revolution how ideological consciousness had been thrown back, not only in the mass organisations but even in the small 'Marxist' and 'Trotskyist' organisations.

The international debate within the CWI has unfortunately already revealed the same tendencies, particularly in the arguments of the 'Non-Faction Faction' on crucial issues such as the consciousness of the working class today and the approach and attitude towards their own class organisations, the trade unions.

This has been clearly demonstrated in the original and later documents of both Kevin McLoughlin on behalf of the Irish leadership and those of Andros Payiatsos on behalf of the 'whole' Greek EC (including himself). Their argument runs that trade unions have been empty over a considerable period – had no real internal life with little or no opposition to the national leadership – and therefore it was correct to concentrate on building an alternative force amongst other movements: women, LGBTQI+, and 'environmentalists' – the new 'vanguard'. Danny Byrne has come up with an additional 'insight;' that this was a 'cunning plan' of the Irish comrades to turn away from dead organisations like the trade unions and assemble a force outside the existing trade union structures from the intervention amongst women and LGBTQI+, 'educate' them and then turn them back to the unions to provide the necessary force to regenerate a rank and file militant union.

In his ignorance of history, he imagines this to be an entirely 'unique' and original approach. Actually, it is precisely pure 'Mandelism' to seek to use radicalised students to enter the unions and 'electrify' the masses. Moreover, it was tried by a motley variety of sects in the past. The only effect it had was to create a mood of suspicion amongst workers of these 'educated' interlopers in the factories, and question why they had deigned to 'provide leadership' to the working class in this way.

Under the whip of our criticism of their abandonment of a class approach, including systematic trade union work, a certain rapid 're-adjustment' by the Greek and Irish organisations took place. Almost overnight, in place of an absence of reports of strikes and intervention on picket lines, now these magically reappeared on their websites.

However, this was just window dressing, as was indicated by the remarks at the debate in Dublin on 18 February 2019 by industrial workers who bitterly complained about the systematic neglect and even abandonment of trade union work over years.

One member of the biggest Irish trade union, SIPTU, pointed to the derogatory attitude adopted towards himself and others who did attempt to pursue regular trade union activity, including challenging the right wing within the union. His report was also vindicated by a number of worker comrades in the course of the discussion, as was the fact that the paper of the Irish organisation was not systematically sold at union conferences and trade union events.

He had been going to SIPTU conferences since 2011, but there had never been an organised party intervention, except for 2016, when it was discussing disaffiliation from Labour. SIPTU is the biggest union in Ireland with a third of all organised workers. The comrade said it was basic to have organised interventions, yet he felt isolated in the union. The comrade did not need reminding that SIPTU was bureaucratic and rotten!

He did not subscribe to the view that we come back when things pick up. The comrade called for an organised approach to the biggest union in Ireland as there are openings and things can be done. For example, the 2013 SIPTU conference saw one third of delegates oppose the property tax despite all of the attacks on the motion. Ten to fifteen Socialist Party members working actively in SIPTU could do great things in the union.

Yet at the 2015 conference despite being 500 yards from our Cork centre there was no party intervention. Two important motions were taken on disaffiliation from Labour and for the union to turn to parties of the left. The comrade felt that a lot of trade union work in the party has been downgraded without consultation. These charges were of course denied by the Irish leadership.

The comrades in Northern Ireland have pursued consistent and effective work in NIPSA, which resulted in a spectacular victory for us and the left. This was achieved despite conflict with and the effective opposition of some of the Irish leadership with leading NIPSA comrades on numerous issues, over a number of years.

However in complete distinction to these denials, we now have fresh confirmation of just how the unprincipled concessions to identity politics made by the leadership of these sections are not restricted to them alone. The corrosive effect is now clearly manifested in other sections who support the orientation of the Irish organisation, of a systematic rejection of effective long-term trade union work, particularly in the US. This has been shockingly revealed in the course of debates between representatives of the International Faction and the 'Non-Faction Faction'.

One glaring example of this theoretical retreat is manifested in a letter which was sent by Andy Moxley (AM) of the US National Committee and part of the national leadership, to Lenny Shail from the England and Wales section and Matt Dobson from the Scottish section, who have given permission to quote from this letter on this crucial issue.

AM firstly reports: "I'm just finishing up being out in Oakland for our massively successful intervention into the teachers strike here." This strike, which has been widely reported in labour movement circles in the US and in the press, is very significant and is not just restricted to the West Coast, but follows a series of strikes by teachers and others in many areas, representing possibly the re-emergence of the US working class. This in turn could hold out the possibility of important gains for a genuine Trotskyist, Marxist organisation which had a clear programme and perspective for the struggle, and seeks to intervene in these disputes in a rounded-out Trotskyist manner.

AM tells us of the intervention in the Oakland teachers strike, but fails to display any of these qualities in his letter. He has certainly not learned the right lessons from the teachers' strikes and those of others in the US recently.

He writes in criticism of us: "The comrades in the faction have retreated into a reactive, mechanical approach towards what is an incredibly complicated period for the working class. I raised at our NC that the risk of Grantism – applying a formula from a past political period to the current situation – is becoming inherent in the approach of the faction … I think this is reflected in the approach comrades have outlined in reference to the trade unions and working class struggle in general. The comparison has repeatedly been made between today's situation and the situation in the mid-late 1960s – a situation in which there existed filled out mass reformist and Stalinist parties, trade unions and most importantly a large activist layer among the working class with a socialist consciousness".

Bryan Koulouris made a similar comparison at our recent National Congress, that in essence 'Mandelism' arose from a previous period, whose chief characteristics according to him are those now described by AM.

Every word here is a mistake, and sometimes two! It is an oversimplification to describe the 1960s in this fashion and to lump in the quite different situation of the US at that stage with what existed in Europe and elsewhere. There certainly was not a 'broad socialist conscious-ness' in the US or elsewhere for that matter. The consciousness in the US was predominantly of reformist illusions in capitalism and it could not be otherwise given the biggest and largest boom of capitalism in its history. Even in Europe it was the ideas of 'socialist' reformism that held sway even, and particularly, in the mass Stalinist parties which were semi-reformist. There was, it is true, a certain support for the long-term idea of 'socialism', particularly amongst the more developed layers of the working class in the trade unions and at the base of the nominally 'socialist' or 'Labour' parties. It was this basic consciousness which led to Gaitskell's attempt in 1959 to eliminate Clause IV, Part 4 of the Labour Party's constitution, which enshrined the basic idea of socialism.

Mandelism is for us as Marxists shorthand for describing how even some formally-speak-ing 'Trotskyists', those who followed Ernest Mandel, sometimes in a 'non-revolutionary' period like the early 1960s can opportunistically and impatiently look for other forces than the work-ing class to play the main role in social change and revolution: the peasantry, guerrillas, students, as 'detonators of revolution'. In so doing, they abandoned in practice a revolutionary perspective. Such opportunist trends can appear not just in periods like the early 1960s but in any period including, and particularly, in a period of social upheaval and revolution. Moreover they can be manifested not just in outright 'reformist' forms but in centrism and the different varieties of centrism. All revolutions, not just the Russian Revolution but also the German and Spanish revolutions have revealed these trends , particularly in the leaderships of revolutionary organisa-tions, which unless defeated and consistently warned against in advance can have disastrous results for the prospects of a future working-class victory. Therefore such ideas in our ranks have to be prepared against by us and fought tenaciously in advance in theory and particularly where they appear as a danger to the prospects of a successful socialist revolution.

AM makes a similarly gross error when he ascribes to supporters of the international faction what he calls 'Grantism' – I believe AM is a former member of the 'Grantite' IMT and is in theoretical flight from his past – which he describes as "applying a formula from a past political period to the current situation". Not everything Ted Grant did was right, but he did play an invaluable role in defending the core of Marxist-Trotskyist ideas and perspectives in one of the most difficult political periods in history. I was at one with him in this and still am in defending the central role of the working class – in opposition to identity politics. AM would not have come across the ideas of the CWI if we – Ted Grant, myself and other comrades – had not walked away from the Mandelites' false ideas and perspectives and turned towards the working class, particularly the youth. Facile throwaway comments about a 'formula' demonstrates that he has understood nothing about the movements of the working class and how they relate to their basic organisations, even in the US. Marxism basing itself on the working class as the main force of the socialist revolution is not a 'formula'. It should be seen as the bedrock of a principled Trotskyist organisation.

He is condemned out of his own mouth when he writes: "Even with some union workers, whose unions are so thoroughly bureaucratised in many instances they ceased to have the characteristics of a workers' organisation (this is the case with much of SEIU on the West Coast, whose biggest revenue comes not from membership dues but through investments in the biggest private hospital group in California – actually causing them to come out against a national single-payer healthcare system! There are some similarities with the UAW in the former auto manufacturing regions, but not entirely). If we were to say in this instance to a radicalising SEIU worker involved in political demonstrations and movements that the trade unions could/should play a decisive role, it would be completely not understood as they don't see their union as a vehicle for struggle. In this way, I think the argument about one third of Irish workers being in unions doesn't mean much if they're so thoroughly rotted that the consciousness is not even seeing them as useful for anything and we have to take that into account even if we know that those organisations could be used in a certain way if they were healthy".

There you have it! Some workers do not see their union as a 'vehicle' for struggle which has ceased to have the "characteristics of a workers' organisation". Some, indeed many, of the unions in the US are bureaucratised, and some of them heavily so. Wow! Really we have to wait for AM to inform us that the unions in the USA are hampered by a bureaucratic caste. So are the unions in Britain, in Europe, in Africa and Latin America, etc. And this is enough for his sweeping conclusion that the official unions are cancelled out as effective weapons of struggle. We should not make demands on these bureaucratic trade union leaders. The message is that it is not possible for workers to fight effectively and reclaim these unions. Is this really the position of the industrial comrades in the US in the Teamsters, ATU and other unions?

Many are fighting to change the unions. AM denies the history of the US organisation and some of its current work. It has laboured away over decades to try and create a basis for Marxism and, of course, successfully linking this in the past to the idea of a new 'labour' or workers' party. There is a clear turning away here from the working class organisations. The unions can play a key role within the socialist revolution, including in the US. In working within these organisations we have recognised the existence of the bureaucratic caste, as in the US, perhaps more so than in other countries. But what we also concluded was that it was still necessary to recognise the unions as having a dual character: bourgeois at the top – 'labour lieutenants of capital' – but resting on a worker base. We have at all times tried to counterpose the base of the unions to the tops in order to push forward independent working class action. We have many examples of success in this regard; witness our successes in the NSSN and the PCS in Britain, and many others.

Moreover, the recent strike wave shows the possibility of this being repeated in the US and elsewhere. Vox, a liberal website based in the US, as have our comrades, reported on the strike of teachers in Oakland California. Vox wrote: "The Oakland strike gives momentum to a national trend playing out in red and blue states across the country. More than 100,000 public school teachers in six states have walked out of class in the past year, rebelling from years of stagnant wages, crumbling infrastructure, and deep budget cuts to education … So far, in 2019, teachers in three major cities have gone on strike, including Oakland, and nearly all of West Virginia's teachers did too. The Los Angeles teachers strike shut down the nation's second-largest school district for more than a week in January… More than 2,000 teachers in Denver went on strike for three days. The school district ended up giving educators an extra $23 million in pay and agreed to overhaul the compensation system, which relied heavily on annual bonuses."

There have also been some informative, good reports on Socialist Alternative's site too. The comrades write: "The Democratic Party establishment, backed by the billionaire class, has had an agenda of privatization and turning public schools into charter schools. Up until recently, this has been done behind closed doors, but the [Oakland Education Association (OEA)] has shed light on their plan and brought it fully out in the open for all of Oakland to now see and understand …

"Attacks on public education are happening all across the state. If the whole labor movement unites behind all teachers union locals, both AFT and NEA, up and down California for a one-day strike or sick-out to undo the state's endorsement of the charterization of public schools, this would be a tremendous first step in building the state-wide movement that is necessary to stop the education privatization agenda of the billionaire class."

In summarising the strike, the comrades write: "Unfortunately, the OEA leadership's present-ing of the TA as a decisive victory for the strike did have the effect of partially undercutting this important democratic measure, but robust discussion and debate occurred anyway. Meetups of teachers at various schools and clusters of schools based on region were set up by rank-and-file teachers, and statements were circulated via email and social media …

"If unions locally and nationally began to use the example set by Oakland teachers we could begin to stop attacks on our living standards and win victories in our workplaces, as we rebuild a fighting labor movement. Both the LA and Oakland strikes, which had a sharp political character and mobilized working class communities in a common struggle to fund public education and end privatizations, also point towards how we build a mass movement centered on the social power of the working class to win Medicare for All, affordable housing for all, free college and an end to mass incarceration."

What is this but a call for the unions at all levels to mobilise for action both locally and also nationally by placing demands on the leadership of the unions at all levels? We support the initiative of rank-and-file activists but we also have to have a perspective for transforming the unions nationally, which AM effectively writes off. Crude rank-and-filism alone will not succeed in Socialist Alternative becoming a major force in the US unions.

AM's letter reveals a disturbing vindication of what we originally raised in relation to Ireland has now spread to other sections, of at best the downgrading of the role of the working class and its organisations, particularly the trade unions and looking towards other forces to do the job. How else to explain his cloudy, not to say inexplicable, 'formula': "We must also avoid the mistakes [?!] of social democracy in looking to subordinate entirely the issue of special oppression, I think the false polarisation by the faction unfortunately has encouraged this. I was extremely disappointed with the balance of the article on Scottish equal pay victory for instance and attribute it entirely to the factional situation."

His points in relation to this battle are farcical and way off the mark. Matt Dobson and Philip Stott have pointed out that our comrades played a leading role in this strike. Through this, we were able to get strikers to attend Socialism 2018 in London. This was a strike mainly of working class women, who instinctively and correctly appealed to the male workers to join them in the struggle. It was not, as Danny Byrne, in his eager embrace of identity politics, suggested, just "a feminist strike". Moreover the strike was successfully led by our comrades in Scotland who quite correctly linked up the movement of the women and demands on conditions, equal pay and so on with the male workers. At the same time they brought forward the 'special oppression' of women in general which resulted in increased support for the strike and the growth in the influence of our party.

The clear suggestion of AM and others who agree with him is that our comrades in Scotland should have artificially injected into the strike additional demands related to 'special oppression' which the women workers had not first raised themselves. These workers understood the vital necessity of firstly winning and maintaining a common front with other workers. We have had a long history in Britain of fighting against separatism and for working-class unity in the workplace: fighting to overcome the splits between skilled and unskilled workers, racial and national divisions, etc. This is in contradistinction to the ultra-left sects who invariably intervened in workers' struggles in a ham-fisted manner, particularly in cases like those in Northern Ireland.

The approach of AM and other US comrades who have attacked our work in Glasgow is no different of that of the SWP and union bureaucrats in Birmingham, who have constantly attempted to divide mainly female striking homecare workers from mainly male bin workers by constant and repeated claims that the homecare workers are only under attack because they are women. This is despite a small number of male homecare workers included in the workforce, and despite the repeated huge attacks facing the bin workers and other sections of the council workforce. Only through our comrades' interventions were we able to win support and achieve a momentous joint strike day with huge hundreds-strong joint picket lines, against the position of the SWP and local Unison bureaucracy.

This letter by AM is a concession to identity politics at a time when the working class is stirring and there is a growing class polarisation which is developing in the US. This is not to 'ignore' or to 'downplay' – as the Non-Faction Faction suggests that we do – the special oppression of all specially oppressed layers, but to skilfully link these together with the general struggles of the working class.

We say frankly that unless the approach of AM is corrected, the US organisation will not be able to face up to the task of winning the decisive sections of the organised working class or the mass of workers to its banner.

On the Glasgow Equal Pay Dispute

Socialist Party Scotland EC

The approach adopted by the Scottish section to the historic equal pay battle in Glasgow has recently come under criticism as part of the international debate. Points of difference were raised at the US National Committee to the effect that we had somehow downplayed or ignored the key gender aspect of the strike.

Similar points have now been elaborated by two US comrades in written comments. The secretary of the CWI, Tony Saunois, received the following question from a US comrade, Josh Koritz, last week: "Hope your doing well. I wanted to ask you a question that I asked at the NC that you didn't get to responding to in your sum up. I read this article ("Equal Pay strike victory: A historic day for the working class in Glasgow!" on SocialistPartyScotland. org.uk) from the Scottish comrades about the Glasgow strike. My opinion is that it down-plays the central aspect of the strike – the gender pay gap – and puts far too much emphasis on the solidarity from male workers. What do you think?"

A leading US comrade, Andy Moxley, has also commented: "We must also avoid the mis-takes of social democracy in looking to subordinate entirely the issue of special oppression. I think the false polarization by the faction unfortunately has encouraged this. I was extremely disappointed with the balance of the article on the Scottish equal pay victory for instance and attribute it entirely to the factional situation."

We assume these criticisms are common currency among the US leadership, and indeed the Non-Faction Faction (NFF) generally. Of course we welcome scrutiny and discussion of our articles, leaflets and our general work by any comrade. Included in this response are references to a range of the material produced before, during and after the historic strike action in October 2018 and the subsequent victory for the working class in Glasgow – a victory that, we would remind the comrades, our party played a very important role in.

Glasgow City Unison branch, within which Socialist Party Scotland members play a lead-ing role, organised thousands of workers who took strike action for equal pay. Regular mass meetings, successfully encouraging women to step forward as shop stewards and spokespeople for the campaign, was central to some of that work. Our articles in the paper, website, and many of our leaflets carried interviews and quotes from women involved in the action, not least to bring out the class anger and determination that formed the backbone of this movement.

The accusation by the comrades in the US that we downplayed the "gender pay gap" is embarrassing and must betray the fact that the comrades have not read the articles we produced. For example read the article headlined "Women have died in this city waiting on equal pay. It's beyond a disgrace."

Josh takes us up for putting "far too much emphasis on the solidarity from male workers." The article he refers to says this on male workers in total: "Some of the women carried placards thanking the mainly male refuse workers who walked out, in defiance of anti-union laws, in support of the mainly female strikers last October. The slogans included "The dust may have settled but we will remember that the dustmen came out!"

We quote a female worker and shop steward, and then our comrade and union leader Brian Smith about what was achieved: "The deal that has been agreed represents a huge transfer of wealth to working-class families in the city and as such represents a seminal victory for the workforce. A victory that would not have been achieved without the marvellous 48-hour strike last October.

"The deal will ensure our members are paid up to March 31, 2018 for the historic pay injustice they suffered. But this is only half the battle as now we need agreements on a new job evaluation scheme going forward.

"As a union we won't accept any attempts to lower wages and conditions for any worker. Or as the equal pay strikers have rightly described it, to 'rob Peter to pay Pauline.' It's vital that we keep our members organised and ready to fight for pay justice for all."

What is the problem with this? Should we have taken out the reference to male workers' solidarity action? The women themselves made the illegal strikes of the refuse workers a key point that they referred to again and again, including after the strike when they plastered posters all around the depots and housing schemes where the refuse workers were based, thanking them for their solidarity.

In criticising us, Josh is actually inadvertently opposing the position adopted by the women workers themselves. Not a good position for a Marxist to be in! Isn't it the role of socialists and Marxists to emphasise the unity of the working class? To emphasise the common features that working-class men and women have in the struggle to end all forms of oppression, including pay inequality? By the way, 10% of the equal pay strikers were male.

Did we, as Andy hints at, ape "social democracy" and, "subordinate the issue of special oppression" when we wrote in our main article for our website and paper ("Glasgow's Equal Pay uprising shows the power of the working class") on the day after the strike that:

"8,500 Glasgow working-class women made history on October 23 and 24. As the BBC news commented, it was 'one of the biggest ever strikes in the UK on the issue of equal pay.' In truth, it was more like an uprising, in which the power of the working class was clearly demonstrated.

"In a phenomenal logistical effort, picket lines were set up across hundreds of primary schools, nurseries, cleansing depots and council buildings. This achievement alone testified to the mass participation that was a hallmark of the strike. A colourful sea of 10,000 strikers, dominated by the flags, banners and placards of Unison and the GMB, as well as fellow trade unionists and supporters, marched in a noisy and vibrant demo on the first strike day, that shook the streets from Glasgow Green to George Square.

"Central to the mobilisation was the tremendous fighting capacity of low paid women workers who make up 90% of the strikers. Betrayed by the previous right-wing Labour council, who presided over the pay inequality scandal for a decade – and the new SNP leadership who promised a just resolution but have dragged their heels – working class women had had enough.

"12 years underpaid and undervalued, the strike reflected the pent up anger, and also the experience of the last decade of vicious capitalist austerity. As one striking marcher interviewed on the rolling news broadcast said: 'We want fairness. I'm a single parent, struggling to support my family on £800 a month.' Striker Carol Qua made the point that she had three council jobs and was still struggling. Finally the frustration was given an outlet, these workers enthusiastically seized their chance to show their working class power."

What we did, at all times, was to underline the potential power of the working class to win using mass struggle. The women workers involved never saw themselves as carrying out a 'feminist strike,' as one leading member of the NFF claimed at the time. It was a working-class strike, led by working-class women, with Marxists playing a key role in facilitating the action.

It was also not lost on the strikers that they were taking action against an SNP council led by a women who describes herself as a feminist, and a council chief executive who is also female. Both of these women were obstacles to the just demands of thousands of low-paid women in Glasgow. It is vital that we make clear our complete opposition to all forms of such pro-capitalist 'feminism' and any idea that their interests are compatible. We instead advocate mass working-class and socialist struggle to defeat them and the system they defend.

Unfortunately, the criticisms of the two US comrades betray, in our view, the influence of identity politics on their outlook. They seem to want to locate the Glasgow strike in the gender category rather than one primarily of class, within which the double oppression of working women gave the movement the character of an 'uprising,' as we emphasised.

This tendency among the NFF to separate off such struggles as feminist, if taken into the working-class movement – whether by us or other forces – can only threaten the unity of the working class and weaken the appeal of Marxism among those moving into opposition to austerity and capitalism.

We would therefore urge the comrades to reconsider their approach.

Other articles on the equal pay strike include: Mass strike wins historic step towards victory in Glasgow equal pay battle; Equal pay strikes and mass teachers' demo opens up a new phase of working class struggle in Scotland; Working class women making history in mass strike for equal pay. All are available on SocialistPartyScotland.org.uk

4. On the NATIONAL QUESTION

Scotland's Referendum: a Working-Class Revolt

Peter Taaffe, Socialism Today 182, October 2014

The independence referendum in Scotland was remarkable for many things: the huge politicisation and class polarisation, combined with the beginning of mass intervention in politics, particularly by the most oppressed sections of the working class, shaping their own destiny. This was hitherto seen as the preserve of the self-appointed, stifling elites who dominate what passes for political discourse in Britain. The referendum, with its heightened passion, has altered the political landscape of Britain: 'things will never be the same again', as even capitalist commentators have observed. One of its most striking results was the effect that it had internationally. A country with a population smaller than the county of Yorkshire, and half that of greater London, albeit with a proud history of working-class defiance, shook Europe and the world to their foundations.

World leaders, from Barack Obama to the Chinese head of state, Xi Jinping, drawing in the Pope on the same side as the Orange Order, were lined up to urge frantically the rejection of Scottish independence. The British ruling class which, within living memory, ruled one quarter of mankind – with its prestige and what remains of its world reputation at stake – was so terrified of a Yes vote that it outdid itself in venom against those advocating independence. "The world is saying No to Scottish separation", shrieked Phillip Stephens in the Financial Times. A few days before the referendum took place, the same journal reflected the sheer terror of the capitalists: "Ruling elite aghast as union wobbles … Business onslaught over Yes vote … Business 90% against Yes".

Surprise, surprise, the International Monetary Fund was also conscripted to the anti-independence bandwagon and warned "Recession risk in markets". Alan Greenspan, former chairman of the US Federal Reserve and fresh from presiding over the greatest financial and economic disaster witnessed since the 1930s, returned from internal exile to warn that "a Yes vote would be an economic mistake for Scotland [and] a geopolitical disaster for the west". And if Scotland had actually voted for independence, it would be punished: "The Scots will discover the taste of austerity", warned the FT.

Why this hysteria, a seeming absence of any sense of proportion when judging the events in Scotland, on the part of these mandarins of capitalism? The explanation is to be found in the opposite yet equally powerful response that events in Scotland have enthusiastically evoked among the masses in Europe and elsewhere, with many countries facing their own explosive national question. Mariano Rajoy, Spanish prime minister, and his foreign minister, with the Catalan masses breathing down their necks, naturally viewed Scottish independence quite simply as a 'catastrophe' which would, they claimed, "worsen the economic slump in Europe and risk the European Union's (EU) disintegration".

In reality, it is the 'Balkanisation' (their word) of Spain, the right of self-determination and independence for the Catalan people and, following them, the Basques, which they mortally fear. The Catalan movement was given a big boost by virtue of the fact that the Scottish referendum was taking place. 'How could Cameron have so miscalculated?' was the snarl, which echoed throughout Europe. It has encouraged the Catalans and other nationalities to demand their own referendum – bitterly resisted by Madrid. Meanwhile, in Italy, there exists a simmering mood in the Alto Adige, the largely German-speaking region, demanding similar rights as the Scots for a say in their future, while the right-wing Northern League is making similar demands for northern Italy.

Socialists and the national question

These examples of the international ramifications of Scotland's intense debate over independence show that there is hardly a country today that does not have, to one degree or another, a national question which threatens to detonate at any time. The onset of a world economic crisis has resurrected the national question in regions and countries where it seemed previously to have been settled.

This means that the labour movement, particularly those who claim to be socialists and Marxists, have to grapple with this issue. In so doing, it is necessary to avoid falling into the pit of opportunism, of accommodating to bourgeois, capitalist nationalism or of adopting an empty, abstract, propagandist approach which can never succeed in connecting with the real movement of the working class, particularly its oppressed layers.

At each stage of developments over the last four decades the forces of Marxism in the ranks of Militant, now the Socialist Party, supported the Scottish people's legitimate demands in the national sphere. While the summits of the labour movement, not just the right-wing but also those then on the 'left' like Neil Kinnock, opposed even limited devolution for Scotland in the 1970s, we unequivocally supported it. We did not engender any illusions though that this was a 'final destination' that could solve all the problems of the Scottish people.

At the same time as defending the right of self-determination for the Scottish people, we did not favour the Balkanisation of countries composed of different national groups. It is absurd to imagine that any country, particularly a small country, can prosper and solve their problems in isolation. In a globalised world, it is not possible to go it alone. The striving for 'unity' of the European capitalists, enshrined in the EU, is an expression of the need for the productive forces – science, technique and the organisation of labour – to be organised on a continental and even a world scale. But the capitalists can never fully overcome the limits of private ownership or the nation state. Only the working class acting together can, through a democratic socialist united states of Europe, achieve this task.

Therefore, while fighting for an independent socialist Scotland we, and particularly our comrades in Scotland, link this to a socialist confederation in the first instance of Scotland, England, Wales and Ireland, as well as a socialist Europe. There were occasions in the past when we argued against independence for Scotland as an immediate demand, particularly as a slogan. This was because independence did not enjoy the support of significant sections of the population. In these circumstances, to advocate 'self-determination', and particularly independence, that is separation, could be interpreted by many Scottish workers as expressing a wish that we, the majority, do not want to live with them in a common state. However, once the idea of independence had gripped the minds of the masses, the support of a majority or a significant and growing minority, we faced a changed situation.

The direction of travel has been clear in Scotland for a long time. The election of the Scottish National Party (SNP) as a majority in the Scottish parliament was seen as a staging post on the way to 'independence', particularly for the most energetic and dynamic sections of the working class who have come to the fore in the referendum campaign. A significant section – oscillating between 40-50% – of young people in particular had already embraced this idea, long before the referendum was agreed. The task of Marxists was to give support generally but seek to give it a socialist content. This was and is combined with warnings about the inadequacies, to say the least, of the SNP's resolve to remain within the framework of capitalism, which would mean that few of the social demands driving the Yes campaign could be realised. On the contrary, savage austerity would have been the future for Scotland unless workers were able to use victory in the referendum to press for a break with capitalism.

Mistakes of the left

The Yes campaign provided a huge opportunity to strike a blow against the plans of British capitalism for systematic attacks on the working class. Hence the Yes placards that declared "an end to Tory rule for ever". Unfortunately, that would not have followed independence automatically, in the sense of an end to cuts and support for pro-big business policies, with an SNP government speaking out against austerity but implementing it in practice while continuing to rule Scotland. But it showed the class feelings behind the demand for independence.

It is incredible therefore that even sections of the left, like George Galloway, bitterly opposed independence on a shared platform with Tories, Liberal Democrats, as well as an increasingly discredited Ed Miliband in the No camp. Despite his heroic stand in the past against the Iraq war, as well as his championing of the general case for socialism, Galloway was roundly booed by significant sections of the young people gathered at the debate for 16-year-olds. But he was not alone, especially when he falsely claimed that "austerity is ending" and "a 1945-style Labour government" was in prospect for 2015.

The Communist Party of Britain (CPB), linked to the Morning Star newspaper, also found itself on the wrong side of history. "A No vote in the referendum has to be made the springboard for the mobilising of the working-class movement at British level to demand real constitutional change", was its position. (Statement on Scottish independence, 4 March 2014) Just how this is possible when you oppose the aspirations of the mass of the Scottish working class remains a mystery. The CPB's reasons for opposing the Yes vote? "Membership of the sterling area which subordinates Scotland to the current neoliberal policies without any power to change them, at the same time seriously erodes the opportunity for united working class action across the nations of Britain ... Worse still, membership of the

EU would oblige Scotland to incorporate in any written constitution the terms of the 2012 Treaty of Stability, Coordination and Governance".

But why does this follow from independence? Surely the working class in an independent Scotland would have the opportunity, perhaps a greater opportunity, to oppose membership of the EU? The CPB demonstrates here a fetish about the sterling area, as well as in relation to the EU. Membership of both has not stopped a united working class in Britain or Europe from fighting the bosses and opposing actual or proposed anti-worker legislation.

The implied argument here is that support for the independence of Scotland automatically divides the working class. Yet it is possible to support independence and fight for and unite the working class. This was answered more than a century ago by Karl Marx and Vladimir Lenin. Indeed, the Marxist movement, from the time of Marx, has a long pedigree on this issue. Marx, in general, stood for a unified state. Yet both he and Engels stubbornly advocated Irish independence. Only after independence, argued Marx, would federation between Ireland and Britain then be posed.

Lenin deepened this approach in educating the workers of Russia to defend the right of self-determination of nations oppressed by tsarism. Lenin argued that only in this way would it be possible to gain the confidence of the masses of the oppressed nations. On the basis of a democratic socialist republic they would not cut away but voluntarily link their fate to that of the masses of Russia. This presentation of the issue was brilliantly confirmed in the course of the Russian revolution. The Bolsheviks recognised the right of self-determination including secession, as was shown by the example of Finland, which separated in 1918.

The arguments of the CPB and the small organisations on the left, including some alleged 'Marxists', are echoes of the approach of Rosa Luxemburg. She opposed Lenin's proposal for the right of self-determination and also the decision of the Bolsheviks after taking power in 1917 to give the land to the peasants. She saw these demands as representing a backward step. On the contrary, the Bolsheviks managed to unite the working class, because they also opposed bourgeois nationalism – as the Committee for a Workers' International (CWI) has done consistently in Scotland.

Lenin explained that, sometimes, you can take one step backwards in order to take two steps forward. Where the land is divided, it is done in order to win the confidence of the peasants who could only be convinced of the necessity of large-scale production in agriculture over a period of time and with their consent. The same applies to self-determination which allows oppressed nationalities to pass through the stage of realising their own demands, allowing them in practice to see the need to unify the productive forces on a bigger scale, thereby arriving at a voluntary confederation.

Only the CWI has had a consistent position on the national question, both in Britain and internationally. The Socialist Workers' Party (SWP), for example, in the 1970s debate over devolution, declared: "If a referendum is eventually held in Scotland and Wales we abstain. This is not a position that means ducking the arguments … Our abstention will mark us out from the rest of the labour movement, retreating in fear before the new reformism, without aligning us with the unionist, British, nationalist camp". (The National Question, September 1977) Like a leaky umbrella that does not work when it is unfolded, this policy was unceremoniously abandoned without explanation.

It is true that the form in which the struggle over independence was conducted was not ideal.

Referendums are not the preferred weapon of the working class and its organisations. Dictatorships or undemocratic regimes often use referendums to bolster their position, presenting a simple choice: yes or no. The labour movement and particularly socialist forces are sometimes compelled to stand alongside of, and share platforms with, bourgeois or pro-bourgeois forces, with the political risk that they will not be able to get over their message and programme.

Referendums can also be a trap for genuine socialist forces if they do not clearly differentiate themselves politically, in terms of perspective and programme, in the course of the campaign from temporary nationalist 'allies'. This does not necessarily involve directly attacking forces with which we are aligned. Sometimes, it is sufficient to just outline our case, which will bring out clearly to workers our differences with the nationalists. If we are skilful enough, audiences, particularly workers, will draw the right political conclusions. However, on other occasions it may be necessary to sharply differentiate ourselves in terms of programme and perspectives from, for instance, bourgeois or petty-bourgeois nationalists – the SNP in this referendum – and also from left nationalism.

The forces of the CWI that participated in the Scottish referendum did not fall into the trap of bolstering the SNP. While energetically supporting the Yes campaign in general, the Socialist Party Scotland (SPS) collaborated in a splendid independent, working-class orientated and effective campaign, which drew in hundreds and thousands of enthusiastic Scottish workers alongside Tommy Sheridan and prominent SPS members. Even Rupert Murdoch, in a backhanded compliment, recognised this when he complained that too many "lefties" were prominent in the Yes campaign.

Moreover, our case was spelt out in some programmatic detail and contrasted with the false perspectives of those nationalists who painted a rosy future for Scotland on a capitalist basis. All the previous capitalist models that the SNP invoked in the past – Ireland, Iceland, and Scandinavia as a whole – are now clearly tarnished as a result of the devastating world economic crisis. The referendum showed a massive rejection of austerity, whether imposed from Westminster or Edinburgh. The demographic breakdown of voting patterns showed that it was the working class, particularly its most deprived and oppressed sections in the areas that voted Yes, in Glasgow, Dundee, West Dunbartonshire and North Lanarkshire, alongside the majority of the 16-17 year-olds, who massively opted for independence.

Tory manoeuvring

If ever there was an example of the kind of 'nationalism', reflecting the "outer shell of an immature Bolshevism", about which Leon Trotsky spoke, it was in the solid working-class vote for Yes in this referendum. 'Independence' was organically linked in the minds of the masses with complete independence from those who imposed the poll tax in the past, the bedroom tax today, the persecution of the disabled and sick, etc.

This mood has not gone away. David Cameron, two weeks before the vote, believed he was facing defeat which would in all probability seal his political fate. Even the Tories were baying for his blood. If Scotland had voted Yes, Cameron's own party would have voted No to him! In the event a massive scare campaign, crucially and massively helped by the intervention of the Labour leadership, particularly Gordon Brown – using up whatever political capital he still possessed – managed to corral the overwhelming majority of the middle-class and the 'don't knows', into the No camp.

The ferocious No campaign in the last stages had an effect. Matthew d'Ancona wrote in the Sunday Telegraph: "Lord Ashcroft's post-referendum polling shows that 19% of those who voted No made their decision to do so in the past month – a vindication of the frantic campaigning by the Unionist side in that period".

However, this has created almost as many problems for the British ruling class as a Yes vote would have done. Cameron, the gambler that he is – 'chancer', according to the Sunday Telegraph – within hours of the result being announced, stated that he would 'honour' his promise to deliver more powers on tax and welfare to the Scottish parliament. But he added the twist that "new powers for the Scots should be balanced by new rights for the English".

There was an implied threat that, if this was not agreed, then the 'vow' of devo-max for Scotland would be withdrawn. However, this would be "incendiary" in Scotland, as the retiring SNP leader, Alex Salmond, said. Cameron has no choice but to give concessions or he will face a bigger uprising than witnessed in the referendum. His proposal is clearly designed, with a general election months away, to appeal to English nationalism, with the added advantage, he believes, of outfoxing Ukip and, at the same time, wrong-footing Miliband and the Labour Party.

He is unlikely to get his proposals passed this side of a general election. However, it is striking how all the Tory voices which appeared on television – Cameron, Heseltine, Hague, etc – under the cloak of 'greater democracy', advocate that the 59 Scottish MPs (41 of whom are presently Labour) should no longer vote on 'English matters' in the House of Commons.

Their reasoning goes that, even if Miliband wins in May next year, he will not be able to implement his programme because Scottish MPs will be debarred from voting on crucial issues – the so-called 'West Lothian question'. Yet Will Hutton in the Observer pointed out: "The McKay commission, on the impact of devolution on British government, pointed out there have only been two electoral periods since 1919 – 1964 to 1966 and between March and October 1974 – when the party in government had not won a majority in England. Moreover, [the online democracy project] mySociety finds that of 5,000 votes in the House of Commons since 1997, only 21 depended on the votes of Scottish MPs".

These proposals have been signed up to by not just Tory luminaries but also Nick Clegg. They include 'greater powers' to cities and regions. This is clearly designed to give more power to the undemocratic, dictatorial mayors like Boris Johnson in London to implement brutal anti-working class measures, such as the assault on ticket offices at the present time on London Underground.

No oversight is really exercised by councillors below the mayors or council cabinets and, indeed, the very creation of these positions is designed to allow these hatchet men to more easily implement further cuts. They are part of the overall programme to further attack the living standards of the working class. They must be implacably opposed and met by counter-proposals by the labour movement. This should include the abolition of mayors and cabinet rule in local authorities. Full democracy and accountability of local councillors should be restored.

Seizing the moment

Cameron was given a bloody nose in the referendum campaign. It is now time to finish off the whole of the Tory gang and all capitalist politicians threatening to drag working people further into the abyss. Scotland has shown that the working class is rotten ripe for a clear political alternative. The events around the referendum, particularly among the working class, show that a potential 'Podemos moment' exists. In Spain, the radical movement around Podemos came from nowhere to capture in six weeks 1.2 million votes in the European elections. Something similar is now possible in Scotland if Tommy Sheridan, aligned with the Marxists and others, particularly the trade unions like RMT, were to take the plunge and create a socialist, radical alternative which would act as a magnet to all of those workers and youth inspired by the independence campaign.

Unfortunately, however, instead of striking out boldly to lay the basis for a new party of the working class, Tommy has now stated: "I suggest we in the Yes movement promote continued unity by backing the most likely independence supporting candidate at next May's general election. In concrete terms that means advocating an SNP vote to try and unseat as many pro-No party supporters as possible".

This statement was made without, as far as we are aware, any serious consultation with those who supported and worked alongside him very successfully in the Hope not Fear campaign. It was the socialist message combined with firm support for independence that attracted thousands who were and remain deeply opposed to and suspicious of the SNP. Now Tommy suggests the lessons of that campaign should be abandoned. The working class should line up behind the SNP despite the fact that it has already carried out cuts and will carry through more, including before the 2015 election.

Thousands of socialists, therefore, will be behind a pro-cuts agenda if Tommy's suggestions are accepted, with socialist policies postponed to an indefinite future in the 'national cause'. What is this except a disastrous repeat of 1918 in Ireland when the Irish nationalists also argued 'labour must wait', and the craven trade union leaders like Thomas Johnson acceded to this? Irish labour left the field free to the nationalists and Sinn Fein with disastrous results for the working class.

Tommy also states: "We should insist all pro-independence candidates in the 2016 Scottish election commit to a March 2020 referendum". How timid! Why wait four years to implement a referendum? Indeed, with a massive new mandate, why would a Scottish government necessarily go for a referendum as the route to independence? But if it did, it would be able to go for it immediately and score a stunning victory.

But his proposals should be rejected for other reasons as well. He states: "Unity is strength. Don't let our differences weaken our cause". But this does not apply between parties based on the working class and those pro-capitalist parties like the SNP who inevitably betray the aspirations of those who are seduced into supporting them. If implemented this would cripple the independence of the Scottish working class and its ability to resist the onslaught of the capitalists politically.

The campaign has shown what an independent socialist campaign could achieve. It is necessary to build on this. This is the real lesson of the Scottish referendum. The idea that independence for Scotland is off the agenda "for a generation", as Salmond said, is totally false. The genie is out of the bottle and the demand for an independent, socialist Scotland will grow in intensity as the crisis of capitalism worsens and provokes a mass revolt.

A Reply on the National Question

Niall Mulholland, for the IS Majority

The Irish NEC majority document, 'The National Question in Ireland and the Dispute in the CWI' contains comments of a general nature regarding a Marxist approach on the national question and Ireland which the IS does not have fundamental disagreement with.

However, the Irish NEC majority also repeatedly asks what differences does the IS majority hold on the national question with the Irish leadership and why does the IS not reveal them. It is claimed that the IS has "suggested political differences with the Irish section on the national question". The IS are told "not to hide differences" and that the "shadow boxing ought to come to an end". In debates, Irish NEC comrades have accused the IS of holding "secret" positions and that we have only embarked on "skirmishes" on the national question.

These assertions are not accurate. The IS majority have openly raised concerns and differences with the Irish leadership for several years. The Irish NEC claims should also come as a surprise to leading Non-Faction Faction (NFF) supporters, such as Danny Byrne (DB – IS alternate) and Tom Crean (TC – US EC), who have been sharply critical of the Irish section leadership regarding the national question (including in IB and IS meetings, in the case of DB). Yet during the current debate in the CWI, there has not been a murmur from these comrades on this subject. TC referred to "differences" he holds with the Irish comrades during his contribution at the November IEC meeting, and then failed to list any single one of these "differences"! It appears that for factional expediency these leading NFF comrades have lost their political memory and voices.

What are the differences?

This document is a reply to the main points made in the Irish NEC majority document; it is not intended as an exhaustive, all-rounded Marxist approach on the national question in Ireland.

The IS never said that its concerns, raised openly, amounts to fundamental or profound differences with the Irish leadership on the national question. But significant differences of emphasis and nuance have arisen and when dealing with the national question these are not unimportant. Any incorrect emphasis or repeated mistakes on this crucial question must be dealt with and corrected or the real danger arises of the development of incorrect political tendencies or positions to emerge.

The following are examples, not exhaustive, of where the IS has discussed and debated the national question and programme with the Irish leadership, over several years:

• The IS proposed a plenary session on the national question on the agenda of the 2014 IEC meeting. This was partly intended to try and encourage Irish IEC comrades to raise any differences they may have had with the IS on the national question, including the position the Scottish section adopted on the independence referendum

• Dublin Easter 1916 Rising 100th anniversary: Phone conference discussion in 2016 between IS comrades and Irish NEC comrades on how Marxists should commemorate and analyse this historic event, followed by, on the initiative of the IS, debates on the same subject at a commission at the 2016 CWI summer school and a commission held at the England and Wales section's 'Socialism' event in November 2016

• Discussion between IS comrades and Stevie Boyd (SB - Ireland) and former Spanish comrades at 2017 IEC meeting regarding Catalonia and programme, and similarities and differences with Ireland

• IS comrades raised concerns about an article published in September 2017 by the Irish section − "Why socialists oppose a border poll" − considering the title and article did not fully take into account sufficiently and sensitively Catholic working-class moods and sentiments, as well as correctly addressing Protestant working-class moods and rights etc

• Niall Mulholland (NM − IS) attended an Irish NC meeting in late 2017 for a special discussion on the National Question and programme, followed up by a visit by DB to an Irish NC in 2018 that also discussed these issues

• NM (IS) attended a March 2019 Irish NC debate on the 'United Front'

• NM (IS) and other IS comrades commented on draft texts of pamphlets and books on Irish workers' history produced by the Irish section, when the texts have been brought to the attention of the IS.

Catalonia

The Irish NEC document refers to the former Spanish section's position on Catalonia. Irish IEC comrades raised questions concerning how IR addressed the question of those workers who opposed independence in Catalonia, and on aspects of the former Spanish section's programme and demands. This included IR's call for a 'workers' or 'socialist republic' of Catalonia and why the section did not bring more to the fore the call for a 'socialist federation' of the region.

Irish comrades have a right to raise these criticisms, of course (though we believe some of the comrades somewhat mechanically transferred the situation in N Ireland to Catalonia). IS comrades had already broached these issues and others with the former Spanish comrades.

The IS cannot answer for the former comrades from IR who have left the CWI, set on a sectarian and ultra-left path, and are no longer taking part in the debate. Previously the IR leadership replied to the comments made by Irish IEC comrades at IEC plenaries and in separate discussions with Irish IEC comrades. They argued that the exact terminology was not critical as long as socialist policies were expressed. They said that given the role of the 'socialist' PSOE it would not be readily understood if they called for a 'socialist' Catalonia and instead called for a 'socialist republic' or 'workers republic' of Catalonia. They claimed that they do stand for a socialist federation, posing it as a "socialist republic of Catalonia and a federal socialist republic based upon the free and voluntary union of the Spanish state, if that is their wish". But IR said that it would have been wrong to bring this slogan to the fore during the huge movements in Catalonia for independence. This, the IR argued, could have implied to workers in Catalonia that we stand for hurrying them back into the Spanish state just as independence is achieved. The leading Irish comrades expressed their satisfaction with the IR's replies.

Scotland

Previously, at the 2014 IEC meeting, SB (Ireland) argued that the Scottish comrades should consider not calling for a 'yes' vote in any new Scottish referendum on independence because of the negative effects a successful 'yes' vote would have amongst Protestants in N Ireland (ie raising fears of the breaking up of the UK will lead towards a united Ireland).

Marxists need to be aware, of course, about the wider effects of their slogans, demands and programme. We stand for the right to self-determination - a democratic demand. This starts from the premise that no nation should be obliged to remain within the borders of a multinational state, contrary to its wishes. While we stand for the rights of national minorities, we also have to take into account the interests of the wider working class. How this is balanced out depends on the concrete circumstances. In the case of Scotland, it would be clearly wrong to suggest that the right to self-determination should be denied by our comrades there because of the possible negative connotations such a demand may have in other parts of the UK. Marxists do not lightly advocate independence, particularly in multi-national states. But where we do take a position in support of independence, not just the right to self-determination – ie where there is a clear desire for separation, as in Scotland - we cannot hold that this is subject to the wishes of other nations or a section of the population, as in N Ireland. Our approach on the national question cannot just be seen through the prism of one country but must be viewed in an all-sided manner, using the method of Marxism.

The working class must have its own, independent position on the national question, as on any other question. In Scotland, our comrades call for an independent socialist Scotland, and a free and voluntary socialist federation of Scotland with England, Wales and Ireland. This is linked to the slogans, "No to the bosses' neo-liberal European Union. For a socialist Europe and a socialist world."

This requires comrades in Ireland to give a careful explanation of our position on Scottish independence; explaining the democratic right of Scottish people to decide their own future while emphasising the class bonds between Scottish workers and workers in N Ireland, both Protestant and Catholic, and the need to build on these in the struggle for socialism across the islands.

Debate on programme

The Irish NEC majority document refers to how in "a series of verbal contributions comrades in the faction have suggested that we are paying too much attention to the rights of one community in Northern Ireland, and not enough to the other". This is a crude interpretation of the position of the IS but it does indeed suggest the concerns the IS has presented. We were under the impression that some Irish NEC comrades agreed that they had "bent the stick too far" on this issue. At the March 2019 Irish NC debate on the 'United Front', some NEC and NC comrades made precisely this point.

The Irish NEC majority poses that it is "possible that comrades are not convinced by our position, adopted 25 years ago, that in certain circumstances Protestants should have the right to opt-out of a socialist unitary state, or believe that this is a defensible position but should not be voiced or raised at this time".

NM (IS) was a member of the Irish NEC, Northern REC, and a FT'er in Belfast during the 1990s, and fully involved in the discussion in the Irish section on the national question and programme. This internal discussion was initiated by the new situation opening up in the North of Ireland in the 1990s (the ending of the 'Troubles' and the start of the 'peace process') and internationally (following the collapse of Stalinism). It was felt necessary and timely to re-examine our analysis of the national question in Ireland and to discuss if we needed to change our programme.

The discussion centred over changes in consciousness amongst Protestant and Catholic workers and the need to update our programme. It was agreed that we had to take enhanced concerns and uncertainty amongst Protestants more into account, to win the ear of the most politically advanced Protestant workers and youth. We needed to express more the 'rights' of Protestants. Some comrades posed the question as to whether we should not only consider the right of Protestants to opt for separation in a future socialist state, if they so wished it, but go further and actually advocate it.

The discussion documents, drafted by Peter Hadden, were discussed and amended and eventually voted on and agreed. The main document was turned into a public pamphlet ('Troubled Times'). The final text clearly stated "… a single socialist state is our preferred op-tion...However given the entirely legitimate fears of Protestant workers that a united Ireland in any form equals coercion, we have to be able to provide an assurance to the contrary. By opposing a capitalist united Ireland we have stood against the forcible coercion of Protestants. Now we need to add the firm guarantee that there would be no element of coercion on a socialist basis either. In practice this means a guarantee that, should the majority of Protes-tants firmly oppose being part of a socialist united Ireland, they would have the right to opt out, that is to establish their own socialist state...Such a solution would pose many difficulties but it would be possible. Precisely because of the complexities and even allowing that two socialist states would have open borders which would give permanence to sectarian division, it makes much more sense to have a single state."

Regarding how the question of Protestant rights is raised, "What we say to Protestants is that it would be better to have a solution which can unite Catholics and Protestants and put old capitalist inspired enmity to the side, but the choice is yours. A socialist society will accommodate you in whatever decision you make. We will always accord this right to Protes-tants, but it may not always be necessary to raise it. The strengthening of class unity, develop-ment of a party of the working class and of a socialist consciousness, may mean that the issue will recede and the idea of a single socialist state will become acceptable without reservation. For now we do not need to present the right to opt out in our list of demands. Rather it is for use when we set about more fully explaining our programme, verbally or in more lengthy written material."

In 2017 the Irish NEC decided it was time to revisit the programme and to hold a series of discussions on the national question and programme in the Irish section. NM (IS) attended an Irish NC meeting in late 2017.

It appeared to the IS that some of the Irish leadership believed that it was necessary to move on from the above formulations and to express in a more direct, public way today the right of Protestants to opt for a separate socialist state. Perhaps some of the comrades believed that we should go further and advocate a separate socialist Protestant state?

Unsatisfactorily, the discussion on the national question and programme initiated by the Irish NEC was never concluded in the Irish section. We were asked to send a IS comrade to another NC, in the first quarter of 2018, for another round of discussion, and DB (IS alternate) attended. At this meeting, however, the discussion on the national question was truncated. The IS never heard a full explanation as to why the discussion ended without conclusion. SB (Ireland) informed NM (IS) at the 2018 CWI summer school in Barcelona that he would write a public pamphlet on the issue but the IS has not seen a draft text.

Two nations?

We are now informed in the Irish NEC document that "...we conclude now that there are not two nations in Ireland but there is a separate Protestant community with democratic rights that must be respected".

From the very start of the Irish section, we rejected the idea of 'two nations'. The first edition of Militant Irish Monthly (1972) carried an article by Peter Taaffe (Two Nations? Bankruptcy of Theories of O'Brien and 'Marxist' Sects') which commented: "The adoption of the 'two nations' theory is born out of a despair that the present religious polarisation in Northern Ireland is fixed once and for all, that real unity between Catholic and Protestant workers cannot be achieved and consequently all that remains is to permanently fix these divisions by recognising two nations and two separate states".

During the height of the Troubles, when the loyalist strand of 'Ulster independence' gained some support amongst Protestants, we polemicized against the ex-Maoist British and Irish Communist Organisation (BICO), which adopted a two nation, 'pro-Protestant' theory. In a letter to Irish Times in August 1974, comrade Peter Hadden wrote: "Blinded by the growth of sectarianism the BICO look for short-cuts. Others seek similar short-cuts amongst the Catholics by clinging to the tails of the Provisionals. What such "socialists" ignore is the urgent need for the uniting of the working class. Socialism will not be built "among the Catholics" or "among the Protestants". Protestant and Catholic workers together struggling against all Tories, Orange and Green and those in Britain – it is for this that socialists must fight."

The national question and consciousness is not static. There have been important changes in society and Catholic and Protestant mass consciousness since 1974 and since Troubled Times was written, 25 years ago, that have to be taken into account. But the IS does not think that they warrant fundamental changes to our programme and how we advocate it. The Irish NEC refers to the lines in Troubled Times that discussed how, theoretically, a separate Protestant 'nation' consciousness could develop, over time, as sectarian divisions deepened and hardened on the back of defeats of the working class. It concluded this point had not been reached. This remains the case. The working class is still divided along sectarian lines, in many ways (in much housing, education and voting patterns, for example) but there are also very important areas where Catholic and Protestant workers mix, most significantly in the trade unions. While Brexit and a 'border poll' pose great dangers of significantly raising sectarian tensions and even renewed conflict, this is not a forgone conclusion. Recent election successes for 'non-sectarian' parties (albeit bourgeois parties) and independents and 'lefts', including our comrade Donal Ó Cófaigh's success in Fermanagh, have also shown a desire by sections of the working class and youth and middle classes to move beyond the sectarian-based parties.

The Irish NEC document raises the dangers of increased sectarianism and potential conflict. It is correct to make these warnings but we need to be measured about it, avoid taking a one-sided, linear approach, and careful not to come across as fatalistic and 'catastrophist'. This is not based on wishful thinking or an empty sentiment about the working class and its organisations. We have always pointed out that there are countervailing class tendencies that point to uniting the working class. Class struggles and the creation of a mass party of the working class will cut across tendencies towards sectarian divisions and a slide to conflict.

Presenting our programme

The Irish NEC document correctly states that referring to the "two communities" in the North today is reflecting realities on the ground (ie working class communities largely divided along sectarian lines) and is not the same as defining them as "two nations", with all the implications that would hold for our programme and demands.

But how we present our programme and demands, and how we portray each "community", are very important. While it is correct to recognise the reality of two 'communities' or 'two traditions' in Northern Ireland – reflecting the sectarian divide – that does not mean that we acquiescence to it or accept that it is permanent. The two communities are separated on many questions, but still united on many other questions. There may be two 'traditions' but there is one class. We have to put forward a programme which recognises and upholds the rights of both these communities, while campaigning for workers' unity on class issues to break down the sectarian barriers. While there are two traditions, there is also a third one, a working class, socialist tradition, and part of our role is to highlight and popularise this class history. We should seek to emphasis unity over division and state clearly our preferred position would be a socialist Ireland, with full minority rights, as part of a socialist federation, on a voluntary and equal basis, of Ireland, England, Scotland and Wales. This will be part of a wider socialist federation of Europe.

For decades we were accused by left republicans and the ultra-left of being "Labour-Unionists" or worse, because uniquely on the left we took Protestant working class concerns and fears into account. We put forward a principled class position, calling for workers' unity and for socialism. While we campaigned against state repression, which was mainly meted out against the Catholic minority, we were adamant in our opposition to the divisive and counter-productive individual terror 'armed struggles' of the republican paramilitaries. The sects opportunistically adapted to the mood in Catholic working class areas and acted as cheerleaders to the Provisional IRA ('Provos'). In effect, these forces capitulated to the sectional struggles of the Catholic oppressed, not connecting this struggle to the general struggles of the entire working class. Our small forces rejected this variant of what today is called 'identity politics'. Our organisation concentrated on youth and trade union work and courageously flew the flag of socialism in elections. Modest but important gains were made, winning Catholic and Protestant working class recruits. Often facing a dangerous and difficult situation, swimming against the stream, our organisation in the North had to consolidate its forces. It was necessary to patiently steel the cadres in the ideas and methods of Marxism and Trotskyism, in preparation for opportunities that would open up for us in the class struggle. Others on the Left took a disastrous opportunist and ultra left path, acted as cheerleaders to the Provos and, not surprisingly, consequently lost cadres to the republican movement.

We should strive to ensure we do not present our ideas and programme in such a way as to give the impression that we emphasis divisions and separateness. It is correct to raise the fears and uncertainties and aspirations that exist in Protestant working class areas. But if this is done in a routine manner, and as the main emphasis, is there not a danger the impression can be given that the party is 'one-sided' and pays less attention to the equally legitimate views and concerns amongst the Catholic working class? Can this give a wrong impression regarding our position of class unity? Does an expressed emphasis inadvertently lead to a misunderstanding of the CWI position? In that sense, we do believe that on occasions "the stick is bent too far".

The NEC document states that "At this point we do not raise the 'right of Protestants to opt out'… however, in the context of an imminent border poll our position on the 'right to opt out' will necessary come more to the fore."

It is not clear what is meant by this statement. Certainly during a period of heightened sectarianism it is necessary to sharpen our demands. The document states, "It will be necessary to explain our position more regularly, more methodically, in discussions, and in longer, more developed article … it will probably be necessary to develop new formulations and new slogans, in order to fully explain our position in the exact situation that unfolds."

We agree that we have to look at the given situation and adjust demands and slogans, accordingly. The rights of both communities need to be expressed from a Marxist point of view. But even then we still need to be extremely cautious about putting forward new demands, slogans or formulations that in any way appear to assume and reinforce separateness and divisions. For many workers, Catholic and Protestant, bringing more to the fore today the idea of a separate Protestant state, even when qualified as "under socialism", implies divisions are today so entrenched and have reached such a qualitative stage that a separate Protestant 'nation' already exists. No matter the intentions of the comrades, if that was to be viewed as the position of the Irish section it would earn the ruinous reputation of being a 'two nations' party.

Border Poll

It is correct to warn about the dangers of a sharp rise in sectarian tensions and conflict surrounding a border poll. But this does not exhaust the matter. It does not automatically mean a straight descent into sectarian conflict and civil war. Given the situation in the North, we have always adopted highly conditional and qualified perspectives, particularly when dealing with previous periods of heightened crises. There are many twists and turns in the situation. Not least, we have to emphasis the role of the working class, especially the organised working class in the unions, trades councils, genuine community groups etc., that can cut across sectarianism. Mass struggles of workers in N Ireland have always tended to push back sectarianism and sectarian forces and open up the possibilities for the development of class based politics. Conversely, the setback of workers' struggles tends to open up the way to sectarianism.

There are many hurdles to be overcome before a border poll is called and no guarantee it would see a majority 'yes' to a united Ireland, north and south, even if Catholics made up a majority in the North. But if a poll is called, and a majority voted for 'unity', what would be our perspectives? It is most likely that there would be strong Protestant reaction, the degree to which we cannot tell beforehand, which could lead to renewed conflict and, in the absence of organised working class movements, can spiral out of control and engulf the North, for a period.

But this is not the only perspective. The working class will not just sit back and allow the situation to deteriorate and for society to be plunged back into armed conflict. It is possible that from pressure below, the union leaders can be forced into organising mass demonstrations and even strikes/stoppages against the bigots, as saw repeatedly in the past.

Neither will the ruling class just sit back and allow a deteriorating situation to unfold, threatening the stable rule of capitalism and profits. It is possible that the main political parties, north and south, under intense pressure from the ruling classes in the UK, Ireland, EU and the US, would draw back from the cliff edge, as has happened before. They could try to cobble together some new constitutional fudge, some form of 'all Ireland' institutional bodies and constitutional arrangements that fall short of a capitalist united Ireland. This would be sold to Catholics as further significant steps towards a united Ireland, which would unfold over a period and which would avoid turmoil and bloodshed. Protestants would be sold the idea that concessions were needed in order to maintain their special relationship with the UK.

These possible perspectives and other variants need to be at least considered and discussed.

In dealing with the issues around a border poll we have to take into account not just Protestant fears and perceptions about what a border poll would mean for them but also Catholic 'democratic sentiments' and desires.

The IS raised with leading comrades in Ireland our criticisms of an article entitled, "Why socialists oppose a border poll". We felt that this title was tone-deaf and tactless, and the article did not sufficiently taking into account Catholics views, consciousness, and concerns. We were told that the title was added on by editors and it would be removed. Yet it still remains posted with this headline on the southern Irish SP site.

It is correct for us to openly warn that a border poll will lead to heightened sectarian tensions, would not see a solution to the national question, and that Protestants cannot simply be expected to accept being 'voted into' a capitalist united Ireland. But we also need to take into account Catholic consciousness on this matter.

Provisions for a border poll are contained in the Belfast Agreement (also known as the 'Good Friday Agreement', GFA). Both Protestants and Catholics believe they made significant 'compromises' to ensure peace. Catholics were told that in return for accepting "Protestant consent" to constitutional change a mechanism for a vote for 'unity' is enshrined in the GFA. This is now posed more sharply and seemingly within reach due to demographic changes and Brexit etc.

We need to be mindful that our section in Ireland gave heavily qualified 'critical' support to the referendum on the Agreement, which was held both North and South. If we had not, our party could have been seen as standing with arch-bigots, on both sides, who wanted a return to war. As we said at the time, the Agreement also opened a window of opportunity to develop class politics in a period of relative peace. We have to therefore explain our opposition a border poll today sensitively and carefully. Catholic workers may well ask our party, why do you not support our democratic right to exercise self-determination enshrined in the GFA? We must honestly warn Catholic workers that a 'majority vote' resolves nothing, that it will only be a sectarian head-count, will worsen sectarian tensions and will not lead to their hopes of a peaceful and prosperous united Ireland. We oppose all attempts to force Protestants into a capitalist united Ireland, either by bombs or ballots, just as we support the right of Catholics to oppose the Northern statelet, no matter how "reformed". We must strive to put forward in the workers' movement and communities concrete working class-based initiatives to really bring the two communities together and to try to resolve the national question etc.

Key to this will be the role of the unions in the North. They are the only mass vehicles bringing together workers from both backgrounds. Unions and trades councils must be the focus of any serious challenge to sectarianism. In the last year, trade unions and trades councils organised against a car bombing in Derry and after the shooting of journalist Lyra McKee – workers' protests in which our comrades in Nipsa, the NUJ and Fermanagh UNITE played a key role. If an 'open turn' had been adopted in the north towards unions, could such initiatives have taken place?

Easter 1916

The Irish NEC majority document does not even mention previous debates with IS comrades regarding the 100th anniversary of the Easter 1916 Rising. In our view, leading Irish comrades tilted towards a revision of the analysis and approach taken by our organisation since the 1960s, when we produced an article on the 50th anniversary of the rising.

In discussions with IS comrades, Irish NEC comrades were much more critical of the rising and the role of James Connolly than has been previously expressed in our articles and publications. Leading Irish comrades said that they thought Trotsky's brief analysis of events in Dublin in 1916 was 'better' - more correctly critical and astute - than the analysis made by Lenin, which we have often cited in the past. An NEC comrade argued that the Rising should not be referred to as an 'uprising' as this was an exaggeration. Several comrades said that 1916 was a 'mistake'. At the summer school commission, a leading Irish comrade remarked it would have been better if the rising had not taken place. An NEC comrade even made heavy weather about Connolly reportedly observing Catholic last rites in prison before he was executed by British forces – the implication being that Connolly was religious and that this somehow cast a negative light on his role (leaving aside the fact that the jury is still out concerning Connolly's attitude towards religion, it is neither here nor there whether Connolly took last rites when appraising his historic role).

The Irish NEC comrades never explained in a coherent way why they had this change in emphasis. Much of this more critical approach appears to have been motivated by the comrades' concerns about how Easter 1916 is exploited and coloured by all stripes of nationalism and republicanism, with particular reference to Sinn Fein, and, linked to this, how Protestants in the North view Easter 1916.

The Easter Rising is a major historical event in Irish history. Each significant anniversary of the event will inevitably see the event analysed and commemorated through the lens of that time. We also have to take current consciousness into account when discussing Easter 1916. But for Marxists, an historic revolt of the oppressed, such as the Easter 1916, must be seen in its time and context, with all the necessary lessons drawn out for the workers' movement today. To describe it as a "mistake" or wish that it had never happened because it was not a clear-cut workers' rising, uniting Catholic and Protestant workers across the island on a socialist programme, is an ahistorical, abstract approach that can alienate the party from advanced layers of the Irish working class.

The decades before the outbreak of world war one saw heightened class struggles across Europe, with Ireland amongst the most explosive, which were cut across by the war and the betrayal of social democracy. The Easter Rising was an expression of a more general radicalisation of the working class brought on by the grinding slaughter of the imperialist conflict. It was part of the class struggle because the struggle for national self-determination was so interwoven with the class struggle. But, as Lenin pointed out, "It is the misfortune of the Irish that they rose prematurely, before the European revolt of the proletariat had had time to mature."

Writing in July 1916, Lenin denounced Karl Radek's position of calling the Easter Rising a "putsch" as a "monstrously doctrinaire and pedantic assessment" of the situation. Trotsky adopted a similar approach as Lenin. He described the Irish rebels as "heroic" and he reproached Plekhanov for his opposition to the Rising.

Lenin ridiculed the notion that, "Very likely one army will line up in one place and say, 'We are for socialism', while another will do so in another place and say, 'We are for imperialism', and that will be the social revolution! Only from such a ridiculously pedantic angle could one label the Irish rebellion a 'putsch'. Whoever expects a 'pure' social revolution will never live to see it. Such a person pays lip service to revolution without understanding what revolution really is."

Trotsky's short article identified the objective pressures that saw Connolly's adaptation to the nationalists but not in a denunciatory manner. Applying the permanent revolution to Ireland, Trotsky outlined the political and historical features that shaped the development of the Irish working class and he posed the role of the Irish working class in future national and social struggles.

In previous CWI articles on Easter 1916, we have never been uncritical cheerleaders of the rising and of the role of Connolly. He took part in the Easter 1916 after defeats and setbacks which profoundly affected him – the 1913 Dublin Lockout and the capitulation of European social democratic leaders in 1914. Yet during 1916 Connolly had not capitulated to nationalism but he was clear that the Rising was an attempt to spark the working class into action across Europe.

The main question is not whether Connolly and the Irish Citizens Army should have thrown their lot in with the middle class radical nationalists but it is the manner in which this was done. In principle, there was nothing wrong with seeking to win the support of the best elements of the Irish Volunteers, which drew its recruits from urban workers and rural poor. But Connolly's orientation involved concessions of a political character. As we have written before, Connolly did not prepare for and appeal for a general strike, make a class appeal to conscripted British troops or issue his own separate class-based and socialist 'proclamation', for example. Connolly was also seriously disadvantaged by not having the sort of revolutionary party that could hammer out programme, tactics and strategy, which only Lenin had fashioned.

It is necessary to address Connolly's mistakes, in order for the workers' movement to learn from them but it is vitally important that we do so in a balanced, proportional manner. We must be careful not to alienate ourselves from Irish workers who rightly regard Connolly as a heroic proletarian martyr and a giant of the labour movement, and the youth, who will increasingly turn to his revolutionary socialist ideas.

Marxists cannot be seen as adopting a 'soft' approach towards imperialism, concerning historic events or by how we take up state repression, today. By the same token, we must use skilled and sensitive terminology, given the sectarian divide in society in the North and how left republicanism debases the content of many slogans.

Defending the CWI programme

As the above comments show, the IS had had concerns on aspects of how the Irish leadership deals with the national question and programme and demands but we have not said this amounts to fundamental or profound differences. The discussions and debates between the Irish NEC and IS comrades have undoubtedly helped to ensure a more balanced position was adopted, for example, regarding the Irish section's publications on Easter 1916 and other historical events.

But we are obliged to pose a stark warning; if the Irish section's present rightward political evolution continues, including opportunist adaptation to 'identity politics' and other alien class ideas, this will inevitably colour the analysis on the national question and the programme and demands.

There are also practical consequences flowing from the wrong approach to unions in the south over the last years. The party has not been able to respond effectively, as could have been the case, to the divisive Sinn Fein-driven, 'Trade Unionists for a New and United Ireland' campaign in the unions because the mistaken 'open turn' policy left us with fewer forces in the unions in the south. Our main opposition to the nationalist campaign, which could pose splitting unions along sectarian lines if it gained strong momentum, was conducted through our base in Nipsa and in Unite in the North.

If the Irish NEC majority continues on its path, away from Trotskyism, they will also inevitably start to depart from the clear independent class, Marxist position on the national question forged by the CWI in Ireland over decades.

The IS will work with all those comrades committed to building the CWI in Ireland, North and South, on a principled Marxist programme, continuing the heroic work started 50 years ago in the white-heat of events in Derry and Belfast.

6.
REFOUNDING
the CWI

WORLD PERSPECTIVES

The following world perspectives document was discussed, amended and passed by delegates and visitors at an international conference, held in London from July 22-25, to re-found the Committee for a Workers' International (CWI). The conference was attended by 200 delegates and visitors from England, Wales, Scotland, France, Germany, Austria, Ireland, India, Sri Lanka, Malaysia, Finland, South Africa, Chile and the United States. Apologies were received from comrades in Nigeria and Israel who had travel and visa problems

The international faction ['In Defence of a Working-Class, Trotskyist CWI'] formulated our platform in opposition to those who wished to nullify the revolutionary perspectives and programme of the CWI, by political opportunism and embracing identity politics. We did this in the full knowledge that mass upheavals loomed and sections of the CWI would be ideologically unprepared for this, and would be facing the wrong way, if we allowed this situation to persist. We therefore tried to correct some of the mistakes of the Irish party on identity politics, the retreat from clear working-class orientation, programme and organisation. To our great disappointment, we found that the malaise was not just restricted to Ireland but had spread to others, who had ideologically bent the knee under the pressure of the prevailing retreat in the workers' movement internationally. They had abandoned a consistent Marxist approach, embracing the ideas emanating originally from US universities, the ideological 'factories' of US and world capitalism.

The ensuing ideological struggle within our ranks has indicated just how far this process has gone, which now necessitates that we reconstitute our International on the basis of revolutionary perspectives and tasks. This has become evident now to everybody in our faction with the disappointing results in the recent elections in Ireland. The ideological retreat evident in a number of sections has meant that we had to struggle to ensure that our International and its constituent parts were ideologically consolidated on clear Marxist and Trotskyist lines. As always, this must be underpinned by clear international perspectives.

Even before the discussion has been exhausted, as we predicted, new mass events are already upon us, unfolding before our eyes, at the same time as the inevitable and growing political divergence with the so-called 'co-ordinating sections' [ie the undeclared opposition faction inside the CWI] takes place.

There is a drastically worsening of economic perspectives for the world economy aggravated by the trade war, which has only just begun, between China and the US. The IMF estimates that the contraction in world trade that has already taken place is equal to the size of the South African economy. This has been accompanied by the outbreak of new mass movements in Hong Kong – which could reverberate in China, opening up entirely new mass working-class movements. Revolutionary movements have erupted in Sudan and Algeria. Erdogan has been soundly beaten in the Istanbul re-run election. A similar process is underway in Eastern Europe and possibly in Russia itself with the outline of the biggest movements for decades, which could shake to their foundations really for the first time the pro-capitalist, post-Stalinist autocracies that have cloaked themselves in a thin veneer of 'democracy'. There is also the possibility of a new conflagration in the Middle East, a small war stoked up by the breakdown in the nuclear deal with Iran and the subsequent clashes in the Arabian Gulf. This could, in turn, have an important economic fallout, not least in spiralling oil prices, which in the past have usually been harbingers of a new economic crisis. A spiralling of world oil prices could feed back into the world economy and deepen the recessionary trends already evident.

These events have very speedily demonstrated beyond doubt the incapacity of the minority opposition faction to face up to the big changes in the world situation which impend. In Ireland, as we anticipated, there have already been setbacks in the electoral field, enormously aggravated through the opportunist peddling of 'identity politics' typified by their one-sided slogan in the European elections: "Vote for a socialist feminist". Sometimes, even a correct programme and a good campaign will not guarantee automatic electoral success if the objective situation is unfavourable. However, problems can be enormously compounded, and therefore lead to a bigger defeat if a campaign is seen as appealing to just one section of the population. The CWI has accumulated enormous experience in different electoral campaigns in a number of countries. In Liverpool, when we effectively controlled the Labour group of councillors and through this the council itself, we never suffered any significant electoral defeats, even when we thought that it appeared not to be the most favourable situation. When the councillors were removed by the government with the help of the Labour right, their replacements were in the same political mould. Therefore the momentum based upon our achievements in terms of real changes in the lives of the working class in the city meant that we did not lose one general council election. In fact our vote consistently held up until the right wing, through expulsions and exclusions, took power into their own hands.

This, unfortunately, was not the case in Ireland because of the narrow approach adopted by the Irish leadership and the concentration on identity politics, which will be compounded even more on the basis of the present trajectory of the Irish party. The electoral defeat they suffered came on the backs of them promising a mass political radicalisation following the victories on abortion and the LGBTQ+ marriage equality. This failed to materialise, with the Greens making the most dramatic gains, and the Irish party suffering big losses.

World economy in stagnation and decline

The world economy has now decisively entered a new phase of stagnation and decline – possibly a serious decline in the next period. The general economic weakness has been enormously aggravated by the colossal rise in inequality which, by cutting the market, cuts purchasing power. The Economist has commented that the current situation stands in stark contrast to the economic position roughly between 1945 and 1980. In this period, governments under mass pressure particularly from a revitalised trade union and labour movement were able to begin to shrink the inequality seen in the past, at least in a relative sense. However, since 1980 up to 2016 the total share of income going to the top 1% in the US and the UK has more than doubled while the incomes of the bottom 90% in the same two countries have barely risen at all over a period of 25 years! At the same time US bosses' (CEOs) 'earnings' were on average about 20 times as much as the typical worker in that period, while today they receive 350 times as much as those at the bottom! World inequality has risen most in the US and UK, while some other countries have seen much smaller increases – Canada, Japan, Italy – and inequality has been stable or falling in others: France, Belgium, Hungary, for example.

Of course, the weaknesses and setbacks of the labour movement in the period from 1980 up to today – particularly the current, seriously weakened trade unions – has enormously helped this process of wealth and power being accumulated more and more into the hands of the rich and their representatives. No wonder Warren Buffett, one of the richest capitalists, brazenly brags that there is certainly a class war and his class is winning! However, the Keynesian bourgeois economist John Kenneth Galbraith in the past also warned the ruling class about the inevitable political threats they will meet from this kind of situation, from an aroused working class and labour movement by seeking to accumulate ever greater piles of wealth. He wrote: "The conspicuously wealthy urge the character-building value of privation for the poor."

This however – even without the intervention of parties and leaders – will inevitably produce at a certain stage the massive outpouring of anger from below. We are now on the eve of such a situation in all parts of the world: "Far from being a golden era for workers, this is actually an age of insecurity," wrote Larry Elliott, the London Guardian economic correspondent. The hollowing out of the car industry in Britain, the former workshop of the world, is symptomatic of the general crisis situation facing European industry. The official jobless rate in Britain is the lowest since 1975 and in the US the lowest since 1969. However, the unemployment rate today is not an accurate indicator of the economic health of capitalism or the living conditions of the masses as a whole.

The situation is characterised by low pay and short time working with an estimated half of young people in Europe affected by this. These low-paid jobs do not adequately compensate for crippling rising costs. There has been the loss of consistent and high-paying jobs. This situation particularly affects youth who are becoming a potentially powerful revolutionary factor with big repercussions politically in the next period.

Also, the real labour market is not nearly as robust as the official figures suggest. This general situation exists not just in the US but in Europe as well, enormously aggravated potentially by the trade war and now by the military posturing and actions of Trump against Iran, which if it results in clashes and a corresponding rise in the price of oil could have the most serious economic consequences for a quarter of a century. Larry Elliott points out (in the Guardian) that these events do not come at the "end of a quarter of a century of strong and uninterrupted growth – as was the case in 1973. It is more like the late 1970s, when the world economy was hit by a second oil shock triggered by the war between Iran and Iraq".

Rising inequalities have also been accentuated by asset price inflation which, as the Financial Times pointed out, "sowed the seeds of today's populism", with popular discontent evident in the growing violent demonstrations and street protests, and the emergence of new political parties mounting a challenge to the institutions of capitalism.

The strategists of capital have themselves been forced to comment on the growth of demands for new measures within the radical wing of even bourgeois parties like the Democrats in America, such as the 'Green New Deal'. This is a form of 'people's quantitative easing' –

money going into trouser pockets rather than lavish subsidies to big business – an increase in state expenditure in order to boost 'demand'. This is roughly along the lines of what Roosevelt introduced in the 1930s through Keynesian-type methods.

Its advocates are prompted to propose such measures because of their fear that the next serious economic downturn can provoke an unprecedented mass radicalisation/revolution, which they will find difficult to contain: "If this much angst and anger has swelled during an extended post-crisis period of moderate growth, what on earth will happen when the next downturn arrives?" writes Elliott. To compound their problems, London specialist financial journal City AM wailed recently: "An all-out trade war is becoming more likely." Iran is already pushing back against the Trump regime and it is not excluded that China will do the same, as could Mexico which is threatening retaliation against the 25% tariffs first suggested by Trump against Mexican imports. This was Trump's answer to immigration from the South, which was largely as a result of the deep crisis which afflicts Latin America, particularly Guatemala, El Salvador and Honduras, the three nations of Central America from where most migrants into the US presently originate. The crippling poverty, corruption and violence have pushed hundreds of thousands to seek escape in the US from this nightmare.

However Trump's measures have engendered opposition not just from Mexico but from the neighbouring US border states that have already been impacted by the retaliation against immigrants by the US federal government. This has added to the growing discontent in the US itself, with what some commentators have inaccurately called a 'new Cold War' – which usually denotes a conflict between fundamentally different social systems. This 'Cold War' is between rival capitalist great powers. It refers to the trade stand-off between China and the US which has severely impacted already on those US states who rely on their agricultural trade with China.

Major world powers in conflict

At the same time it has ratcheted up the great power conflicts throughout the world. Putin remarked that the US attempts to block China's technology giant Huawei and to stop the Nord stream gas pipeline to Europe are "economic raiding and will lead to trade wars". Ominously, while trying to cement new ties with China to their "highest level in history", he also warned that Trump's actions "are a road to endless conflicts, trade wars and maybe not even only in trade … Figuratively speaking, an all-out brawl with no rules". He also indicated a new attempt by Russia to cement relations with China in opposition to the US. This is part of a process to reorient Russia's economy towards Asia and the Middle East that has already led to trade between both countries rising by 24.5% last year. Putin further commented: "We do not have a relationship as deep and broad as we do with China with any other country in the world today."

The assertive combative approach of Trump, which was initially welcomed by big business, is now raising questions about his strategy. For instance Morgan Stanley has warned that a full-blown trade war would be "a disaster that could tip the US into recession". And very significantly, it went on to say that tariffs are hidden, regressive taxes that are paid for by US businesses and consumers. It also referred back to the Smoot-Hawley Tariff Act of 1930 and warned of any repeat today: "Unilateral tariff strategies have no record of historical success and have always led to unintended consequences", something that we have consistently warned could happen prior to Trump going down this road.

At the same time there is a growing opposition to Trump and his proposals, both domestically and internationally. This is summed up by the fact that only 17% of Americans say that they trust Washington most or all the time. As the writer Janan Ganesh has warned in the Financial Times: "If there is to be a lasting struggle with China, the US public, who can vote for something else whenever they want, will have to consent. This implies an open-ended public tolerance for economic disruption, military expenditure and the sheer psychic burden of conflict, with its high-risk moments." He compares the scenario to the conflict with Russia during the Cold War when he claims: "then deference to government was near unanimous". That is clearly not the situation today in the US.

On the contrary foreign wars or even military conflict can quickly become unpopular, particularly if it is a question of 'guns or butter' which impacts on the well-being and living standards of the US population. Statistics show that job creation slowed sharply in May as corporate confidence weakened. At the same time stories of increased poverty have inevitably crept into the press. One woman in Seattle told a journalist that the only items left in her kitchen were pickles and eggs because she could find so little work! This is in one of the hi-tech capitals of the US and the world in which increasing layers of workers are living from hand to mouth. These are the ingredients for a massive eruption socially of the US workers in the next period.

Sabre rattling – particularly in the South China Sea and the Arabian Gulf – is accompanied with threats of an economic war by Trump against China and Iran, and the looming threat of a real war in these contested areas. The basis for this is the attempt by Trump to contain China – and particularly for what he calls its decades-old tactic of "stealing" the technology of the US. This is no different to the similar threats that were made by Britain against the rising power of Germany in the 19th and the 20th-centuries. That eventually culminated in the First World War. Any prospect of a real war today would spill over into nuclear exchanges with enormous repercussions not just in these regions but throughout the world.

While this confrontational posture and the actual small clashes which have taken place in the Gulf emanate primarily from Trump himself and his circle, nevertheless, even without his presence, American capitalism – as it did in relation to a rising Japan in the 1980s – would have come increasingly into conflict with China. The increased economic prowess of China – combined with its growing military reach, and therefore economic influence as well – would inevitably lead to conflict. The difference between most of the American bourgeois and Trump is that the former wish to 'contain' China largely by diplomatic means bolstered by overwhelming military power, whereas Trump is an adventurer who is not averse to flexing his military muscles. However, this could, even inadvertently for Trump, turn into an armed conflict with serious consequences in the Middle East, an area not yet remotely recovered from the devastating wars in Syria and Iraq and the terrible fall-out from these in almost every state in the region. Moreover there would be consequences in the US even for the deployment of relatively small numbers of US troops for a president who promised to "bring all our troops home".

This was already an empty promise because the US is now an imperialism of permanent military bases, a policeman ready to intervene in 'emergencies'. They are kept in reserve, ready to safeguard, through military, 'police-type' intervention if need be, imperialism's and particularly the US's interests in the neo-colonial world. They are kept in readiness to be deployed as firefighters in preparation for the inevitable conflicts which are already breaking out in some countries in the Middle East and the neo-colonial world.

Revolutionary wave in Sudan and Algeria

In Algeria and Sudan the first sparks of a new revolutionary wave have been unleashed with power in Sudan being exercised by the masses on the streets and in the factories while the army was compelled to observe for a time an uneasy stand-off. The military, while compelled to retreat in the face of the mass movement, is still playing for time. They are afraid that power exercised by the masses would result in a thoroughgoing investigation of army atrocities under the Nimeiry regime which took power in 1969 in a military coup and was toppled in 1985. Elections were held a year later but the military took control again in 1989. Forced to retreat in the face of a colossal mass movement, including demands for a general strike in late May and early June, the military once more opened fire on the masses and opposition figures were arrested. But the military faced a call for the masses to answer this with "the tools of civil disobedience in the general political strike". Sudan has a history of independent workers' movements – to a certain extent more potentially powerful, with once having a mass communist party, than elsewhere in the region – which can develop once more in the heated political situation that is unfolding.

However if the masses' gains are not cemented through independent class action, including a properly prepared political general strike with the idea of workers' and poor people's power invested in popular committees of the masses, then revolutionary gains will be inevitably undermined. If this is not done, the army tops, which have been biding their time, will once more unleash their thugs and militias against defenceless, vulnerable sections of the masses. The call should be made for the general strike to drive out the military and establish popular elected committees including rank-and-file soldiers with real power vested and backed by a democratic armed militia and the demand for a revolutionary constituent assembly. The lessons of recent events in the rest of the Middle East is that unless a revolutionary process is completed – through a 'general strike' or insurrection, led by the working class in the towns but spreading to the countryside, with revolutionary students playing a key role – then counter-revolution will inevitably strike back. The aim should also be to create a genuine, democratically controlled revolutionary party as a guiding force to complete the victory.

In Egypt in 2011 a convulsive mass revolutionary movement swept away the Mubarak dictatorship. However, because no force – a mass revolutionary party – existed to generalise the experience of the masses in the form of a programme and perspective, then reaction, first in the form of Morsi and the Muslim Brotherhood and then the direct dictator Sisi through 'elections', managed to take power. A successful workers', students' and youth movement in Sudan can play an enormously regenerative role in the Middle East for revolutionary prospects throughout the region, including a revival of revolutionary forces and events in Egypt and elsewhere in the Middle East.

A similar situation could open up in Algeria, which seemed to be hardly touched by the revolutions of 2011 and later. Indeed, it is striking that it is those countries that did not seem to be as affected by the events of 2011 and subsequently which are now in the forefront of revolutionary struggle, with Sudan in the vanguard. In Algeria the effects of a past 'civil war' primarily between the state and the Islamists, involving bloody repression with hundreds of thousands of casualties held back protests against the army-backed regime. Now, however, the masses appear to have lost the fear of the military and repression. The army tops have even admitted in interviews in the Western bourgeois press that, in their age-old tradition, they have been tempted to use force against the mass movement but are not certain of the 'loyalty' of the rank-and-file troops to carry it out! When the army is no longer reliable, when it threatens to break into pieces, then the army tops are beginning to lose control and that is the unmistakable sign of coming revolution!

And it is not just in North Africa, which has been a cockpit for the competing powers, involving intervention from the different imperialist forces, including also Russia. Russia is seeking to bolster its presence in at least 13 countries in Africa, striking military deals and grooming the new generation of 'leaders' and undercover agents. However, Putin's Russia, playing 'catch up' with China and the US amongst the competing powers, has already established a strong presence throughout Africa and has generated in the process growing hostility to itself. Chinas' rapacious, exploitative policies will meet further resistance in Africa. The Belt and Road Initiative, involving the building of an energy pipeline and new trade routes from Asia to the heart of Europe, has already invoked similar opposition in Europe, with opposition to China also growing in Africa and parts of Asia.

The search for new markets – new outlets for capital – has resulted in a new 'scramble for Africa'. However the continent faces colossal challenges from climate change, aggravated by population increases which will, as part of the worldwide population explosion to an estimated 9.7bn in 2050, reach 2bn in sub-Saharan Africa. This will put huge pressure on the continent as a whole in terms of food production, control of climate, natural disasters as well as the multiplicity of accumulated national, tribal, class and other divisions. The present bourgeois regimes, from the weakest to the strongest, face inherent instability on the basis of a perpetuation of the present parasitic exploitative regimes throughout the continent.

Nigeria and South Africa

We have a presence in the two most important countries in Africa: South Africa and Nigeria. Although small in numbers, we have managed to build a considerable political influence in South Africa, the most economically developed, and in Nigeria, the most populous. This has been achieved over decades at the cost of great individual sacrifice financially and personally of leading comrades who have managed to assemble a small but important force of cadres which remain under our banner.

The current conjuncture in South Africa is complicated, but full of enormous potential. The May general election has deepened the crisis of political representation for all classes. The ANC and main opposition Democratic Alliance both suffered a loss of electoral support – the former its biggest loss since 1994, and the latter its first electoral reversal since it was formed, significantly under its first black leader. Despite a modest increase in its vote, the Economic Freedom Fighters (EFF), amidst more allegations of corruption, has failed to position itself as an alternative, especially amongst organised workers. Its shift to the right continues, revealing its petty bourgeois character. The Socialist Revolutionary Workers Party, formed as a 'Communist Party Mark II' by the dominant grouping in the leadership of the metalworkers' union, NUMSA, was humiliated and did not win a single seat, failing to break-out of the narrow circles of the NUMSA bureaucracy.

Nevertheless, in South Africa there is a burning class anger and determination to act, reflected in record levels of strikes and community protests. But the high levels of militancy are not yet matched by a generalised political understanding of the nature of capitalism or what it will take to replace it with socialism. The process of realignment in the trade union movement that has been underway for a number of years – especially the severe weakening of the ANC-aligned Cosatu federation and creation of the new Saftu federation – has broken some of the chains of class collaboration. But the continued dominance of leaders shaped and schooled in the pre-Marikana period has limited this. The vacuum in working class political leadership is felt more and more sharply by the working class as they look for a means to fight back. We are confident that the working class will in time lift up a leadership worthy of it. To assist and prepare for this, it is vital to defend and sharpen our own political clarity and ideological firmness against the different reformist and neo-Stalinist tendencies in the trade union bureaucracies. Any blurring of the lines for short-term gain would prove disastrous in the long-term. This has emerged as the political fault line in the South African section, with those on an opportunist trajectory on this issue grouping around the undeclared right-ward moving faction.

Nigeria – once one of the most favourably placed countries in sub-Saharan Africa because of the seemingly priceless asset of considerable oil resources – decades after gaining 'independence' is now locked in a spiral of decline and impoverishment. The Economist compares the Nigerian economy to a stranded truck with average incomes having fallen for four years and the IMF believing that it will not rise for at least another six. The latest figures for unemployment are 23% compared with 10% at the beginning of 2016, and the government expects it to reach 33% next year as the population continues to rapidly expand. Inflation is 11% with some 94 million people living on less than $1.90 a day, more than in any other country, certainly in Africa, and the numbers are swelling. Horrendously by 2030 a quarter of the very poor people of the world will be Nigerian according to the World Data Lab.

Now, once again, an economic recession is demonstrating the fragility of Nigeria's economy and its dependence on the world economy. The fall in the price of oil has hit Nigeria as oil accounts for over 90% of Nigeria's export earnings and around two thirds of government income. This plunged the economy into the "worst recession in 25 years", between 2016 and 2017, with negative GDP growth for five consecutive quarters. An immediate consequence of the economic crisis is widespread non-payment of wages, especially in the state sector, and a continuation of the deindustrialisation that began with the austerity policies of the 1980s. The election of Buhari to the presidency in 2015 has aggravated the disaster and has made the position immeasurably worse with the masses calling him 'Baba go slow' because he has done little or nothing for them! But because of the absence of a mass workers' political alternative to challenge for political power, Buhari successfully won a re-election, in February of this year, giving him a mandate to rule till 2023.

Nigeria has a powerful working class which has many times demonstrated its potential to draw all sections of the oppressed masses and youth behind it in struggle. Between 2001 and 2012, there were at least 10 general strikes over demands for reversal of fuel price hikes and for an increase in the national minimum wage. Some of these general strikes were forced on the labour leadership and often the question of political power was posed but there was no force large enough to build support for a programme that the workers' movement could have used to take power. But since the January 2012 general strike and mass protest, which represented a peak in the strike movement, there has been a steep decline in workers' struggles, partly due to frustration of the workers and poor masses with the absolute spinelessness of the labour leadership to actually fight energetically and consistently. Since then, most of the labour leadership have not even raised a finger of serious activity. In May 2016, a "general strike" called over a fuel price hike ended in fiasco. This strike was not seriously mobilised for and was only called as a gesture; its outcome further weakened labour's reputation.

Despite these reversals in labour's fortune, the Nigerian CWI section has never given up on arguing for the rebuilding of a fighting, mass-based and democratic labour movement, armed with a programme and strategy to overthrow capitalism, as the only way to ensure the winning of any minimum lasting concession. The current absence of significant workers' struggles is allowing ethnic and other issues to come to the fore, coupled with growing signs of restlessness amongst the unemployed or underemployed youth. At the moment, the labour movement is locked in negotiations with the Federal Government over how the new national minimum wage of N30, 000 ($82 USD) is actually implemented. Given the position of the Nigerian economy, which faces new economic upheavals, this battle can become the new focal point of the class struggle over the next period.

The question of maintaining a consistent orientation to the working class and its mass organisations is very relevant to the work of our small forces in Nigeria. Without this, we could not have been able to build and sustain the section in the twists and turns of the anti-military struggles in the 1990s. Now this work is even more required and runs alongside the section's campaign for "a mass workers' political alternative". The Socialist Party of Nigeria (SPN), which the DSM comrades successfully registered and then contested in the 2019 general elections, can play an important part in this. We have to combine the building of the SPN, which has opened a new periphery for our work, with rebuilding our base in the workers' movement and intervention in struggles.

India and SE Asia

Undoubtedly the recent election in India was the most important development for Asia and has effects on the world. We have dealt with this in some detail in the recent podcast organised by our Indian comrades, so this document will just touch on the most important issues here. Modi and the BJP emerged strengthened from the elections, although it was not a crushing victory by any means, with the vote for the BJP increasing from 31% to 38%. The Congress party, in the past the main electoral vehicle for Indian capitalism, suffered again a serious defeat while the CPM, the main workers' party, actually lost votes and seats in former strongholds like West Bengal, indicating a complete demoralisation of their base – the product of consistent retreats over years. Some, including CPM members, even sought refuge in rallying to the BJP banner.

However, the BJP failed in its first term to solve any of the major issues facing Indian society with a majority of its estimated 1.34 billion people still languishing in poverty. It is unlikely to make a serious dent in the accumulated problems of Indian capitalism. The doom-laden pessimistic perspectives of most commentators of a continuous strengthening of the BJP will be undermined by the march of events in the next period. Of course we cannot underestimate the ability of the BJP to seek to reinforce communal division in order to perpetuate its rule. The other side of this however is that it will provoke, at a certain stage, a mass movement from below particularly in protest against deteriorating wages and living standards, and the inability to solve the land question. A repetition of the last massive general strike cannot be ruled out through the increasing class polarisation in Indian society. Our forces are well-placed to intervene in this process against the whipping-up of sectarian tensions and in the inevitable battles of the working class. We need to put squarely on the banner of the Indian labour movement the idea of new mass workers' parties. This will be to the fore if the Communist Parties continue with their present spiral of decline; they could even completely disintegrate. Since the election the economic growth rate has further slowed which has necessitated the Central Bank to cut the main interest rate for the third time this year. This indicates that economically the shine is coming off Modi's India.

In neighbouring Pakistan Imran Khan has desperately sought relief from literally anywhere – particularly the Muslim countries of the Gulf – in order to shore up his rickety regime. Class movements in both India and Pakistan, including a revival of the workers' movement, will develop at a certain stage, as will movements against communalism and we must seek to put ourselves at the head of such a movement. The brutal Hindu centralism of the Indian government will also stoke up the fires of opposition to national oppression and the long-expected Balkanisation could, after 75 years of 'independence', once more come onto the agenda, with serious implications for the rest of South Asia.

We have an important presence in other countries in Asia particularly Sri Lanka and Malaysia, which we must nurture, and build a strong base for the coming upheavals in the region. Sri Lanka still remains an important base for the CWI with a very complicated political situation following the recent Isis attacks on the island, which were clearly aimed at racially and ethnically polarising Sri Lanka and creating an atmosphere of fear. The mass movement is presently somewhat restrained by this; however this will give way to a new mood of struggle with important opportunities for the CWI to grow substantially.

The nature of the Chinese and North Korean regimes

The issue of China, which has been dragged into our internal dispute by the "coordinating sections" undeclared opposition faction, is worthy of a separate extensive analysis, which is not possible within the limits of this relatively short document. Suffice to say that some of our opponents are in the process of rewriting the history of our analysis of the character of the Chinese state, both in the past and in the current situation. Such disputed issues as Tiananmen Square and what it represented were extensively analysed and reported on in the past. We intend to fully document the consistency of our analysis and the inconsistency of the undeclared opposition faction.

Some of them crudely described China as a finished capitalist regime when we upheld it was in transition, still a 'hybrid' with big features of capitalism but retaining some of the elements from the planned economy of Stalinism. Many discussions took place again and again at IECs with no resolution of the issue. The suggestion by the IS that we should put forward the formula that China was 'state capitalist of a very special kind' was accepted by all. A recent book, 'The State Strikes Back' argues persuasively that "China has moved away from market oriented reform towards a more state-controlled economy, partly in order to strengthen the central role of the party state".

North Korea also now falls into the category of a former hard-line Stalinist type state which has 'evolved' to where it is no longer a clearly Stalinist regime. Since the 1990s, the 'market economy' has begun to play an increasingly important role. The government did not determine how this process evolved and even until recently did not really approve of it, but rather largely ignored the emergence of an increasing number of private businesses that often register as 'state-owned enterprises'. With the introduction of capitalism – still supervised and managed by a monstrous bureaucratic machine – all the inequalities under Stalinism are battened on to a developing capitalist economy which as one commentator put it means that "inequality is staggering; both 'old inequality' between party apparatchiks and commoners … and the 'new inequality' between entrepreneurs and commoners, created by the revival of capitalism."

This means massive increased luxury for the tops including the Kim family with their fabulous eating habits and $48 prime steaks, New York style – a price equal to the average monthly income of a North Korean family! On the other hand general living standards have gradually increased but the growing contradictions mean inevitable social and political explosions in North Korea, which could also reverberate in China. Possessed of nuclear weapons both Trump for the US and Xi Jinping for China have courted North Korea in the recent period. This is an attempt to nullify any nuclear armed threat to South Korea, Japan and East Asia as a whole, and for the Chinese regime to ensure its support for North Korea in the event of a serious conflict with the US.

Latin America – an explosive situation

The defections of our former comrades in Brazil involved a complete capitulation to identity politics – which the country is riddled with – by the leadership of our former section. However, there will be an inevitable questioning of them – their lack of political backbone to withstand pressures – when the harsh reality of the objective situation and a colossal outbreak of the class struggle will take place not just in Brazil but throughout the Latin American continent. The plunge downwards in the economic situation is illustrated by the recent catastrophic power failure across South America. This left Argentina and Uruguay in particular in almost complete darkness – with only the archipelago of Tierra del Fuego reported to be unaffected. The ineptitude of the Argentinian Macri government – which faces elections – was indicated by the lines of cars marooned at traffic lights in a blacked out capital city. This was described by a leading newspaper as a "desert". It was fortunate that this incident took place at the weekend because during a working day the resulting chaos would have been even greater! The government gave timely advice: "Don't panic. Find a torch, preferably one with a new battery, check your water supply"! This incident comes just over three months after blackouts began to blight crisis-stricken Venezuela, plunging millions of its citizens into darkness for days at a time. Latin America at this rate vies for the title of the 'dark continent' once bestowed by imperialism to Africa!

The continent is faced with a multitude of crises with Brazil, Venezuela and Argentina at the centre of events. With the victory of Bolsonaro in the Brazilian elections it was expected that the new period of reaction would open up not just in Brazil but this would set the tone for the whole of the continent. The counter-revolution prepared to overthrow the Maduro regime and it was quite clear that Trump and Bolton had approved plans for a military intervention if necessary to supplement the armed counter-revolution that was planned in

Venezuela. Moreover the economic meltdown in Venezuela, with an inflation rate of one million percent, a shortage of even the essentials for basic living, and millions of refugees fleeing – with 1.2 million going to neighbouring Colombia alone – the ground seemed to be set for the defeat of Maduro. But the counter-revolution did not succeed for a number of reasons. The army and police in the main, tied as they are to the record and privileges of Maduro – and before him of Chavez – feared that they would be more secure staying with him than facing an uncertain future on the basis of a US/Colombia armed overthrow of the regime. The reserves of support for the Chavista regime were also enormously bolstered by Trump threatening intervention which aroused the bitter opposition of the Venezuelan masses to imperialist intervention. This is a powerful issue throughout Latin America – and in the land of Bolivar it is especially pronounced.

The attacks of the regime in Brazil have begun to whip up new mass movements in the cities and, in particular, in opposition to the hooligan rape of the rainforests which has been unleashed by the measures of the government. No less important are the big movements which impend in both Argentina and in Chile which will allow us to re-build some support among the more durable layers of the working class. The new movements which will develop will inscribe on their banners class demands, including those of women, particularly working-class women, supporting at all times principled points of agreement and solidarity between all genders under attack but firmly opposing those separatist ideas which split workers in struggle through identity politics.

The victory of the right in a series of Latin American countries flowed from the failure of the "left" governments like Lula/Dilma and also the more radical regimes of Chavez, Morales and Correa. However, the new right-wing governments have lacked a solid social base to rest upon. This is reflected in the speed with which mass opposition has developed to them. In Argentina Macri has had to confront five general strikes. Bolsonaro has now had to face a mass general strike which was estimated to have been supported by 45 million workers. This is an indication of the limits of reaction although it can assume a repressive and authoritarian character. However, the lack of a mass revolutionary socialist alternative is reflected in the swing back to the Peronists in Argentina despite the growth of the FIT and some other 'Trotskyist' forces which, despite winning significant support have not proved able because of their sectarian approach to win the support of significant ranks of dissident Peronist workers. The explosive situation which exists in Mexico, especially since the coming to power of Lopez Obrador, AMLO, opens a new chapter for the working class there which is going to have repercussions in Latin America and north of the Rio Grande in the US.

The US – crucial for the international working class

The political upheavals in the US are of crucial international importance for the working class. These are taking place against the backdrop of a polarised political and social situation. The US has seen positive labour developments sparked off by the 2017 wildcat, rank and file organised West Virginia teachers' strike. While overall union membership did not increase in 2018, there was a 400,000 increase in the number of union members under the age of 35. The developments around the Sanders campaign, although it is not simple repetition of 2016, pose important issues of a programmatic and tactical character for revolutionary socialists. It is important that we avoid the pitfalls of opportunism and sectarianism. What are the best, most appropriate slogans and demands in relation to the US presidential elections and specifically is it correct for us to support radical figures such as Bernie Sanders in the Democratic Party primaries? These issues are presently under widespread discussion and debate both in and around the Democratic Party and among others outside the Democratic Party.

The US Democratic Party is clearly a capitalist party, moreover with a pernicious record of consistently opposing the interests of the American working class. Our aim is to ultimately replace this with a new mass workers' party, which could provide the American working class with the necessary experience for them to draw radical and revolutionary conclusions and create a socialist party built on firm Marxist foundations. However the route to such a party is not at all straightforward. Sometimes sections of the working class have to pass through the experience of a radical bourgeois party, or at least the wing of such a party, before they are prepared to break and create a party. This in turn may mean sometimes giving critical limited support to elements moving in such a direction – not necessarily advocating a vote for them as such – but assisting those attracted to them, through appropriate slogans to find the road to a complete breach with the bourgeois parties.

For instance, Engels was prepared to discuss with the early socialists and other radicals in Britain, even with Keir Hardie when he was still a Liberal party agent, in order to help him in the direction of breaking from liberalism. He duly did, helped form the Independent Labour Party, in 1893, and later became the first leader of the new Labour Party, in 1906. Similarly, Papandreou in Greece evolved from the leader of the liberal Centre Union party towards the founder of Pasok, at one stage a very radical socialist party. We encouraged this and participated in this new party very successfully for a period. But it later collapsed through gross opportunism.

Similarly, in 2016, we gave a certain critical support – in the sense of encouraging Sanders to stand in opposition to the openly bourgeois wing of the Democratic Party and demanding he break from it and launch a new party. But we drew the line at publicly advocating a vote for Sanders while he remained in the Democratic Party and opposed urging people to register as Democrats. Some in our ranks, who have now departed, did advocate a vote for Sanders and supported him in an opportunistic manner.

In the current situation in the Democratic Party, where the primaries for the 2020 presidential elections are being prepared, it is necessary to intervene in the movement around Sanders' campaign. When pressed he defends the idea of "democratic socialism" although explains this as the "Scandinavian welfare state" and more recently FDR's 'New Deal' in the 1930s. This is in contrast to Elizabeth Warren who comes out with certain radical demands but specifically states that she is not a socialist but believes in a reformed capitalism. We have to seize the time provided by the enormous political ferment taking place in preparation for the next elections. Millions are mobilising on how best to defeat Trump. We have to audaciously pose the unequivocal demand for a new mass party of the working class. In a skilful way it is necessary to raise our criticism of the inadequacies of Sanders' programme, which is to reform in the direction of a more humane capitalism.

Our criticisms need to include Sanders' failure to take the necessary steps to break from the Democrats and build a new party. Indeed, Sanders argues that he is "in a good position" to bring people, especially youth and people of colour, "into the Democratic party". Our former supporters in the US fail to do this and, generally speaking, in their material, only call for Sanders to take such a step if he is blocked in the Democratic Party.

The call for a new workers' party needs to be done in a sensitive and skilful manner and to take into account the illusions which have probably grown that it is possible to transform the Democrats. This flows from the powerful "get Trump out" mood which will become even stronger as the 2020 election approaches. It has also probably been re-enforced by the successful election of DSA member Alexandria Ocasio Cortes ('AOC') to Congress and others to other public positions. However, despite this it is correct for us to sensitively raise our position on the need for a new party in articles and propaganda – not necessarily as slogans or demands – but to point to what is needed and also why we argue that such a new party fights for a socialist alternative. It is not sufficient just to have a perspective, but also a worked out programme is needed. This should be linked to the present consciousness of the American working class and their active layers – preparing the ground for mass political action, separate and distinct from the increasingly discredited bourgeois parties.

Turmoil in Europe

The lessons of the recent European elections reported on our website sum up well the mood that is developing in Europe at the present time. The elections have confirmed the turmoil that exists throughout the continent, which is one of chronic political, economic and social instability. This was reflected in some countries in a surge for Green parties, helped by the recent popular movements demanding action against climate change and, on the opposite side, a growth of right-wing nationalist and far-right parties. The traditional ruling parties generally suffered massive losses, as did a number of recent new formations that have sprung up in recent years. This was strikingly reflected in Britain by the six-week-old Brexit party coming top of the polls in the European elections while the 'governing' Conservatives came fifth with 9.1% of the vote, the lowest share in their over 200-year history.

In many countries in Europe the initial reaction to the crisis of 2007-08 was resistance to the ruling classes' attempt to make the working and middle classes pay the price of the most serious economic recession since the 1930s. This resistance took different forms, including the growth of often new parties on the left which promised to stop austerity and to take measures against the super-rich.

However, in most cases these parties did not carry out what they said, or implied they would do, and in a number of countries the consequences were seen in the European elections. The most shameful and spectacular case was that of Syriza in Greece which came into government in early 2015 promising to end austerity, but which, within a matter of months, capitulated. Syriza gained just over 26% of the vote on 26 May this year, compared with the over 36% it won in the two 2015 general elections. The conservative New Democracy party topped the polls. New elections have been called in Greece which are likely to see Syriza replaced by the right-wing New Democracy.

In Spain, Podemos, emanating from the Indignados movement that began in 2011, scored 20.6% in the first general election it contested in December 2015. However, the leadership's lack of a clear alternative socialist policy, and increasing willingness to subordinate itself to the pro-capitalist leadership of the Spanish social-democratic PSOE, has since dented its support. Podemos, in alliance with the United Left, won just 10.1% in this election, half its 2015 score.

This has allowed PSOE to temporarily make an electoral recovery. In Portugal the 'Left Block', by propping up the Socialist Party government, has assisted the PSP in maintaining its electoral support. This can rapidly change with the onset of a more severe economic crisis and attacks against the working class in both Spain and Portugal. In Germany support for Die Linke, the Left party, has stagnated for similar reasons to Podemos.

The Socialist Party in Ireland also suffered a setback as its vote in the Dublin seat dropped to 4,967 (1.36%), compared to 29,953 five years ago, and 50,510 (12.4%) in 2009, when Joe Higgins won a Euro seat.

In many countries right-wing nationalists and the far right have stepped in to try to take advantage of this situation, on an increasingly populist programme. These right-wing demagogic opponents of the EU have been helped by the fact that most leaders of European trade unions and 'left' parties support the capitalist EU.

This is the background to these elections seeing in a number of countries a strengthening of the far right, with Salvini and the Lega in Italy scoring 34.3% of the vote and topping the poll, as did Marine Le Pen's 'Rassemblement National' (the renamed National Front) when it beat President Macron's En Marche to the top spot.

In some countries far-right parties did not do well. In the Belgian general election it was mixed where simultaneously the right-wing nationalist New Flemish Alliance, which has been in government, saw a sharp drop in its support in the Flemish region as the far-right Vlaams Belang more than doubled its vote to 18.5%.

These elections have opened up a period of uncertainty in many European countries. The big drops in votes for the German ruling parties raise the question of whether the coalition there will continue until 2021. The German Social-Democratic Party (SPD) suffered its worst percentage vote, 15.8%, since the 1887 election when it was still an illegal party.

Some capitalist commentators consoled themselves with the fact that, in France, Macron's party was a narrow second behind Le Pen's. But the fact remains that the French president's own party was only supported by 22.4%, roughly the same percentage that backed him in the first round of the 2017 presidential election. Macron has no solid base, something seen in the 'gilets jaunes' (yellow jackets) protests. While the French left had a poor result – Mélenchon's 'France Insoumise' gained just 6.3% – there is still a potentially explosive social situation which can result in further movements.

In a number of countries the votes for the Greens did represent a search for an alternative, particularly by the young and the middle class. However, many of those looking to the Greens today will be disappointed by them tomorrow.

In Germany they have no problem forming coalitions with Merkel's pro-capitalist party and previously helped Schröder's right-wing SPD government carry through neoliberal austerity measures. Most Green leaders see themselves as working within, rather than challenging, capitalism.

What is clear is that growing numbers of people in Europe are rejecting the old order, whether it is in their own countries or in the shape of the EU. There is a developing mood that the system is rigged against ordinary people, that their views are ignored and their living standards cut as the rich get richer, along with growing opposition to what is rightly seen as rule from above, whether it be governments or big corporations.

This is an explosive mixture which does not just herald movements within countries but also clashes between competing nations. The catastrophic situation facing the Tory party in Britain and the unprecedented crisis within it in the recent leadership elections represents an historic turning point for this, the most successful capitalist party which is faced with splits and possible disintegration. The ruling class are also desperately worried at the prospect of a Johnson-led government. The crisis surrounding Brexit and the Tory party is a product of the decline of loss of power of British imperialism. The EU is not simply a single united bloc. The rival capitalist classes have their own agendas. Some capitalist world powers, whether it be the US, China or Russia, will also intervene in pursuit of their own interests.

Against this background the Euro elections offer both positive possibilities and a warning. Positively they showed again how the old order is being questioned and that there is a search for an alternative. Negatively it showed that unless the workers' and socialist movement can offer an alternative, and seriously struggle for it, then reaction will seek to exploit the situation to build support.

The dramatic drop in support for the social democracy in Germany is part of a European-wide process in most European countries. A harbinger of what is coming is indicated by the fact that some commentators have been going back – a long way back – in studying those conditions that existed at the period of revolution in Britain. One, John Harris in the Guardian, stated: "I have been reading Christopher Hill's 'The World Turned Upside Down' [a spell-binding account by a 'Marxist', albeit Stalinist, historian of England's own revolution]. He has also dipped into the experience of the Chartists in 19th-century Britain, the first independent working class political movement in history, which in the space of ten years or so went from the peaceful petition to the idea of a revolutionary general strike against the capitalist system!

This is just one indication of the massive upheavals that impend in Britain: that a commentator invokes England's 17th century revolution as a warning of what could happen! Trotsky did the same in 'Where is Britain Going?'. The same warnings apply to all the other countries of Europe. Moreover this process will not just be restricted to Western Europe. It is already beginning to unfold in Eastern Europe, as indicated by events in Poland and the Czech Republic, where it exceeds in its potential the movements that developed at the time of the so-called 'Velvet Revolution'. All the past 'certainties' of Poland, particularly the influence of the Catholic Church which historically developed as a symbol of Polish nationalism, are being challenged by the impressive and unprecedented movement against its influence in favour of the liberalisation of LGBTQ+ rights – hitherto not seen in Poland on such a scale as now. In Russia the early release of the opposition journalist is an indication of the growing sensitivity of the Putin regime to the opposition that is developing on democratic rights from below. Movements within the trade unions will follow.

Mass strike in Switzerland demands equal pay

The massive strike in June and demonstrations of women in Switzerland, which are symptomatic of this new period, was the biggest industrial action in that country since the 1912 general strike, and even bigger than its 1991 predecessor. Unlike Germany, it was taken up not only by left wing organisations but also called for by the largest SDB/USS trade union federation. The strike was called specifically to demand higher pay, greater equality and more respect for women in one of the world's wealthiest countries where half the population –

women – are in their own words "treated unfairly". Incredibly women only got to vote in federal elections in 1971, decades after most of the Western world, and until 1985 needed their husband's approval to work or open a bank account! Even more scandalous was the fact that statutory maternity leave was only introduced in 2005. Moreover professional women earn on average nearly 19% less than men and 8% less with the same qualifications! Amnesty International found that 59% of Swiss women have experienced sexual harassment! However, workers have led the way in fighting these conditions. Some employers let female staff off to join the protest while others even supported them.

Yet several firms told female employees they would have to book any time off as a holiday, and Switzerland's main employers' organisation stated that it was against the movement, despite opinion polls showing more than 63% of Swiss backing the campaign. This demonstrates that women in Switzerland have the same general problems of women's oppression inherent to class society and inadequate low pay as elsewhere in Europe. The Swiss strike was preceded by the Glasgow homecare battle on pay and conditions of a predominantly female workforce. Nevertheless, they resorted to traditional working class action through a strike and sought to link up with working class men in a common struggle to change conditions. The movement in Switzerland developed such a momentum that even established politicians, like Zurich's social democratic mayor, Corine Mauch, joined the protest. However these forces joined the protest to limit its demands and derail the movement towards women's quotas in company managing boards instead of economic demands. The movement, therefore, needs a clear orientation in demands and programme.

This year has seen almost monthly demonstrations and protests against the threat of devastating climate change. The "youth strikes for climate" brought thousands of young teenagers – and sometimes even younger – out of the classroom and onto the streets demanding action to halt and reverse climate change. Greta Thunberg, the Swedish teenager first sparked off support and called for the general strike for the climate. This was unfortunately more advanced politically than the party in Ireland who did not even see the need for the campaign in support of the right of to abortion to make broader class demands, including the idea at least of a demonstrative "general strike" of women, young people and workers together. After Thunberg's appeal the idea of a general strike has been echoed by Jeremy Corbyn and John MacDonnell and has caught on among layers of activists. Now there is a demand for "an earth strike" – a general strike for the climate. This shows a very positive mood when young people are talking about workers taking strike action and using the language of mass struggle. It points in the direction of the force in society that has the power to decisively change things – the organised working class. It is an instinctive appeal by young people to the working class and its organisations. The youth strikes now taking place are the biggest of young people since the student demonstrations in the winter of 2010 against tuition fee increases. This was linked to the battle to defeat austerity.

If this movement would appeal consistently to workers by putting demands on trade union leaders and linking it with the fight for guaranteed jobs for those affected by climate change, it could help to build an unstoppable movement from below. But the consciousness in the movement is mixed. Some layers orientate towards consumer change, veganism and other individual measures to stop climate change. This is used by the tops of the movement, generally undemocratically run by NGO representatives, to orientate the movement to vote for the green parties. Groups like 'Extinction rebellion' attract a radical layer with proposals for direct action. However without a clear political orientation, the working class driver of a car which has been blocked by sit-ins can become the 'enemy' rather than the coal company owners which make huge profits by the destruction of the planet. When it comes to the demand for strike action, we need to link up the climate protest with the working class movement. At the same time we pointed out there is a difference between a protest strike and an all-out general strike which poses the question of power, of who runs society. So such a demand should not be lightly raised. Moreover the difference between the protest strike and a general strike must be stressed. However, even a one-day strike could have colossal consequences in weakening further weak governments. A one-day general strike in Britain could bring down the hated Tories and propel a Corbyn-led Labour government to power. It would also enormously enhance the case for decisive action against climate change. We are sure that similar actions will be taken by the different sections of the CWI.

Marxists, socialist consciousness and building a revolutionary workers' International

These developments in Europe and internationally indicate that a new explosive era has already begun. There are still the obstacles that arose from the consequences of the collapse of Stalinism and its effects on the workers' organisations and the throwing back of socialist consciousness which will need to be overcome by big events. This issue has also featured during the course of the struggle inside the CWI. As we pointed out, there was a radicalisation following the 2007-08 crisis. We had initially anticipated that it would lead to the emergence of a more pronounced socialist consciousness. However, as we have explained, this did not happen. The lack of a generalised, sustained movement of the working class, has led in the recent period to a more complex and contradictory situation in Europe and internationally.

The sectarian split we experienced in Spain tried to deny reality as they buried their heads in the sand ignoring the complexities of the situation which had arisen. The right-ward split, grouped in the so-called "coordinating sections" – an undeclared faction – has reacted to it by an opportunist adaptation. In recognising the complexities we must not underestimate the explosive situation which still exist in society in Europe or internationally. The onset of a new economic crisis following the experience of 2007-08 will lead to an even more polarised explosive situation in which a more pronounced socialist consciousness can emerge. Our forces can assist this process in some countries. This development will enable us to strengthen our forces and recover the losses we have suffered.

Experience has shown that the opposition faction – alongside other sectarian organisations – is utterly incapable of seizing the opportunities that will develop in the next period. It is left to us as the bearers of the real Trotskyist fighting traditions of the CWI to intervene and win the next generation to our banner.

Rotting capitalism can offer no way out for the masses of the world. They cannot harness the colossal potential which is being built up by the development of new technology – information technology in particular. Pessimists such as Paul Mason believe that unless we abandon Marxism and embrace 'humanism' we will be taken over and enslaved by new "more intelligent machines", the product of the development of artificial intelligence. Another scenario, he writes, will see Trump and reaction – including fascism – as the future for humankind.

We reject all these pessimistic scenarios. It is entirely feasible that the fourth Industrial

Revolution, the huge development of information technology, including the creation of intelligent machines, can go hand-in-hand with the control and management of the means of production for the benefit of all on the basis of a planned democratic socialist society. The instruments to create this are mass revolutionary parties and revolutionary workers' international, the outlines of which we will build, despite all the obstacles, in the next period.

BUILDING THE CWI

Following an intense and polarised factional struggle in the last twelve months, an international conference was convened by the International Secretariat in London in July 2019. This very successful and optimistic meeting agreed to re-constitute the CWI. The conference was attended by 200 delegates and visitors from England, Wales, Scotland, France, Germany, Austria, Ireland, India, Sri Lanka, Malaysia, Finland, South Africa, Chile and the United States. Apologies were received from comrades in Nigeria and Israel who had travel and visa problems. This meeting endorsed the document below as a balance sheet of the conflict, and prospects for building a revolutionary Trotskyist international organisation.

The CWI has faced a political division and split with those who have capitulated to the pressures of opportunism, identity politics and turned away from systematic consistent trade union work. Identity politics is a weapon of world capitalism to divide the working class by reinforcing separatism. This has posed the need to reconstitute the international organisation on a firm Marxist and Trotskyist basis. This is an historic task which confronts us in preparation for the eruption of big class battles in the coming period as a consequence of the profound crisis facing global capitalism.

The debate which has raged during the last seven months has revealed an ideological and programmatic corrosion and collapse that has taken place in sections and groups of the CWI. This is defended by the opportunist trend which has crystalised, represented by the leadership of the Non-Faction Faction (NFF) opposition grouping. It is now clear, as we have explained in many documents produced by our faction, that the fundamental principles upon which the CWI was founded in 1974 have been abandoned by the NFF leadership. In order to defend the principles which built and maintained the CWI it is necessary to reconstitute the international to build a working class, revolutionary Trotskyist international organisation.

The crisis began with a clash with the Irish organisation over the use of alien, profoundly undemocratic underhand methods which broke with democratic centralism. Together with this huge breach in the methods of the CWI, the Irish party had moved away from a strategic, consistent orientation and intervention in the trades unions and buckled to the separatist pressures of identity politics. The defence of our revolutionary socialist programme and transitional method was abandoned in the mass and semi mass work undertaken by the Irish party. Reflecting these political and ideological retreats the profile and concept of building a revolutionary party were largely lost.

When the IS raised these issues with a view to correcting them, a series of leaders of sections, which later grouped together in the NFF, rose up to defend the Irish organisation. As the debate ensued it became clear that the same ideological and political corrosion which had infected the Irish organisation was also present in other sections of the NFF.

This development represents a set-back for the struggle to build a revolutionary socialist workers' international. However, it would be fatal to ignore the political reality which exists

– that of a political rupture in the CWI as it was formerly constituted has taken place. In this situation it is necessary to re-establish ideological, political and organisational clarity In order to defend the programme of the revolutionary party – which is the International – to actively intervene in the intense political polarisation and working class struggle that is already unfolding.

The ideological and political collapse which has taken place in many sections, and on the left in general, is, at root, a reflection of the objective pressures which exist. The main element that has given rise to a more complex and contradictory period since the 2007-08 crisis has been the absence of the working class, in general, clearly putting its stamp on the situation either politically or in struggle. This is reflected, as we have explained, in the extremely weak and inadequate character of the new left parties which have developed at this stage. These are politically weaker than even the left reformist trends in the 1970s and 1980s. They have so far in the main assumed more the character of left-populist rather than "socialist" parties. We are confident that this situation will change in the coming period. The first winds of the impending storms to come have already arrived. However, the recent conjuncture has resulted in the short term in a certain impasse in the class struggle, reflected in the growth in some countries of the right-wing populists and far right, which have been able to partially step into the vacuum. This can rapidly change, as has been recently illustrated in Brazil. The crisis now facing the Bolsonaro regime following the general strike of 45 million illustrates this.

Pernicious role of identity politics – a Trotskyist approach

However, in the situation which has existed, the growth of the pernicious ideas of identity politics has been a test for revolutionary socialists. The question is not if it is necessary to intervene in the women's, LGBTQ+, environmental or other movements. We fully support and must energetically intervene in these movements. The question is how? As Marxists we must realistically appraise the positive feature of these movements and also recognise the limitations of them, including their multi-class character. It is necessary to intervene in them on a class basis with the socialist programme which we defend. It is not the duty of revolutionary Trotskyists to buckle to the petty bourgeois and bourgeois pressures of identity politics and separatism as the NFF faction and its leadership has done.

The petty bourgeois pressure of identity politics has provoked a crisis not only in the CWI but throughout the revolutionary left. It was a major factor in the implosion which has taken place in the ISO in the USA. It has affected the SWP in both Britain and Ireland. It has provoked debate and upheavals throughout the Morenoite organisations in Latin America. These petty bourgeois ideas have also been imported into the broader workers' movement, including trade unions and left parties in some countries.

Faced with the threat of this political virus infecting the revolutionary and workers' movement, it is crucial that we combat it ideologically and withstand the alien class pressures which flow from it.

This is a test for revolutionary socialists which the NFF have failed as reflected during the debate. They buckled to the pressure of identity politics in the hope of finding a short cut to win radicalised layers from these movements but without raising our socialist programme. The recent Euro and local council elections in Ireland, which were a disaster for the Irish party, were partly the fruit of these opportunist ideas and methods.

The trade union question – a crucial issue for Trotskyism

The question of the trade unions and the need to undertake consistent systematic work in them is decisive for a revolutionary Trotskyist organisation. It was one of the conditions for affiliation to the 3rd International and a condition of membership of the 4th International when Trotsky helped to found it in 1938. The CWI has always defended and maintained this approach. Yet this cardinal principle has been abandoned by the Irish, Greek, Swedish and other sections. They have justified this because of the degree of bureaucratisation and low level of active membership and low level of unionisation.

These problems are real as we have commented in previous documents and our political analysis. However, they are not justification for a revolutionary Trotskyist organisation to turn away, (albeit for a "temporary period") from undertaking patient and consistent work within the trade unions. It is not enough simply to visit picket lines – important though this is. We must also, through consistent work, build a base in the trade unions and work places, developing opposition groupings, together with other workers, to fight the trade union bureaucracy. Initiatives to build trade unions amongst the new unorganised sections of workers is also a crucial task facing the working class which CWI members and sections need to engage in. We entirely reject the claim that we have adopted an "Anglo-centric" attitude towards trade union work. The exact tactics we deploy or advocate in any particular country has always been extremely flexible, to take into account the differences which exist in. The bureaucratised nature of most of the trade unions and low level of active membership is an international feature of the current situation. However, despite the obstacles and problems that arise it is entirely wrong to use this as an excuse to turn away from official trade union organisations, even in some countries with "yellow unions" or unions integrated into the state machine, as Trotsky pointed out in the 1930s. Work in the official unions does not preclude, when the situation warrants it, supporting or initiating movements or organisations outside the official union structures. This aspect of the work of the CWI is central for building a revolutionary party.

The Transitional Method and the CWI

The defence of the 'Transitional method' and programme is another aspect of the struggle we have ferociously defended. The transitional method recognises the existing consciousness of the working class, and seeks to link it with the idea of the socialist revolution. As Trotsky explained, it is necessary to raise demands that correspond to the current consciousness and through a series of transitional demands construct a bridge which will assist workers concluding the need for a socialist programme to break with capitalism. In the course of the recent struggle, some in the NFF have not adopted this approach. The idea of "socialism" is abstractly tagged on the end, with no preceding demands or argumentation leading to such a conclusion. Or, where it is explained, it is done in articles in journals or web-sites but not raised in propaganda material when intervening in mass movements. The use of the transitional programme and method is a crucial weapon to build a revolutionary party based on the working class. It will be necessary in the reconstituted international for every section and group to produce a programme, to be reviewed and discussed not just by each section but in the international organisation itself.

The degree of divergence on these issues, and also democratic centralism between us and the NFF, is fundamental for Trotskyists. They represent a political rupture. The roots of the current crisis in the CWI are to found in the objective situation. However, this explanation of the ideological collapse in some sections is not an excuse for some long- standing former cadres of the CWI who have capitulated to the pressures of the objective situation in an opportunistic way.

Building a revolutionary International

This crisis in the CWI is not the first time that objective conditions have provoked a crisis and collapse of Marxist cadres and workers' leaders. Although on a much more serious and dramatic manner and under different conditions we saw the collapse of the 1st, 2nd and 3rd Internationals. The 2nd and 3rd Internationals were mass organisations unlike the small but significant forces in the CWI at this stage. The USFI capitulated under the opportunistic pressures of the objective conditions of the post-war boom and then looked towards students and the guerrilla movements as a more immediate "revolutionary force" at the time. Then it was necessary for the comrades to break from this organisation and take the necessary steps to re-build the movement. Without this bold step the powerful base we built in the 'Militant', leading the mass poll tax movement and the struggles in Liverpool, and the building of the CWI, would not have happened. The method and approach adopted in that period needs to be reconquered through the political and organisational re-founding of the CWI and applied to the new world situation we face with the historic crisis of global capitalism.

There can be no guarantees how any individual, party or International organisation will face up to the pressures of opportunism or sectarianism which inevitably arise during the class struggle. However, it is crucial that we learn lessons from the recent experiences we have had as an international. Some sections in the recent period have recruited from a layer of youth, mainly from university backgrounds. It is necessary for any revolutionary organisation to build a base in the universities, which will include a layer of the petty bourgeois. However, we need to ensure that they are steeled in the ideas and methods of Bolshevism and put themselves on the standpoint of the working class. Comrades recruited from this milieu need to be tested out through intervention in the class struggle and imbued with the spirit of self- sacrifice in time, sub payments and commitment to building the revolutionary party. This has not been done with many of those recruited from this background in the recent period.

In part, this was inevitable given the current stage of the class struggle in many countries. However, we must draw the lessons from this and test out youth from such a background over a period of time. We should try to avoid putting even some committed and self-sacrificing young comrades into leading positions before they have been tested and developed through self-sacrifice and intervention in the class struggle. We should strive to apply Trotsky's advice to the US SWP, in the 1930s, that comrades from a petty bourgeois background are regularly involved in recruiting workers to the party.

This is crucial if we are to build a solid cadre in the sections and an International that is able to face up to the challenges the class struggle will bring with it in the coming period.

With workers we need to take a more flexible approach to recruitment. We still need to sustain an audacious attitude towards recruitment. However, at the same time, as part of the struggle to rebuild the revolutionary movement, we should return to the concept of a period of discussions with contacts and new recruits with a systematic plan of political education coupled with intervention in the class struggle.

Whilst we need to build a base amongst the students it is also crucial that our youth work involves a plan to win young workers to our ranks.

The building of a section of our International will go through many different stages. There is nothing wrong with a small group beginning with a base amongst a layer of students understanding the role of the working class. However, then it needs to turn towards intervening amongst the working class and begin to recruit workers and educate them with our programme, methods and traditions and begin systematic consistent interventions into the trade unions, work places and communities.

We are and will emerge from this crisis as a more hardened revolutionary International both politically and in the spirit of self-sacrifice needed for party building. We must never allow again the situation to arise as it did in southern Ireland where a national section becomes entirely dependent on income from the state rather than the subs and money raised from the working class. Any money accrued from the state or other sources must be separated out and put under the control of the party structures. We must ensure that the full timers, which are essential to build the party, are a lever for party building and not a substitute for the party. We should ensure that the ratio of full timers to party members is of a healthy political balance. Flexibility is needed, especially in the neo-colonial world but in the initial stages of building a revolutionary party a ratio of 30 subs paying members per full timer is an approximation we should aim for.

This conference of the international faction drawing on the lessons and experience of the struggle in the CWI during the last seven months therefore concludes:

• That we reconstitute the CWI as a revolutionary Trotskyist working class international.

• We stand on the principles and methods of Marx, Engels, Lenin and Trotsky, the first four Congresses of the Comintern, the founding documents of the fourth international and the founding documents, programme and congresses of the CWI.

• All members and sections of the refounded CWI are committed to defending these ideas and programme; work amongst the youth including students and young workers; undertake systematic work in the trade unions and amongst the working class; audaciously intervene in the womens, LGBTQ+, environmental and other such movements on a class basis, defending a revolutionary socialist programme and combating the ideas of separatism and identity politics and all alien ideas; struggle to build revolutionary parties and a world party of revolution.

We are confident that the forces of the CWI will play a crucial role in the struggle to build a mass revolutionary socialist international. At this stage our forces on a world scale are limited numerically but with enormous potential and can make significant gains. We can be strengthened in the coming period given the crisis that confronts capitalism. The building of the CWI into a more powerful force will not be done on the basis of lineal arithmetical growth. It will involve a process of coming together through principled political agreement with other revolutionary socialist organisations and parties and new parties that are seeking a revolutionary way to break with capitalism. It will involve unifications and also splits.

This conference, therefore, agrees that the International Secretariat should be mandated to convene a world congress in 2020 for the parties and groups which stand on the central tenets of the CWI. Other revolutionary organisations and groups which are prepared to seriously and honestly engage in debate and collaboration about the building of working class revolutionary socialist parties should also be invited.

We agree to elect an international council representing the sections and groups present at this conference. The International Secretariat who are members of the international faction should continue to function as the IS and bring proposals to the 2020 congress regarding structures and functioning of the international.

In refounding the CWI, including comrades present at its foundation, as a majority of the membership we agree that we continue to use the name, Committee for a Workers' International, as the defenders of the methods, tradition and programme that it was founded on in 1974.

Appendices

WOMEN AND OPPRESSION IN CLASS SOCIETY

Adopted by the CWI World Congress, 2016

This statement draws out some general points on the situation facing women, the perspectives for struggle and our programme and approach. However, the enormous variation between different countries means that perspectives and approach to struggle will also vary considerably across the globe.

Movements against different aspects of women's oppression have been a feature in a number of countries in recent years. They include the mass demonstrations against rape in India and Turkey, the movement on abortion rights in Ireland and the million men and women back in 2011 who marched in Italy against the sexism of the then President Berlusconi.

As so many times before in history, we have seen working women start uprisings, with the Mahalla textile district base for the Arab Spring being a case in point. The female brigades in defence of Rojova have, during the last years of counter revolution, constituted an important contrast to their direct enemies in ISIS, whose state is conducting massive trade in sex slaves.

The control of women's sexuality has been at the core of women's oppression since it first emerged. Today there is an increase in the struggle for women's right to their own bodies. In the US a student-based movement has arisen against rape. In Latin America a number of movements have taken place. The continuing women's and workers' movements have also produced progress, such as increased access to contraception in Africa and growing questioning of female genital mutilation (FGM). The halving of the rate of maternal deaths in the last 25 years and the shrinking of the gender gap of children entering education in many 'developing countries' also constitute a basis upon which more struggle for equality can develop.

Struggle against the old order also tends to act to boost LGBT struggles, as we have seen globally. Fifteen years ago the Netherlands became the first country to allow same-sex marriage. Today it is legal in thirteen European countries – although accompanied by growing polarisation and backlashes, particularly in Eastern Europe. Often a growing feminist awakening emerges with a growing LGBT consciousness, and these movements tend to intersect and mutually reinforce one another. In recent years, transgendered persons have raised their voices to a larger extent than before in some countries.

All of these struggles reflect an increased confidence to fight against oppression among broad sections of, particularly younger, women. In many countries capitalist propaganda suggests that women have a right to expect equality. However, this is contradicted by reality. Women have won greater rights in parts of the world in recent decades. Nonetheless, the oppression of women continues to exist in every country.

The family and capitalism

The oppression of women developed alongside and intertwined with the development of class society, linked to the development of the family which has, in different forms, acted as an important agent of social control for all class societies. As Engels correctly explained in the nineteenth century, the bourgeois institution of the family had the weakest hold over the working class and oppressed. Nonetheless even today, while many peoples' own experience of family is positive, often the people closest to them in the world, the hierarchical nature of society is echoed in the structure of the traditional family, with the man as head of the household and women and children obedient to him. This puts the primary responsibility on individual families to bring up the next generation of workers. It acts to oppress women, but also puts an enormous burden on men to materially provide for their family.

However, while the family remains a vital institution for capitalism, at the same time the capitalist system itself tends to undermine it. As women are drawn into the paid work-force in large numbers their increased confidence and financial independence mean that they are less willing to accept being treated badly in the home and in personal relationships, and have more possibilities to leave. Nonetheless, the idea remains deeply ingrained that women are possessions of men who need to be loyal and obedient to their partners. The whole of society is permeated with propaganda endlessly re-emphasising the 'proper' role of women – as home-makers, mothers, sexual objects, peacemakers and so on.

Women and the workforce

The situation facing women varies considerably in different countries worldwide. In some European countries women now make up more than half of the workforce (although a much greater percentage of women than men work part-time). Globally 50% of women of working age are working, a small fall of around 2% since 1995. The fall is accounted for by the huge increase in unemployment among young people of all genders, particularly in Europe. But it also reflects a fall in women's participation in the labour force in China and India where, between 1995 and 2013, it declined from 72% to 64% and from 35% to 27% respectively. The UN puts the change in China as a result of "significantly fewer government-sponsored child-care facilities" with the "proportion of more affordable state-owned and community-based childcare centres decreasing from 86% in 1997 to 34% in 2009". This is a graphic illustration of the negative consequences of the destruction of vestiges of the planned economy!

Even where women make up a smaller percentage of the workforce they have often still played a central role in class struggle, just as it was women textile workers who began the February revolution in Russia 1917. In Bangladesh in 2013 there were massive strikes in the overwhelmingly female garment industry. In Nigeria, where just under half of working age women work, women have been at the forefront of successive general strikes. While the double oppression that women face can be a major extra obstacle to becoming actively involved, when struggles erupt women workers are often the most militant and determined.

The gender pay gap remains global. Even where there is a high level of participation in the workforce by women only a tiny number at the top have closed the pay gap. In some developed economies the pay gap has narrowed, but this is partially caused by the fall in real terms of the pay of working class men as a result of the destruction of manufacturing industry rather than by an increase in women's pay. In 2011, the World Bank reported that women globally still earn between 10% and 30% less than men, and the gap is no smaller in richer countries than in poor ones. Women remain concentrated in the service sector. In Latin America and the Caribbean, more than 70% of employed women work in the service sector. This is also true in Eastern and Southern Europe. This work – often related to the domestic tasks of 'cooking, cleaning, caring and catering' – is almost always low paid.

Nonetheless, overall, where women have been drawn into the labour force in increasing numbers there have also been improvements in the general situation of women in society. Even then sexism remains ingrained into the fabric of capitalism. It is now less socially acceptable in many countries to openly state that women are the possessions of men. But this idea – and that it is acceptable to enforce it with violence or the threat of violence – remains deeply embedded and was enshrined in law until relatively recently. Marital rape only became illegal in Britain in 1991, Spain in 1992 and Germany in 1997. While no longer legal, or openly acceptable, marital rape is still widespread and rarely punished. The same applies to rape in general. It is estimated that in Britain only 15% of all rapes are reported to the police and only 7% of those result in conviction. According to the UN, of all the women killed globally in 2012, almost half were killed by their partners or family members. In contrast, only 6% of killings with male victims were committed by intimate partners or family members.

Domestic labour

In many neo-colonial countries, the oppression of women is more brutal and severe than in the economically developed countries. There has been a wave of propaganda in Europe and the US attempting to link the brutal treatment of women to Islam, particularly using the horrendous treatment of women by ISIS. However, while there is no question about the barbaric practices carried out by ISIS in the name of Islam, it is wrong to link the degradation of women to Islam in particular. Historically, practices such as honour killings or FGM have been carried out by all religions. Even today these horrendous practices and others – like enforced suicides of widows and dowries for brides – are carried out under the banner of different religions. There are many factors, including the degree of religious influence in society or in government and the level of class struggle, which affect the degree of women's oppression in particular countries, but in general it is the predominance of semi-feudal economic relations rather than any particular religion which is central.

In all countries women continue to bear the brunt of domestic responsibilities, despite increasingly also going out to work. In many cases women are still, as Trotsky put it, the 'slaves of slaves'. In countries where the working class and poor cannot afford the labour-saving devices of modern capitalism – washing machines, fridges, vacuum cleaners and so on – and often do not have an electricity supply to power them, the domestic burden on women is back-breaking. In the economically developed countries, the combination of labour-saving devices and an improvement in social attitudes means that there has been some lessening in the domestic burden on women. In Britain, for example, most studies show men accepting that they should do an equal amount of domestic chores as women, although there is still a considerable gap between intentions and reality. One survey about Britain showed that on average women did 17 hours a week of domestic chores (excluding childcare) whereas men did less than six.

The uneven division of domestic work contributes to women generally having lower wages, less leisure time and worse health than men, but the main gain is for the capitalists. By putting the main burden of domestic life, the bringing up of the next generation and caring for the sick and elderly on women, they are removed from the responsibility of society as a whole.

While historically the development of capitalism has generally led to progress for women in comparison to previous class societies, it has now largely been exhausted. Twenty-first century capitalism, far from taking steps towards lessening the domestic burden on women, is heading in the opposite direction. The relentless cuts in public services taking place across the economically developed countries are destroying the childcare, care for the elderly and other social services which previously partially relieved the burden on working class people, particularly women. Women are also more likely to work in the public sector and therefore to lose their jobs as a result of cuts. Rising housing costs and the closure of refuges in many countries make it more difficult for women to leave violent partners.

At the same time the fall in real wages and cuts to social benefits means that there is no prospect for most working class and many middle class women of choosing to leave the workforce to concentrate on domestic tasks. To bring a family up on the basis of one breadwinner is increasingly becoming impossible. On the contrary, both parents often have to work in more than one job each. This is creating the basis for huge social explosions over cuts to public services, housing and pay. Women will be at the forefront of these, as they have been with the $15 an hour movement in the US.

Women's liberation and class struggle

We also have to be prepared for further mass movements relating to the specific oppression of women. In general the capitalist class is divided on how to deal with the question. A section would support a major offensive against women's rights, linked to propaganda about the importance of the family, women's role in the home and so on. However, there is a realisation from others that this would jar too sharply with social attitudes and would provoke mass movements. This was the case with the huge demonstrations in Spain against attempts to severely curtail the right to abortion, which successfully defeated the proposed law. In fact the increased confidence of woman globally means that we can also see offensive movements, such as in Ireland, to improve women's rights. The demonstrations against rape in India are also an indication of the kind of struggles that can develop in the neo-colonial world.

The struggle for women's liberation is, at root, part of the class struggle, in which the struggles by women against their own specific oppression dovetail with those of the working class in general for a fundamental restructuring of society to end all inequality and oppression. We disagree with bourgeois and petit-bourgeois feminism because it does not take a class approach to the struggle for women's liberation. This does not mean, of course, that only working-class women are oppressed. Working-class women are 'doubly-oppressed', both for their class and gender, but women from all sections of society suffer oppression as a result of their sex, including domestic violence and sexual harassment.

However, at root, to win real sexual equality for women, including women from the elite of society, a complete overturn of the existing order is necessary in every sphere: economic, social, family and domestic. The necessary starting point for such an overturn is ending capitalism. The working class is the only force capable of leading a successful struggle to overthrow capitalism and therefore the struggle to end women's oppression and the class struggle are intrinsically linked.

To say this is not to suggest that we take a dismissive attitude towards a new generation of women who enter struggle initially around their rights as women and who do not, as yet, have a class approach. Recognising that you are oppressed, and that you can fight against your oppression through a common struggle with others who share the same oppression, is an important step forward. In that sense what can broadly be described as identity politics are an inevitable part of the political awakening of many members of oppressed groups within society. However, the history of struggle against oppression shows that, on the basis of experience, those participating tend to go beyond identity politics as they recognise that the root cause of their oppression lies in the structure of society.

Our role has to be to intervene skilfully, in a transitional way, to link the struggle against women's oppression to the struggle for socialism. This includes being prepared, where necessary, to clearly oppose the ideas of bourgeois and petty-bourgeois feminism, not least the idea held by many feminists that the blame for the oppression of women lies in the innate character of men rather than the structure of society.

Of course, that does not mean we do not combat sexist behaviour in this society, not least within the workers' movement. In arguing that the working class is the only force capable of fundamentally changing society, we are not in any way blind to the prejudices, including racism, sexism and homophobia, which exist among all classes including the working class and which we have a proud record of combating.

Violence against women

If workers' organisations in general and, above all, revolutionary parties are to succeed in unifying the working class in the struggle to change society it is vital that they champion the rights of women and all oppressed groups. We do not take the crude position that has historically been adopted by some revolutionary organisations; for example the International Socialist Tendency (IST – the international followers of the British SWP). When the CWI in Britain initiated the Campaign Against Domestic Violence, (CADV) the SWP initially reacted by arguing that raising male violence against women in the trade unions was divisive. This flowed from their mistaken theoretical position on how the workers' movement should deal with women's oppression.

In his book 'Class struggle and Women's Liberation', Tony Cliff, founder of the SWP, argued that the women's liberation movement was wrong to focus "consistently on areas where men and women are at odds – rape, battered women, wages for housework – while ignoring or playing down the important struggles in which women are more likely to win the support of men: strikes, opposition to welfare cuts, equal pay, unionisation, abortion". We countered this narrow approach. Of course it is vital for the workers' movement to take up economic issues such as opposition to welfare cuts and equal pay. In fact these issues are also central to a campaign against domestic violence. The CADV campaigned, as the Socialist Party and other CWI sections do today, in opposition to all cuts in sexual and domestic violence services, for a huge expansion in the number of women's refuges and for a mass council house building programme in order to make it possible for women to live independently.

However, we fight for the maximum unity of the working class, not by trying to brush issues relating to the specific oppression of women under the carpet, but by campaigning to convince the whole workers' movement that it is necessary to take these issues seriously. The CADV played a vital role in convincing every major trade union in Britain to adopt a national policy against domestic violence. This demonstrates, contrary to Cliff's views, that the big majority of working class men can be won to a position of opposition to domestic violence.

Workers' organisations exist within capitalism. They are not the model for a new society, but tools to aid the struggle to create one. This is not an excuse for avoiding dealing firmly with all cases of sexual harassment and abuse, but rather a recognition that such cases will sometimes occur. It is utopian to imagine it is possible to create a model of a socialist society within capitalism. Even the most thinking class-conscious elements of the working class are products of capitalism, with all of the distortions of the human personality which that creates. We cannot expect that our members – especially new members – come into the party fully-formed with a complete understanding of every issue, including of sexism. The aim of socialists in the workers' movement should be to raise understanding of all issues over time, including the oppression of women and taking a position of confronting any instances of sexual harassment and abuse.

The struggle for greater participation by women

We also have to fight for greater participation by women in both the CWI and the workers' movement as a whole. First and foremost this is a political issue. It is by adopting and fighting for a programme that is in the interests of working class women that the workers' movement will attract more women to its ranks. We need to ensure that our discussions on perspectives and programme include a socialist gender perspective. This does not mean that a correct programme will – in and of itself – overcome the problem.

In every country the double oppression that women face means that they have extra obstacles to overcome in order to be active, especially in periods where there is not an upsurge in struggle. If this is true for the workers' movement as a whole it is even more the case when it comes to women joining the CWI while we are still a relatively small revolutionary minority in society. Particularly in societies where the oppression of women is most brutal, it is a major achievement to build a female cadre in the organisation, even if they are – at this stage – a small minority of the party.

It can sometimes be necessary to hold separate party meetings for women, particularly new members, but of course these should always be a transitional measure with the aim of building branches that involve both men and women. We should strive towards half – or even a majority, as with the current Executive Committee in England and Wales – of our leading bodies at local, national and international level being made up of women. We also have to fight for women comrades to play a role as public representatives for the CWI, where they can often be extremely effective, as we can see in the US and Ireland. However, these goals cannot be achieved artificially, but have to be on the basis of developing a female cadre over time. It is crucial that we put extra effort into developing the political understanding and particularly the political confidence of female comrades. CWI sections should regularly assess and discuss what measures can be taken to involve more women in the section and in the leadership.

Women's self-organisation within left parties and the workers' movement is very important for combatting the idea that women's oppression is natural and to strengthen the contribution of women to the class struggle and assist them to reach their full potential. This can be done through organising women's commissions or caucuses where women can meet to discuss and formulate policies – specific, as well as general, points from a women's perspective. This creates an environment for women to feel more comfortable and strengthen their ability to intervene elsewhere. These commissions are not decision-making bodies; it is the branches, aggregates, committees and congresses which make the decisions. Women are half the working class but are under-represented, especially on the leading bodies of parties and trade unions. We do not believe we will solve this problem or overcome discrimination against women by these measures alone, but they can be of great assistance in fully involving women in the struggle.

While our scarce resources mean it will not always be possible to do everything required, we have to strive to take practical measures to make it easier for women to be active, such as the provision of childcare, safe accessible venues and so on. At the same time we have to fight for the workers' movement to do the same.

Quotas

In some countries the workers' movement has adopted quotas or reserved seats as a means to ensure women are represented within the leadership. Such measures do not, on their own, overcome the obstacles that the mass of women face in becoming active in the workers' movement and can even act as a hindrance. In some trade unions in Britain, for example, token measures have been taken which increased the number of women in their leadership bodies, but are also used by the right wing of the union to strengthen their grip on the leadership. As a result of the unions' woeful failure to fight, the mass of women are undoubtedly less likely to become active in the union, despite having women in the leadership.

Nonetheless, because of the perception that they can act as a tool to increase women's participation in the movement, we usually do not oppose quotas, especially where they have already been introduced. In some instances, CWI sections have supported the introduction of quotas in workers' and left organisations, for example in PSOL in Brazil, where today the leadership is made up of 50% women, and it has played some role in increasing women's involvement. However, there can be occasions when we do oppose particularly token measures. In all cases we have to make clear that quotas will not solve the problem and that a fighting programme in the interests of working class women, and practical measures to aid women's involvement such as childcare, are central.

The CWI has a proud record of campaigning on issues relating to the specific oppression of women and also of developing women into the leadership of the CWI. However, what we have achieved so far is only a small beginning. By intervening energetically, with a clear programme, into the struggles that will erupt, including those that relate to the specific oppression of women, we will be able to win many thousands of working-class women fighters to our ranks.

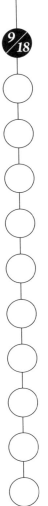

IS PROPOSED STATEMENT

Following 13 & 14 September 2018 meeting with the Irish leadership

This statement was proposed to the meeting mentioned above. However, the Irish leadership refused to support it.

The IS and the whole CWI recognises and salutes the tremendous achievements and work of all the comrades in the Irish section over a period of decades, and in particular in the struggle over the water charges and the tremendous victory we played a crucial role in; scoring the victory in the repeal referendum. Nothing must be done to sully these achievements in the current discussions. These achievements have been the result of the sacrifices and struggles of all the comrades in the Irish section together with the CWI.

However, a crisis has developed. The IS and representatives of the leadership of the Irish section have met to have extensive discussion to try and find a principled solution to the problems which have arisen.

This meeting followed the revelation that a comrade, had [carried out a hack]. The IS totally condemns these actions and finds them reprehensible. We agree that this needs to be reported and discussed by the NC of the Irish section, which should discuss and agree what disciplinary sanctions should be taken.

However, the IS is also of the view, that mistakes were made by the Irish leadership in handling this issue. There are political questions and aspects of party building methods which comrades have raised which need to be discussed out further within the section involving the IS. We urge all comrades in the leadership to work constructively to try and positively engage in discussion to resolve these issues. Comrades in the course of these discussions have the right to discuss with all comrades as part of this process. Any discussion on a more organised basis amongst comrades should only be done on the basis of informing the appropriate structures and leading bodies of the party.

The IS will participate in these discussions with the view of trying to assist the comrades to overcome the current crisis and move forward.

LETTER FOR DISCUSSION

Hannah Sell, on behalf of the IS, to Laura Fitzgerald, IEC (Ireland)

S orry for not replying yesterday, I was out of the centre speaking in Leeds. As requested below I've listed a very brief summary of issues we would like the Irish NC discussion on 14 October to address, hopefully in order to clarify the issues and reach agreement. And, of course, as we have made clear, our questions on these issues in no way undermine our recognition of the fantastic victory achieved in the referendum campaign.

We know that comrades on the Irish NEC have questions over the approach of the IS to struggles relating to women's oppression. At the meeting in London on 13 and14 September Kevin McLoughlin said that he 'didn't think the comrades had engaged in a serious way with the women's movement as it has emerged over the last two years' and that he thought we were 'hesitant' on it but didn't know why. We don't agree but think it would be useful to discuss this issue out. You, of course, should explain your criticisms of our approach, including what concrete measures you think were needed and not taken by the international. We would also like to hear your assessment of the different struggles that have developed around various aspects of women's oppression globally, including the factors that have led to them taking place now and what you see as the perspectives for such movements in the coming period.

We would also like to discuss how you see the connection between women's and LGBTQ+ oppressions and radicalisation. At the [CWI European summer] school [in Mid-July 2018] you and other leading Irish comrades seem to argue that if we didn't 'put these issues central' we would be cut off from radical young people. In addition some young comrades from Ireland appeared not to understand the centrality of the working class. We, of course, agree that we have to stand in defence of women's and LGBTQ+ rights in every country. However, we would not agree that these are the central issues, above all others, leading the broad mass of young people, and working class young people in particular, towards anti-capitalist conclusions at the moment, nor would we agree that that the section of society who are radicalised initially on these issues are the single most important section for us to orientate to either in Ireland or internationally. That is not to dispute that an important section can be radicalised around these issues, particularly where movements take place and where we intervene in and attempt to give leadership to them, as we correctly have done in Ireland and other sections. We would like your views on these questions.

We would also like to discuss concretely what measures the comrades took during the referendum campaign to raise the potential role of the working class in fighting for women's rights. For example what demands did we put on the trade union leaders, what activity did we conduct at workplaces, and how did we use the positive example of the water charges victory?

Finally, we would like to discuss how comrades see the role of Rosa both currently and in the future, and how that relates to the role of the party and future class struggles. We would also like to know if the comrades view Rosa as an applicable model for our work internationally regardless of circumstances which, if so, we would not accept.

For background on our general approach it might be worth looking at an article I did for Socialism Today [see page 83].

Even though these points are very brief I think it would be worth circulating them to the NC for their information.

I hope that is helpful, look forward to seeing you at the weekend.

Following the Irish NC - Hannah Sell,
on behalf of the IS

The National Committee mentioned in the previous document was scheduled to discuss identity politics. However, this discussion was postponed, due to the debate around the hack and the NEC majority's handling of it. This is why, in this email to Kevin McLoughlin, Hannah concludes by mentioning written material on the question of identity politics.

This is a brief reply to your note to Tony Saunois (TS) on the recent NC meeting. TS is currently in the US so I am replying on behalf of the IS. I don't have the addresses of all the NEC members but please forward this to them.

We don't agree with your assessment that the NC was 'a fair debate and airing of the issues'. Many of the contributions from the NEC majority included misinformation. You, for example, finished your introduction by saying that the IS had said it "suspected a clique was running the Irish organisation", despite TS having made clear at the 21 September NEC meeting that was not our view.

Unfortunately, in the course of the discussion there were also comments from leading comrades that were alien to the traditions of the CWI and, rather than engendering fair debate, created an atmosphere where supporting the NEC majority resolution became a matter of party loyalty.

Joe Higgins (JH) argued that it 'was not credible' that the leadership of a party which had played a leading role in numerous movements including against water charges and for abortion rights could have made the serious mistakes in the investigation which were alleged by the IS. He went on to criticise the letter Philip Stott (PS) wrote to you, Danny Byrne and Paul Murphy in February 2016 which raised concerns about the deficiencies of the electoral programme put by our TD candidates in that year's general election. Comrades assert they have no problem with debate on political issues but Joe said he was 'indignant' at PS's letter because he 'had just finished three full Dáil terms on behalf of the Socialist Party and CWI' and it was 'not credible that we were hiding our policies'. He finished with appeals to the NC comrades to listen to 'the real comrades'.

Joe has rightly got authority in the party as a result of the important role he has played over a long period of time which unfortunately, in our opinion, he misused. This was followed later in the meeting with a contribution a full timer where he declared that, 'If Joe Higgins has a problem with how IS comrades have conducted themselves, I have a problem in how they have conducted themselves'.

Stephen Boyd was one of the last speakers in a two-day long discussion and raised criticisms of the IS which had not previously been raised by Kevin McLoughlin or Ciaran Mulholland in their introductions or by other NEC members supporting the majority decision, all of whom had already spoken in the discussion. This gave the IS limited opportunity to respond. Incredibly, he also attempted to answer the criticisms of numerous comrades – who were supporting the NEC majority, but thought the IS should have been informed of the situation in mid-July when the hack was first discovered – by saying our response when they finally approached us on 8 September proved they were right not to do so earlier!

However, we of course agree that it is now crucial we discuss the key political and organisational issues that have arisen including the national question, the united front, our approach to Sinn Féin, identity politics, our demands in relation to Brexit, and the party's structures. We will be producing some written material beginning with outlining our views on identity politics to aid discussion including at the NC in November [page 91].

We think it is essential a report of the discussion is given at the IEC but will get back to you on how we propose to do this once TS has returned from the US.

DECLARATION OF A FACTION

In Defence of a Working-Class, Trotskyist CWI

*F*ollowing a week of intense discussion and debate at the December 2018 IEC it is clear that there are now two trends emerging within the CWI. Following the majority leadership of the Irish section breaking with the democratic principles of our party, fundamental differences have emerged, including methods of building and character of a revolutionary party and international based on democratic centralism.

There are differences on programme, tactics, united front methods, the national question, orientation to the working class, how we intervene in the women's movement and orientate in particular to working-class women and youth. All of these issues need to be fully discussed to clarify these questions. We will produce a platform explaining in more detail our approach to these questions and in defence of the traditions and methods of the CWI in preparation for future storms.

We appeal to all IEC comrades and members of the CWI to discuss all these questions. Should comrades agree with the main issues and methods being defended by this faction then we invite them to support and join us to defend the methods and traditions of the CWI. The discussion throughout the CWI should be discussed out in a principled and structured manner through the structures of the CWI and its sections.

Signed by full CWI IEC members and alternate members:

Weizmann Hamilton (South Africa), Michael Koschitzki (Germany), Philip Stott (Scotland), Clare Doyle (IS), Peter Taaffe (IS), Sascha Staničić (Germany), Hannah Sell (England & Wales, IS), Judy Beishon (England & Wales, IS), Shaun Arendse (South Africa), Babara Areal (Spanish state), Juan Ignacio Ramos (Spanish state), Victor Taibo (Spanish state), Carla Torres (Mexico), Miriam Municio (Spanish state), Miguel Campos (Spanish state), Félix Martínez (Venecuela), Christine Thomas (Italy), Jagadish Chandra (India), Niall Mulholland (IS), Ravi Chandra (Malaysia), Srinath Perera (Sri Lanka), Siri Jayasuriya (Sri Lanka), Bob Labi (IS), TU Senan (IS), Tony Saunois (IS).

FACTION RESOLUTION

Put to the IEC by the IDWCTCWI faction – defeated 21—24 (full IEC members)

This IEC has had a full and extensive discussion on the crisis which has developed between a majority of the Irish leadership and the IS. During the debate between the Irish section and the IS and at the IEC meeting, the IS and some IEC members believe that fundamental political issues of difference have emerged. Other members of the IEC did not agree. These involve the questions of programme, tactics, orientation and the concept and methods needed to build a revolutionary party and international, based on the methods of democratic centralism. The IEC agrees that a full discussion needs to take place in the international on all these issues.

The IEC unreservedly condemns the [hack]. The IEC believes that the response of the leading Irish comrades, while rooted in genuine concern for safeguarding and defending the party, was deficient in a number of important aspects. The IEC feels there were mistakes, in particular the length of time that there wasn't a formal democratic oversight by the NEC of the investigation; not to work through the holiday and conclude the investigation quickly to establish the facts; not to inform the IS in July. The IEC recognises that the leading comrades in Ireland accept these points.

We therefore agree that this debate take place in 2019 in a structured manner through the structures of the sections of the CWI. The issues under dispute are: 1) On programme and orientation and the issue of the centrality of the role of the working class and our approach to the trade unions; 2) Identity politics and the international women's movement; 3) Methods of building the party and the International; 4) Perspectives.

The IEC agrees that a World Congress of the CWI shall be conveyed in January 2020 to debate all of these and related issues and an IEC in August.

For the preparation of this congress we agree to form a congress organising committee to oversee all aspects of the pre-congress debate period starting now, up to the congress. This committee will be comprised of 6 members on the basis of parity between the recently formed faction and other IEC members. We agree 3 members – Tom Crean, Danny Byrne and Eric Byl – from the IEC meeting and 3 from the faction.

THE FORMATION
OF A FACTION

An explanation for Scottish members -
Philip Stott, IEC member (Scotland)

A major dispute on, in my view, fundamental issues arose at last weeks' IEC meeting. A range of documents and correspondence on these issues is available and is essential reading for comrades. Much of it relates to issues arising from before the IEC and not what happened at the meeting. I want to explain from my point of view what took place at the IEC and why a faction has been formed involving a section of the international leadership, which I have joined and fully support.

The IEC meeting agreed a period of structured debate through the sections of the CWI, culminating in a world congress in January 2020. There were two different resolutions put forward on this. I supported the one which was narrowly lost but which made clear our view that these differences are fundamental [see page 236]. The alternative resolution said they're not serious differences.

Divergences

The divergences, in one sense, began over a crisis that arose in Ireland over the summer/autumn period. The reprehensible actions of a comrade were responded to by a small group in the Irish leadership who carried out an investigation. The comrades involved did not inform their leading body, the NEC. Nor, crucially, did they inform the International Secretariat (IS), even though they had significant evidence of who was responsible by mid-July. By not seeking democratic authorisation and oversight for their actions they broke with the democratic norms of the CWI and set a very bad precedent.

It was not, in fact, until September that the comrades informed the IS of the situation, seeking support for their actions. To make matters worse, in presenting a report to the IS in September they made clear that part of their investigation was to find evidence of an 'undisclosed opposition group' in the party. They believed at that stage that a leading NEC comrade had also been involved and was part of a 'clandestine group' that was hostile to the party. This turned out to be baseless. Such behaviour by leading comrades in Ireland is completely alien to the methods of the CWI. If there is a grouping you think is operating in the party, ask for a discussion with the comrades involved. Ask them to engage openly in a discussion on their differences. Comrades who have differences should also openly declare them and be encouraged to do so.

The IS, the elected leadership body of our international, did not support the actions of the Irish majority leadership and said so. This led to an escalation of the differences. The IS asked to raise its concerns at the Irish NC meeting in October, which I also attended along with a number of IS comrades. Both myself and the IS condemned unreservedly the actions of the comrade who carried out the original attack on the party.

At that meeting a case was put forward by the leading Irish comrades in defence of the actions of the Irish NEC majority. The debate was not just about the serious incident but also touched on the mistakes I believe have been made in Ireland on programme, how we intervene in movements, elections, identity politics, the united front and so on.

More worryingly was the way many leading comrades intervened at the NC meeting to support the leadership by leaning on the success of the party in Ireland. That the NEC majority comrades in Ireland could not be making mistakes because of our achievements in elections, the water charges struggle, the Repeal movement etc. This shocked me and reminded me of the methods used by the Scottish Militant Labour majority (our then CWI section) during the Scottish debate between 1998 and 2001.

We cannot forget that Militant in Scotland and SML also achieved stunning success for a period. It led a mass movement during the poll tax battle and had tremendous electoral achievements on its CV. Yet the mistakes made by the leadership led to the collapse of our section in Scotland and also, eventually, the ruination of the SSP which they led into a re-formist and nationalist dead-end. There is an element of the Scottish situation also being present in this debate and the dangers of adapting to opportunist pressures in a complicated objective situation.

The NC in Ireland voted by a large margin to support the Irish NEC majority. It was agreed that a debate on identity politics and the role of the CWI in the developing women's move-ment – again asked for by the IS – would take place at the November NC meeting in Ireland. The IS, as is normal in our international, asked for the situation in Ireland and Identity Politics to be placed on the agenda of the IEC.

During the run-up to the meeting, IEC comrades from Sweden, Belgium, Greece and co-thinkers in the US – in a coordinated move, in my retrospective opinion – expressed their opposition to the IS and the way they were handling the situation - which is their right to do so.

They claimed the IS was pushing for a split in the CWI, or that the IS had over-reacted to the situation. In fact the IS was proposing no action against the Irish leadership of any kind. When I arrived at the IEC it rapidly became clear that a grouping was operating in opposition to the IS. Many meetings and sidebar discussions were taking place and as the IEC began the issues began to crystallise.

In essence, as well as a majority of the Irish IEC members, the comrades from the already mentioned sections supported the Irish leadership. They raised little or no opposition to the clear breaches of democratic centralism that had taken place in Ireland. The same unprinci-pled method they also applied to the obvious mistakes in Ireland over programme and how we have intervened in the women's movement.

Political roots of this crisis
Every time a major debate has opened up in our sections and/or international it has always had political roots. This equally applies to the collective history of the revolutionary movement.

Political clarification is essential to ensure the sharpening of our tools; programme, tactics, strategy and sticking firm to our central orientation - which is to the working class and its organisations. Our debate will centre on these questions, along with how we build our party and on what layers, as well as in defence of democratic centralism.

The political foundations of the debate in the CWI are rooted in the objective situation we are in. The delay in the emergence of a distinct socialist outlook by broad layers of the working class and youth, or even its advanced section, following the 2007-08 crisis has applied opportunist pressures on the forces of revolutionary socialism.

Many so-called Marxist organisations have taken to the road of dissolving themselves in broader movements or have adapted to the prevailing consciousness, including the watering down of their programme. We are not immune from these pressures. The current debate reflects the reality of these pressures. And in particular the delay in the working class moving in a mass and sustained way to challenge austerity and capitalism.

The fact that the working class entered the crisis a decade ago still impacted by the consequences of the collapse of Stalinism, and without being armed with even a broad socialist outlook, or in most cases a party of its own, has impacted on our international and our sections. In some cases, and this was clear from the IEC, some of our sections have adapted in a negative way to these pressures. As a result the working class and revolutionary character of the CWI and its sections is part of this debate.

Ireland

Our Irish section has achieved many outstanding victories over decades. It has been rightly held-up as an example across our international. This should be fully recognised. The successes of the Irish section are not under debate. What is under debate are the mistakes that have been made recently. I participated in the general election campaign in the south of Ireland in 2016. During my visit, and again after the election, I raised with the leading Irish comrades a series of criticisms, including about the lack of a socialist programme in our election material.

I wrote to the IEC comrades in Ireland in early March 2016. "As you know I raised questions over the approach we adopted through the AAA on programme during the election campaign. Essentially, in all of our election materials and the majority of our media appearances, we put forward to a mass audience the central demand for tax rises on the corporations and the rich. In general there was no call for public ownership and the wider measures that need to be taken to deal with the inevitable steps that the capitalists would take in Ireland and Europe against such a government. Especially important following the experience of Greece."

"The idea that tax rises and a fairer distribution of wealth - in effect a more progressive capitalism - would be a solution to the economic and social crisis in Ireland was pronounced. I think this was a mistake and should be recognised as such.... In essence did we not make too many concessions to what we might see as the 'current consciousness' and ended up by, objectively speaking, arguing for a fairer capitalism?"

The comrades responded in a negative way to these criticisms initially. However, after discussions initiated by the IS, the comrades said they accepted mistakes had been made, although they said it was due to pressure of work in a very frenetic election campaign. No doubt this may well have been a factor. However, the comrades dismissed the idea that they had adapted to opportunist pressures of electoralism and of watering down our programme. Yet this tendency is still evident today, with Solidarity leaflets in some of our key areas still not putting forward a clear socialist position and an absence of demands for public ownership.

Electoral pressures

One of the other issues I raised in my letter was fears over the lack of party profile and the evident distortion in how reliant we are in the south of Ireland on the public positions. "The huge pressure of electoral work, which is almost all-encompassing, has – as the comrades know – led to a very large part of our apparatus and cadre being consumed with this work, the public positions etc."

What was evident at the IEC was just how reliant we are on the elected positions. We have 25 full timers – soon to be 27 – and half of the full-timers (FTers) are linked to the work in the Dáil and council positions. This means we are dangerously over-reliant on whether we can keep the elected positions to fund the party. Moreover, our subs-paying base is only just over 100 comrades in the south of Ireland. This means that FT comrades have a far too great a specific weight compared to a narrow base of active party members. And that FT comrades play a disproportionately large role in the NC, compared to non-FT members and workers.

This reality can and is leading to a tendency that adapts our programme to a far lower level than is acceptable - especially when we are intervening in mass campaigns like elections. This tendency was also evident in the intervention we made in the historic victory over the right to abortion earlier this year. None of the posters in the referendum we produced were in the name of the party. They were all in the name of Rosa and Solidarity.

Rosa – our socialist feminist platform – was the main vehicle through which the Irish comrades participated in the movement. Yet the primary Rosa campaign leaflet was completely devoid of any mention of socialism, capitalism or even of the working class. It did not include any of Rosa's anti-capitalist and anti-austerity demands, or explain how the fight for a woman's rights to choose is also a class issue and is linked to the fight for better childcare, healthcare and a living wage etc.

This tendency to downplay class and socialist demands is evident again and again in the Irish comrades' material when they engage in mass campaigning. Rather than use the mass audience they have to raise consciousness as to the tasks the working class face in the struggle against capitalism - there is a tendency to do the opposite. These were the issues I and the other comrades who subsequently formed the faction were challenging.

What we faced, as I have said, was an opposition tendency in the CWI who wanted to shield the Irish leadership from criticism. To cover up the extent of the problems that exist in the Irish section and the evident dangers we face if this goes unchecked. When I spoke at the IEC I concluded by explaining that if the Irish leadership did not change their approach, the revolutionary character of the section in Ireland would be diminished.

Working class orientation

The title of the faction statement is "In Defence of a Working-Class, Trotskyist CWI". Why do we say "working class". Perhaps the most shocking development arising from the discussions was the extent to which the idea that the CWI orientates consistently to the organised working class has been undermined in practice.

One Irish comrade intervened in the discussion to say that the comrades in the south had drawn the conclusion in 2009 that the mass anger at austerity would not be reflected in the trade unions because of the sell out by the leaders. Another leading comrade from Ireland said they had taken a turn away from the unions, with a plan to return later, and equated it to the open turn away from the bourgeoisfied Labour party that we executed in the early 90s.

Frankly, this is breathtaking in its mistaken approach. The trade unions, and this includes in Ireland, even with their pro-partnership approach, are still mass workers' organisations. Unless we have a plan, an organised, consistent and patient approach to the workplaces and trade unions, we will fail as a revolutionary organisation.

Even if we begin to build our sections amongst young people, we must always turn them to the idea, in practice, of orientating to the working class. That the working class is the decisive force that will change society. In reality the comrades in the south of Ireland have had no consistent work in and around the unions for years. This can and has led to a miseducation, especially of young comrades as to the tasks of our party and who we base ourselves on and why.

It became clear at the IEC that some comrades who support the Irish NEC majority and opposed the IS' criticisms have also made similar mistakes. Not necessarily consciously. Perhaps because of the low level of struggle and the objective difficulties in building. Nevertheless, the pressure of the period was evident when comrades began to criticise the IS for failing to take up properly the issues of the women's movement, refugees, LBGTQ+ oppression etc.

The CWI as a whole, including the comrades who support the faction, have a very good record of orientating and intervening in these types of movements. Our only insistence is that when we do we raise our programme, we link the fight against oppression to system change and socialism, and point to the working class and its organisations as the decisive force in achieving this in a transitional way. This approach is not widely accepted in these cross-class movements where identity politics and petty bourgeois ideas are quite widespread. There is more on this in the debate on identity politics, which comrades must read, alongside the article on socialist feminism in the current issue of Socialism Today [see page 75].

The IS have argued that there is an element of Mandelism in the approach of some IEC comrades. This is the idea that while basing yourself on the working class in words, in practice there is increasingly an emphasis to orientate to cross-class movements, including on issues of oppression, without raising a clear Marxist programme. The faction in the international is arguing in favour of intervening, building from and taking initiatives in these movements, but in a way that does not result in the diminishing of either our transitional programme or its primary orientation which is to the working class as a whole.

Democratic centralism

The breaches of democratic centralism in Ireland by the leadership is one thing. The attempts to defend their actions by some IEC comrades during our meeting is another thing altogether. One leading comrade, in moving the alternative resolution on how to proceed, even went as far as to say that the IS should have accepted the decision of the Irish NC in October and move on. Just imagine if the IS has just accepted the 1998 Scottish conference decision of SML to effectively begin steps to dissolve our revolutionary organisation. If it had not launched a struggle against this and gone to the World Congress decision in 1998 to get support for its position. Where would we be now?

The CWI is not a federation of parties and groups. We are a democratic centralist revolutionary international. The leadership bodies don't turn a blind eye to serious mistakes or errors. And certainly not if they threaten the viability of our revolutionary forces. From its formation, the CWI has been based on mutual learning and, where necessary, criticism.

We elect leadership bodies to take care of and develop the international between congresses. Most often to handle the day-to-day work, draw up analysis on fast-moving events and for liaising with our sections. Sometimes, like now, to fight to correct mistakes before they have even more serious consequences.

We have a duty to seek to correct mistakes. The CWI and its membership must now use the period of debate that will open up to examine all of the questions under debate. Not to score cheap points and argue over secondary questions but to fight for the future direction of the CWI. To ensure our international sharpens our instrument for the next stage. One which will see the working class emerge as the decisive force to take on capitalism and fight for a socialist future.

Two tendencies have now emerged. This is not unusual in the history of the Marxist movement. The one represented by the newly formed international faction, I believe, has the correct orientation that will allow us to successfully face up to the challenges of the next period.

January National Committee Resolution

Passed by the England & Wales NC
37—4, with 2 abstentions

Following two full days of debate on the issues, at successive NC meetings, this NC declares its political solidarity with the recently formed international faction, 'In Defence of a Working-Class, Trotskyist CWI'. We will organise a full and democratic debate and encourage every member to participate and to weigh up the arguments for themselves. Nonetheless, given the important political and organisational issues involved, we believe it is necessary for us to declare our view at this point as the leading body, between congresses, of the England and Wales section.

March Congress Resolution

*This is the amended, final resolution which was passed unanimously
at the England and Wales Congress*

This congress recognises the democratic right of the faction 'In Defence of a Working-Class, Trotskyist CWI' to have been formed, and of our National Committee – which had two debates on the issues – to have taken a view. We also recognise the right of comrades to raise questions and criticisms of the formation and views of the faction. Congress believes the debate will be strengthened by comrades discussing and exchanging ideas throughout the CWI. Of course, as the NC resolution made clear, the section as a whole is still in the process of discussing its view.

We recognise that many comrades in England and Wales and internationally have not yet drawn conclusions on the issues.

Clearly, it is vital that a full and democratic discussion is organised in order to assess the nature and depth of the serious differences that are emerging with the aim of reaching clarity and principled unity throughout the CWI. The key issues include the centrality of the working class, the transitional approach, democratic centralism and the methods needed to build a revolutionary party and international. We agree to organise a full and democratic discussion, including debates in every region with supporters and opponents of the faction, and to encourage every member to participate and to weigh up the issues involved. In addition we resolve to call on the NC to, if necessary, organise a special congress towards the end of the year, first to try and draw some conclusions on the debate and secondly to ratify our delegates to the world congress.

MAY NATIONAL COMMITTEE RESOLUTION

Passed 35—7 by the England and Wales NC

*I*n the view of this NC, during the last five months of debate the two main trends in the CWI have continued to diverge. It is clear that there are decisive differences on the crucial issues of orientation, perspectives and programme as has been outlined by 'In Defence of a Working-Class, Trotskyist CWI' in its statement 'For a Trotskyist International – against opportunism and ultra-leftism'. [see page 21] The 'NFF' has tried to rally support on the basis of appeals for 'unity', but they evade engaging in a serious political debate because to do so would reveal their opportunist trajectory away from the political approach and methods of the CWI, including turning away from a serious orientation towards the trade unions and succumbing to the pressures of identity politics.

We therefore agree that the England and Wales section will sponsor the conference of the 'In Defence of a Working-Class, Trotskyist CWI' faction taking place in July 2019. We believe that this is the way forward towards building a powerful Trotskyist international based on the working class, and the founding principles and methods of the CWI.

Instead of seriously engaging with the political issues, the NFF focus on allegations against the 'regime'. They are now attempting to insist an IEC takes place in August, despite the IS having called one for November. It is clear that the NFF see an August IEC as a step towards a 'regime change' in the leadership of the CWI on an unprincipled political basis. They wish to use the currently unrepresentative character of the IEC – where, for example, England and Wales has 4 members as does Greece with 309 members, Russia with 24 members has 2, and Cyprus with 21 members has 1 – as a means to carry out a fundamental shift in an opportunist direction which would destroy the CWI as a viable Trotskyist international.

This NC therefore will not recognise any attempt by the NFF to declare a meeting of IEC members as a meeting of the CWI's IEC. If such a meeting takes place, the England and Wales section of the CWI will not attend it, and will view it as, in reality, declaring a split from the CWI on an opportunist political basis.

July Special Congress Resolution

Agreed 173 to 35

Six months ago a serious crisis broke out in our international. The period since then has demonstrated with clarity that leaderships in a number of the national sections are breaking with the theoretical foundations of the CWI forged by more than 45 years of work and sacrifice. The reasons for this political degeneration are the complex and contradictory objective situation facing Marxists over the past period.

This opportunist grouping has buckled under these objective pressures and is moving in a rightward direction away from Marxism. Starting as a political drift, an adaptation to the relatively low level of socialist consciousness and the failure of the working class to decisively put its stamp on events over ten years on from the financial crisis of 2007-08, the past six months of debate has seen the emergence of a distinct crystallised international tendency, the non-faction faction (NFF), which at the end of May 2019 very belatedly took the decision to set up a faction in England and Wales.

The events of the last six months have vindicated the formation of the In Defence of a Working-Class, Trotskyist CWI (IDWCTCWI) faction at the IEC in December 2018 in order to defend the CWI against this degeneration. This has proved to be a correct and necessary measure as has the decision of the England and Wales NC in January 2019 to declare itself in political solidarity with that faction.

The continuation of a healthy revolutionary international is at stake and, after six months of intense and democratically organised debate in England and Wales, this special congress of the Socialist Party confirms the following:

1. The platform and documents written by the IDWCTCWI faction and the IS majority, along with the material contained within the publications of the Socialist Party, represent the orientation, programme and methods that underpin a principled revolutionary international. In the faction, and in the work of our party, we recognise the clearest and most consistent expression of the CWI and its founding ideals.

2. The approach as outlined in the documents and debates by the NFF would lead to a decisive weakening of the foundations of our Marxist and Trotskyist international and of the Socialist

Party. We reject the turning away from consistent work in, and orientation to, the mass workers' organisations, the lowering of the socialist transitional programme when intervening in movements, elections and struggles, and the incubation of alien class ideas, particularly elements of identity politics, by the NFF which, if applied in England and Wales, would completely change the character of our party.

3. We agree with the decision of the NC to sponsor the international faction conference, taking place from 22–25 July in London. We will support all efforts to ensure the continuation of a principled revolutionary international. A prerequisite for this is defending and building on the theoretical and organisational foundations conquered by the CWI over the last 45 years.

4. We also agree with the decision of the NC not to recognise any meeting of IEC members called by the NFF. It is clear that the NFF are taking steps to build an alternative organisation. Some sections have not paid their full international dues over months, now NFF supporters – including IS member Danny Byrne – have called, in writing, for sections to stop paying their international dues, a decision which has been implemented by the Austrian NC. The NFF wish to use their meeting in August, and the World Congress in January 2020, to create an international that is completely outside the current political framework of the CWI, including changing the composition of the IS in order to achieve this. These meetings will therefore become a cover for the false and damaging policies and orientation of the NFF who wish to turn the CWI into an international in their own image and the Socialist Party will not participate in them.

This special congress of the Socialist Party calls on all members, whether or not they have joined the IDWCTCWI faction, to continue to help build the Socialist Party as part of a healthy Trotskyist international organisation in order to prepare for the mighty class battles ahead. The Socialist Party will collaborate with all genuine Marxist parties, groups or individuals who are in agreement on the central tenets of the CWI's approach including the centrality of the working class, consistent work in and orientation to the mass workers' organisations, and the necessity of the transitional method.

We are confident that the overwhelming majority of Socialist Party members will wish to participate in this historic task. If a small minority decides instead to build an alternative organisation, based on the opportunist policies of an NFF international, they will have to do so outside of the Socialist Party, where they will have the opportunity to test their ideas against the reality of the class struggle.

While the last six months of debate have been difficult, we are confident that we have come out of them politically strengthened, with greater cohesion and determination, and are therefore prepared for the coming convulsions in Britain in which we will have opportunities for dramatic steps forward.

Democratic Structures & Acronyms

The Socialist Party and the Committee for a Workers' International operate on the principles of democratic centralism, developed by Lenin and the Bolsheviks, and the subsequent Marxist movement. This is reflected in how the structures of the Socialist Party and CWI work. The CWI is composed of **sections**, parties that organise on a national basis, including the Socialist Party of England and Wales.

The basic unit of the Socialist Party is the **branch**; members are part of their local branch. Branches elect delegates to **congress**. Congress is the most direct expression of the membership collectively, and is the highest decision-making body of the party. Congress will usually meet once a year.

The congress elects a **National Committee (NC)**. In between congresses, the NC is authorised to act on behalf of the congress. The NC brings together leading comrades from across the section to discuss the central political and organisational questions. It usually meets roughly four times a year. Congress can replace or modify the NC as it sees fit. Some sections of the CWI refer to their NC as a **Central Committee (CC)**. A special congress can be called at any time by the NC; which the NC is obliged to do so if requested by a third, or more, of branches.

The NC elects an **Executive Committee (EC)** from its ranks. Members of the EC are based at our national office and provide the Socialist Party's day-to-day leadership. The EC usually meets weekly, but, because it is based in our national offices, there is the flexibility to meet more frequently if necessary.

While CWI-wide structures are comparable to the above, because of the nature of assembling socialists from across the world, there is usually a longer timescale. A **world congress** brings together delegates from all full sections. The last three happened in 2016, 2010 and 2007. The world congress elects an **International Executive Committee (IEC)**, which usually meets every year. The IEC elects an **International Secretariat (IS)**, which in practice acts as the day-to-day leadership of the CWI. The CWI also holds **International Bureau (IB)** meetings. The IB is a body of staff who work directly for the international, to discuss the day-to-day work.

Other meetings take place outside of these structures. Mentioned within this book are the CWI **European School** and the **Asia Bureau**. These are not formal decision-making bodies, but play a role in facilitating discussions amongst comrades. As explained elsewhere, the aim of the Asia Bureau is to bring together leading comrades from CWI sections across Asia. The European School brings together a much broader layer of CWI members from across Europe, and beyond.

Some activists are employed directly. Every member is encouraged to be active within the movement and within the party; so to distinguish staff members, they are colloquially referred to as **full-timers, or FTers**.

CHRONOLOGY

This book is presented within thematic sections. Below is a list of the debate documents in chronological order. This does not include the Socialism Today articles included within the book.

FURTHER READING

Marxism in Today's World • Peter Taaffe

The Rise of Militant • Peter Taaffe

From Militant to the Socialist Party • Peter Taaffe

Liverpool: A City That Dared to Fight • Peter Taaffe & Tony Mulhearn

Socialism and Left Unity: A Critique of the Socialist Workers Party • Peter Taaffe

A Socialist World is Possible: The History of the CWI • Peter Taaffe

It Doesn't Have to Be Like This: Women and the Struggle for Socialism • Christine Thomas

The Origins of the Family, Private Property and the State • Friedrich Engels

Marx and Engels on the Trade Unions • Karl Marx & Friedrich Engels

What Is to Be Done? • Vladimir Lenin

The Right of Nations to Self-Determination • Vladimir Lenin

Left-Wing Communism: An Infantile Disorder • Vladimir Lenin

The First Five Years of the Communist International (two volumes) • Leon Trotsky

The History of the Russian Revolution • Leon Trotsky

In Defence of Marxism • Leon Trotsky

The Transitional Programme • Leon Trotsky

Trade Unions in the Epoch of Imperialist Decay • Leon Trotsky

The Programme of the International • Ted Grant

These and more available from

left books

leftbooks.co.uk

socialist books

Socialist Books is the publishing house of
the Socialist Party of England and Wales

To find out more information about
Socialist Books, view other titles
or get in contact, see
socialistbooks.co.uk

For more information about
the Socialist Party, visit
socialistparty.org.uk

For international news, analysis
and reports, or to sign up to
support the CWI, go to
socialistworld.net